THE CULTURAL VALUES OF EUROPE

THE CULTURAL VALUES
OF EUROPE

Edited by Hans Joas and Klaus Wiegandt
Translated by Alex Skinner

Liverpool University Press

First English edition published 2008 by
Liverpool University Press
4 Cambridge Street
Liverpool L69 7ZU

Originally published as *Die kulturellen Werte Europas* (Frankfurt am Main: Fischer, 2005)

British Library Cataloguing-in-Publication data
A British Library CIP record is available

ISBN 978–1–84631–138–3   cased
      978–1–84631–139–0   limp

Typeset by Carnegie Book Production, Lancaster
Printed and bound by Bell and Bain Ltd, Glasgow

Contents

List of Figures and Tables   vii

Notes on Contributors   viii

Foreword   ix
    Hans Joas and Klaus Wiegandt

The Cultural Values of Europe: An Introduction   1
    Hans Joas

1 The Axial Age in World History   22
    Shmuel N. Eisenstadt

2 The Judeo-Christian Tradition   43
    Wolfgang Huber

3 The Greco-Roman Tradition   59
    Christian Meier

4 How Europe Became Diverse: On the Medieval Roots of the Plurality of Values   77
    Michael Borgolte

5 Freedom, Slavery, and the Modern Construction of Rights   115
    Orlando Patterson

6 The Value of Introspection   152
    Kurt Flasch

7 Rationality – A Specifically European Characteristic?   166
    Wolfgang Schluchter

8 The Affirmation of Ordinary Life   187
    Wolfgang Reinhard

9   Inner Nature and Social Normativity: The Idea of Self-Realization   217
     Christoph Menke

10   The Status of the Enlightenment in German History   253
     Reinhart Koselleck

11   The Dark Continent – Europe and Totalitarianism   265
     Mark Mazower

12   Value Change in Europe from the Perspective of Empirical Social
     Research   277
     Helmut Thome

13   The Realities of Cultural Struggles   320
     Dieter Senghaas

14   The Contest of Values: Notes on Contemporary Islamic Discourse   338
     Gudrun Krämer

15   Does Europe Have a Cultural Identity?   357
     Peter Wagner

     Glossary   369

     Afterword   372
     Klaus Wiegandt

List of Figures and Tables

Figures

7.1	Currents within Western Christianity	181
7.2	The Protestant ethic and the 'spirit' of capitalism	183
7.3	Comparison of types of Christian asceticism	184

12.1 Percentage share of postmaterialists minus materialists in eight age cohorts in six western European countries, 1973–94   285

12.2 Position of 65 countries in relation to two value-dimensions   291

12.3 Change of values in Federal Republic of Germany 1949–80   296

12.4 Educational goals in the federal states over the course of time   297

12.5 Agreement with equality of outcomes in the new Federal Republic, 1991–2000   304

Tables

12.1 Value type according to occupation and age group   289

12.2 Claimed superiorities of the German Democratic Republic over the Federal Republic of Germany   306

Notes on Contributors

Michael Borgolte, Professor of Medieval History at Humboldt University, Berlin.

Shmuel N. Eisenstadt, Professor Emeritus of Sociology at the Hebrew University, Jerusalem.

Kurt Flasch, Professor Emeritus of Medieval Philosophy at the University of Bochum.

Wolfgang Huber, Protestant Land Bishop in Berlin and Brandenburg, Chair of the Council of the Protestant Church in Germany, formerly Professor of Protestant Theology at the University of Heidelberg.

Hans Joas, Director of the Max Weber Centre for Advanced Cultural and Social Studies in Erfurt and Professor of Sociology at the University of Chicago.

Reinhart Koselleck, Professor Emeritus of Modern History at the University of Bielefeld, deceased 2006.

Gudrun Krämer, Professor of Islamic Studies at the Free University of Berlin.

Mark Mazower, Professor of Modern History at Columbia University, New York.

Christian Meier, Professor Emeritus of Ancient History at the University of Munich.

Christoph Menke, Professor of Philosophy at the University of Potsdam.

Orlando Patterson, Professor of Sociology at Harvard University.

Wolfgang Reinhard, Professor Emeritus of Modern History at the University of Freiburg and Fellow at the Max Weber Centre for Advanced Cultural and Social Studies in Erfurt.

Wolfgang Schluchter, Professor of Sociology at the University of Heidelberg, founder and first Director of the Max Weber Centre for Advanced Cultural and Social Studies, Erfurt.

Dieter Senghaas, Professor of Sociology at the University of Bremen.

Helmut Thome, Professor of Sociology (methods of empirical social research) at the University of Halle.

Peter Wagner, Professor of Sociology at the University of Trento (Italy).

Foreword

Hans Joas and Klaus Wiegandt

From 26 to 31 March 2004, the third conference of the foundation 'Forum for Responsibility – Foundation for Post-Professional Education' (Seeheim-Malchen) took place at the European Academy in Otzenhausen (Saarland) on the topic 'The Cultural Values of Europe' with around 160 participants from all fields of society.

The present work documents the talks given at the conference, supplemented by the contribution by Gudrun Krämer. This third volume continues the series 'Forum for Responsibility', which accompanies the conferences, a series which began with the publications *Evolution* (2003) and *Humanity and the Cosmos* (2004).[1]

The foundation's future activities will also focus on some of life's most fundamental issues along with pressing social problems, which will be presented in an interdisciplinary vein by internationally renowned scholars and discussed with participants within the framework of conferences.

With the topic 'The Cultural Values of Europe', we enter for the first time the field of the humanities and social sciences after two conferences of a natural scientific tenor. Many important political debates are currently raising the issue of values and Europe's cultural identity. We need think only of the debate on a European constitution, particularly its preamble and the question of how to formulate a reference to God. The issue of the limits to the expansion of the European Union, as arising, above all, in connection with possible Turkish accession, has focused new attention on the issue of Europe's identity. The need to redefine Europe's relationship with the USA also makes this issue unavoidable;

---

[1]   A fourth and fifth volume have now been published on *The Future of Our Planet* (2006) and *Secularization and the World Religions* (2007). An English translation of the volume on secularization that we have edited will be published by Liverpool University Press.

in recent times, it has for example led to the impossible-to-ignore plea from such well known contemporary thinkers as Jacques Derrida and Jürgen Habermas for the 'rebirth of Europe'. The rapid processes of modernization beyond Europe, under radically different cultural conditions, also make it imperative for contemporary Europeans to look at themselves in new ways; not least, the crucial issues of the dark sides of European history, whether in the shape of the totalitarianisms of the twentieth century, or the older history of European intolerance and European expansion within the context of colonialism and imperialism, represent a challenge. A smoothed-over view of European history is of no use to us here; there is no longer any possibility of reviving the idea of the Christian Occident, opposed to an (uncomprehended) Orient and viewed as a stronghold of reason and true freedom.

We have succeeded in fleshing out the conception of the cultural values of Europe (discussed in more detail in the chapter by Hans Joas) over the course of our conference because, happily, an outstanding expert declared his or her willingness to take part in the discussion of each sub-topic. These great scholars also did their best to express their thoughts in generally comprehensible language. Readers can judge for themselves how far they succeeded in this; but there should be no doubt about their intention to link together intellectual innovation and general comprehensibility for the benefit of a broad public.

Like its predecessors, which dealt with 'Evolution' and 'Humanity and the Cosmos', this conference also concluded with a panel discussion. This was dedicated to the subject: 'Is the Clash of Civilizations Unavoidable? Values in an Age of Globalization'. Rather than documenting this discussion, we have supplemented the talks given during the conference with a contribution by one of the panellists, namely the remarks made by the Berlin Islamic Studies scholar Gudrun Krämer on the topic 'The Contest of Values: Remarks on Contemporary Islamic Discourse'.

Our thanks go to the conference participants for their profound interest and critical questions, which not only invigorated the conference, but also led to later modifications in the written versions of the various talks. Two of the participants, Wolfgang Reinhard and Peter Wagner, offered their advice as early as the planning stage, and we are especially grateful to them for this. The Swedish Collegium for Advanced Study in the Social Sciences (SCASSS) in Uppsala offered Hans Joas the opportunity to make the finishing touches to this volume under optimal conditions; our thanks go to its director Björn Wittrock.

Seeheim-Malchen and Uppsala
Autumn 2004

The Cultural Values of Europe:
An Introduction

Hans Joas

In Joseph Roth's novel *Die Flucht ohne Ende* (*Flight without End*), the main character Franz Tunda ends up in Berlin in the 1920s, in the aftermath of the unspeakable turmoil of the First World War and the Russian Revolution. Here, he gains entry into the high society of the leading lights from the fields of industry and diplomacy. As it has a direct bearing on our topic, let us eavesdrop on a conversation that takes place during one of their get-togethers:

> At solemn moments they all spoke of the commonalities shared by European culture. Once Tunda asked: 'Do you think you could manage to tell me precisely what constitutes this culture which you claim to defend, even though it is in no way threatened from outside?'
>
> 'Religion!' said the President, who never went to church.
>
> 'Morality', said the lady, whose illicit relations were common knowledge.
>
> 'Art', said the diplomat, who had not looked at a single picture since his schooldays.
>
> 'The European idea', said a gentleman by the name of Rappaport cleverly, because vaguely.
>
> The aristocrat, however, contented himself with the remark: 'Just read my magazine!'
>
> 'You want', said Tunda, 'to uphold a European community, but you must first establish it. For this community does not exist, otherwise it would already know how to maintain itself. And it seems to me very doubtful whether anyone can establish anything at all. And who would attack this culture anyway, even if it did exist? Official Bolshevism, perhaps? Even Russia wants that culture.'

'But may want to destroy it here in order to be the sole possessor!' exclaimed Herr Rappaport ...[1]

This passage contains many characteristics related to today's debates about Europe, its culture and identity. The variety of competing criteria regarding what precisely represents Europe is as familiar to us as the hypocrisy of those who loudly proclaim that Europe's identity consists of attributes and values which they themselves do not possess. We are also familiar with the way qualities are vaguely attributed to European culture without first examining whether these do or do not exist in other cultures. It comes across as slightly forced when someone asserts that a certain identity already exists, but that it is also something which can be produced – as though the speaker knows exactly how this can be done: generating a commitment to values and constructing an identity. External enemies of European culture are adduced, even if it is not very clear where they are to be found and whether imagining such opponents of European values might not easily distract from the fact that these supposed enemies often employ for their own purposes certain suppressed components of the European ideational heritage or merely react to European claims of power and self-interest. There was one subject not mentioned at Roth's soirée which would be inescapable today: the distancing from America. Here, even the *type* of distancing is at issue – from America as an extension of Europe or a model example of western values, to an additional and even dangerous threat to European culture.

Thus, we do not seem to have progressed much in this debate since Joseph Roth's time. Yet how can we progress, how can we escape the blind alleys of argumentation, which we ourselves have recognized as blind alleys? How can we arrive at a definition of Europe's cultural values, one that abstains from any self-adulation or creation of an enemy-image and which is sufficiently precise so as not to dissipate into obscure generalities? A definition which is clear and yet will satisfy the historical and geographical variety of Europe, which will avoid illusions of feasibility and still function as guideline at a time when decisions of great historical import have to be made at the European level?

This contribution will attempt to adumbrate just such a definition. This can only be done with recourse to the prior academic work of many scholars – that is, at least the concept of this volume and the symposium on which it is based. But before proceeding any further, we need a brief explanation of the term 'value', since it is equally controversial and is in danger of being applied as haphazardly as the term 'Europe' has been.

---

[1]   Joseph Roth, *Flight without End*, trans. by David Le Vay in collaboration with Beatrice Musgrave (Peter Owen: London, 2000), pp. 116–17; originally appeared as Joseph Roth, *Die Flucht ohne Ende* (1927) (translation modified).

In order to approach the term 'value' and to arrive at a viable definition, it is best to begin with two observations that indicate how difficult it is to precisely define what is meant by this term.[2] The first observation is that our bonds to the 'Good', as we all know, are not the result of our intentions. Moral preachments are one of the least effective ways of successfully educating people, and our resolutions are usually very short lived. Yet why? The reason lies in the fact that our commitment must contain a passive aspect: we have to feel committed and not commit ourselves. Two venerable German words describe this particularly well, *Ergriffenwerden* or *Ergriffensein*, approximately translated in English as 'being captivated by'; these terms should be used when speaking about the commitment to the Good, and not concepts such as choice and decision, as though we could merely have an external and distanced, playful or experimental relationship to our commitments.

The second observation concerns the apparently paradoxical fact that we do not feel limited or constrained by commitments that have been constituted by *Ergriffenwerden*. One might even assert that the stronger our commitments, the more intense our feeling of being at one with ourselves. Remember the classic scene from European cultural history that symbolizes this intertwining of commitment and freedom: Martin Luther's refusal to recant his heresy at the Diet of Worms, where he spoke the legendary words, 'Here I stand. I cannot do otherwise. God help me. Amen.' These words form the cornerstone of the founding myth of Protestant individualism – but perhaps not only of Protestant individualism. And even if Luther did not actually say these exact words, there are plenty of other passages in his writings which confirm that he was, in fact, very aware of how self-destructive an action is that contradicts one's own notions of Good and Evil, or, in other words, is opposed to one's own conscience. His 'I cannot do otherwise' does *not* refer to an external force to which he was subjected: the social pressure to which he was exposed, enormous in its magnitude, went in the opposite direction and was aimed at compelling him to recant. Nor was it an internal compulsion as many are inclined to believe today, since, for Luther, the voice of conscience is not a fixation that should be cured through therapy. Because he followed his conscience, aware of the great risk of persecution and even death, the rebel or reformer remained at one with himself.

On a small scale, we are all well familiar with this problem. If both of the aforementioned observations are plausible, then values are phenomena that captivate us, not something we can directly strive to adopt; yet when they do

---

[2]   Below is an outline of the basic ideas of my book *Die Entstehung der Werte* (Frankfurt am Main: Suhrkamp, 1997); English translation: *The Genesis of Values* (Cambridge: Polity, 2000).

captivate us, they lead to a specific experience of freedom that continues to exist even under conditions of external compulsion.

If we shift from this experiential to a more conceptual level, then value is a term that must be separated from two other expressions, which are often uttered in the same breath. Values are different from norms because norms are restrictive and values are attractive. Norms reject certain modes or goals of action as morally or legally impermissible. By comparison, values do not limit the scope of our actions, but rather expand it. Only certain actions become conceivable for us because of our commitment to values. Since we may wish to be different from that which we already are – by, for example, emulating role models – we are able to transcend ourselves. If values are described as constitutive and attractive and hence differentiated from norms, a new danger of confusion emerges. They can seem like mere variations of the desires that unquestionably also describe that which attracts and drives us. Values thus seem more long-term, perhaps more stable than and superior to momentary desires – but not essentially different from them. It is, however, a grave mistake to think along such lines. While desires merely consist of what is desired, values express our notions of what is for us desirable. The difference between 'desired' and 'desirable' has been emphasized in American philosophy ever since John Dewey.[3] Our values cause us to appraise our desires. We might subsequently reject certain desires or, conversely, we might desire to be someone for whom certain actions are completely natural. Values are not merely conceptual notions about desirability we can easily renounce if challenged. Values are *emotionally laden notions of that which is desirable*. Or at least this is the definition I hold to be correct and which serves as the basis for this essay.

If then we have arrived at a more precise definition of the value phenomenon – although without dealing with a series of questions about, for instance, the consequences brought on by value commitments for the norms we consider appropriate, or about the possible dangers of identifying absolutely with certain values – then the next question to be posed would be how value commitments emerge and are subsequently transformed. And since value commitments cannot be commitments to values that exist as values if absolutely no one feels any commitment to them, then we can ask ourselves how values emerge and transmute. This is not the place to examine the issue of what we already historically and sociologically know about the dynamics of the emergence of values and their transformation. It should, however, be mentioned that we do have to analyse a specific type of human experience, which I call the experience

---

[3]   John Dewey, 'Theory of Valuation', in *International Encyclopedia of Unified Science*, vol. 2, no. 4 (Chicago, IL: University of Chicago Press, 1939), p. 31. This difference can be traced to Dewey's earlier writings as well.

of self-transcendence. If we are not thinking about the values that we somehow receive automatically in our childhood – through identification with our parents or a previous generation – we have to inquire into what moves us to consider something as desirable, that is, what makes a certain idea of the good subjectively evident and emotionally captivating. In order to understand this question, we need an elaborate phenomenology of the experience of self-transcendence, of being catapulted beyond the limits of our previous self, and of the interpretation of such experiences. Only then can we understand the biographies of specific individuals or the history of certain cultures not as linear, but as distinguished by the imposition of unforeseeable events, by the emergence of new and unprecedented interpretations of experiences and by an open interplay between mankind's need for interpretation and the cultural interpretations on offer.[4]

We now return to the question of the definition of European values. If the aforementioned description is adequate, then we may begin our exploration from two opposite poles. Notions of what makes something desirable can then be pushed to the fore, the propositional content of the values, so to speak, or, alternatively, the specific communities and traditions in which the emotional attachment to such content becomes identity-shaping. An examination of Europe can thus be based either on a complex of characteristic values, or, alternatively, on vital cultural traditions. Moreover, these two approaches do not exclude one another and can be pursued simultaneously. The most popular term for Europe's supposed complex of characteristic values is 'freedom'. The traditions repeatedly drawn upon to define Europe are the 'Greco-Roman' on the one hand and the 'Judeo-Christian' on the other (even if the construct 'Judeo-Christian', which emphasizes the commonalities between Judaism and Christianity instead of what divides them, is a product of the twentieth century and stems from an opposition to anti-Semitism and Christian-based anti-Judaism). None of these typical characterizations should be missing here. Yet I propose two intellectual moves that will show these distinctive and not inappropriate views in a different light. Before examining the Greco-Roman and Judeo-Christian traditions, there will be an analysis of the so-called 'axial' breakthrough to the discovery (or invention) of transcendence, which simultaneously gives us a frame of reference for non-European 'high cultures' and 'world religions'. And the European tradition of freedom will be explained in a different light by addressing the constitutive relationship between the slave experience and the emergence of the value of freedom. On this basis, an attempt will then be made to isolate certain specifics appertaining to Europe's cultural 'value system'. The decisive impulse for

---

[4]   For more on this, see Hans Joas, *Braucht der Mensch Religion? Über Erfahrungen der Selbsttranszendenz* (Freiburg: Herder, 2004); English translation: *Do We Need Religion? On Experiences of Self-Transcendence* (Boulder, CO: Paradigm, 2008).

the main distinctions here come from the Canadian philosopher Charles Taylor's major work, *Sources of the Self*.[5] In his book, Taylor's aim was to elaborate the basic structures of modern identity as such, rather than pinpoint certain specifics of European culture. Yet, inasmuch as Europe undoubtedly spearheaded the process of modernization for several centuries (however we want to characterize this), it is quite justified to reinterpret his findings in view of our present objectives. And doing this does not result in trivial claims. 'Inwardness', 'the affirmation of ordinary life', and 'self-realization' emerge as core European cultural values. I will return to these three later in more detail. Yet they have to be seen in the context of two other values that are often claimed to be characteristic of Europe. One must therefore ask whether we can really speak of 'rationality' as a specific European trait and whether a willingness to 'accept pluralism' can also be deemed a hallmark of Europe. The second value's somewhat complicated formulation is meant to imply a slight difference vis-à-vis the term tolerance; for this reason, this volume will examine how Europe became aware of its diversity in the Middle Ages. If the guideline here is value complexes, then at least two important 'movements' of European intellectual and political history should be addressed independently: the eighteenth-century Enlightenment and twentieth-century totalitarianism. Is there an enlightened tradition upon which Europe can draw today? And how does our image of Europe change if we not only remember the good and beautiful aspects, but also the crimes and horrors of the twentieth century, which prompt historian Mark Mazower to label Europe the 'dark continent'?

These are some of the many questions that must at least be addressed when attempting to establish a substantive characterization of Europe's cultural values. Although this alone threatens to exceed all frameworks, there will, of course, still be gaps in our analysis. Thus, even with such a vast and ambitious approach, we still lack a perspective on Europe in light of its outward expansion, above all through its colonial history. Our perspective on Europe also lacks consideration of the settler communities that came from Europe, in the United States for example, whose identity was partially constituted by the struggle for independence from Europe. These questions will be treated only with regard to the issue of Islam and whether we are presently witness to a 'clash of civilizations'. And one could certainly pursue in an even more detailed manner the internal diversity of Christian as well as non-Christian religious traditions in Europe. In our opinion, two further approaches must be taken into account. Firstly, one must remember that most sociological research on values and their transformation is not carried out in an historical, hermeneutic manner, but rather

---

[5]   Charles Taylor, *Sources of the Self* (Cambridge, MA: Harvard University Press, 1989).

in a quantifiable one. What can we learn from this type of research, and how can we apply that knowledge to questions concerning today's values? Second, among the many individual findings, we must consider the crucial question: does Europe have a cultural identity at all? In what sense can one speak of Europe as a community of shared values?

As already noted, the concrete elaboration of this research agenda surpasses the knowledge of any individual scholar in a scientific community that has become increasingly segmented. However, an independent attempt at synthesis, based on the previous work of others, can and should be undertaken.

The first step consists of characterizing Europe as an 'axial age' culture. This term has not yet become a part of everyday language and thus calls for explanation. It was coined by the philosopher Karl Jaspers in his 1949 book *Vom Ursprung und Ziel der Geschichte* (*The Origin and Goal of History*), which was based on earlier observations by previous authors. Jaspers pointed to the fact that the origins of *all* major world religions, and even ancient Greek philosophy, can be traced to the period between 800 and 200 BC, what he calls the 'axial age':

> The most extraordinary events are concentrated in this period. Confucius and Lao-tse were living in China, all the schools of Chinese philosophy came into being [...] India produced the Upanishads and Buddha and, like China, ran the whole gamut of philosophical possibilities down to scepticism, to materialism, sophism and nihilism; in Iran Zarathustra taught a challenging view of the world as a struggle between good and evil; in Palestine the prophets made their appearance, from Elijah, by way of Isaiah and Jeremiah to Deutero-Isaiah; Greece witnessed the appearance of Homer, of the philosophers – Parmenides, Heraclitus and Plato – of the tragedians, Thucydides and Archimedes.[6]

These parallel intellectual processes, which occurred largely independent of each other and so did not influence each other, yet which had an enormous effect on our civilizations, on India, and China, succeeded – according to Jaspers – a mythical age and introduced an age of systematic reflection on the basic conditions of human existence. Jaspers cannot and does not wish to explain how this parallelism of developments came to be. It seems more important to him that a mutual understanding between these axial age civilizations is possible, because though there is no common origin, there are very similar questions at issue.

But Jaspers gives us only a very vague description of the origins of this

---

[6] Karl Jaspers, *The Origin and Goal of History* (London: Routledge, 1953 [1949]), pp. 2–3.

axial age problematic – apart from hinting at an intense reflection on the human condition as such. In the 1970s, when the idea of the axial age resurfaced, a certain consensus between the participating historians of religion and theologians emerged, according to which the over-arching trait of all these religions and philosophies could be best described by the term transcendence. Formulated another way: thinking in the categories of transcendence was and is characteristic of the axial age cultures. Yet what exactly is meant by 'transcendence?'

This term implies that a distinct, quasi-spatial separation between the worldly and the divine emerged in those religions and philosophies, and that ideas were developed around the existence of the otherworldly, transcendent realm. While previously, in mythical times, the divine was in the world and a part of the world, in other words, while there was no real separation between the divine and the mundane, and the spirits and gods could be directly influenced and manipulated just because they were a part of the world – or at least while the realm of the gods functioned, more or less, along the same lines as the earthly realm – with the new redemption religions and the philosophies of the axial age, a major gap was created between the two spheres. The fundamental idea here is that the divine is the actual, true, irrefutable Other, and the mundane in comparison can only be inferior.

Such a difference is not only descriptive. An unprecedented tension develops between the 'mundane' and the transcendent – a tension with major consequences. The notion of a divine ruler, for example, can no longer be compatible with such a distinction. The worldly ruler can no longer be god-like because the gods have another place – in the realm of the transcendent. Moreover, the ruler might even be forced to justify himself before the divine commandments. The ruler is of this world – and must justify himself to the true otherworld. A new form of criticism (of authority) is now possible, which introduces a completely new dynamic into the historical process because people can always point to the fact that the ruler may not satisfy divine commandments. At the same time, it becomes possible to argue in a much more radical and tenacious way about the right god or the right interpretation of the divine commandments, which would sooner or later lead to conflicts and differentiations between various ethnic and religious collectives. Intellectuals – that is, priests, prophets, etc. – now play a much more important role compared to pre-axial age times, because they now have the difficult task of interpreting the inaccessible will of the gods, a will no longer easily understood within mundane categories. These ideas of transcendence opened history to completely new areas of conflict. Formulated somewhat more abstractly: with the notion of transcendence, the idea of a need to fundamentally reconstruct worldly order was born. From then on, social order was perceived as something that could changed in line with divine principles; for the first time, deliberate revolutions re conceivable. The tremendous impact of ideas originating in the axial age gave birth to a new social dynamic. In this regard, the great Israeli sociologist Shmuel Eisenstadt outlines a broad, dynamic and innovative comparative research project.

Thus can the axial age character of the traditions that have hitherto shaped Europe be summarized. It would be easy in this context to elaborate a link with Islam or Buddhism. Yet in Europe we are not dealing with one such tradition but instead with many different traditions, and with massive tensions between them. Europe has often been viewed, and with varying evaluations, as torn between Athens and Jerusalem; yet, if we look at this more closely, a distinction has to be made between Athens and Rome on the one hand, and between Judaism and Christianity on the other. Still, if we hold to this simplification, then with regard to the Judeo-Christian heritage one must consider that this merging of two traditions may, from the Christian point of view, present a welcome overcoming of anti-Judaic tendencies, but could be seen from the Jewish perspective as a renewed absorption of Jewish thought. Wolfgang Huber, following Dietrich Ritschl, thus does well in his contribution to first review the various perspectives from which we might reinterpret 'the relationship between the Jewish and the Christian traditions, between the people of Israel and the Christian churches' ([CREF] in this volume). In particular, he attacks the so-called substitution model, according to which the people of Israel lost their special status as God's covenant partners because they failed to embrace Jesus as the Messiah. Huber takes his cues from the two great Jewish religious thinkers, Franz Rosenzweig and Martin Buber, when they speak of 'two modes of faith', two paths to the one God, which are not to be lumped together, but can instead be seen as converging one with the other at the end of the eschatological timeline.

Every attempt to articulate that which embodies (with all the well-known scholarly qualifications) the 'values' of the religious traditions called Judeo-Christian will immediately encounter the problem that religion is more than a collection of statements with evaluative validity claims; faith consists of stories, myths, rituals, and experiences, which can never be reduced to a clear-cut formula. Yet it would be irrational not to at least attempt to identify the basic motifs of a certain religious faith, motifs which can then become important to the rational discourse on values. I consider Wolfgang Huber's attempt to emphasize four basic motifs convincing. First, the world and mankind are seen as a creation; that means that everything in the world is seen as a gift from God, including man's freedom and inborn and inviolable dignity. Secondly, God is not only thought of as a personal entity to be feared and loved, but as a personal God that loves and who turns to man with love. To fail to recognize this motif of the loving God, in my opinion, is to miss the true, emotionally intense core of this religious tradition. This motif has very frequently been understood as a radical discontinuity between Judaic law-based morality and the Christian ethos of love; but there can be no question that the Hebrew Bible was already familiar with the idea of a loving God. Surely, this core feature of the biblical message, the belief in God's goodness, is interpreted in the New Testament in a new way – in the sense of God becoming a person accepting man without reservation: Jesus Christ. Huber interprets the third motif, hope, as not only pertaining to the future, but also to the present: the permanent presence of God in the world. And the fourth motif, self-transformation, describes how man's orientation towards a loving God can unlock his own power to love, as long as God's implied invitation is accepted. These are the four main motifs of this tradition. But, as Ernst Troeltsch had already clearly recognized, there can be no unambiguous translation of these fundamental Christian motifs into a political ethical code. Even the organizational forms of the community of religious believers are therefore always disputable, even more so the ideal political order that is considered by believers to be appropriate and acceptable in a religious sense. Huber makes a significant attempt to argue in support of the constitution's privileging of human dignity and the values of tolerance and democracy, and in support of a relativization of law through brotherly love, as values that can be justified by basic Christian principles. But this is not about the logical deduction of fundamental political values based on faith, but finding a creative solution to the ineradicable and strained relations between world and faith.

Let us turn from Jerusalem to Athens. Medieval and modern Europe was undoubtedly deeply influenced by the Greco-Roman tradition, not just once or twice, when, for example, Christianity became the state religion of the Roman Empire or during the so-called Renaissance, but again and again, and in the most varied and contradictory ways. The existence of strained relations between the Judeo-Christian and the Greco-Roman traditions cannot be denied. Up to and including the present, these strained relations have sometimes been exaggerated to the point of antagonism, for example by Cornelius Castoriadis or Michel Foucault; they are then exploited in the sense of using one tradition as a means of overcoming the other. It is beneficial, therefore, to look at the non-Christian, that is to say Arabic, reception of the Greek tradition, which was far more one-sided and superficial than that of predominantly Christian Europe. Christian Meier asks why 'the classics' were able to establish themselves, despite frequent intense resistance, more solidly as a model here in Europe than in the Arabic world (in this volume, pp. 60–1):

> How was this possible? Were Christian Europeans simply more open, less clever, or more unformed and less fixed in their thinking than the Arabs? Does it make a difference whether you get the ancient sources via living people, the Greeks of the Byzantine Empire – or merely from books and other remnants? Did the Church allow for more room for manoeuvre in

its approach to the Holy Scriptures than did Islam with respect to the Koran?

Or did western, Latin Christianity willingly or unwillingly make medieval and modern Europeans highly receptive (and sometimes addicted) to the ancient sources? Was this because it did, despite all the ruptures with tradition, in fact entail plenty of Greek and Roman elements and transmit them further, thus laying the foundation for the revival of the ancient, a foundation on which it could ceaselessly stimulate new impulses, a foundation which enabled people to feel a sense of affinity with it? This was not entirely disconnected from the fact that the ancient texts were constantly being copied and handed down in the monasteries. The Gospels and the Pauline epistles were in Latin; the theology of the Church Fathers was full of borrowings from ancient philosophy, while canon law and the practice of administration owed their existence to the Roman Empire. In brief, the question arises as to whether the legacy of the ancient world met with such tremendous and, over the long term, such widespread receptivity in Europe, in contrast to the Islamic world, on the basis of factors inherent in the Church or generated by it.

If this is the case, then medieval and modern Europe are connected with Antiquity far more directly than is commonly assumed. Rather than preceding the history of Europe, the ancient world constitutes Europe's early history. On this view, Christianity not only fought against and eliminated many ancient elements, but in fact, and above all, saved and passed on many such elements, and not only in terms of outward appearance.

No matter how much one emphasizes the continued impact of Greek culture in Europe, it does not lessen the inherently strained relationship with Judeo-Christian culture. What then is the character of the particular, unique, and still vital aspects of the millennium-old cultural innovations of the Greeks? Christian Meier summarizes it with the phrase, 'cultural development on the basis of freedom rather than domination'. The culture of the Greek city-state was not shaped by the imposition of a strong regime and its administrative and representational requirements, but through the preservation of many small, independent political units and the development of a form of life in which at first the leading stratum of society, but soon more and more members required autonomy and independence themselves. This autonomy was seen as a prerequisite for the all-round development of the human being and a shared attempt to solve the problems that arose among these freemen. Meier not only claims that this basic structure underpins the culture of public and rational argumentation, but also historiography, architecture, literature, and even science, which manifested themselves in an exceptional period of human creativity that even became conscious of itself. Of all the types of human potential that it is possible to realize, this one was of such clarity of form that it became a continual point of reference for future ages.[7]

'Cultural development on the basis of freedom' – this not only implies an empirical claim regarding the connection between Greek city-state structures and ancient Greek culture but, of course, a certain value as well, of 'freedom', or at least a certain understanding of this value. Orlando Patterson, the Jamaican-born American sociologist, an important authority on the history of slavery in both his country and worldwide, developed the thesis, in his impressive work on the history of the value of freedom,[8] that we can only explain the emergence of freedom from the history of slavery. He means this not only in the widely known sense that freedom was not enjoyed by all Greeks and that to a considerable extent the foundations of the city-state economy lay in slavery; that may be true, yet this has too often been alleged as if it indicated a deficiency in the Greek interpretation of freedom (and democracy as such). Patterson sees slavery not only as an enabling condition or as a restrictive framework for freedom, but as constitutive of it: 'Slavery had to exist before people could even conceive of the idea of freedom as value, that is to say, find it meaningful and useful, an ideal to be striven for' (in this volume, p. 117). Without 'the absolute, unprotected, unmediated power of life and death of one person over another' (p. 117) as it was institutionalized by slavery, the idea would never have arisen that it might be good to be free of any and all constraints. In other societies that held slaves, there may also have been approaches to the idea of freedom, yet in ways which allowed this idea to be immediately devalued as 'slave value',

> something desired only by the once-fallen, the debased, or the perverted. Thus in all non-Western cultures, where it was found necessary to find a word for freedom, that word always had connotations of loss, unredeemable

---

[7]   Regarding the culturally second-rate quality of the Romans, compared to the Greek formation of culture through freedom and the religious departure of Judaism, Rémi Brague developed the theory that Europe could mostly be understood in terms of 'Romanity': Rémi Brague, *Europe, la voie romaine* (Paris: Criterion, 1992); *Europa, Eine exzentrische Identität* (Frankfurt am Main: Campus, 1993); English translation: *Eccentric Culture. A Theory of Western Civilization* (South Bend, IN: St Augustine's Press, 2002).

[8]   Orlando Patterson, *Freedom*, vol. 1: *Freedom in the Making of Western Culture* (New York: Basic, 1991). On Patterson's line of thought, see Hans Joas, 'Der Wert der Freiheit und die Erfahrung der Unfreiheit', in Hans-Richard Reuter *et al.* (eds), *Freiheit verantworten. Festschrift für Wolfgang Huber* (Gütersloh: Gütersloher Verlagshaus, 2002), pp. 446–55.

failure, nastiness, delinquency, debasement, and licentiousness. Only in the west did the word come to be cherished as the most precious in the language, next only to the sound of the name of God (pp. 117–18).

According to Patterson, the shift in how freedom is assessed, from a fearful social detachment to a desired independence, was due to a specific political-economic constellation in Athens, an alliance of masters and others versus the slave class. 'The *demos* became a free *demos* vis-à-vis the unfree aliens, with a shared power vis-à-vis the powerless and dominated slaves' (p. 118). Yet the type of political institution that grew out of this division of power further develops the notion of freedom in the sense described by Christian Meier. Patterson emphasizes, however, that Christianity, as the first and only world religion, declared freedom to be a religious goal, even intellectually and spiritually 'sacralized' it, and this most impressively in Paul's Epistle to the Galatians.

In view of these considerations of the emergence of the value of freedom, we have already shifted from reconstructing the strained relations between Europe's foundational traditions to examining the individual values that – presumably or actually – characterize Europe. 'Freedom' is certainly such a value – and Patterson's analysis thoroughly confirms this European specificity, although he justifiably addresses the establishment of this value in the USA as well as the universal discourse on freedom which America begat. The other most frequently named European values are diversity and rationality. If we follow medieval historian Michael Borgolte's argument, then one must first consider religious diversity in order to understand European diversity. He presents important arguments as to why the discourse on Christian Europe, such as Novalis' dream about the time 'when *one* Christendom dwelt in this continent shaped by human hand', always fell short. The medieval period was far more 'a period characterized by a number of cultures, which were influenced by monotheistic religions: Christianity in its Roman and Orthodox variants, Islam and, of course [...] Judaism' (in this volume, p. 79). He is exploring a theory that has repeatedly resurfaced for decades, at times carelessly, yet one that was revived by Jan Assmann's new and brilliant arguments. Assmann's theory proclaims that monotheism brought intolerance to the world, or more circumspectly put, that monotheism's tendency to deal violently with religious conflicts is greater than that of ancient 'polytheistic' paganism.[9] Borgolte contradicts Assmann in both aspects of this theorem. Ancient paganism was neither limitlessly tolerant, nor was monotheism manifestly intolerant. Borgolte writes:

---

[9]   See most recently Jan Assmann, *Die Mosaische Unterscheidung oder der Preis des Monotheismus* (Munich: Hanser, 2003).

Assmann, like other contemporary authors, suggests that monotheism, in its concern for unity, could lead only to division and not to the embracing of diversity. I reject this view. The profession of faith that belief in a single God demanded, and the religious differences and frictions it provoked, were certainly a nigh-on inexhaustible source of conflicts; but with its uncompromising approach, monotheism was also an invaluable school for the perception of the other, which could certainly lead to acceptance. As religion affected everybody and monotheism forced everyone to make a decision, everyone could come to know religious diversity. Even in cases where no clashes occurred between Christianity, Judaism, and Islam, and where they were not in competition, people were always concerned with the correct faith; schisms and heresies are the clearest manifestations of the potential for difference within the world of orthodox belief shared by Christians, Jews, and Muslims. On the other hand, and this is often underestimated, religious differences by no means led inevitably to conflicts or murderous attempts to annihilate other groups. Europe's survival, but, above all, its culture, rests to this day upon the toleration of differences between groups (in this volume, pp. 100–1).

'Toleration of differences' is definitely not the same as tolerance in the fullest sense of the term, namely with regard to standing up for the freedom of others. Thus, the history of tolerance does not begin until after the Middle Ages. Hence, it would be misleading to consider tolerance – rather than merely 'tolerated difference' – a value that traditionally holds sway in Europe. The notion of tolerance stems from the specific way in which religious conflicts in Europe and North America were dealt with; as a concept with a history, it thus sensitizes us to its traces in the Middle Ages.[10]

And 'rationality'? It was the great Max Weber who drew attention to 'the *distinctiveness* of Occidental rationalism, and within it that of modern Occidental rationalism',[11] asking how its emergence might be explained, or why this same process of 'rationalization' did not occur in other regions of the world such as China or India. It is not only the term 'Occident' that is worthy of discussion, however, but, above all, the terms 'rationality' and 'rationalization'. Weber could easily be misunderstood as having a one-sided understanding of these terms

---

[10]   On the history of tolerance, see Rainer Forst, *Toleranz im Konflikt. Geschichte. Gehalt und Gegenwart eines umstrittenen Begriffs* (Frankfurt am Main: Suhrkamp, 2003) and Perez Zagorin, *How the Idea of Religious Toleration Came to the West* (Princeton, NJ: Princeton University Press, 2003).

[11]   Max Weber, *Gesammelte Aufsätze zur Religionssoziologie*, vol. 1 (Tübingen: Mohr, 1920), p. 12.

and, hence, as failing to adequately understand that which led to the triumphal march of modern capitalism and which hindered (yet later enabled) this same triumphal march in other world regions. It is not possible here to address the mountain of literature dealing with the interpretation and empirical testing of the so-called Weber thesis regarding the link between Protestant ethics and the spirit of capitalism. Let us rather follow Wolfgang Schluchter, perhaps the greatest contemporary authority on Weber, and his analysis of Weber's concept of rationality, which provides a highly differentiated picture, both analytically and evaluatively (in this volume, p. 185):

> A specific process of rationalization is undoubtedly associated with the modern European cultural world, whose outcome is a theoretical and, above all, practical rationalism of world mastery. Its origins lie in that religious world, and it was from there that it spread around the world. It became universally significant, but is it also generally valid? In light of the history of violence that accompanied this process of rationalization, there is good reason to doubt that it is. Max Weber did so as well.

This is at the very least an ambivalent if not tragic judgment on Europe's history of rationality; it is anything but a triumphal claim to Europe's superiority with regard to reason (conversely, though, neither does it amount to self-hatred or the self-damnation of Europe or of rationality).

'Freedom', 'toleration of difference', and a 'practical rationalism of world mastery' – although requiring more precise description – are the three qualities we have identified as being fundamental to European cultural values. 'Inwardness', 'the affirmation of ordinary life', and 'self-realization' are three other values (or value complexes) which developed during certain phases of European history and have today become a cultural matter of course. The development of the idea of inwardness from Platonic philosophy to the intellectual milestone of Augustine's thought (and his autobiography) has been outlined by Charles Taylor (and many others before him); there is no need to repeat this here. The particularities of a Christian understanding of inwardness become completely apparent only when compared to the concept of inwardness found in other world religions. But the argument here concerns a certain reflexive relationship to the very value of inwardness. If the exploration of the inner person, the intensity of the 'experience of oneself', and a distancing from the world is seen as valuable, how does this relate to our practical relationship to the world? Is it then less valuable? Can one claim that Europe is dominated by the practical rationality of world mastery *and*, at the same time, the culture of inwardness? The topos for the debate on the value of inwardness in the Christian tradition is the passage on sisters Martha and Mary in the Gospel of Luke (10:38–42), who kindly give shelter to Jesus.

But only one of the sisters, Martha, prepares the food, while Mary just sits at Jesus' feet, listening to him. Martha says to Jesus: 'Lord, do you not care that my sister has left me to serve alone? Tell her then to help me.' But the Lord answered her, 'Martha, Martha, you are anxious and troubled about many things, but one thing is necessary. Mary has chosen the good portion, which will not be taken away from her.' This passage is always (and in all likelihood justifiably) considered a clear expression of Jesus preferring inner religious contemplation to external occupation. Yet one of the greatest medieval thinkers, Meister Eckhart, added an ingenious spin to this passage in his interpretation, and Kurt Flasch has impressively drawn attention to it. Meister Eckhart sees Martha as the superior of the two. She understands well the experiences religious contemplation can offer and how valuable these are, yet she also knows that we cannot be idle in the mere cultivation of our inwardness. 'The truly wise life', according to Flasch, 'consists not in contemplative pleasure, but in arranging activities in the outer world in line with the best that we know, the best that love demands' (in this volume, p. 162). Mary and her contemplations are therefore a good thing, to be encouraged and defended; yet external occupation, being the level before contemplation, does not imply that a culture of inwardness is the highest level. The freeing up of the person in order to *act* thus goes beyond any cultivation of inwardness. In Flasch's interpretation, Meister Eckhart comes across as a pragmatist *avant la lettre*. Hence, the European tradition was not alone in discovering inwardness; it did, however, reflect on this in a particular manner and, also in a particular manner, heightened the tension between inwardness and activity. As a result, any simple appeal for a return to inwardness essentially fails if it does not radically reassess this same tension.

'The affirmation of ordinary life' – this sounds rather strange as a definition of a basic European value. To illustrate what is meant, Charles Taylor quotes Puritan preachers such as one Joseph Hall:

> The homeliest service that we do in an honest calling, though it be but to plow or dig, if done in obedience and conscience of God's Commandment, is crowned with an ample reward, whereas the best works for their kind (preaching, praying, offering Evangelical sacrifices) if without respect of God's injunction and glory, are loaded with curses. God loveth adverbs, and cares not how good, but how well.[12]

Another illustration of this point might be Dutch still-life painting from the early

---

[12]   Taylor, *Sources of the Self*, p. 224 (here the reference to Charles H. George and Katherina George, *The Protestant Mind of the English Reformation* [Princeton, NJ: Princeton University Press, 1961], p. 139).

modern era, which did not depict saints, kings, or mythological figures, but ham, grapes, and glasses of wine. Meister Eckhart held the view that a life of activity in the world with God as one's spiritual reference point was more valuable than world-forsaking inwardness, and his view can be seen as heralding this powerful transvaluation as it took place during the Reformation. For it was indeed a transvaluation when the everyday reality of work and sexual reproduction was no longer considered tedious or base, in contrast to the 'higher' or valuable activities of the noblemen or clergy, but was now viewed as at least equally valuable or even superior, since the simple content of an activity no longer determined its value, but rather the manner of its execution. The dual notions of an enhanced evaluation of one's professional occupation on the one hand, and religious support for one's financial aspirations on the other, also play a key role in Max Weber's description of Protestant ethics. Wolfgang Reinhard goes beyond this analysis of Taylor's in two respects. Reinhard, a leading authority on the Catholic 'Counter-Reformation', is one of a handful of scholars to finally put an end to the serious use of this term, having showed that Catholic reactions to the Reformation can in no way simply be interpreted as an attempt to defeat or 'roll back' the Reformation. The Counter-Reformation was itself often a kind of Reformation, that is, it was concerned with Catholic modernization and individualization[13] – Reinhard makes an effort to consider these Catholic variants of the affirmation of ordinary life. In 1609, in his *Introduction to a Devoute Life*, Catholic bishop François de Sales sounded not so different from Puritan preachers when he wrote (quoted by Reinhard in this volume, p. 201):

> Of the virtues, we must give preference to those which correspond to the duties of our vocation [...]. The great opportunities to serve God are rare; there is never any lack of small ones. But he who is faithful over a little, the Saviour tells us, will be set over much. Thus, do everything in the name of God and it will be done well. Whether you are eating or drinking, resting or cooking: if you do your work well, you will be of much use before God, if you do everything because God asks it of you.

And the founding of the Jesuit order, the new religious order of the time, produced a religious elite trained to perform its duties within the secular world rather than turn away from it in contemplative detachment. The second area in which Reinhard first develops and then goes beyond Taylor is the greater attention he pays to sexuality and love in everyday life – and the transvaluation that this

---

[13]   See his collected essays: Wolfgang Reinhard, *Ausgewählte Abhandlungen* (Berlin: Duncker & Humblot, 1997).

realm of life underwent during the same period (fourteenth to seventeenth century). The gradual valuing of partnership in marriage and the legitimization of sexual desire remain – from today's perspective – quite restricted; but they, too, experienced a real boost with the Reformation, and not only among Protestants. With these analyses, a multifaceted image of the 'emancipation' of the early modern layman takes shape. Reinhard, however, ends on a very pessimistic note. He views the present as characterized by the predominance of work, the market, and sexuality over other values, which has turned the old devaluation of everyday life on its head.

The value of 'self-realization' is the most recent European value to be discussed here. Its emergence can be traced back to the late eighteenth century; the term itself, however, is even more recent and was first applied by Hegel. Charles Taylor, in his important Hegel monograph,[14] analysed how the notion of a telos embedded in different living forms of nature (the apple tree in the apple seed) was understood by thinkers such as Rousseau and Herder as a proactive process – the fulfilment of the telos in human beings was no longer thought to occur through a straightforward process of maturation, without any active effort, but rather to require the engagement of the individual and their self-knowledge. This proactive turn also involves a process of individualization: my preordained developmental goal is different from yours and everyone else's. Yet that which became an important impulse for the *Sturm und Drang* movement, Romanticism and the bohemian milieu, often in a misunderstood way, long remained primarily a phenomenon of the elite. This does not mean that the ideal of self-realization was restricted to power or social elites, but that it could be turned against them. It was not until the 1960s that this value unfolded in a truly broad sense in European (and North American) societies. There is consensus on this point among sociologists of culture. More difficult than clarifying the social distribution of this value is the conceptual explanation of what the rather paradoxical expression 'self-realization' actually implies. Christoph Menke investigates with great perspicuity the hidden traps associated with this term. The assumption of a hidden 'inner core' existing within us is not defensible on closer examination. Yet how might we then imagine the still unrealized self, which, at the same time, determines the direction of one's self-realization? Unmistakable here is the link to the topic of value-constitutive experiences. The need to clarify these conceptual questions is urgent because it is the only way to avoid misunderstanding the ethos of self-realization as underwriting narcissistic self-referentiality.

The value of self-realization has a complex relationship to that philosophical movement of the eighteenth century that serves as an indubitably positive normative point of reference for many in today's discussion on Europe's cultural

---

[14]   Charles Taylor, *Hegel* (Cambridge: Cambridge University Press, 1975).

values: the Enlightenment. 'Self-realization' is very much a counter-notion to the (Kantian and classical Enlightenment) notion of 'self-legislation' – yet not a counter-notion in the sense of hostility, but of enhancement, which desires to go beyond moralizing and the subjection of the self to rules (even if they are self-imposed). It would be very wrong to force this oppositional model – which has continued to occupy major thinkers ever since the eighteenth century and has occasioned attempts at synthesis – into the format of good Enlightenment versus dangerous Romanticism (or vice versa). In our volume, consequently, the analysis of self-realization is followed by the drawing up of a balance sheet for the 'Enlightenment' by one of its prime authorities among contemporary historians. Reinhart Koselleck attacks the central hallmarks of what one could call the mythos of the Enlightenment. The 'Enlightenment' was neither the self-designation of the most significant thinkers associated with this term today, nor, for most of its representatives, did it imply antireligious sentiments or an excessive faith in mankind's power to shape his own history. What is correct, however, is that the term arose around 1780 and was a historical novelty insofar as it was applied by contemporaries to identify their own time. Because we ourselves are so steeped in ever-changing labels for our own times, it is hard for us to perceive how new this phenomenon was in the eighteenth century. Koselleck sees genuine novelty in precisely this dynamization of the understanding of time and history. For centuries, history was understood as a teacher (*magistra vitae*), in part because one assumed that mankind was fundamentally unchangeable; one could therefore draw lessons from actions, events, and circumstances in Antiquity, lessons of eternal validity. One arrives at a far more radical historicization of human self-understanding if this notion is abandoned and the uniqueness of each historical moment, primarily the present, is taken into account. Koselleck, in his writings and in the large collective project *Geschichtliche Grundbegriffe* (Fundamental Historical Concepts) has comprehensively explored this turning point, coining the expression 'saddle period' ('Sattelzeit') for the age in which it took place. He is referring to the period between 1750 and 1850 in Germany, in which a new understanding of history penetrated the deep strata of human consciousness – an understanding of history that continues to shape us today and which entails the risk that it might be used for ideological purposes. Without this turning point, according to Koselleck, the secularized hopes for redemption through totalitarian movements that arose in the twentieth century would never have been possible.

Even these totalitarian movements are a result of Europe. It would be all too convenient to trace them to the 'half-Asian' character of Russia or to the German *Sonderweg* and thus reserve only positive connotations for modern-day Europe. Mark Mazower has no illusions when he points out that twentieth-century Europe was no sanctuary of freedom, but rather a hotbed of totalitarian ideologies and experiments and a multifarious mixture of democracy and dictatorship. If Europe, by contrast, now defines itself in opposition to such ideologies and regimes, this has something to do with the reinterpretation of the experiences associated with totalitarianism. An idealized image of Europe, however, does not strengthen, but rather weakens this reinterpretation. Mazower is optimistic that the age of totalitarianism in Europe has been overcome and is worried only that new totalitarian movements might emerge outside of Europe. This, of course, leads immediately to the question of what repercussions such a renewed totalitarian threat might have for Europe.

This completes our overview of the cultural values of Europe. The remaining contributions in this volume relate the question of these values to the current state of empirical social research (Helmut Thome), the 'Realities of Cultural Struggles' (Dieter Senghaas), the strained relations between the 'West' and Islam and the inner-Islamic discourse on fundamental values (Gudrun Krämer), and the question of a European cultural identity as a whole (Peter Wagner). It is not necessary to make any further reference to these essays here. In these contributions, broadly conceived cultural diagnoses will be related to precise quantitative findings; sensationalist theses concerning the imminent 'clash of civilizations' are refuted by drawing on advanced research on peace and development; assumptions of an inherent Islamic incapacity for democracy and human rights are repudiated, and, finally, the essential features of a European identity are based on an experiential history of the continent's divisions.

Peter Wagner ends his contribution with an appeal not to imagine Europe along the lines of a nation-state model, 'as a territorial, political, and cultural unity in the world, which distances itself from others and opposes them. This would be to repeat the disastrous intra-European trends of the nineteenth and twentieth centuries on a global scale' (in this volume, p. 368). We encounter here an ambiguity which was always inherent in the question of Europe's cultural identity and European values. Is this question aimed at elucidating values that Europeans hold in common or which link them in a unique way?[15] The values we are dealing with here, even if they are accepted by all Europeans, must go beyond the European context, must even achieve universal validity. Hence, there is something that binds us Europeans together, but which we do not want to keep to ourselves. One must understand that this is not a paradox for the sole reason that values themselves do not create systems or exclude others, but are believed in, upheld, and transmitted by people. We should not be misled by terms like value systems or cultural systems here. The constitutive relation of values to experience and interpretation, as addressed above, makes it possible to connect the particularities of the contingent experience of history with claims

---

[15]   I thank Christof Mandry for pointing out this ambiguity.

for a universality of values. An exemplary attempt not only to posit this on a philosophical-programmatic level, but also to formulate it in a concrete manner was, in my opinion, made by the Polish writer Stefan Wilkanowicz; his proposal for the preamble to the European constitution was not accepted, but it expressed better than any other how an attempt at a definition of European cultural values, far removed from self-adulation and self-hatred, and informed by an acute historical consciousness, could have gained legal form:

We, Europeans,

- aware of the richness of our legacy, which draws on the achievements of Judaism, Christianity, Islam, Greek philosophy and Roman law as well as a humanism rooted in both religious and nonreligious traditions;

- aware of the value of Christian civilization, the main source of our identity;

- aware of the frequent betrayal of these values, by Christian and non-Christian peoples alike;

- aware of the good as well as the harm we have brought to the peoples of other continents;

- grieving over the human catastrophe wrought by the totalitarian systems conceived within our civilization,

[...] desire to build a common future.[16]

---

[16] Quoted from Adam Krzeminski, 'Nicht in jeder Verfassung', in Der Tagesspiegel (Berlin), 12 December, 2003, p. 6. The complete text can be found in the liberal Catholic weekly publication Tygodnik Powszechny, 6 June 2003 (see the English translation in the World Press Review 50, 2003, no. 9).

1

The Axial Age in World History

Shmuel N. Eisenstadt

I

In this article I want to analyse the distinctive characteristics of the 'axial civilizations' – those civilizations which are identical with Max Weber's Great Religions. They constitute one of the most important scenes in world history and in the discourses about values of the modern world.

I shall first analyse some of the common characteristics of these civilizations and then proceed to analyse some of the major differences between them – indicating how both these common characteristics, as well as the differences, have greatly influenced, to a high degree, indeed, shaped, many of the common characteristics of modernity.

By 'axial civilizations' we mean those civilizations that crystallized during the time from 500 BC to the advent of Islam in the seventh century AD – a time when new types of ontological visions, of conceptions of basic tension between the transcendental and mundane orders emerged and were institutionalized in many parts of the world: in ancient Israel, later in Second Commonwealth Judaism and Christianity, ancient Greece, very partially Zoroastrian Iran, early Imperial China, Hinduism and Buddhism, and, beyond the axial age proper, Islam.[1]

The crystallization of such civilizations can be seen as a series of some of the greatest revolutionary breakthroughs in the history of mankind, which changed the course of human history. The central aspect was the emergence and institutionalization of the new basic ontological conceptions of a chasm between the transcendental and mundane orders. These conceptions were first developed among small groups of autonomous, relatively unattached 'intellectuals' (a new

---

[1]   S. N. Eisenstadt (ed.), *The Origins and Diversity of Axial Age Civilizations* (Albany, NY: State University of New York Press, 1986).

social element at the time), particularly among the carriers of models of the cultural and social order, before they were ultimately transformed into the basic 'hegemonic' premises of their respective civilizations, that is, before they were institutionalized and became the predominant orientations of both the ruling as well as of many secondary elites, fully embodied in the centres or sub-centres of their respective societies.

The development and institutionalization of the conception of a chasm between the transcendental and the mundane gave rise to attempts to reconstruct the mundane world-human personality and the socio-political and economic order according to the appropriate transcendental vision, to the principles of the higher ontological order formulated in religious, metaphysical, and/or ethical terms – or, in other words, to implement some aspect of such vision in the mundane world.

The Specificity of the Axial Complex
II

The crystallization of the axial civilizations constitutes a specific and – until the emergence of modernity – probably the most radical pattern of decoupling of various structural and cosmological dimensions of the social order, a decoupling which constitutes the core of social and cultural evolutionary tendencies.

The core of this specific 'axial' decoupling has been – to follow Johann Arnason's formulation – the radical 'distinction between ultimate and derivative reality (or between transcendental and mundane dimensions, to use a more controversial formulation)',

> connected with an increasing orientation to some reality beyond the given one; with new temporal and spatial conceptions; with a radical problematization of the conceptions of cosmological and social order, and with growing reflexivity and second order thinking, with the resultant models or order generating new problems (the task of bridging the gap between the postulated levels of reality).[2]

At the same time, a far-reaching decoupling of many aspects of the social structure had occurred, leading to the release of free resources, which could be organized in many different ways and the carriers of which constituted challenges for the hitherto institutional formations.

---

[2]   Introduction by J. P. Arnason in Arnason, S. N. Eisenstadt and B. Wittrock (eds), *Axial Civilization and World History* (Leiden and Boston, MA: Brill, 2004).

The development of such cosmological conceptions on the one hand, and, on the other, the decoupling of many aspects of the social structure took place, at least to some extent, independently of one another, driven by their internal momentum – albeit continually reinforcing one another in a variety of ways. At most, a certain affinity developed between cosmological visions and the type of structural differentiation or decoupling; the different dimensions of the social order – political formations and discourse, constitution of collective identity or economic formations – developed a high degree of autonomy. Thus, within these societies, multiple constellations of power, collective identities, and economic formations developed, each with its own dynamics. These very dynamics opened up the possibility, the quest for some type of reconnection – giving rise to the different modes in which they were interwoven with different axial cosmological orientations, and to the different institutional patterns.

The most important manifestation of such a quest for connection was the emergence of a new view on institutions, the common institutional core of which became the broadening, the opening-up of the range of institutional possibilities and options – from the emergence of new conceptions and patterns of political order and collective identities, to the weakening of their perception as being 'naturally given', which, in turn, even opened up the possibility of contesting their very foundations.

This new view on institutions entailed strong tendencies to reconstruct mundane life – social order, personality, as well as cultural activities; and second (closely related) to develop conceptions of a world beyond the immediate boundaries of those societies – a world open, as it were, to such reconstruction.

III

The most important among such broader institutional tendencies that developed within all axial civilizations were strong tendencies to construct a societal centre or centres to serve as autonomous and symbolically distinct embodiments or implementations of the transcendental visions, as the major *loci* of the charismatic dimension of human existence. These centres attempted to permeate the periphery and restructure it according to their own autonomous visions, conceptions, and rules. Concomitantly and in close connection with the institutionalization of axial cultural programmes, axial civilizations developed a strong tendency to define certain collectivities and institutional arenas as the most appropriate ones to represent the broader transcendental visions. These new 'civilizational' – 'religious' – collectivities were distinct from political and 'primordial', 'ethnic' local or religious ones, yet they continually impinged on them, interacted with them and challenged them, generating continual reconstruction of their respective identities. Such processes were affected by the continual interaction between the various autonomous cultural elites, the carriers of solidarity, and political elites of the different continually reconstructed 'local' and political communities. Under these circumstances, new patterns of cultural creativity developed that were closely connected to the new patterns of reflexivity. On the purely 'intellectual' level, it was, above all, theological or philosophical discourse that flourished and became constructed in much more elaborate and formalized ways, organized in manifold disciplines and generating continual developments within such frameworks.[3] The problems that were addressed within these discourses were the result of the autonomous developments in different arenas of cultural creativity and of the constitution of collectivities and the relations between them. They concerned, for example, the conception of cosmic time and its relationship to the mundane political reality, different conceptions of *historia sacra* in relation to the flow of mundane time, or sacred space in relation to mundane space. As a result, they gave rise to the construction of new types of collective memories and narratives thereof.[4]

It was the bearers or carriers of these visions who were of crucial importance for the emergence of axial civilizations. They represented a new social element, namely a new type of cultural elite – religious or secular – that transformed the nature of other political and economic elites and of the carriers of the solidarities in different collectivities. They were autonomous – even if in different degrees in different civilizations – intellectuals or *Kulturträger* such as the ancient Israelite prophets and priests and later on the Jewish sages, the Greek philosophers and sophists, the Chinese literati, the Hindu Brahmins, the Buddhist Sangha, and the Islamic Ulema. Initially only a small nucleus within society, these cultural elites or intellectuals developed the new cosmologies, the new transcendental visions and conceptions – and thus became of crucial importance in the development of the new 'civilizational' institutional formations and the concomitant new patterns of collective identity and world visions in these societies. As they succeeded in becoming highly influential or predominant – even hegemonic – in their respective societies, as they forged new types of coalitions with other elites, their respective institutional visions materialized and developed into distinct institutional patterns. However, the institutionalization of such visions has been dependent on a certain openness in the social structure, on the existence of free resources and a public opinion that made broader strata receptive to the visions promulgated by such elites.

---

[3]   S. N. Eisenstadt and I. Friedrich-Silber, *Cultural Traditions and Worlds of Knowledge: Explorations in the Sociology of Knowledge* (Greenwich, CT: JAI Press, 1988).

[4]   B. Z. Kedar and R. J. Z. Werblowsky (eds), *Sacred Spaces: Shrine, City, Land* (Basingstoke: Macmillan and The Israel Academy of Sciences and Humanities, 1998).

IV

The societies that developed within the framework of axial civilizations were very diverse. They could be fully fledged empires – indeed a great variety thereof (for example, the Chinese, Byzantine, or Ottoman Empire), rather fragile kingdoms or tribal federations (ancient Israel), combinations of tribal federations and city-states (ancient Greece), the complex decentralized pattern of the Hindu civilization, or the imperial-feudal configurations of Europe. Each of these types varied with regard to structural differentiation and cosmological visions as carried by different elites, and the coalitions forged by them.

The concrete contours of these societies, their centres and their dynamics, varied considerably according, as indicated above, to the structure of the predominant elites and their coalitions, the cultural orientations they promulgated, and the modes of control they exercised. In India, for instance, a very high degree of autonomy among religious elites stands in contrast to a lower degree among political elites. While there was a relatively small degree of differentiation of political roles among the broader strata, European societies developed a much greater degree of autonomy and differentiation among all elites. Similarly, within the imperial agrarian regimes, as the comparison between the Byzantine and Chinese Empires clearly indicates, far-reaching differences existed in the structure of their centres and the mode of their differentiation, despite the fact that they shared rather similar degrees (and relatively high ones for historical societies) of structural and organizational differentiation in the economic and social arenas. These centres also varied, of course, according to the different organizational, economic, technological, and geopolitical conditions of their respective societies.

As we have seen, the major dimensions of the social and cultural order – the cosmological visions and the different aspects of social structure – developed, at least to some extent, independently of each other, each pushed by its own momentum.

Contrary to the presuppositions of classical evolutionary approaches, which have also influenced, if only implicitly, the major analyses of axial civilizations, the different dimensions of structural differentiation and disembedment of cultural orientations and the growing problematization of the perceptions of the sources/dimensions of human existence do not always go together in a clearly predetermined way. At most, there is a certain affinity between institutional choices on the one hand, and cosmological visions and the type of structural differentiation on the other. Indeed, axial civilizations developed a high degree of autonomy with regard to the different dimensions of the social order – be it political formations and discourse, constitution of collective identity, or economic formations – a development, however, that was to some extent independent of, even if closely interwoven with, the distinctive axial cosmologies.

At this point, the comparison of similar power-structures – be it patrimonial, feudal, imperial, or city-state – in non-axial and axial civilizations is of special interest. Many institutional patterns that developed in axial societies could be very similar to those in non-axial ones, often attesting to the 'persistence' of non-axial components within axial civilizations. But the crucial component that distinguished axial civilizations was the possibility of dissent and heterodoxy, the possibility of change as a result of struggles over power, resources, and ideological contours. It is of special interest in this context to note that many of these heterodoxies or sectarian activities were among the most important carriers of the broader, often universalistic, cosmological and institutional visions. As a result, institutional constellations not only varied between different axial civilizations, but they could also change dramatically within them, giving rise to a much greater range of variability and changeability than in non-axial civilizations. In Johann Arnason's words:

> [T]he relationship between Axial cultural horizons and the structures of social power is profoundly ambiguous. New and more elaborate patterns of legitimation are counterbalanced by new possibilities of articulating dissent and protest as carried by different elites and coalitions, whose composition varies from one case to another, act as 'carriers' of the axial paradigm.[5]

Thus, for example, with respect to the constitution of different patterns of collective identity, the very distinction between different collectivities generated the possibility that primordial, civil, and sacred themes could be re-combined on the local, regional, and central level in ever new ways and be reconstructed in relation to sacral civilizational themes – including the possibility of continual confrontation between them. No single locus, not even the centres of the most centralized European Empires, could effectively monopolize all these themes. Rather, they were represented on different levels of social organization by different collectivities – 'ethnic', political, civic, and religious – each with relatively high levels of self-consciousness and different conceptions of time and space in relation to other collectivities.

The relations between different collectivities and political and economic formations, the struggles and contestations between their respective carriers thus constituted the particular dynamics of axial civilizations, giving rise to the concretization of different institutional patterns, to different, as it were, institutional 'choices'. The concretization of any such choice could be long-lasting

---

[5]   Introduction by Arnason in Arnason, Eisenstadt and Wittrock (eds), *Axial Civilization and World History*, pp. 19–49.

(as was the case in China) or, as in other cases, of a much shorter span. In any case, they were greatly dependent on political or ecological settings and other historical contingencies, which certainly were not fore-ordained in either the cosmological vision or the 'original' ecological setting.

Of special importance from the point of view of the relation between 'cosmological' visions, ecological settings, and institutional formations is the case of what Talcott Parsons called 'seed-bed societies' – early ancient Greece and ancient Israel as prime illustrations.[6] The characteristic feature of these seed-bed societies has been the very discrepancy between the potential institutional range of their basic visions and the concrete possibilities of their institutionalization – resulting in the fact that many of the institutional potentialities of their visions were in a sense 'stored', to be transmitted as components of institutional settings and dynamics of other civilizations.

V

The processes of reconstitution of institutional formations within axial civilizations were reinforced by the fact that, with the institutionalization of these civilizations, a new type of inter-societal and inter-civilizational world history emerged. To be sure, political and economic inter-connections between different societies existed throughout human history. Some conceptions of a universal or world kingdom emerged in many pre-axial civilizations, like that of Genghis Khan, and many cultural interconnections developed between them, but only with the institutionalization of axial civilizations did a more distinctive ideological and reflexive mode of expansion develop.

In close connection with their tendencies to reconstruct the world, these civilizations developed a certain propensity to expansion, in which ideological, religious impulses were combined with political and, to some extent, economic ones. Although often radically divergent in terms of their concrete institutionalization, the political formations which developed in these civilizations – and which can be seen as 'ecumenical' – comprised representations and ideologies of a quasi-global empire, and some, at moments in their history, even the reality of such an empire. This mode of expansion also gave rise to some awareness of creating possible 'world histories' encompassing many different societies. These 'world histories' or, rather, the different conceptions of world histories, clearly had an impact on the constitution and institutional formation of collective consciousness and identities of the different societies.

---

[6]   T. Parsons, *The Evolution of Societies* (Englewood Cliffs, NJ: Prentice Hall, 1977), p. 13.

VI

The multiplicity of different modes of 'decoupling' between the components of social actions and structure within axial civilizations makes a more differentiated analysis necessary, especially of the relations between non-axial and axial civilizations.

In large parts of the literature on the axial age, pre-axial civilizations were presented as a sort of residual category, as failed axial civilizations or as their precursors. Their crystallization, self perpetuation as well as their changeability, dynamics, and tendencies to expansion were not, on the whole, analysed in their own terms. In this way, very important dimensions of world history (or histories), and of the place of these civilizations in them, were lost. This is especially true of the analysis of these distinct ontological visions and patterns of reflexivity that developed within non-axial civilizations.

Peter Machinist,[7] for example, has shown with respect to Assyria and Babylonia that the cultural orientations which were prevalent within these civilizations were not just precursors of the axial ones, or failed axial ones. The specific cosmological conception which can be designated as proto-axial orientations and the patterns of reflexivity which developed in these civilizations were not simply unable, as it were, to develop into axial ones, but evinced a continuity and dynamics of their own. These orientations and their bearers were very influential in shaping institutional and intellectual spaces in which distinct patterns of intellectual and cultural creativity and reflexivity developed. Moreover, within non-axial cosmologies, the different components of such visions could be combined in very different ways. Of special interest from this point of view has been the Ahmenid case, in which very strong universalistic orientations developed, but without the attempt to reshape the social and political order according to some transcendental visions. Japan is probably the most vivid illustration of a case in which relatively high levels of structural differentiation and 'non-axial' cosmological orientation go together with the continual encounter with great axial civilizations (the Confucian or Buddhist), giving rise to highly developed 'non-axial' patterns of reflexivity.[8]

In all these civilizations, the elements of structural differentiation, cosmological visions, and elite function were combined in different ways. Each civilization developed a dynamic of its own, which was of great importance on the world

---

[7]   P. Machinist, *Mesopotamia in Eric Voegelin's Order and History* (Munich: Eric-Voegelin-Archiv, 2001).

[8]   S. N. Eisenstadt, 'Japan: Non-Axial Modernity and the Multiplicity of Cultural and Institutional Programmes of Modernity', in J. Kreiner (ed.), *Japan in Global Context* (Munich: Iudicium, 1994), pp. 63–95.

historical scene and which continued to be of great importance even once axial civilizations took over the playground, as it were. Even in the new axial settings, such non-axial orientations and their carriers constituted important components of the cultural and institutional dynamics – creating autonomous spaces which could indeed be very influential, albeit, of course, in different degrees in different civilizations and within the new axial frameworks, often persisting, as has been the case in Egypt, through changes in the dominant axial civilizations.

A differentiated approach to the analysis of basic cosmologies makes it also necessary to go beyond the distinction between 'this-worldly' and 'otherworldly' orientations – a distinction that has its roots in the Weberian programme and that constituted a basic component of studies on axial civilizations in the 1960s.[9]

Kurt Raaflaub has shown, for example, that the Greek–Hellenist–Roman complex constitutes a distinctive case – very different from the other major 'this-worldly' civilization, the Chinese. The critical difference between these two civilizations: although transcendental orientations as a guiding principle for the constitution of the social and political order were relatively weak in the first case, it nevertheless developed a very strong reflexive and critical discourse about the social and political order, in many ways unequalled – at least until modern times – in any other axial civilization. It is this difference which is probably of great importance in explaining at least some of the distinctive characteristics of the Hellenistic and Roman civilizations, especially the specific tendencies to imperial expansion. It was this case on which Arnaldo Momigliano based his assertion that polytheism is good and monotheism bad for empire building.[10]

In all these cases, the interrelation and contacts between different axial civilizations and between axial and non-axial civilizations – each with its own claims for some universality– constituted one aspect of their dynamics. This aspect has been neglected in many analyses, to some extent probably because of the tendency to the conflation of axial civilizations with that of an axial age.

Such contacts did not only lead to the exchange of central cultural tropes and, consequently, to different patterns of syncretization, they also gave rise to new, both pre-axial and axial civilizations. That was the case with the Ahmenid and Hellenistic cultures as well as with several south east and east Asian civilizations, and of course with Islam.

---

[9]   S. N. Eisenstadt, 'This-Worldly Transcendentalism and the Structuring of the World: Weber's "Religion of China" and the Format of Chinese History and Civilization', *Journal of Developing Societies* 1 (1985), pp. 168–86; reprinted in Eisenstadt, *Comparative Civilizations and Multiple Modernities* I (Leiden and Boston, MA: Brill, 2003), pp. 281–306.

[10]   A. Momigliano, *On Pagans, Jews and Christians* (Middletown, CT: Wesleyan University Press, 1987), ch. 9: 'The Disadvantages of Monotheism for a Universal State', pp. 142–58.

All these cases, as well as the study of the Parsonian 'seed-bed civilizations', open new vistas in the analysis of the interrelations and influences between different civilizations, indicating that such influences are not only to be found in already-concretized settings or in the impingement on the systemic boundaries of the respective institutional formations, but rather in a multiplicity of ways and channels cutting across such borders.

The Constitution of Collective Identities and Constellations of Power in Axial-Age Civilizations
VII

The institutional contours of the major social formations that developed within axial civilizations were continually reconstituted. Several, often overlapping, but never fully identical directions in which these reconstructions could develop can be identified. One such direction was generated by the civilization of heterodoxies and sectarian tendencies. The possibility of dissent and its impact on the dynamics of their respective societies is an inherent feature of axial civilizations, but, as indicated above, the concretization of such possibilities, the patterns in which collective identities and constellations of power were reconstructed, vary greatly between them. Examples are the crystallization of Jewish identity in the Second Temple and in exilic times,[11] the Iconoclasts in the Byzantine Empire,[12] the great divide between Sunni and Shiite Islam,[13] and Protestantism in Europe.[14]

---

[11] S. J. D. Cohen, 'Religion, Ethnicity and "Hellenism" in the Emergence of Jewish Identity in Maccabean Palestine', in P. Bilde *et al.* (eds), *Religion and Religious Practice in the Seleucid Kingdom* (Aarhus: Aarhus University Press, 1990), pp. 204–24; S. N. Eisenstadt and B. Giesen, 'The Construction of Collective Identity', *European Journal of Sociology* 36 (1995), pp. 72–102.

[12] S. N. Eisenstadt, *Power, Trust and Meaning: Essays in Sociological Theory and Analysis* (Chicago, IL: University of Chicago Press, 1995), ch. 11: 'Culture and Social Structure Revisited', pp. 280–306; Eisenstadt, *Comparative Civilizations and Multiple Modernities* II (Leiden and Boston, MA: Brill, 2003), ch. 24: 'Origins of the West: The Origins of the West in Recent Macrosociological Theory: The Protestant Ethic Reconsidered', pp. 577–612.

[13] S. N. Eisenstadt, 'Sectarianism and the Dynamics of Islamic Civilization', in G. Stauth (ed.), *Islam: Motor or Challenge of Modernity* (Hamburg: Lit-Verlag, 1998), pp. 15–33.

[14] S. N. Eisenstadt, 'The Protestant Ethic Thesis in an Analytical and Comparative Framework', in Eisenstadt (ed.), *The Protestant Ethic and Modernization: A Comparative View* (New York: Basic, 1968), pp. 3–45; Eisenstadt, *Comparative Civilizations and Multiple Modernities* II, ch. 24.

All these cases also showed a strong tendency to redefine the identities of their respective collectivities – and even to give rise to the construction of new, distinct civilizational, political, and ethnic identities.

A second direction of reconstruction was generated by the emergence of autonomous political actors who attempted to redefine the scope of political communities in relation to the broader ecumenical ones. This was the core of the imperial formations constituted by distinct political entrepreneurs within major axial civilizations – such as the Byzantine in the framework of Christian axiality, or the different imperial formations within the framework of the Islamic civilization.[15]

The third direction, often connected with the former, yet in principle distinct from it, was generated by 'vernacularization'.

These changes occurred in different axial civilizations in different ways. They entailed the (re)construction of constellations of power, of political regimes, and of different collectivities and collective identities as well as the relations between those 'identities' – especially between the 'local', 'civic', ethnic, and the civilizational sacral identities with their strong universalistic orientations. The differences were shaped, first, by the basic premises and cultural programmes of these civilizations, especially by the ways in which the relations between attributes of the sacral, cosmic, and social order on the one hand, and the basic attributes of the primordial ascriptive collectivities on the other hand, were represented within the cultural programmes and perceived by hegemonic elites. Here, three typical constellations can be distinguished. The first, most fully illustrated by the Jewish and, in a different way, by the Hindu case, has been characterized by the vesting of ascriptive collectivities with sacral attributes. The second one, most fully illustrated in ideal typical way in Islam and Buddhism, occurs when there is a total disjunction between the two. The third possibility, most fully developed in parts of Christianity and, in different ways, in Confucian societies, arises when these attributes of the 'universalistic' and the primordial collectivities are conceived as mutually relevant, each serving as a referent of the other or as a condition of being a member of the other without being totally embedded in it. Such a partial connection usually means that the attributes of the various ascriptive collectivities are seen as one component of the attributes of sacrality, and/or conversely, that the attributes of sacrality constitute one of the attributes of such collectivities.

Second, these directions of change were greatly influenced by the historical experiences and political ecological settings of these civilizations, especially if they were, as was the case in Europe and India, politically decentralized, or if

---

[15]   S. N. Eisenstadt, *The Political Systems of Empires* (New York: Free Press of Glencoe, 1963); new edition with a new introduction (New Brunswick, NJ: Transaction Publishers, 1993).

they were more centralized, as was the case in China, the Byzantine Empire, and later in Islamic Ottoman and Safavid Empires.

VIII

Given the constraints of space, we shall limit ourselves to a more detailed comparative analysis of two major decentralized axial civilizations – Christian Europe and India. Throughout the Middle Ages, up to the early modern period, both civilizations developed different patterns of pluralism, of dispersed centres and collectivities that were, however, bound together by orientations to a common civilizational framework.[16]

In India and Europe, major collectivities and central institutions were continually constituted in a variety of ways, all of which entailed different combinations of the basic terms and codes of collective identity: primordial attachments and traditions, transcendental as well as traditional civic criteria. The continuous restructuring of centres and collectivities revolved in Europe around the tension between the sacred, primordial, and civil dimension. While, for instance, many collectivities were defined and legitimated mainly in primordial terms, they also attempted to arrogate sacred and civil symbols of legitimation; they all contained strong territorial and political orientations – orientations that were also shared by many of the sectarian and heterodox groups that developed in Europe.

The relations between the broader civilizational and 'local' primordial collectivities developed in a different way in India, in close relation to its distinct cultural programme. The major difference was the weaker emphasis on territorial and political orientations. This was due to the fact that in 'historical' India, the political arena, the arena of rulership, did not constitute – as it did in monotheistic civilizations or in Confucianism – a major arena for the implementation of the transcendental visions predominant in this civilization. Indian civilization, as it was understood and promulgated by its bearers, did not contain a strong political component, again in contrast to Europe, to other monotheistic religions (Judaism and Islam), and even more so to China. It is only recently that strong tendencies among some political groups have emerged to promulgate a specific Hindu political identity and to define the Indian civilization in political terms.

In India, the patterns of collective identity were closely related to political dynamics. The conceptions of the political arena and of legitimation of rulers were closely related to the theory and practice of sovereignty, which, in turn, is of great importance for the understanding of the Indian political dynamics,

---

[16]   S. N. Eisenstadt, *European Civilization in a Comparative Perspective* (Oslo: Norwegian University Press, 1987).

especially of its pragmatic attitudes and accommodative stances. As Wink,[17] the Rudolphs,[18] and others have shown, these conceptions emphasized the multiple rights – very often defined in terms of various duties – of different groups and sectors of society rather than a unitary, quasi-ontological conception – real or ideal – of 'the state' or of 'society', thereby giving rise to fractured sovereignty. The organizational dimension of this picture is, on the face of it, similar to the one that prevailed in Europe throughout the Middle Ages and the early modern period. The crucial difference is, however, that in Europe the ideal of political unification – symbolized in the ideal of re-establishment of the Holy Roman Empire, however fragile its institutional bases were – constituted an ideal model. In India – at least until recently – such an ideal was at best very weak. While the 'fractured' sovereignty that developed in India was often combined with a tendency to far-reaching civilizational expansion, especially on the subcontinent, it did not give rise – as in the monotheistic civilizations or in China – to the construction of autonomous, often imperial, political centres, distinct from the periphery, attempting to impose on the periphery through distinct political activities and organizations, political religious conceptions, or a distinct civilizational vision. In India – despite its 'empires' – there neither developed a conception of statehood as a distinct, absolutized ontological entity, nor an absolutist conception of politics. Although India knew states of different scope, from semi–imperial centres to small patrimonial states, the overall Indian cultural tradition was never identified with any of them. Indian polities were characterized by predominantly personalistic and patrimonial categories. Rulers relied, above all, on the support of the various particularistic communities and, to some extent, especially in some of the later developments, as among the Mauryas, on personal loyalty and ties for recruitment of personnel and for contacts with different sectors of society.

In contrast to Europe, the reconstruction of the major collectivities and the development of new types of social organization in India was not, on the whole, connected with radical shifts in the modes of their legitimation or with principled struggles concerning the bases of such legitimation. The bases of legitimation of the various mundane, political or economic, activities were – defined in terms of their respective dharmas and auspicious performances

[17]   A. Wink, *Land and Sovereignty in India* (Cambridge: Cambridge University Press, 1986).

[18]   S. Hoeber Rudolph and L. I. Rudolph, *In Pursuit of Lakshmi: The Political Economy of the Indian State* (Chicago, IL: University of Chicago Press, 1987); Hoeber Rudolph and Rudolph, *Essays on Rajputana: Reflections on History, Culture and Administration* (New Delhi: Concept Publishing Company, 1984); L. I. Rudolph (ed.), *Cultural Policy in India* (Delhi: Chanakya Publications, 1984); S. Rudolph, 'The Princely States of Rajputana: Ethnic, Authority and Structure', *The Indian Journal of Political Science* 24 (1963), pp. 14–31.

– relatively continuous throughout Indian history, even if their actual applicati
were often rather flexible.

IX

The basic definitions of ontological reality prevalent in India did not generate strong alternative conceptions of political order. The sectarian movements that developed in the framework of Indian civilization were not so strongly connected with the reconstruction of the political realm as they were in Europe, and the process of vernacularization developed in India in a different direction than in Europe.[19] Consequently, the principled, ideological reconstruction of the political (or economic) arena did not constitute, as it did in Europe, a major focus of protest movements or the numerous sects that developed within Hinduism – Bhakti, Jain, Buddhism, and others – even if segments of such movements participated in the changes of political regimes and the wars between different kings and princes.

Many of the visions promulgated by these movements emphasized equality, but it was, above all, equality in the cultural or religious arena, with respect to access to worship, and only to some extent equality in the political community. Thus, although some of the heterodox movements with their egalitarian orientations sometimes became connected with rebellions and political struggles, they were not characterized by the strong articulation of new political goals, nor were they linked with many attempts to restructure the basic premises of political regimes. Only in some popular uprising against alien or 'bad' rulers did such goals crystallize for a short while.

Movements which were focused on the reconstruction of ascriptive civilizational symbols and collectivities could become connected with the extension of the borders of political communities, with the establishment of new political communities, or with changes of dynasties, but rarely with the reconstruction of the premises of the political centres. Buddhism did give rise to such new premises, but they became fully institutionalized only outside India, in the new Theravada Buddhist polities of south east Asia and in Mahayana Tibet.

---

[19]   S. N. Eisenstadt and H. Hartman, 'Historical Experience, Cultural Traditions, State Formation and Political Dynamics in India and Europe', in M. Doornbos and S. Kaviraj (eds), *Dynamics of State Formation: India and Europe Compared* (New Delhi: Sage Publications, 1997), pp. 27–55; L. Dumont, *Homo Hierachicus: An Essay on the Caste System* (Chicago, IL: University of Chicago Press, 1970); J. C. Heesterman, *The Inner Conflict of Tradition: Essays in Indian Ritual, Kingship and Society* (Chicago, IL: University of Chicago Press, 1985); G. Goodwin-Raheja, 'India: Caste, Kingships and Dominance Reconsidered', *Annual Review of Anthropology* 17 (1988), pp. 497–522.

Throughout its long history, India has witnessed far-reaching changes in its political and economic organizations, in technology and in levels of social differentiation, as well as the redefinition of boundaries of political units, some restructuring of the economic sphere, and changes in social and economic policies – all effected by coalitions of entrepreneurs rooted in different caste networks, economic groups such as merchants. But except for the ultimately unsuccessful attempt of Ashoka, most of these movements of change did not succeed in – and possibly did not even aim at – restructuring the basic premises of the political arena or the basic centre-periphery relations.[20]

These characteristics of the major religious and popular movements, their relations to the political centres and the institutional and symbolic characteristics of the political arena explain one of the most interesting aspects, from a comparative point of view, of Indian medieval and early modern history, namely the absence of wars of religion, of the type which characterized Christianity and Islam – that is, wars in which political goals were closely interwoven with, and legitimized by, attempts to impose by political fiat a religion on the community or on the political realm, even if the relations between different sects or groups were often very far from amicable. While India saw many, often brutal struggles and contestations between different religious groups, these conflicts never developed into wars of religion. Even if the recent emphasis on the relatively peaceful symbiosis of Muslim and Hindu groups in the Mughal realm is probably exaggerated, the numerous, often intensive conflicts between them did not lead to forced conversion or total confrontation between the two religions – which has been an important component of the situation within and between monotheistic religions.

X

The patterns of relations between primordial and sacral themes developed differently in the more centralized political systems among the axial civilizations: a range of empires such as the Roman, Chinese, and Byzantine Empire. In these empires, power was much more concentrated and centralized. Consequently and in contrast to the situation in India or Europe, their political centres developed a relatively strong tendency to regulate the combination of different collective identities. Such regulation did not usually entail – with the partial, but indeed only partial, exception of the Byzantine Empire and of other Christian kingdoms (such as the Ethiopian or the Armenian Kingdom) – the appropriation of all major – sacral, civil, and primordial – themes, rather on the macro-societal

---

[20]   D. Lal, *Cultural Stability and Economic Stagnation: India c. 1500 BC–AD 1980* (Oxford: Clarendon Press, 1988).

level but certainly not on the local level. Different 'ethnic' civil, local, and even religious communities were allowed to maintain and develop quite far-reaching distinctiveness, autonomy, and self-consciousness – a process that was indeed enhanced by the encounter with the broader civilization in so far as their basic tenets did not, as was the case within Judaism in its relations to the Hellenistic and Roman Empire, negate the basic legitimacy of the imperial order.[21]

However, the relation between the centralistic tendencies and local autonomous formations differed greatly between these empires – very much in line with the basic cultural programmes, the social imagery, and their distinct historical experience (the detailed analysis of which would be beyond the scope of this article).[22]

A Comparative Note: The Constitution of Collective Identity in a Non-Axial Civilization – Japan through the Tokugawa Period
XI

Japan provides a most instructive illustration of the crystallization and continuity of a distinct type of collective identity in a non-axial civilization. Japan successfully maintained its collective identity, despite the continual confrontation with two axial civilizations, Confucian and Buddhist, and later the ideological, military, political, and economic systems of western civilizations.[23]

A distinct type of collective consciousness or identity developed early in Japanese history. It was a political and ethnic identity that was couched in sacral-primordial terms [24] and that did not – as was the case in Europe or China, Korea,

---

[21]   Cohen, 'Religion, Ethnicity and "Hellenism" in the Emergence of Jewish Identity in Maccabean Palestine', in Bilde *et al.* (eds), *Religion and Religious Practice in the Seleucid Kingdom*, pp. 204–24; Eisenstadt and Giesen, 'The Construction of Collective Identity'.
[22]   Eisenstadt, 'Culture and Social Structure Revisited'.
[23]   Eisenstadt, 'Japan: Non-Axial Modernity and the Multiplicity of Cultural and Institutional Programmes of Modernity', in Kreiner (ed.), *Japan in Global Context*.
[24]   J. M. Kitagawa, *On Understanding Japanese Religion* (Princeton, NJ: Princeton University Press, 1987); G. Rozman, *The East Asian Religion, Confucian Heritage and Its Modern Adaptation* (Princeton, NJ: Princeton University Press, 1991); M. Waida, 'Buddhism and National Community', in F. E. Reynolds and T. M. Ludwig (eds), *Transitions and Transformations in the History of Religions* (London: E. J. Bailly, 1980); J. R. Z. Werblowsky, *Beyond Tradition and Modernity* (Atlantic Highlands, NJ: Athlone Press, 1976); C. Blacker, 'Two Shinto Myths: The Golden Age and the Chosen People', in S. Henny and J. P. Lehmann (eds), *Themes and Theories on Modern Japanese History* (Atlantic Highlands, NJ: Athlone Press, 1995).

and Vietnam – develop within the framework of a universalistic civilization with strong transcendental orientations. Japan, to be sure, was greatly influenced by its encounter with Chinese Confucianism and Buddhist civilization. However, in contrast to axial civilizations, Japan resolved its confrontation with universalistic ideologies by apparently denying them rather than attempting to relate them to its primordial symbols.

This collective consciousness was constructed around the idea of a sacred liturgical community and the uniqueness of the Japanese collectivity or nation. The concept of a divine nation, or – to follow Werblowsky's felicitous expression – of sacred particularity, did not, however, mean that Japan thought of itself as being uniquely 'chosen' in terms of a transcendental and universalistic mission or as having a responsibility to God to pursue such a mission.

Japan's conception of sacred particularity usually held its own when confronted with successive waves of universalistic ideologies (Buddhist, Confucian, then liberal, constitutional, progressivist, or Marxist), all of which seemingly called for a universalist redefinition of the symbols of collective identity. With the exception of small groups of intellectuals, such a redefinition did not take hold in the Japanese collective consciousness. Instead, the premises of these religions or ideologies were continually reconstructed and combined with sacral, primordial, and natural terms.

Reformulations of the Japanese collective identity entailed very intensive orientations to 'others' – China, Asia, the West – and an awareness of other encompassing civilizations claiming universal validity. But that did not mean that Japan wished to participate in such civilizations, to reconstruct its own identity according to these universalistic premises, or to become a part, whether central or peripheral, of such a universalistic system. In extreme form, Japan asserted that it was its own collectivity that embodied the pristine values enunciated by other civilizations and wrongfully appropriated by them. This yielded a very strong tendency – which played an important role in Japanese society from the Meiji up to the contemporary period – to define the Japanese collectivity in terms of 'incomparability', very often couched in racial, genetic terms or in terms of some special spirituality. Such definitions made it impossible to become Japanese by conversion. The Buddhist sects or Confucian schools – the most natural channels of conversion – could not perform this function in Japan.

The ability of Japanese elites to promulgate and 'reproduce' such extreme denial of the universalistic components of other axial civilizations has its roots in some of their basic characteristics, the most important of which, from the point of view of our analysis, is that these elites were not strong and autonomous. They were embedded in groups and settings (contexts) that were mainly defined in primordial, ascriptive, sacral, and often hierarchical terms, much less in terms of specialized functions or universalistic criteria of social attributes.[25]

True, many cultural actors – priests, monks, scholars, and so on – participated in such coalitions. But with very few exceptions, their participation was based on primordial and social attributes, on criteria of achievement and social obligations issuing from the different particular contexts that shaped these coalitions. It was not based on any autonomous criteria rooted in or related to the arenas in which they were active. These arenas – cultural, religious, or literary – were themselves defined in primordial-sacral terms, notwithstanding the fact that many specialized activities developed within them.

Such construction of the overall Japanese collective identity allowed, especially in the pre-modern period, the development of a wide scope for local and regional identities, which were also defined mostly in particularistic primordial terms, though with lesser emphasis on sacral components that were mostly vested in the centre, thus enabling a relatively high degree of porousness of these respective boundaries.

Such porousness became already weaker in the Tokugawa period when the first attempts were made to establish more rigid boundaries for the overall Japanese collectivity; it became even fuller versed with the crystallization of the Meiji state.[26]

The Axial Component or Dimension in World History
XII

The preceding discussion provides some important indications for a much more differentiated analysis of the relation between non-axial civilizations, axial civilizations, and world history. Earlier analyses of axial civilizations entailed a very strong – if implicit – evolutionary assumption of potentially universal stages of world history. The recent discussion calls for a much more diversified approach. Instead of assuming that the crystallization of axial civilizations entailed the emergence of a distinct, more or less uniform axial age in world history, it is better to analyse the different developments within their own contexts, focusing on the variety of factors that contributed to them.

The preceding discussion of the development of different axial civilizations indicates that their cultural programmes and institutional patterns were not the

[25]   S. N. Eisenstadt, *Japanese Civilization: A Comparative View* (Chicago, IL: University of Chicago Press, 1996).

[26]   D. L. Howell, 'Territoriality and Collective Identity in Tokugawa Japan', *Daedalus* 127.3 (1998), pp. 105–32.

result of natural evolutionary potentialities of these societies – or of all human societies – even if they were greatly influenced by the patterns of decoupling between different dimensions of the social order within these societies. Rather, such programmes and patterns, as is the case with other institutional formations in the history of mankind, were shaped by the continuous interaction between several factors, the most general being the various constellations of power, that is, the modes of elite contestation and co-optation in different political systems, the cosmological conceptions, and political ideologies.

Or, in greater detail, these programmes were shaped, first, by basic premises of the cosmic and social order, the basic 'cosmologies' that emerged within these societies – in 'orthodox' and 'heterodox' formulations. A second shaping factor was the pattern of decoupling between the different dimensions of the social order and of institutional formations. The third set of factors was the internal tensions, dynamics and contradictions that developed in these societies in conjunction with the structural-demographic, economic, and political changes, and between these processes and the basic axial premises of these civilizations. A fourth factor was the encounter with other societies or civilizations. The different – continually changing – axial programmes were shaped by the ways in which the different societies and civilizations were incorporated into the international frameworks which developed as a result of the processes of their expansion. A last factor was the continual confrontations between, firstly, different interpretations of the basic premises of axiality as promulgated by different centres and elites and, secondly, the real developments, conflicts, and displacements that accompanied the institutionalization of these premises. These confrontations activated the consciousness for the contradictions inherent in axial cultural programmes and the potentialities generated by their openness and reflexivity; and they gave rise to the continual reinterpretation of the major themes of the axial programmes, of the basic premises of their civilizational visions, and their grand narratives.

The axial syndrome does indeed constitute a very crucial component in the development of human societies. It could develop in different ways in different contexts; and it could become connected in different ways with other axial as well as non-axial societies or civilizations.

All these considerations seriously question the conflation between the crystallization of axial civilizations and an 'axial age' or 'ages'. They clearly indicate that the extent to which the developments in different parts of the world converge into a 'global' or 'semi-global' axial age has yet to be explored and investigated – and not as a given. While there is no doubt that the institutionalization of different axial civilizations created new visions of possible world histories, it does not mean that any one such vision became hegemonic and necessarily excluded other visions. Indeed, these considerations attest to continual contestations between these visions and the civilizations in which they were initiated; and to the fact that not all societies were incorporated into the frameworks of axial civilizations and were indeed 'taken over' by them. Rather, they were able to develop their own spaces with distinctive dynamics. They could also, as the case of Japan shows, create their own very important niches in international frameworks dominated by axial civilizations.

XIII

Following these considerations, the relation between axial civilizations and modernity should be reconsidered at least on two levels. On the first level, it should be stressed that the emergence of modernity should not be considered a natural outflow or outgrowth of the potentialities inherent especially in European axial civilizations. Following Weber's general insights into comparative history, it should rather be seen as contingent on the combination of various 'accidental' historical developments.

On the second level, the close affinity between the analysis of 'multiple axialities' and that of 'multiple modernities' should be recognized.[27] Here, the distinction between primary and 'later' modernities is of special importance – which brings us again to Max Weber and two different readings of his work.[28] The first reading, apparent in the way in which the Protestant ethic thesis has been interpreted in recent decades, emphasized Weber's concern to explain the nature of the specific mode of rationalization that developed in the West – a problem succinctly analysed by Wolfgang Schluchter.[29] In the 1950s and 1960s this concern gave rise to a search for equivalents of the Protestant ethic in other civilizations – one of the best, and first, of which has been Robert N. Bellah's *Tokugawa Religion*.[30] Bellah assumed, if only implicitly, that it is insofar as such equivalents of the Protestant ethic develop in other civilizations that they will really become modern. If one emphasizes only this reading of Weber, it is seemingly irrelevant

---

[27]   S. N. Eisenstadt, 'Multiple Modernities', *Daedalus* 129.1 (2000), pp. 1–29; L. Roniger and C. H. Waisman (eds), *Globality and Multiple Modernities: Comparative North American and Latin American Perspectives* (Brighton: Sussex Academic Press, 2002).

[28]   S. N. Eisenstadt, 'The Protestant Ethic and Modernity: Comparative Analysis with and beyond Weber', in K. S. Rehberg (ed.), *Soziale Ungleichheit, kulturelle Unterschiede* I (Frankfurt am Main: Campus, 2006), pp. 161–84.

[29]   W. Schluchter, *Die Entwicklung des okzidentalen Rationalismus: Eine Analyse von Max Webers Gesellschaftsgeschichte* (Tübingen: Siebeck, 1979); Schluchter, *The Rise of Western Rationalism: Max Weber's Developmental History* (Berkeley, CA: University of California Press, 1981 [2nd edn 1985]); Schluchter, *Rationalism, Religion and Domination: A Weberian Perspective* (Berkeley, CA: University of California Press, 1989).

[30]   R. N. Bellah, *Tokugawa Religion* (Glencoe, IL: The Free Press, 1957).

to the contemporary world of multiple modernities. There is, however, another reading, which is highly relevant to an understanding of multiple modernities. This is the reading of the *Gesammelte Aufsätze zur Religionssoziologie* as studies of the internal dynamics of the various Great Civilizations – in their own terms, in terms of their distinctive rationalities, with special emphasis on the role of heterodoxies and sectarian movements. Such a reading of Weber is reinforced by the fact that these 'new' multiple modernities are, as it were, 'late' modernities. Weber focused his analysis on the development of the first – western, European – modernity, but he did not assume that later modernities will necessarily develop under the same conditions. Reading Weber in this way leads almost naturally to the question of how the specific historical experience of a particular civilization may influence – certainly not determine – the distinct characteristics of the modernities that develop within these civilizations[31] – thus bringing us to the analysis of multiple modernities.

---

[31]   Eisenstadt, 'Multiple Modernities'; Eisenstadt, *Die Vielfalt der Moderne* (Weilerswist: Velbrück Wissenschaft, 2000).

2

The Judeo-Christian Tradition

Wolfgang Huber

I

Europe is not a 'Christian club', countered Turkish Prime Minister Recep Tayyip Erdogan, when Angela Merkel, chair of the German CDU at the time, brought Europe's Christian character into play as one of the objections to Turkish membership of the European Union. The Turkish politician's disparaging reference to a 'Christian club' was certainly somewhat unfortunate; and the chair of the former Central Council of Muslims in Germany, Nadeem Elyas, was also rather careless when he adopted the same term. But it is true that it is impossible to account for the cultural character of Europe, during any era of its history, solely with reference to its Christian – or Judeo-Christian – roots. In fact, both types of claim are correct: in contrast to all other continents, Europe has been a primarily cultural rather than geographical entity from the very beginning. And from the beginning, its cultural character has been determined not by one, but several formative factors. No reference to Christian Europe or the Christian West, no matter how commonplace, can and should obscure this fact. The notion of Europe's Christian character can therefore never be intended in an exclusive sense or with any claim to a monopoly.

Only Europe's cultural and religious history explains why we call Europe a continent. Three names are crucial to its cultural and religious character: Athens, Rome, and Jerusalem.

Europe has Greece to thank for the spirit of philosophy, the awakening to science, the openness to the arts. This is a legacy, as it happens, passed on to a significant extent by medieval Islam. It is to the Romans that Europe owes the establishment of a legal system, a sense of appreciation for political unity and organized rule. Finally, Europe is indebted to Jerusalem for the Bible, its characteristic religion, the determining notion of the relationship between God and humanity. Christianity emerged from Judaism; the Bible of the Christians incorporates the Hebrew Bible. Jesus, Peter, and Paul – to mention just these three – were Jews. Whenever Christianity has tried to emancipate itself from these Jewish roots, the consequences have been terrible. For the future, therefore, the only legitimate Christianity is one that is aware of its origins in Judaism.

Anyone referring to Europe's Christian roots must consider its relationship to the antique legacy together with the Jewish and Islamic influences on the development of Europe. There is no justification for marginalizing Europe's Christian character, and equally little for equating it with Christianity. For no era of European history is this appropriate.

II

The fact that this Christian character owes its origins to Judaism was, of course, long suppressed, indeed denied. Nowadays we refer with seeming matter-of-factness to the 'Judeo-Christian tradition'. Yet in the twentieth century, almost no-one in Germany would have used such a term. Only after the horror of the Shoa, the murder of European Jews decreed by the Nazi state and for which many people bear a degree of responsibility, has a shift in thinking begun. Only with the Second Vatican Council has the Roman Catholic Church set about redefining its relationship with the people of Israel. The admission of guilt by Pope John Paul II in Yad Vashem in 2000 was a moving illustration of this shift. At the same time as the Vaticanum Secundum, efforts to develop a 'theology after Auschwitz' gained traction among Protestant theologians. Such endeavours are a far rarer occurrence within the various types of Orthodox theology. Yet even where they do occur, such efforts cannot obscure the fact that reference to the 'Judeo-Christian tradition' points far more to a still-open wound than a relationship that has already been resolved.

This is because there are (at least) four perspectives from which the relationship between the Jewish and the Christian traditions, between the people of Israel and the Christian churches is viewed. Dietrich Ritschl has distinguished between a history-of-religion perspective, a substitution model, a *Heilsgeschichte* model of continuity, and the model of the two paths.[1]

The starting point for the *history-of-religion perspective* is the thesis that the Judaism of the last few centuries before the birth of Christ was on the wane and grown rigid with age. In contrast, early Christianity constituted a counter-movement; it brought about a renewal of the faith in one God as well as a shift beyond the Jewish people. While Pharisaism may have been an important reform movement within Judaism, the Jesus movement set in motion a reawakening in a quite different way. On this view, Jesus' interpretation of the law in the Sermon

---

[1]   See Dietrich Ritschl, *Theorie und Konkretion in der Ökumenischen Theologie* (Münster: LIT, 2003), pp. 73ff.

on the Mount or the interpretation of the fate of Israel set out by Paul the apostle in chapters 9 to 11 of his Epistle to the Romans are considered key points of reference. They rest on a perspective that subsequently guides a particular approach to the history of Christianity as well. This history, too, features the alternation of acquired rigidities and reawakenings. If we follow this idea, we can refer to a Judeo-Christian tradition in the first place only if we also pay heed to the process of ceaseless renewal. This renewal not only has the character of an *aggiornamento*, a process of responding to the needs of the time, but is also characterized by a return to the roots, a movement 'back to the sources', a reformation in the sense with which the sixteenth century endowed this word.

Alongside this perspective, and unquestionably overlapping with it, is the *substitution model*, sometimes also referred to as a model of disinheritance. Theologically, this model picks up on the idea of the covenant which God makes with humanity. This idea is based on God's covenant of creation, renewed after the Flood through God's covenant with Noah. Through the Sinai covenant, the people of Israel are chosen and acknowledged as God's people in an exclusive sense. The Torah and, at its centre, the Ten Commandments, the Decalogue, become the document of this covenant. Yet Israel itself loses this special position as God's people by failing to open itself to the coming of the Messiah, refusing to recognize Jesus as such. Since then, the Christian Church has replaced Israel as God's covenant partner. The Church is called into the 'new covenant', which replaces the 'old covenant'. It calls itself the people of God and thus takes the place of the old as the 'new people of God'. The Hebrew Bible is called the 'Old Testament' because it has now been superseded by the 'New Testament'. The relationship between the two is one of promise and fulfilment or of law and gospel.

We must recall this interpretive schema in order to understand the debate rekindled by Mel Gibson's much-discussed film *The Passion of the Christ*. In a case such as this, the accusation of 'anti-Semitism' tends to obscure rather than do anything to clarify the point at issue. This is not a matter of racial anti-Semitism, but of whether the depiction of Jesus' trial by the then-local Jewish aristocracy and of the mob with its cries of 'Crucify him!' apportions blame for the condemnation of Jesus in a way that might justify the notion of the disinheritance of Israel, of the end of the covenant that God made with this people. Here, of course, we must keep in mind that such anti-Jewish sentiment undoubtedly played into the hands of the racial anti-Semitism on which the plan to annihilate European Jews was subsequently based.

The opposition between 'old' and 'new' deployed within the concept of substitution is, of course, already found in the Hebrew Bible itself. Now it is applied to the Church's succeeding of Israel as God's covenant partner. One radical interpretation that failed to take hold went further and even transferred the inherent dualism to the concept of God itself. The Old and New Testament, this interpretation tells us, do not refer to the same God at all. Rather, the antagonism between Israel and the Church reflects the opposition between two different Gods. It was Marcion who, in the second century A D, produced this interpretation and logically called for the removal of the Old Testament from the Christian canon. He failed to get his way; yet similar ideas were to flare up time and again. This occurred in a particularly depressing way during the 'Third Reich' among the so-called German Christians, who adopted the idea of eradicating all Jewish elements from the Christian Bible – without considering that they were thus removing Jesus himself from the Bible. For Jesus of Nazareth was a Jew.

However untenable this substitution model may be, it stubbornly persists. Especially within Judaism itself, many people continue to believe that the Christian churches are characterized by such a view. Many Jews are correspondingly reluctant to engage in theological discussion. From a Jewish perspective, there is still something very strange about references to a 'Judeo-Christian tradition'.

However, in light of the biblical findings and the necessary theological distinctions, the substitution model is untenable. Rather, from a Christian perspective, it is vital to affirm that the special relationship of covenant that the God of Abraham, Isaac, and Jacob entered into with the people of Israel, was not annulled, but confirmed by the revelation of God through Christ. And it must also be affirmed that the Christian Church is the younger sister of this covenant people of God, and as a result the former's relationship with the latter is one of grateful dependency rather than competition.

Running counter to the idea of substitution, a *Heilsgeschichte conception* emphasizes the idea of continuity. This continuity may be emphasized so strongly that it indeed excludes entirely the idea that the Church is replacing Israel. On this view, God's engagements with his people in the 'Old Covenant' retain their validity undiminished. However, this very idea also suggests that one covenant follows another, replacing it. It is impossible to avoid a *Heilsgeschichte*-based notion of progress, according to which God's covenant through Christ revises and thus relativizes the other covenants in its finality and universality. But then the question arises of how, from a Christian perspective, the existence of post-biblical Judaism is to be assessed. As a consequence, the subsequent dual history of the Hebrew Bible in its Christian and Jewish interpretation entered the Christian consciousness only very late. In this respect, the fact that Christian exegesis long described the Judaism of the last few pre-Christian centuries as 'late Judaism' speaks volumes. The relationship between the Old and New Testament was conceived in terms of 'promise' and 'fulfilment' and the continued existence of a Jewish community, now scattered across the continents over the course of millennia, made no theological sense. Thus, even the concept of *Heilsgeschichte*, despite the continuity that it asserts, could not overcome the latent or manifest anti-Semitism of Christian theology.

It can be overcome only by a *model of the two paths*. In its most simple form, which goes back to Franz Rosenzweig and was incorporated into Martin Buber's 'two types of faith', it states that there are two paths to the one God.[2] The Jewish path to God is through Moses and the Torah, the Christian path to God is through Jesus and the Gospel. The consequences of this model for the understanding of the person of Jesus Christ, particularly when it is adopted by Christians, are far-reaching. For on this view, even from a Christian perspective, Jesus is not to be regarded as the messiah of the Jews. But this is a conclusion clearly out of sync with statements made in the New Testament, particularly in the letters of Paul, but also in the Gospels.

On the other hand, if we take Paul's reflections in the lengthy section on Israel in the Epistle to the Romans (ch. 9–11) as our starting point, the separate paths converge from an eschatological perspective. The fact that the people of Israel, so Paul tells us, are still cut off from the Gospel, changes nothing about the fact that 'as regards election, they are beloved for the sake of their forefathers. For the gifts and the calling of God are irrevocable' (Romans 11:28 and following). The idea that the separation of the Church from the heathens and the people of Israel will be overcome for the sake of Christ is carried further in the Epistle to the Ephesians. In the faith that Christ 'is our peace', the author sees reason for the certainty that the barrier of enmity that still separates Jews and Christians will be torn down (Ephesians 2:11–22). Here, it is not hostility, but reconciliation, not destruction, but conviviality that forms the perspective from which the relationship between Jews and Christians must be seen.

The dismantling of the wall that separates Jews and Christians from one another was, however, superseded by a history of pogroms and the Holocaust. This made it all the more urgent to redefine this theological relationship in a fundamental way. It was vital that respect for the two paths and the obligation to pursue reconciliation become constitutive features of Christian theology. Only from this perspective can contemporary Christian theology dare to speak of a 'Judeo-Christian tradition'.

III

But what does this tradition consist of? How can it be described? What is its essence? Taking the model of the two paths seriously means admitting that one is coming from a particular perspective. This single tradition with its dual fountainhead can be described only from one of the two perspectives – the Jewish or the Christian; no-one can claim to represent both in the same way.

---

[2]   See Martin Buber, 'Zwei Glaubensweisen', in Buber, *Werke*, vol. 1 (Munich and Heidelberg: Kosel, 1962), pp. 651–782.

And we must immediately add: no Christian can negate the internal plurality of Christianity. No-one is capable of simply unifying the different denominational traditions into a single, integrated picture. Even if ecumenical developments justify the statement that what Christians share in terms of faith is now more important then what divides them, even this shared profession of faith will always be expressed in a particular way, partly coloured by the speaker's denomination. However far we expand our horizons, viewing Christianity as a universal entity, all of us are concurrently influenced by one of the many 'Micro-Christendoms' which have developed throughout the course of Christian history.[3] Religious, cultural, social, and political factors have interacted in the development of these Micro-Christendoms. It will thus come as no surprise in what follows if I discuss the Judeo-Christian tradition from a Christian perspective and if this Christian perspective is in turn of a Protestant character, influenced by the 'Micro-Christendom' in which I myself am at home: German Protestantism.

With this proviso, I shall dare to set out concisely, against the background of the Jewish tradition, what I consider to be the organizing principle of the shared Christian tradition – I might also say: the motivating force of the Christian faith.[4] I illuminate this organizing principle through reference to four basic motifs: of creation, love, hope, and the changing of ways.[5]

I begin with the *motif of creation*. It is fundamental that the human being is perceived as part of the world created by God. He shares in the goodness of Creation. Gratitude for the gift of life is thus a key feature of human existence. Because of this, human freedom can also be considered an inviolable good because it has the character of freedom owed to God. For in the face of all human selfishness and guilt, God still keeps faith with his Creation; human beings thus remain destined for freedom. Before he can avail himself of the freedom to do things of his own accord, he is freed by God to make something of himself. To honour God is thus the first task of human life. To accept and acknowledge the dignity bestowed by God is the second. This dignity is not acquired through human achievement, nor is it forfeited through human error. It is in precisely

---

[3]   See Peter Brown, *The Rise of Western Christendom* (Malden, MA, and Oxford: Blackwell, 1995), p. 216.

[4]   This accords with the ideas laid out in my book: *Kirche in der Zeitenwende. Gesellschaftlicher Wandel und Erneuerung der Kirche* (Gütersloh: Bertelsmann, 1999), pp. 115ff.

[5]   Gerd Theißen has put forward numerous proposals for identifying such basic motifs of the biblical message. There are many more of them in his case; I attempt to focus on four such motifs. See Gerd Theißen, *The Sign Language of Faith* (London: SCM, 1995), pp. 17ff; Theißen, *Zur Bibel motivieren* (Gütersloh: Gütersloher Verlagshaus, 2003), pp. 131ff.

this sense that it shows itself to be inviolable and inalienable. In the most unusual of circumstances as well as in the midst of everyday life, in his strengths and weaknesses, and in the face of guilt and death, it is God's grace that provides the human being with sustenance and support.

From a biblical perspective, this grace is the pledge of God's love. The *motif of love* occurs in this tradition essentially as an account of a divine emotion expressed towards the human being and only secondarily as a human emotion. The grace in which this divine love finds expression is already discussed in the Old Testament, in the Hebrew Bible. 'Grace' is part of the vocabulary of the people of Israel. This people knows not only the experience of blessing, which is associated with the Creation and its continuity: 'While the earth remains, seedtime and harvest, cold and heat, summer and winter, day and night, shall not cease' (Genesis 8:22). It also knows the experience of salvation, God's liberating intervention in history, the beginning of something new, possible only thanks to God's loving attention to humanity. The Exodus out of bondage in Egypt became a fundamental experience of divine grace for the people of Israel: 'In the future, when your son asks you [...] tell him: "We were slaves of Pharaoh in Egypt, but the Lord brought us out of Egypt with a mighty hand"' (Deuteronomy 6:20–1). God's love for his people is apparent in this act of redemption. The aim of God's commandment is that the people themselves live up to this love. To comply with this commandment has no other meaning than to respond to God's grace and keep faith with His covenant. 'He has told you, O man, what is good; and what does the Lord require of you but to do justice, and to love kindness, and to walk humbly with your God?' (Micah 6:8). It is this correspondence between God's loyalty to the covenant and the human response through obedience to the divine commandment in which the historical texts of the Old Testament – including the major legal texts – meet with its prophetic message. And it is already a hallmark of Old Testament prophecy that it not only proclaims God's judgment of Israel's misdemeanours, but takes refuge in the forgiving God who makes it possible to start afresh (Micah 7:18–19):

> Who is a God like you, pardoning iniquity and passing over transgression for the remnant of his inheritance? He does not retain his anger forever, because he delights in steadfast love. He will again have compassion on us; he will tread our iniquities underfoot. You will cast all our sins into the depth of the sea.

But the New Testament gives this fundamental aspect of the biblical message a name – which is particularly striking in certain parts of the Prophetic tradition, in the second part of Isaiah for example. God's grace takes the form of a person. His unconditional affirmation of humanity despite all its obvious godlessness is given the name of Jesus of Nazareth. The fact that God Himself may be recognized in him is the revolutionary new feature of the New Testament. Indeed, God is recognized in him not only in his suffering and resurrection, but also in his earthly activities and preaching. In both respects, the New Testament ascribes to him the biblical title of the Son of Man, that is, the guarantee of God's eschatological presence. The image of God and of human beings conveyed in Jesus' activities as well as his suffering and death is expressed in particularly vivid form in parables. Two of these – the parable of the prodigal son and the parable of the good Samaritan – express with exemplary intensity how God's proximity transforms human beings' basic situation; the Sermon on the Mount is another way of articulating the same point. The faith that God's proximity will persist beyond the period of Jesus' earthly activities finds expression in the hope that His spirit remains.

The motif of love is thus bound up with the *motif of hope*. The prospect of God's future yet to come is linked with the confidence in his dynamic presence in time. The divine spirit is the pledge of His presence. This idea of a dynamic presence of God – not only in the blessing of His Creation, but in His merciful attention to human beings even in their forlorn state – gives rise to the complex and fascinating idea of the unity of God in the three persons of the Father, Son, and Holy Ghost. The doctrine of the Trinity, regarded by some as near-incomprehensible speculation, is intended to make clear that God as the Creator and the Elector of Israel, the one revealed in Jesus of Nazareth and present in the spirit is the same God. At issue here is the sameness of God in the dynamism of His presence in the world.

This brief review concludes with the *motif of the changing of ways*. Jesus' preaching has a clear centre. The proclamation of God's proximity is linked with an invitation to a life which is moulded by the love of God, love of one's neighbour and of oneself. Those who become aware of their dignity and experience freedom through faith are at the same time turned towards their neighbour. A life that is human and humane is one characterized by relations of mutual recognition among equals. The perspective of the Christian faith thus entails a practice aimed at justice, at conditions of equal freedom and mutual recognition. For a practice such as this, the hardest challenges lie in the experience of imposed inequality, that is, in which recognition is refused. Faith thus perceives social reality from below, from that perspective which has been summed up as 'putting the poor first'.

Only in response to one-sided interpretations of human dominion over Creation, as associated in the modern era with the dynamism of scientific development, has a perspective gained acceptance which long lay submerged. It does not limit putting the weak and humble first to one's fellow human beings, but includes the non-human natural world. The more expansive the human capacity and human aspirations to exercise power over the world and over life become, the more apparent it is that the self-limitation of human claims to disposal and the responsible use of human means of domination are key aspects of faith in God as the creative spirit present in His Creation. Compassion for those suffering and actions taken on behalf of future generations and the non-human natural world emerge as important dimensions in the Christian understanding of human existence.

All four of the basic motifs that I have spotlighted are informed by two conditions: the assumption that there is one God and that His relationship to the world is that of Redeemer. Monotheism traces everything that happens in the world back to the one God and evaluates it in light of Him. But this monotheism comes up against the contradiction of evil and the implacable fact of death. Belief in salvation renders these forces of secondary import. And it makes the one God, who revealed Himself to the people of Israel, universal, the God of all peoples. But the belief in salvation is subordinated to monotheism. Jesus Christ is not a second God, for 'nothing can stand next to God, other than God Himself'.[6] This linkage of monotheism and belief in salvation determines the development of the Christian faith in the triune God and thus the Christian understanding of God as a whole.

IV

What I have described as basic motifs of the Judeo-Christian tradition may be interpreted in a variety of ways.[7]

These motifs may be linked with a notion of the community of believers whose institutional character is so highly developed that the individual's relationship to God is made dependent on his relationship to the Church.[8] It is the Church's significance to the faith of the individual as an institution acting on her behalf that is at issue in the debate on the *Catholic* model of the Christian tradition. From the perspective of other traditions, it is confronted with a questioning of excessive *institutionalism*, which runs the risk of erasing the difference between a commitment to God and commitment to the Church.

But these motifs may also be linked with a version of the Christian faith

---

[6] Theißen, *Zur Bibel motivieren*, p. 137.

[7] In what follows I draw on a typology also found in the work of Theißen: *Zur Bibel motivieren*, pp. 253ff.

[8] See Friedrich Daniel Ernst Schleiermacher, *The Christian Faith* (Edinburgh: T. & T. Clark, 1999 [1831]), p. 103. He states that 'the antithesis between Protestantism and Catholicism may provisionally be conceived thus: the former makes the individual's relation to the Church dependent on his relation to Christ, while the latter contrariwise makes the individual's relation to Christ dependent on his relation to the Church'.

that concretizes the roots of this tradition in the biblical texts in such a way that literal statements of truth take the place of a truth that is understood and that is acquired through lived experience. It is the process of living acquisition of this tradition that is at stake in the *fundamentalist* versions of the Christian tradition, which turn the living character of these texts along with their inherent tensions into mere *literalism*.

Finally, this tradition may also be linked with a conception in which moral positions are no longer a human response to the promise of divine grace, but themselves become the key means of human salvation. In the attempt to come to terms with the moral failings of the Church itself, such forms of *social morality* have also made their presence felt in the interpretation of the Christian tradition, sometimes in recent forms of Christian expression. These attempt to articulate the biblical ethos as a critical response to the history of the Bible's impact and to liberate themselves from its anti-Jewish, repressive, and patriarchal interpretations; yet such efforts run the risk of descending into a moralism that makes certain values and deeds criteria of salvation. It is thus the given nature of salvation that is at issue in the critical debate on such moralism in the interpretation of the Christian tradition.

Where is the Protestant form of the Christian tradition located within this spectrum? We may understand the 'Protestant principle'[9] in such a way that it provides guidance on the capacity for discrimination. The feats of discrimination characteristic of a Protestant world view are anchored in the Reformation's rediscovery of the Pauline message of justification.

In Martin Luther's interpretation, the idea of justification is that only through the gift of faith and not through one's own efforts is the human being recognized and justified before God. This biblical insight, placed back at the centre of the Christian understanding of faith by the Reformers, gives rise to three feats of discrimination which Protestantism emphasizes in a special way.

The first is the fundamental *distinction between God and human being*. That wanting to be as God is a fundamental distortion of human existence is clearly evident in the excesses of the present era: in the presumptuous aspiration to create human life itself, and in the tendency to realize the claim of disposal over the lives of others by means of violence and to engage in excessive public displays of such violence. Only through the distinction between God and human being can we conceive of two things between which a state of tension otherwise inevitably prevails: the finite nature of the human being and the inviolability of human dignity. Only if this dignity is based on its status as addressed by God rather than its own achievements can it avoid shattering as a result of errors and guilt. Only

---

[9]   See Paul Tillich, *Der Protestantismus als Kritik und Gestaltung* (Munich and Hamburg: Siebenstern, 1966).

if human life is given a promise not dashed on the finiteness of this life can we refer to human dignity strictly understood. In this sense, the human being is an 'end in itself'. Two hundred years after the death of Immanuel Kant it is crucial to underline that the human being must not be degraded and used as a means. Human dignity is inalienable. This conviction fuses both the Christian legacy and secular legal ethos. In the constitution of the Federal Republic of Germany this is apparent in the link between the profession of responsibility before God and the human being on the one hand, and the inviolability of human dignity on the other. How to express something similar in the treaty on a European constitution is the subject of debate.

Second, the *distinction between the individual and her deeds* goes hand in hand with this. The human being is more than she makes of herself. She is more than her deeds or misdeeds, her accomplishments or mistakes. Everyone's life depends on the blessing of the new beginning, on the gift of forgiveness. I shall illustrate this through an example. It was the churches who made it clear, in the depressing days following 26 April 2002 in Erfurt, that however much grief and rage might be felt at the deeds of the deranged gunman Robert Steinhäuser in the Gutenberg high school in Erfurt, he, too, is in need and is worthy of intercession. Just as no-one is denied God's love, love should also be indivisible among human beings. This is an impulse on which humane and solidarity-based interaction depends. This is one of the reasons why people point out that in Jesus' interpretation, love for one's neighbour finds its clearest expression in love for one's enemy.

The third distinction concerns the *Christian understanding of hope*. The Christian faith leaves the ultimate truth to God and thus safeguards itself against all attempts to impose ultimate truths through violence and to postulate and implement totalitarian doctrines of salvation of the kind we have experienced over the past century, particularly in Germany. Christian hope distinguishes between God's future, the only context in which we can expect the revelation of a final truth by God, and the organization of the earthly future, which must always remain provisional and is dependent on responsible human action. Through this distinction, the Christian Church is helping humanize how people deal with the future.

These three distinctions between God and human beings, between the individual and his deeds, and between time and eternity open up a perspective on humanity in which the *human being is perceived as a relational being*. Neither what the human being possesses nor what she makes of herself is decisive. Rather, her humanity is anchored in the web of relations within which life takes place: the relations to God and to one's neighbour, to the society in which one lives and to oneself constitute human existence. This notion of the human being combines individuality and sociality, freedom and responsibility. Autonomy and self-determination are an essential component of this notion of the human being;

but they are not interpreted in such a way that the person's relationship to herself is detached or isolated from her relationship to her fellow human beings, the society in which she lives, and to God. Rather, this tradition privileges the idea of a human being aware of herself, oriented towards living in a community, and open to God. From the perspective of this tradition it is necessary to set in motion processes of education in which this notion of the human being is renewed, its sources recalled, and the cultural forms in which it has found expression understood.

The Protestant form of the Christian faith has from the outset tended to feature an alliance between faith and education. It favours a faith understood by individuals and for which they themselves take responsibility. But at the same time it tends to neglect the forms of religious communitization. If the institutionalism of the Catholic model of the Church faces critical scrutiny from the Protestant perspective, the latter must also consider, in self-critical fashion, the widespread indifference to the forms of religious community and their enduring institutional shape. For whenever such indifference holds sway, Protestantism fails to take seriously the fundamental insight inherent in the view of humanity which characterizes Protestantism itself: if it is an essential feature of the human person that she lives in relationships, then she is not merely accidentally but fundamentally a creature of community. If this is so, then the relationship of faith to the community is just as constitutive as is its character as personal conviction.

V

There is more to the Christian faith than cultural values. Its core is the relationship to God and thus a 'value-free truth'.[10] When we look into the contribution of the Judeo-Christian tradition to the cultural values of Europe, we must always keep in mind that the relationship between the truth of faith and the values which emerge from it is not reversed. If that were to happen, faith would make itself seemingly superfluous. But the values championed in its name would lose their foundation. The moral significance of the Christian faith inevitably depends on its transmoral core.

What values are at issue here? What values and norms are at play when, for example, Germany's Federal Constitutional Court states that we must continue to recognize the 'outstanding influence' of the Christian faith and the Christian churches on political life?[11] The highest of these values is *human dignity*, anchored

---

[10]   See Eberhard Jüngel, 'Wertlose Wahrheit. Christliche Wahrheitserfahrung im Streit gegen die "Tyrannei der Werte"', in Jüngel (ed.), *Wertlose Wahrheit. Zur Identität und Relevanz des christlichen Glaubens* (Munich: Mohr, 1990), pp. 90–109.

[11]   The crucifix ruling of 1995 features the following statement: 'Even a state which

in the fact that the human being was created by God and is called to respond to God's call and rendered capable of doing so through the Word of God.[12] God addresses everyone in the same way; this is the basis of the fundamentally equal legal status of each individual. This gives rise both to the idea that no-one should be denied the right to have rights and to an approach to human rights that links freedom and equality. It is true that for the most part human rights were initially formulated and implemented in opposition to or at arm's length from the churches; yet they owe their existence to impulses inextricably bound up with the Christian view of the human being.

Much the same may be said of the *principle of tolerance*. In the Christian understanding, its origins lie in the notion of 'divine tolerance'. This means that God 'tolerates' the human being who in his godlessness has turned away from Him, that is, God does not abandon him to his godlessness. As no-one is excluded from this divine tolerance, the Christian faith features a genuine route to tolerance, anchored in the fact that every human being – regardless of his subjective convictions, including the convictions of his personal faith – exists within the radius of action of God's love. But this principle of tolerance had to be brought to bear in opposition to an intolerance practised in the name of the Church itself throughout the history of intra-Christian conflict. Here, individuals and Christian minorities have blazed a trail for the major churches. The advocates of tolerance could rightly point, above all, to the Christian reform movements, including the Reformation of the sixteenth century. As a result, Luther's thesis of the freedom of the conscience, bound by the Word of God, influenced the development of modern political culture in a particular way.

It is true that Luther's own utterances – particularly about the Jews, the papists, and the peasants – were not exactly imbued with tolerance; and the Reformation as a whole led to acts of profound intolerance, including the burning of dissidents. But the basic idea of the Reformation, if applied consistently, entails not only the possibility of tolerance but the obligation to practise it. This is anchored in the manner in which obligation on the basis of conscience and freedom of conscience are linked already in Luther. This occurs in a way that

---

fully guarantees freedom of religion and thus commits itself to religious and ideological neutrality cannot cast off the culturally mediated and historically anchored values and attitudes on which social cohesion is based and on which the fulfilment of its own tasks depends. The Christian faith and the Christian Churches, however their legacy is judged today, have exercised an outstanding influence in this regard. The state cannot be indifferent to the traditions of thought, convictions and patterns of behaviour derived from them' (German Federal Constitutional Court 93, 1, 22).

[12]   See Trutz Rendtorff and Jürgen Schmude, *Wie versteht die evangelische Kirche die Rede von der 'Prägekraft des Christentums'? Einige Sätze zur Orientierung* (Hanover: EKD, 2004).

rules out all religious despotism. The Church's assignment is to stand up for the truth of the Gospel 'without human power, but by the Word of God alone'.[13] But with respect to the state, Luther leaves us in no doubt that its legitimate power ends where the individual's obligations on the basis of conscience begin; thus, as soon as it attempts to coerce people in matters of faith, one has no obligation to obey it.[14] 'Here I stand, I can do no other': it is quite legitimate that Luther's statement before the Diet in Worms in 1521 was declared the starting point of a culture of freedom of conscience and tolerance. If we look at the subsequent development of the idea of tolerance, we can systematically distinguish between three levels: the personal, the social, and the political.

Personal tolerance is to be understood as based in conviction rather than indifference. For otherwise this would not be a tolerance ensuing from freedom of conscience; personal tolerance is, after all, a matter of the freedom to form one's own convictions and commit to them. The aim of the *social tolerance* to which personal tolerance gives rise is mutual respect for convictions and ways of life rather than their renunciation. Finally, the purpose of *political tolerance* is to facilitate such social tolerance, to create a societal space in which convictions can develop and unfold. This end is served by the guaranteeing of religious freedom, which not only means, negatively, freedom from religion, but also, positively, freedom for religion.

Such a concept of tolerance implies a *relationship between state and church* that goes beyond a mere laicism and which, on the basis of mutual independence and the religious neutrality of the state, makes possible the state recognition of lived convictions and their social significance. The prerequisite here is the non-identification of the state with such convictions. This requires the representatives of the state to exercise restraint in advocating and presenting their personal religious views. It is this relationship between positive religious freedom and the need for moderation that is at issue, for example, in the dispute over the wearing of headscarves by Muslim teachers. Here, the future of tolerance is at stake in a very specific way.

The way in which freedom and commitment or, to put it in more modern terms, *freedom and responsibility* were linked by the Reformation through the concept of conscience, has contributed to the linkage of self-responsibility with solidarity and justice with respect to social action in general. This has influenced both the view of marriage and family, taking all the changes these have undergone

---

[13]   As stated in the Augsburg Confession of 1530, Art. 28; Evangelical Lutheran Ministerium of Pennsylvania, *Luther's Small Catechism with Additions including the Augsburg Confession* (Philadelphia, PA: Lindsay & Blakiston, 1855), p. 106.

[14]   Martin Luther, *Von weltlicher Obrigkeit, wie weit man ihr Gehorsam schuldig sei*, ed. by Delius *et al.* (Leipzig: EVA, 1996 [1523]), vol. 3, pp. 27ff.

into account, as well as the concept of a 'social market economy', in whose development thinkers motivated by Christianity played a significant role. The churches thus have a special affinity to the task of developing and preserving a socially just society and socially just state. Alongside this focus on the tasks of social justice, the responsibility to work for peace and the conservation of nature have become tremendously important in the Christian social ethos of the last few decades.

In this view of the human being, freedom and responsibility must go together. To link them is also the basic idea of democracy. Now that the collectivist view of the human being has died away with the demise of the communist dictatorships in Europe, our great task is to develop and promote a view of the human being that sees freedom and responsibility in their mutual imbrication. The fact that collectivism is a thing of the past does not necessarily mean that we must now leave the field to an isolated individualism. A notion of freedom in which the essence of freedom consists in its arbitrary expression not only cuts all ties with a Protestant concept of freedom, but also with the European tradition as a whole. The Enlightenment, for example, acknowledges that the rational enjoyment of freedom is not opposed to the life that we share with others. Her very freedom points the individual person towards the reality of living together with others. The notion of the autonomy of the free and independent person thus establishes her responsibility for the life of the community rather than nullifying it. In this sense, responsibility arises from freedom.

Finally, the Christian faith also brings the *motif of neighbourly love* into the world of law, the exercise of power and the pursuit of one's own advantage. Among its basic impulses is the call for a shift of perspective that requires you to look at a situation from the perspective of the other, the underdog, the weaker. The Golden Rule — which states that you should treat others as you would wish to be treated yourself (Matthew 7:12) — has surely become the most effective of moral principles, one which, though not of solely Christian origin, was imparted by Christianity. The culture of helping, promoted above all by the charitable institutions of the Christian churches and still represented on a large scale by such institutions today, is an indispensable pillar of humanity within society.

VI

But are there enough opportunities nowadays to bring the impulses of this Judeo-Christian tradition to bear amid processes of general communication? Empirical studies indicate a remarkable state of tension with respect to this issue. On the one hand, particularly in the middle of Europe, we are observing a process of declining commitment to the Church, which has as yet by no means run its course, a process which is often interpreted as an expression of general secularization; on the other hand, in many parts of the world people are turning towards religion, which may, conversely, point to a process of desecularization. We are seeing many people break away from tradition, expressed on the individual level, for instance, in the tendency to take one's membership of the Church less seriously or to withdraw from it entirely; a significant proportion of the population – particularly in eastern Germany – grows up without any ties to the Church. Yet calls for a new ethical stance grow ever louder. Here, even people who do not themselves belong to a church and who have not so far developed an inner relationship to Christian beliefs are emphatic about the churches' responsibility for the development of value-based convictions and attitudes. Many people describe German society as a multicultural one; but just as many observe that a society that has become religiously plural is in particular need of binding values and norms.

At least one conclusion can be drawn from these seemingly contradictory observations. The general thesis of an irreversible process of secularization does not do justice to this predicament. In light of this, some have begun to refer to a post-secular situation. Such a term is not very precise though, as Hans Joas in particular has shown.[15] For it is based on the assumption that a process of, as it were, complete secularization has first occurred, which is now being transcended by a further step into a post-secular reality. But this notion suffers, above all, from the fact that it confuses the transition to a secularist legal system – which has in fact, happily, occurred – with a secularization of society that has fully run its course. Yet the profoundest meaning of the enlightened secularity of the political order lies in the creation of a free social space for the profession of faith and the practice of religion within the community. The secular state thus protects society from the need to be secular. It is in fact the space in which guaranteed freedom can develop as the freedom to practise religion as well as the freedom from religion. It is a blessing that this is the case. For even secular institutions exist on the basis of conditions which they cannot themselves produce. The more secular institutions tend to put such conditions at risk, perhaps even destroy them, the more urgently they require the preservation of the forces which renew such conditions – including the forces of religion. In the present era, with its numerous tensions, we thus not only have the opportunity to bring the characteristic values of the Christian faith to bear. We have an obligation to do so.

---

[15]   See Hans Joas, 'Post-Secular Religion? On Jürgen Habermas', in Joas, *Do We Need Religion? On Experiences of Self-Transcendence* (Boulder, CO: Paradigm, 2008).

3

The Greco-Roman Tradition

Christian Meier

I have difficulties with the term 'values'. If I were to list the ancient 'values' that are thought to have defined Europe, it seems to me that I would have to bottle up all kinds of things (sealing them hermetically inside) which have in reality come together to form a broad stream and have had their effect within it.

Just as an example, let's take democracy. It would seem inherently obvious that it has come down to us as a 'value'. However, most of our sources were written by men who held a generally sceptical view of democracy (and of the 'people'). And this has long determined western opinion. At most, as they liked to believe, such a thing was possible in small polities, in cities, but not in the states of their own era. It was only with much effort that the idea took hold, particularly in the United States of America, that a democracy in which the people ruled through representatives was possible. But even there, people were generally hesitant to talk of democracy. A republic, according to Kant the 'only perfect civil constitution', that was something else: it was a mixed constitution. Even Jefferson's party was initially called republican, and switched over to the term 'Democrats' only in the nineteenth century. Even then, democracy was far from becoming a universal 'value'. That happened only in the twentieth century.

Nonetheless, ancient democracy has probably played a role in the medieval and, above all, modern history of Europe whose importance can scarcely be overstated. But in rather indirect fashion: through all those things bound up with it, which it brought about, through all the ways its ongoing effects were felt. If Plato, for example, did a good deal to ensure that democracy was nothing less than feared, in my opinion his entire philosophy was nonetheless conceivable only in light of the huge challenge represented by this very democracy (in its Attic form), together with all the things that came into being as a result of it.

In essence, democracy was a part of that current which led from Antiquity – albeit via certain processes of narrowing and, above all, certain detours – to the modern era and which, whatever one may think of 'values', made the ancient world a role model for medieval and modern Europe in a huge variety of ways, helping determine its ideals, convictions, key ideas, and thus its central motifs.

How this has panned out in detail is something the ancient historian is not competent to say. For at issue here is not what Antiquity produced, what it was; but how it was assimilated, that is, received. Every reception entails selecting certain elements and produces misunderstandings. What one picks out of the cake of the historical record depends far more on the one doing the picking than on the cake, especially given that the picker adds various elements of his own, an aroma, as it were, which ultimately determines his taste in (and his notion of) the thing itself.

One thing is clear: the ancient sources had a profound impact on medieval and modern Europe, through an endless series of large-scale, small-scale, and very small scale processes of reception, sometimes directly, sometimes indirectly. Why was this? We could try to identify the characteristics of the ancient legacy that might have radiated particular fascination. But there are always two parties involved in fascination. It requires receptivity.

By way of comparison, let's consider another case of reception of the Greek sources, that of the Arabs. They assimilated these sources far earlier than the Christian West, and translated a good deal of them, so that a number of Greek texts reached us only in Arabic translation. Yet, first, they selected specific texts concerned primarily with philosophical and scientific texts (mathematics, astronomy, medicine, etc.); second, once they had mastered these texts, with a few exceptions, they hardly ever consulted the Greek originals again (with very few exceptions, they did not learn the ancient languages); and third (and this is certainly linked with the selection they had made), they did not allow the Greek texts to challenge key aspects of their worldview. To the extent that this did occur, it was quickly nipped in the bud or prevented from gaining traction.

Medieval and modern Europe, meanwhile, constantly studied the Greek – and, before that, the Latin – sources, and indeed in the original. And not only the scientific and philosophical sources. Time and again, Europeans took the Greeks and Romans as role models for their own lives and action as well as their own social order. Sculptors took their lead and learned from the ancient works, as did architects, lawyers, historians, writers, scholars in the widest range of disciplines, orators, politicians. Many young people learned Latin and Greek at school, enabling them to cope with, indeed live in, the ancient sources. And as 'the ancients' became major role models or at least highly respected authorities, people questioned their assumptions in light of them. Often, this occurred in opposition to the Christian sources, which, despite sometimes intense resistance, were unable to prevail against this tendency.

How was this possible? Were Christian Europeans simply more open, less clever, or more unformed, and less fixed in their thinking than the Arabs? Does it make a difference whether you get the ancient sources via living people, the Greeks of the Byzantine Empire – or merely from books and other remnants? Did the Church allow for more room for manoeuvre in its approach to the Holy Scriptures than did Islam with respect to the Koran?

Or did Western, Latin Christianity willingly or unwillingly make medieval and modern Europeans highly receptive (and sometimes addicted) to the ancient sources? Was this because it did, despite all the ruptures with tradition, in fact entail plenty of Greek and Roman elements and transmit them further, thus laying the foundation for the revival of the ancient, a foundation on which it could ceaselessly stimulate new impulses, a foundation which enabled people to feel a sense of affinity with it? This was not entirely disconnected from the fact that the ancient texts were constantly being copied and handed down in the monasteries. The Gospels and the Pauline Epistles were in Latin; the theology of the Church Fathers was full of borrowings from ancient philosophy, while canon law and the practice of administration owed their existence to the Roman Empire. In brief, the question arises as to whether the legacy of the ancient world met with such tremendous and, over the long term, such widespread receptivity in Europe, in contrast to the Islamic world, on the basis of factors inherent in the Church or generated by it.

If this is the case, then medieval and modern Europe are connected with Antiquity far more directly than is commonly assumed. Rather than preceding the history of Europe, the ancient world constitutes Europe's early history. On this view, Christianity not only fought against and eliminated many ancient elements, but in fact, and above all, saved and passed on many such elements, and not only in terms of outward appearance. Just as Christianity owed its success to needs which ancient society itself ultimately brought about and could no longer satisfy, it itself ultimately brought into being a number of needs which it was unable to satisfy, which then caused people to turn time and again to the ancient sources.

I am unable to answer this question; to the extent that this is possible at all, it would require comparative studies on a huge scale. I would nonetheless like to underline the continuity between ancient and medieval/modern Europe, at least hypothetically. My thesis is that something quite new entered world history with the Greeks, and that this was a core element of that which has marked out Europe since then, for at least two and a half millennia. We are dealing here with a highly chequered history, in which the Greek was at its most productive in association with the Roman and the potential for continuing the ancient legacy and taking it up afresh was largely transmitted through Christianity.

The new element that the Greeks brought into the world was the development of culture in the absence of a monarchy playing any truly influential role. To put it crudely: cultural development on the basis of freedom rather than domination.

What this means is best shown in connection with the other question of how this came about, in other words, historically. I leave to one side the further question as to the extent to which Greek culture should be seen as an axial age culture. In at least one respect, it surpassed all the others, namely in this absence of an influential monarchy and, as a result, in the fact that it made democracy possible.

By 'Greeks' I mean here those who began afresh following the collapse of Mycenaean culture and a number of severe traumas.

In the first centuries, about which we know little, many of them, especially those living near the coast of the Aegean, became aware that they lived in small independent polities in as-yet embryonic form; while they were ruled by monarchs, these were merely *primi inter pares*.

This situation could endure over the long term only because no external power was interested in the Aegean region. It is true that over time there were ever tighter commercial links with the east. Phoenician merchants came to the Greeks, and they themselves travelled to the Levant coast and, at some point, to Egypt as well. They adopted an enormous number of things from the advanced eastern civilizations: goods, knowledge, images, ideas, myths, ways of worshipping the gods, the symposium, technologies, experts, and, not least, aspirations (to wealth, wisdom, literature, culture in general). The development of their thought, their knowledge, their imagination, was largely determined by the Orient.

But peculiarly, their political structure, indeed their approach to life, was hardly influenced by the east. To be more precise: at most, the initial political influence from the east may have consisted in learning, for example, from the Israelites and perhaps also from the Phoenicians, that monarchy is a dubious thing.

But this they could work out for themselves, and the problem cannot have seemed especially important to them, as their monarchs were in any case very weak.

At all events, the result of Greek activities and developments, which probably intensified from the late ninth century (together with all the changes triggered by them), was very peculiar. That which was increasingly being acquired on a large scale through trade, robbery, and intellectual stimulation benefited a broad class, roughly speaking the nobility, rather than the monarchs. The monarchs in fact receded into the background as the situation became more dynamic; they were not even strong enough to be associated with any profound upheavals as was the case, if we can trust the historical record, with the fall of the kingdom in Rome a good two centuries later. Monarchy was therefore absent as an agent of cultural development.

Religious authorities, too, played no significant role in this regard. Priests never exercised power among the Greeks. Even Delphi, and here we have to make a distinction, had very little power, but a great deal of authority, which was essentially rooted in intellectual superiority and was focused on the giving of advice.

Above all, with the exception of Sparta and, to a more limited degree, Athens, there were almost no attempts to conquer other polities, in other words, to establish larger polities. The Greeks liked to make war, but instead of conquering, they at most made others dependent on them, and the wars largely had the character of tournaments. The problem of the surplus of people without enough land of their own, which got worse in the eighth century, was solved by founding colonies hundreds of miles away, that is, other small, independent polities.

The early world of the polis thus achieved stability. And a unique polis-like culture began to emerge; common to the Greeks between southern Italy (later Marseilles) and Cyprus, between Cyrene in North Africa and the Crimea – though they did not think of uniting politically.

Now the polis-based culture, that is, retention of the many small independent poleis and the development of the associated ways of life, was possible only if the influential members of the poleis (initially 'nobles' for the most part, joined by others later on) got used to the idea of viewing this way of doing things as self-evidently appropriate to them, or were able to do so as a result of certain attitudes and preferences. The geography of the region, with its numerous small territories and islands, may well have made it seem advantageous to limit the polities spatially. But the Greeks need not have submitted to this. And there were notable exceptions in which geography did not prevent expansion.

The Greeks *wanted* this form of political organization (with whatever degree of awareness). It was matched by a particular type of disposition, initially within the influential class; its members wished to be as independent as possible, autarkic (as it was later called – and still valued), their own masters. A house of one's own (farm and people) served as the economic basis for this. But this independence also required a minimum of restrictions imposed from above. Consequently, the Greeks were keen to concede as little power as possible to the office-bearers; over time, they placed these alongside the monarchs, then replaced the latter with the former. It was significant that the Greeks thought that freedom included not paying taxes (at most, if the polity was very poor, a tithe was taken for the cult of the gods). Expenses arising from the holding of office and the waging of war, plus armaments, one paid for oneself. If there was a need for greater expenditure and public revenue was insufficient, then the members of the community contributed on an ad hoc basis. There was a good deal of 'sponsorship'. And public tasks were, as far as possible, taken care of by the nobles as a group (later, as far as possible, by the assembly and council). For this, though, the polity could not be too large. Had it been, then the individuals would, as it were, have become smaller, losing the ability to directly affect things – unless they had attained a certain stature via function or hierarchy, in other words, in mediated fashion, or via wealth or specialization, that is, in an unbalanced fashion. But this is just what they did not want.

Independence led to a corresponding striving for all-roundedness, for comprehensiveness with respect to human abilities. If you are unwilling to entrust office-bearers and specialists with much power, you have to be capable of doing many things yourself – or at least to do what you can to achieve such capability. The Greeks did appreciate the works produced by specialists, but not the specialists themselves, at least not as citizens. For they withdrew from the agora, and that was more important than the pleasant or indeed essential things their works may have contributed to it. It is better not to consent to your daughter marrying the fortress builder, as useful as he is to the city – if you are a citizen.

These poleis also featured a major role for the public sphere, in a very literal sense: the spaces in which people spent a great deal of time in order to meet, talk, show themselves, keep up to date with events, advise, and make decisions; to distinguish themselves, but also to monitor each other; the spaces, also, in which people celebrated religious festivals with singing and dancing (and in which they practised for such events) and where they engaged in sport. These public spaces, however, were made up entirely of men; women were, if possible, to avoid spending time there other than during religious festivals.

I am unable to describe here *in extenso* this Greek form of the person and the poleis. I shall limit myself to one or two more sentences. In these small polities, in which the elements of domination were, relatively speaking, developed very little, a large number of tasks, otherwise delegated to specific institutions, were shared between citizens (initially the nobility), that is, entrusted to their combined efforts. It was down to them to ensure the necessary degree of affective control. They could cure themselves of the urge to do everything themselves only on a mutual basis, or were quite unable to do so, and could merely reduce or resist it on a case-by-case basis. This was difficult and could succeed only to a limited degree and gradually. Consequently, despite all the individualism, the members of these polities needed a highly developed capacity to strike a balance, which was put to the test again and again. The large number of things that could go wrong and how well the Greeks were aware of these problems is portrayed in the *Iliad*, the epic that relates Achilles' rage. We could also mention the many accounts in which, even in the Classical period, Greeks expressed their demands for revenge in an open and undisguised fashion.

In brief, these polities featured a breed of people who wanted to be free and to freely live out their impulses – people who were also capable of dealing with the resulting abuses among themselves to some extent, to develop over time, for example, mechanisms of arbitration and skills of persuasion (together with a certain elegance of manner and language, of which there is such a wealth of evidence).

This early world of the Greeks was perhaps not terribly unusual in comparison to other early peoples, apart, that is, from individuals' private ownership of land and from the fact that lineages or clanship played practically no role. But what was unusual was the fact that the Greeks developed an advanced civilization out of this early peculiarity and through its preservation. This was unique in world history, as far as I can see. It was a cultural development which did *not* feature the following tendencies:

- expansion of public duties and tasks or only on a negligible scale;

- the ambitious reorganization of the political unit, its embodiment in specific personnel and its becoming independent from the bulk of the citizenry, improved technology, enormous buildings, the development of infrastructure, increased productivity;

- functional differentiation, specialization, that is, the tendency to create unbalanced individuals;

- hierarchies or the like;

- in line with this, the members (or subjects) of the political units tended not to become economically and mentally dependent on the functioning of complex apparatuses and power centres standing apart from the whole.

No, the Greek cultural development that began here was aimed at improving the lives of those largely independent men in their small cities in accordance with their needs, and that meant equipping them with ever more knowledge, abilities, and institutions, that is, cultivating them.

This cultural development served, for example, to further expand the public sphere in a concrete sense, in other words, sport (and contests, as in Olympia), for another feature of this breed of people was that much energy and ambition was diverted into competition. This was something specifically Greek; it existed elsewhere, but only here did it play such an important role. This does not mean that the Greeks did not strive to gain power. Quite the opposite. But it meant that even power and domination were largely regarded by them merely as objects of competition; the same applied to wealth. What they were scarcely capable of doing on the other hand (and were unwilling to do) was to build power structures, conform to the necessities of power building and keep power. In a nutshell: they lacked the willingness to serve power, their own or that of another.

But the Greek development of culture also aimed at special forms of expression, of communication (such as lyric poetry), the deepening and spreading of knowledge and the development of abilities such as that of composing and writing down an epic of more than 15,000 verses soon after the adoption of writing; the exploration of new possibilities of art, the elaboration of a certain luxury, finding better ways of interaction between the poleis, and of limiting war. The new room for manoeuvre which was obtained (through the founding of colonies for example) was not only an expression of new competence in itself, but also required new abilities in order to keep in check the associated freedom.

In brief, what the Greeks had been and wanted to be, they wished to be in ever better, more intelligent, artistic, cultivated ways. This was the initial priority. This only consolidated further the unique character of the Greeks – with the help of the Orient.

Crisis eventually struck. Tellingly, it broke out around one hundred years after the foundation of the first colonies, when space for settlements became scarce. There were major economic problems, tensions between upper and lower classes, ambitious men united the poor and needy, the dissatisfied, under their leadership and founded tyrannical regimes. This, one might have thought, would have opened up the possibility of obtaining power not only in the city, but beyond it – by establishing larger polities. Key developments of relevance to the future would, one might think, perhaps have turned out differently.

Yet all expansion of power remained temporary and highly restricted. The tyrants managed neither to give the polis a fundamentally different structure nor to establish larger polities. Sooner or later, all were deposed. Above all, the polities were consolidated without a monarchy.

Admittedly, the tyrants did contribute a fair amount to this process of consolidation, that is, to economic improvements, to diminishing the tensions between upper and lower classes, as well as to expanding the infrastructure, and to some extent even to the cohesion of the citizenries (through the establishment and provisioning of cults and festivals). They also erected a shelter, as it were, for the suffering cities during stormy periods, which after their fall (and once the weather had calmed down) could be cast off entirely (in contrast to the absolute monarchs of the modern period who created a state that was capable of surviving their fall).

That things turned out this way may have been determined, first, by the fact that while the tyrants could win and secure power (the latter by means of body guards for example), they were unable to lastingly objectivize and consolidate it. They were unwilling and/or unable to carry out those duties essential to such power (or to find people willing and able to do so). At bottom, they themselves wished to be as independent and free as possible – by increasing the extent of their power.

But second, over time – in light of the repeated experience of arbitrary rule, which tyranny was generally quick to degenerate into – the conviction took hold among Greek political thinkers that a just polis-based political order excluded any kind of monarchy.

Here, another major step in the development of political culture was taken, seen most clearly in the fields of political thought and philosophy. Entirely new intellectual possibilities were developed, again to some extent through borrowings from the Orient, but for the most part anchored in the specific needs of Greek society – which now meant not just the upper class, but at least the middle class as well.

This society was faced with enormous tasks: the socio-economic crisis persisted in places. In Athens for example, violent conflicts threatened to break out early in the sixth century, as experienced already in other cities. People had reason to fear that tyranny would be established as a result. How could this be prevented? In any event, it was not just a matter of satisfying specific legitimate interests, but of stabilizing the polity, which had been turned upside down; that is, of conceiving and enforcing an order without having (or wishing to have) an authority which could have guaranteed it. This had to be a self-sustaining order – anchored in its citizens' teamwork.

In light of such problems, the essential thing was to identify causalities, the laws governing the life of the polis, and to find some kind of equilibrium. This was possible only if people assumed that the world is amenable to explanation. This opened up a more general problem, that of understanding the interconnections between the various forces at work within the polis, which was conceived as a kind of cosmos in miniature. Solon of Athens tried to solve this problem at the level of the polis. Two generations later, we find the same model being applied to the cosmos itself by Anaximander: how does the Earth stay up, given that no-one is holding it? His answer was: through a system of equilibrium that it forms with the planets.

This, in my opinion, is the origin of early Greek philosophy, based on numerous templates from the Orient (which may have influenced Solon) – but with a specifically Greek mode of questioning, aimed at discovering natural laws and possible equilibrium.

Perhaps I may be permitted to insert some remarks on the role of reason (*nous*) among the Greeks. In his sociology of religion, Max Weber pointed out that reason and processes of rationalization occur in all civilizations. Reason is part and parcel of the human being and tends, somehow, to develop. But processes of rationalization proceed in different directions, have different starting points, differ in scope (that is, affect the different areas of human life to varying degrees), and are radical to differing degrees.

Among the Greeks, they affected the entire order of the polity and its foundations, as well as the order of the world itself, early on, even in archaic times. The polis, the – free, male – citizenry and private ownership, as a rule including ownership of land, was the presupposition of all Greek thought. But everything else is disposable. Since even Solon's one true order could be achieved only through changes, all templates were up for discussion from the outset and indeed *coram publico*, that is, entrusted to reason to a particularly great extent. As the citizens had to be won over to this order, it had to be communicated to them rationally – a far cry from all secret and specialist knowledge (which was, of course, nonetheless rampant in certain circles). 'If one wishes to speak with reason (*xyn noi*), one must hold fast to that which is common (*xynoi*) to all, as a city holds fast to the law, but much more strongly', concluded Heraclitus.

The Greek understanding of order was hindered very little by the internalization of aristocratic superiority or religious requirements. On the contrary, a great deal of religion became imbued with rationality. The world of the gods, generally irrational in itself, was modified by the belief that the weather god Zeus was responsible for justice – and what justice is became at once a question of political theology and political philosophy: a thoroughly rational matter, in other words. In this sense, rationalization was taken particularly far here; it also determined the character of the citizenry as a whole, both upper and lower classes.

The domestic economy also underwent a certain rationalization among the Greeks. But this occurred to a far lesser degree than in the organization of the polis.

As in the polis and cosmos, objective standards were also sought in architecture: the individual elements of the building had to stand in a precise relationship to one another. This was later to define the building of temples – rather than factors such as tremendous size and splendour, as had been the central concern of the tyrants for a time.

Measurements, laws, and natural laws – all of this constituted, as it were, the correlate of freedom. Objective realities – it was these to which the free Greeks, with such limited tolerance for subjective power, were most likely to sign up. Later, this gave rise to the belief in the possibility of the rule of law.

It was nonetheless difficult, at least in a number of particularly troubled places, to domesticate the free nobility. They were all too quick to use their power, often in arbitrary fashion, against the members of the middle and lower classes, which were sometimes also affected by their factional struggles, by revenge and counter-revenge. There was only one antidote: the strengthening of the broader classes. The precondition for this, however, was that they themselves could make their presence felt in the public sphere, and indeed on a regular basis – if possible in the people's assembly or in committees, or in councils that would need to be established. The elite learned that the poor and needy could not simply be suppressed. This would perhaps have been possible through a stronger form of rule, which was just what they did not want. On the other hand, it wouldn't do to deal with the poor's vociferous complaints and uprisings anew every time they arose. It was therefore necessary to attempt to provide them with institutional means of making their voice heard.

But the functioning of such institutions required the development of an awareness of civic responsibility. From the time of Solon, we see the political thinkers reminding people of the importance of responsibility. That the willingness to exercise such responsibility did develop was facilitated by the fact that the urban public sphere, as the domain of the nobility, was highly attractive. It made sense, assuming that one was reasonably available, to neglect one's own household to a degree in order to be a somebody in public life.

There thus arose the early forms of democracy, civic responsibility, civic equality, a political equality, and thus the discovery of the citizen. The Greeks had finally progressed far beyond Israel and the Phoenicians.

But the crucial test of the world of the Greek polis was yet to come. In 480 BC, the Persian superpower attempted to subjugate the Greeks west of the Aegean. There was now a power in the east interested in the Aegean. There were many reasons to capitulate. The conventional wisdom was that the Persians were vastly superior to the Greeks. But Sparta, Athens, and about thirty other smaller cities resisted – and won. A David defeated a Goliath, with far-reaching consequences for world history.

The Earth was divided into two halves, for the first time as far as I am aware. There was Europe and Asia. And an awareness grew that they were different parts of the world in terms of the nature of society as well: there obedience holds sway, here freedom.

Athens was transformed from a canton to a world power overnight. Much of Greece's energy and many of its problems came together there. Classical Greek culture develops; apart from Homer, who came earlier, and Plato and Aristotle, who came a little later, everything which the broad western public has absorbed from the Greeks came into being then. Classical sculpture, the great temple of Olympia, the buildings of the acropolis. Much of this was entirely new (such as the writing of history, sophistry, Socrates' questions) or essentially new, such as classical tragedy and comedy. Incidentally, it was the only period when democracy (represented by democratically composed commissions) sponsored the creation of outstanding architecture. The *demos* of Athens also made up the audience of the dramas, and to some extent the audience of the sophists, Herodotus, and Socrates as well. Advanced culture and popular culture came into contact, became more tightly enmeshed in fact than at any other time in history.

This makes sense only if we assume that the citizenry, as a whole and in its various parts, needed all the cultural phenomena generated at the time.

Quite suddenly, people experienced an extraordinary expansion of their scope for action. They became aware of the scale – and monstrousness – of human ability to a degree otherwise unknown before the modern era. But the triumphs, the successes, also awoke doubts and fears. Questions about questions arose. The most difficult of decisions had to be made with respect to foreign policy and military matters. New claims took hold within the domestic political sphere. Here, the audacity of one innovation in particular can scarcely be overstated: the introduction of unrestricted, radical democracy, in which the most difficult of decisions were made in the people's assemblies, which met very frequently, decisions which shoemakers, tailors, and linen weavers could play a far from insignificant role in shaping.

All of this threw up a ceaseless torrent of new practical questions, which the Athenians, at least for a time, solved with a relatively high degree of success; they benefited a great deal from their dynamism, and the unfamiliar nature and speed of their actions. Even when they were overly audacious, they often won because others were unable to respond fast enough.

But there was another dimension to these decisions. Questions arose on another level as well. That which the Athenians knew, the traditional knowledge in which they were rooted, quickly proved inadequate – in light of the rapid changes. What should be their touchstone? Time and again, there was a gaping chasm between the time-honoured and the appropriate in which it was all too possible to come to grief. What was just? What was permitted? What was right? It was often necessary to do things that would traditionally have been seen as unjust, impermissible, or wrong.

A multitude of questions of an ethical, indeed philosophical nature opened up, affecting large numbers of people. We know this because we are familiar with some of the attempts to grapple with these questions – through tragedy in particular, the sophists' discussions, and the Socratic questions, attempts, that is, made within the public sphere of the day.

But the question went much further still. What was human reason capable of, as magnificent as it had quite unexpectedly shown itself to be in recent times, if it succumbs time and again to *ate*, blindness, or even to pathological learning? What are human beings really capable of, if they fail so often despite all their abilities and perhaps even because of them? What is the lot of the human being, what is the human being in the first place? What do the gods do, what do they want, how do they operate? Or do they not even exist? Does human action have meaning, is injustice punished? One assumes so; such assumptions endow the world with order, and one can believe it possible to act meaningfully within it. But the more one believes this to be possible and the more one extends the scope of one's action, the higher the aspirations, the more one becomes aware of meaninglessness – and of the wretchedness of human beings, with whom the gods play their cruel game. Other questions were concerned with knowledge.

To what extent was it even possible, when experience shows that everything is relative and seems different to different people.

The atmosphere was replete with these and similar questions at the time. They were taken up by art and literature, history and intellectual discourse, which were challenged to come up with answers in the various languages and media known to human culture. But the questions vibrate within the answers, and often enough the answers entailed pushing the questions further, often culminating in aporias. This was matched by the favoured forms for expressing the great diversity, the conflictual nature, or the sheer ambivalence of human affairs: drama, with its great variety of roles, the use of dialogues in the writing of history – beginning with Herodotus' debate on the constitution, through those in which the sophists and Socrates engaged, to those through which Plato developed his (and his adversary's) ideas. At work here is nothing less than a passion for questioning, a willingness to be disturbed, but also a wealth of expectation, throughout the citizenry, that things could be understood.

This, it seems to me, is what makes the legacy of this century so fascinating, so accessible, and also of such consistent relevance to the present.

- This is a relatively young culture full of freedom and potential for development.

- Its citizenry is as democratic as it is possible to be (if one leaves aside the fact that political rights were restricted to male citizens).

- Thanks to its tremendous victories, this is a self-confident society, alarmingly so, even to itself; one full of expectations, audacious, but, of course, also exposed to a whole welter of uncertainties.

- This society is defined (and frequently afflicted) by a sense of responsibility, open-minded, since everything is new, unencumbered by the ideas that traditionally dominated, one that does not easily lapse into a new routine.

- Because it is constantly required to judge and decide about the most important and difficult of matters, time and again its citizenry is dependent on arguments, rather than relying, as so often, on experience; not easily satisfied either with recklessness or resignation, these citizens are consistently restless and stirred up.

In other words, these were citizens who not only wanted to engage in politics, administer their city and wage war, but who also wanted (and needed) to know what was happening around them, who wanted to understand, that is, relate the new things that they did, suffered, and experienced to what they knew and believed.

This was the ambience, this defined the atmosphere, this made up the horizon of experience, this generated a good portion of the problems within which the writers, artists, and intellectuals moved as well. And as they necessarily referred to (and shared in) the inescapable fact of this citizenry, as some of them (like the writers of tragedy and comedy) were in direct competition with one another, and were also members of a highly competitive world, they had to be understandable, their work had to be accessible – and demanding.

This is what they all shared. Over and above this, the different genres were directed towards different ends. The sculptural image of the human being was concerned, to put it in a nutshell, with the ideal of the multi-skilled person, the body thoroughly trained, like an athlete, capable of defending itself, poised and, at the same time, ruled by reason. Naked and far removed from any notion of one-sidedness, specialization, or class distinctions, this was nothing but a human being, but in its highest form. In tragedy, it was the human being in relation to the tension between greatness (often presumption) and the ties of fate, often enough failure, that tended to be the focus of interest. Tragedy was also defined by the issue of the meaningfulness of events (which ultimately led to manifestations of the most terrible meaninglessness). Finally, in the writing of history, the question of meaning was held in check – in order that one might get at the actual events and causalities and at contingency (which did not stop Thucydides' history from concluding with the tragedy of Athens). In addition, because it explored the anxiety that held sway during this era, tragedy mercilessly exaggerated traditional myth (and transformed it into highly impressive stories and images).

At all times, and this was an expression of Greek rationality, a certain reduction was at work, a focussing on the essential, natural laws, proportion (expressed particularly in the struggle with disproportion).

I don't know whether we should assume that 'the Greeks' were especially gifted artistically or were particularly good at producing great artists. But it is clear that artists and writers were challenged in fifth-century Greek society in a very specific way. According to Jacob Burckhardt, it is possible for certain places to 'produce [...] a disproportionate number of important individuals' from among its citizens.[1] He suggests that this is a matter of the highest of human powers, awoken by the extraordinary.

The legacy of this century forms a single great overall complex, made up of the great victories of the Greeks (Marathon, Salamis), the splendour that they displayed, and a hugely fascinating variety. The whole range of experiences which a culture facing challenges on all sides had with itself and the world found expression in this variety. This complex is comprehensible,

---

[1]   Jacob Burckhardt, *Über das Studium der Geschichte* (Munich: Beck, 1982), p. 181

then incomprehensible, initially convincing, then questionable again, attractive and hard to escape from because it constantly draws you in; in a word, it is fascinating the moment one allows oneself to be captured by it.

This was the first major cultural manifestation – one of a unique kind – of a very free, very independent, very open, and thus self-questioning culture in a world of action, very intensive action that could be questioned, but action that featured a growing awareness of its own questionable nature.

The Classical period came to an end with the defeat of Athens in 404 BC. It bears all the hallmarks of an exceptional era. Never again was an entire citizenry able to produce and maintain such a culture. But the great philosophy, whose character was profoundly determined by the questioning of the fifth century, only began at this time. And the heights of rhetoric, of language, of science were also still to come. This language yet to develop was intended, in significant part, to persuade a people's assembly and popular court.

Shortly afterwards the world was conquered by the Macedonian, Alexander. What the Greeks managed to do in the fourth century and through Hellenism made it easier for the Romans and, later, medieval and modern people to access their classical works. But the Greek impact really began in the fifth century.

This culture of freedom, responsibility, and openness, of reason applied both extensively and deeply, and of the willingness to question radically the world of people and gods, to question oneself, laid the foundations for western Europe and moulded it in crucial ways. It was for long far superior. It allowed people to say, shape, think, and ask that which they themselves were hardly able (or at least less able) to say, shape, think, and ask. And it was highly provocative. Thanks to the diversity of its perspectives, thanks to the ambivalence through which it came to know itself, one could and still can discover it again and again. Time and again, Antiquity has seemed more contemporary than the most recent version of modernity, as the most recent appropriation of ancient materials and ideas. In particular, people needed to look back at the ancient world in order to generate something new, to advance into the unknown and to think in new ways in light of surprising changes. The ambiguous universal, which the Greeks and later the Romans sought to decipher, could in time always assert itself anew alongside the unambiguous particular, alongside specialization, as it were.

Certainly, in other times, including our own, people have progressed far further in many respects, have had a great number of other experiences and sought to express them, experiences which are, however, more specific, more individual, often crueller, and at any rate more defiant of linguistic expression (and mostly related more strongly to the particular circumstances of a given era), together with the experience of being stretched between opposites, of inner turmoil, alienation, isolation, and radical doubt. But alongside these things, I believe that the more universal focus of the ancient world, though this universality was constantly taken to the extreme, can hold its ground as long as people are prepared to truly question themselves and their world.

* * *

Rome, first of all, supplemented the Greek legacy in highly fruitful fashion with certain elements rooted in its own special soil. Second, it took over the Greek inheritance, using it to mould a Roman culture of its own. Greek artists contributed a good deal to this. What Rome produced in terms of the use of form, architecture, sculpture, history, literature, philosophy, rhetoric, bore a strong Greek influence everywhere and in ever new ways – yet was nonetheless Roman. In a certain sense it was a Greco-Roman culture with which the Imperium Romanum was imbued, in the east far more Greek, in the west more Roman. And it cannot be denied that things Greek could be spread further and more easily in Latin and thus take hold more deeply in the west as well.

But the Romans' most important contributions to the legacy of the ancient world were those that they largely produced themselves (albeit with some Greek influence).

First came the republic, that specifically Roman political order, which combined strong leadership with opposition, privileges for the nobility with civil rights for all citizens, which got by without monarchs, conquered the entire Mediterranean world, and proved extraordinarily stable, and was consequently much admired and consistently regarded as exemplary. In addition, in sharp contrast to the Greek polis, this republic was capable of extending Roman law to allies and the conquered, on a sometimes grand scale.

Unlike the polis, the *res publica* had a distinct centre, which raised it as a whole far above its members (as, *mutatis mutandis*, the state was later to do, first in harness with the monarchs, then other representatives). It was characterized partly by the kingdom of the early years (of an Etruscan hue), partly by unquestioned convictions, and, finally, partly by the common will of the ruling aristocracy, which was constantly reinforced and thus objectivized and safeguarded by appropriate mechanisms.

Though the aristocrats did not actually represent the *res publica*, they did identify with it in a special way. And they called the shots within it, though their power was not unlimited. In line with this, the Roman concept of the citizen could not be defined (at least not to a large extent) by participation and having a say in the polity, as was the Greek. It was initially strongly marked by the military, by obedience (though there were certain rights of opposition), and later, above all, by rights or claims to respect (as well as to support within the framework of clientelism). This is why it was far less difficult, relatively speaking, to grant citizenship to others. Because of this capacity for extension of citizenship to others, and the correspondingly minor political importance associated with this status, though emphasis was placed on certain freedoms (and a certain degree of help in times of need), the Roman concept of the citizen is a particularly good model for the EU, which now covers a geographical area similar in size to the Imperium Romanum, though some of the regions included are different.

After the republic came the rule of the Caesars – a thread picked up by the medieval emperors (initially prompted more by the synchronous Byzantine Empire). This is one tradition that has petered out. Much the same may be said of the Roman imperial tradition, which was so significant in the Middle Ages and the early modern period. It is concentrated in the myth of Rome, the holy and eternal city, a myth which benefited the papacy so greatly over the long term (nurturing the highly consequential and productive tension between spiritual and temporal power). Various elements of governmental and administrative organization inherited from Rome, such as the concept of office and the architecture and symbols of domination, have long since ceased to play a significant role.

But there is one thing of Roman origin that is still alive and well, and this is undoubtedly by far the most important, lasting element of Roman tradition: Roman law. It is the product of a nearly 1000-year history, made possible by the specific order of the republic, which extended far into the imperial period in this respect, essentially the work of many generations of Roman legal practitioners (with occasional contributions from Greek thought) and in particular the work of the incredibly long period during which this highly sophisticated law developed very gradually out of the practice of jurisprudence and legal assessment; essentially, it consisted of a great number of legal opinions. The way in which the law was summarized and ordered in the Digest constituted nothing less than the systematic ordering of the most important pronouncements.

As a consequence, the reception of Roman law necessarily gave rise to a science of law. It is impossible to assess how history from the high Middle Ages would have gone if rulers, cities, subjects, merchants, and ultimately the state had lacked this tool, this science with all its potential for depersonalization and reaching decisions. It is, in any event, sufficient to say that this legal tradition was and is of extraordinary significance to Europe (and ultimately the whole world).

I conclude with just two further remarks.

Firstly, the Greco-Roman tradition played a highly significant role in European history not only thanks to much of its form and content, but also because, for a very long time (perhaps even, albeit in a very diluted way, until recently), it represented a unifying transnational element (extending to Russia and including those states created through European emigration). We might think here of the Western Church, not only its Catholic variant, the university, the Latin of science and, above all, the education of the bourgeoisie, which, alongside property, was to become the foundation of its self-confidence vis-à-vis the aristocracy. Here, many elements of ancient tradition made their presence felt, both regularly and in intense phases; albeit much was often lost to philistinism.

Secondly, it is an open question to what extent the entire Greco-Roman tradition (along with many other things) has outlived its usefulness. In an era moving so rapidly away from all tradition as ours, would it perhaps be interesting to study another era which, as a result of the yawning chasm between the traditional and the appropriate, was also unnerved and rendered capable of the most fruitful creations? Drawing on Antiquity has always been interesting in the context of new beginnings. But perhaps now is not the time for new beginnings, but merely for stumbling onwards? We can, perhaps, be sure of just one thing. The Austrian minister of educational and cultural affairs has recently asserted that schools must be as up to date as possible. In light of the current pace of change, this means that what they teach is out of date before the pupils have left. In what sense are the last decades of contemporary history of interest in light of the entirely new problems of terrorism, and the drastic reversal, apparent in every sphere of life, of a centuries-old tendency (understandable only in light of these centuries) towards mass affluence, mass education, and mass political participation? Compared with this, the Greco-Roman tradition is probably of greater contemporary relevance than contemporary history.

4

How Europe Became Diverse: On the Medieval Roots of the Plurality of Values

Michael Borgolte

The editors of this volume have commissioned contributions extending from the axial age in the sixth century BC to the present day. This is the first to mention Europe by name in its title.[1] This volume has been conceived in such a way that the question of how Europe became diverse is to be answered by a medieval historian. It is in fact possible to take the view that Europe, as the historical entity familiar to us, first emerged in the Middle Ages; on this view, despite the fundamental achievements of Greco-Roman Antiquity and the ongoing impact of the old religions, it was the dissolution of the Mediterranean cultural entity last represented by the Romans, and the development of a political and cultural centre of gravity north of the Alps, that created 'Europe'.[2] From this perspective, the Germanic and Slavic migrations played a decisive role, causing a multiplicity of states to take the place of a single empire;[3] the conquest of Asia Minor and North Africa by Muslim Arabs and Berbers, it is argued, had much the same

---

[1] The present text is based on a talk given on 28 March 2004 in Otzenhausen, expanded in places and with footnotes added. I have thus consciously refrained from modifying references to the present to fit the state of affairs at publication (see nn. 41–3 below).

[2] See Jacques Le Goff, *The Birth of Europe* (Oxford: Blackwell, 2004); discussed by Michael Borgolte, *Frankfurter Allgemeine Zeitung*, 24 March 2004, p. L 17.

[3] Most recently: Walter Pohl, *Die Völkerwanderung. Eroberung und Integration* (Stuttgart, Berlin and Cologne: Kohlhammer, 2002); Klaus Rosen, *Die Völkerwanderung* (Munich: Beck, 2002); Norman Davies, *Europe: A History* (Oxford and New York: Oxford University Press, 1996, 1997), pp. 215ff.; Edgar Hösch, *Geschichte der Balkanländer. Von der Frühzeit bis zur Gegenwart* (Munich: Beck, 2002), pp. 37ff.

effect, turning the Mediterranean into a religious and cultural boundary, though Islam also spread to Spain and southern Italy.[4]

Nevertheless, the question arises as to whether and in what sense the events of the third to eighth centuries really produced Europe as a specific entity. A medieval historian has recently cast doubt on this assumption with a new account of late Antiquity and the early Middle Ages.[5] Berlin medievalist Ernst Pitz called his book a 'history of the Mediterranean region between the Atlantic and the Indian Ocean', avoiding the name 'Europe'; he thus designated the subject of his work as the region around the Mediterranean, familiar as the Greco-Roman ecumene of the ancient period. Rather than having fallen along with Rome, this *orbis terrarum* is said to have continued. But the circum-Mediterranean region did not stay the same over the centuries of Antiquity and the Middle Ages. Rather, from the late third century onwards, the peoples living on the fringes of the ecumene dissolved the unity of the old culture, initially causing a division into Occident and Byzantium and then, through the division of the East into Greek Christianity and areas under Muslim rule, the tripartite Mediterranean world. Pitz therefore refers to the 'three cultures of the Middle Ages'. While these medieval cultures competed with one another around the Mediterranean, they were able to retain the old unity on account of their common origins in the Greco-Roman world. This, it is suggested, applies all the way down to the present.

In the view of this contemporary author, we can no longer, like the German Romantic writer, dream of the Middle Ages as the 'beautiful, splendid times

---

[4]   Heinz Halm, *Der Islam. Geschichte und Gegenwart* (Munich: Beck, 2002), pp. 24ff.; Tilman Nagel, *Die islamische Welt bis 1500* (Munich: Oldenbourg, 1998), pp. 1ff.; Günter Kettermann, *Atlas zur Geschichte des Islam* (Darmstadt: Primus, 2001), esp. pp. 19ff. On the famous thesis put forward by Belgian economic historian Henri Pirenne (d. 1935) that Mohammed, or rather the Islamic conquests in the southern Mediterranean region, were the prerequisite for the rise of Charlemagne, that is, the development of the 'west' in north-western Europe, see the following recent contributions: Richard Hodges and William Bowden (eds), *The Sixth Century: Production, Distribution and Demand* (Leiden, Boston and Cologne: Brill, 1998); S. T. Loseby, 'Marseille and the Pirenne Thesis, II: "ville morte"', in Inge Leyse Hansen and Chris Wickham (eds), *The Long Eighth Century* (Leiden, Boston and Cologne: Brill, 2000), pp. 167–93; Hans Werner Goetz, *Europa im frühen Mittelalter, 500–1050* (Stuttgart: Eugen Ulmer, 2003), p. 342.

[5]   Ernst Pitz, *Die griechisch-römische Ökumene und die drei Kulturen des Mittelalters. Geschichte des mediterranen Weltteils zwischen Atlantik und Indischem Ozean 270–812* (Berlin: Akademie, 2001). The following draws on Michael Borgolte, 'Mediävistik als vergleichende Geschichte Europas', in Hans-Werner Goetz and Jörg Jarnut (eds), *Mediävistik im 21. Jahrhundert. Stand und Perspektiven der internationalen und interdisziplinären Mittelalterforschung* (Munich: Fink, 2003), pp. 313–23, esp. pp. 316ff.

when Europe was a Christian land, when *one* Christendom dwelt in this continent shaped by human hand';[6] it was instead a period characterized by a number of cultures, which were influenced by monotheistic religions: Christianity in its Roman and Orthodox variants, Islam and, of course – I would add – Judaism as well.[7] This perspective on our past has become possible because Pitz seeks to grasp the Euro-Mediterranean region rather than Europe as a spatial and historical whole. But is such a notion of wholeness itself justified? If we bear such doubts in mind as we consider this new book,[8] we are faced with motifs which recur in the structure of the present anthology and its chapters.

Ernst Pitz has produced European history as universal history, and it is evident that he subscribes to the Enlightenment dream of cosmopolitan unity and a universal community of all people. As he states, the conditions for realizing the cosmopolitan ideal, through an empire bringing peace to the entire inhabited world, have never been more favourable than they were in the countries around the Mediterranean.[9] But apart from his recourse to the philosophy of nascent modernity, this historian also believes that there is an empirical basis for his universal aspirations. With Karl Jaspers, Pitz assumes that around 600 to 480 BC in different parts of the world, and independently, a breakthrough occurred in the understanding of the human being, its potential and limitations, which laid the groundwork for the advanced civilizations and universal religions.[10] Jaspers, of course, fascinated by the parallel occurrences in Hellenism, in the religions of Persia, India, and ancient Israel, in the doctrines of virtue in China and in

---

[6]   Novalis, *Philosophical Writings*, trans. and ed. Margaret Stoljar (Albany, NY: State University of New York Press, 1997), p. 137. Michael Borgolte, '"Europa ein christliches Land". Religion als Weltstifterin im Mittelalter?', *Zeitschrift für Geschichtswissenschaft* 48 (2000), pp. 1061–77.

[7]   See Michael Borgolte, 'Kulturelle Einheit und religiöse Differenz. Zur Verbreitung der Polygynie im mittelalterlichen Europa', *Zeitschrift für Historische Forschung* 31 (2004), pp. 1–36; Borgolte, 'Die Komposition Europas', in *Enzyklopädie des Mittelalters*, ed. Gert Melville (Darmstadt: Primus, forthcoming).

[8]   See Michael Borgolte, 'Mittelalterforschung und Postmoderne. Aspekte einer Herausforderung', *Zeitschrift für Geschichtswissenschaft* 43 (1995), pp. 615–27; Borgolte, 'Das soziale Ganze als Thema deutscher Mittelalterforschung vor und nach der Wende', *Francia* 22:1 (1995), pp. 155–71; Borgolte, 'Einheit, Reform, Revolution. Das Hochmittelalter im Urteil der Modernen', *Göttingische Gelehrte Anzeigen* 248 (1996), pp. 225–58.

[9]   Pitz, *Die griechisch-römische Ökumene*, p. 25.

[10]   These world historical parallels were first observed by Ernst von Lasaulx in the mid nineteenth century. See Pitz, *Die griechisch-römische Ökumene*, pp. 524, 540, as well as *Saeculum Weltgeschichte*, vol. 2 (Freiburg, Basle, and Vienna: Herder, 1966), pp. 9, 151ff., 253ff., 286ff., 317ff., 382.

the activities of the wise King Numa of Rome, referred to the axial age of world history, basing upon it his 'article of faith', namely 'that mankind has one single origin and one goal'.[11] Pitz has cited this statement;[12] it is at the heart of his view of history. This conscious turn to reflexive thought is claimed to have opened the way to mutual understanding among people. According to this medievalist's view of the course of world history, 'by incorporating ever more peripheral barbarian peoples into their sphere of influence, the advanced civilizations inevitably came into contact'.[13] His book is devoted to the beginning of this segment of world history in as much as Europe was affected by it; it begins with the advance of the nomads, particularly the Sarmatians from Central Asia, into the Mediterranean world[14] and with the resistance of the Emperor Aurelian, praised in a Roman inscription as *restitutor orbis*.[15]

As alluring as this cohesive conception of history may be to some, it invariably provokes resistance. Criticism will be directed against the aspiration to totality that marks this historiography, against the holism of a universal history that wishes to understand the world as a whole and as a unity.[16] This way of thinking has been located in the tradition of Christian *Heilsgeschichte*, whose secularized version it is claimed to be; the unilinearity of the historical process, it is argued, scarcely conceals the Eurocentric perspective that underpins a global history of this kind. Christian Meier abandoned the idea of a universal history as a coherent whole, which eliminates the histories and the great achievements of the individual world cultures, as early as 1988, referring instead to 'a world of histories, of pasts'.[17] Instead of the old world history, our concern from now on is with a history of ecumenes, of the inhabited world. Meier adds the significant comment: 'The direction of this history is unclear, its unity [...] is] just beginning to take shape.' In the same spirit as historian of Antiquity Meier, the historian of the modern world Reinhart Koselleck states that the new historiography is returning to the state of affairs that pertained in the late eighteenth century, when the

---

[11]   Karl Jaspers, *The Origin and Goal of History* (London: Routledge, 1953 [1949]), p. xv, see also pp. 19ff.

[12]   Pitz, *Die griechisch-römische Ökumene*, p. 540.

[13]   Pitz, *Die griechisch-römische Ökumene*, p. 26.

[14]   Pitz, *Die griechisch-römische Ökumene*, pp. 39–40.

[15]   *Der Kleine Pauly. Lexikon der Antike*, vol. 1 (Munich: DTV, 1979), col. 763.

[16]   See Wolfgang J. Mommsen, 'Geschichte und Geschichten. Über die Möglichkeiten und Grenzen der Universalgeschichtsschreibung', *Saeculum* 43 (1992), pp. 124–35, esp. pp. 126–7 (with reference to Karl Popper, Theodor Schieder, and so on).

[17]   Christian Meier, *Die Welt der Geschichte und die Provinz des Historikers. Drei Überlegungen* (Berlin: Wagenbach 1989 [talk from 1988]), p. 12 (also the source of the following quotation); Mommsen, 'Geschichte und Geschichten', p. 124.

historia universalis still consisted of an infinite multitude of narrated histories.[18] The collective singular 'history' took hold only between 1760 and 1780; as the many histories were unified into a single history, the modern era, it is claimed, had an inexorably standardizing, universalizing, and totalizing effect. If we take these insights seriously, and I do not doubt them, then in the case of the Middle Ages, and with respect to pre-modern times in general, it is not appropriate to refer to a single, self-contained, and coherent history. When Pitz referred to three cultures of the Middle Ages, rather than just one, he took this fact into account. But by fitting the history of late Antiquity and the early Middle Ages into an intentional continuum of the Euro-Mediterranean region, aimed at establishing global unity, he contradicted it.

But in dropping the idea of historical wholeness and totality, should we surrender all notion of unity? Would every history of Europe and its values from its beginnings to the present day be an unscientific undertaking? It would indeed, some commentators have recently answered. One feminist historian has rejected the conventional notion of general history for its privileging of unity, opposing it with 'a programme of history free of notions of unity'. On this view, we should assume a multitude of histories rather than the unity of history; the priority is to do justice to the 'many histories of local and worldwide processes of historical change specifically with respect to their contradictoriness, lack of uniformity and difference'.[19] Hierarchy as an organizing principle is inherent in the concept of the unity of history, critics continue, a principle that privileges the logic of the ruler or rulers. In contemplating the causes of the unity syndrome, our author hit upon the traditions of universal and national history. After the search for a universal history in the spirit of the ideals of humanity and Enlightenment had been broken off without result in the early nineteenth century, she tells us, the modern discipline of history focussed on the nation and national history. Historical research and representation discovered effective principles for establishing meaning, of organizing the relevant and the irrelevant.[20] As a

---

[18]   Reinhart Koselleck, *Futures Past: On the Semantics of Historical Time* (New York and Chichester: Columbia University Press, 2004), pp. 194ff.; see Mommsen, 'Geschichte und Geschichten', p. 131.

[19]   Karin Hausen, 'Die Nicht-Einheit der Geschichte als historiographische Herausforderung. Zur historischen Relevanz und Anstößigkeit der Geschlechtergeschichte', in Hans Medick and Anne-Charlott Trepp (eds), *Geschlechtergeschichte und Allgemeine Geschichte. Herausforderungen und Perspektiven* (Göttingen: Wallstein, 1998 [talk from 1996]), p. 35. Here I follow the contribution by Michael Borgolte, 'Vor dem Ende der Nationalgeschichten? Chancen und Hindernisse für eine Geschichte Europas im Mittelalter', *Historische Zeitschrift* 272 (2001), pp. 561–96, esp. pp. 584ff.

[20]   Hausen, 'Die Nicht-Einheit der Geschichte', p. 34.

foil, the unity of history is said to have served to demarcate a particular type of history as general history vis-à-vis various other histories, which could then be marginalized as specialized history. The postulate of unity served, not least in the classroom, to enforce a general view of history and furnish society with a historically substantiated identity.[21] This critique of national history applies to European history as well, which also remained obsessed with unity.[22]

What are we to make of this fundamental critique, which rejects the prevailing practice of historiography and aspires to show the way to a radically pluralist view of history?[23] It is, of course, true that a demand for unity is well suited to the instrumentalization of history. With respect to Europe, its history, present, and future, it is, for example, highly controversial whether we can talk of an identity and what this might be based on. There is consensus only about the fact that we can regard as a unity a Europe based on its western portion or a western community of values. But if, like Pitz and others, we include the world of Orthodoxy and Islam, with its bases in the west and east of Europe, as well as Judaism, this Latin-centric idea of unity no longer holds up.[24] Calls for an 'equality of differences' are thus quite justified.[25]

However, I consider the abandonment of all notion of unity unsustainable. It is plainly and simply the mission of academic research to bring order to the great diversity of phenomena and to produce unity. In the chaos of specifics, one leading scholar has warned, history would become a madhouse.[26] Admittedly, it is always an imaginary unity with which history is concerned, a hypothetical model, rather than unity as an objective, 'ontic' phenomenon.[27] This imaginary unity will always be imperfect and must always leave room for alternatives. Thus, apart from the internal discrepancies found in every model of unity, the important

---

[21]   Hausen, 'Die Nicht-Einheit der Geschichte', p. 38.

[22]   Hausen, 'Die Nicht-Einheit der Geschichte', p. 37. On the 'obsession with unity', see Borgolte, 'Mittelalterforschung und Postmoderne', p. 619.

[23]   On what follows, see Borgolte, 'Vor dem Ende der Nationalgeschichten?', pp. 586ff.

[24]   See the account by Michael Borgolte, *Europa entdeckt seine Vielfalt, 1050–1250* (Stuttgart: Eugen Ulmer, 2002).

[25]   Hausen, 'Die Nicht-Einheit der Geschichte', p. 24.

[26]   Arno Borst, *Der Turmbau von Babel. Geschichte der Meinungen über Ursprung und Vielfalt der Sprachen und Völker*, vol. 4 (Stuttgart: Hiersemann, 1963; reprinted Munich: DTV, 1995), p. 1998.

[27]   See Otto Gerhard Oexle, '"Der Teil und das Ganze" als Problem geschichtswissenschaftlicher Erkenntnis. Ein historisch-typologischer Versuch', in Karl Acham and Winfried Schulze (eds), *Teil und Ganzes. Zum Verhältnis von Einzel- und Gesamtanalyse in Geschichts- und Sozialwissenschaften* (Munich: DTV, 1990), pp. 348–84.

thing is to have a plurality of concepts of unity. In as much as we can make any predictions, for the time being the discipline of history cannot aspire to write the history of Europe, but only histories – plural – of Europe, or in other words, it can only produce views of history which, precisely because of their unavoidable distortions, provoke alternative concepts.[28]

Every historical conception or account of Europe rests on a construction which holds up only to the extent that we accept its premises. The freedom to invent is, however, limited; experience and convention guard against the arbitrary.[29] This is apparent in the endless attempts at least to determine Europe's geographical form. As long as two and a half millennia ago, the Greek Herodotus criticized the division of the inhabited world into three continents, given that Europe, Asia, and Libya, that is, Africa, actually formed 'a single land-mass'.[30] He was also unclear, he added in bafflement, as to 'why [...] the Nile and the Phasis [...] should have been fixed upon for the boundaries [between Asia and Libya and between Asia and Europe, respectively] [...]. Nor have I been able to learn who it was that first marked the boundaries, or where they got the names from.' Thus, like Asia and Africa, Europe was an anonymous invention; it did not and does not exist in nature, but only in people's heads. It cannot be determined scientifically, but neither can it be arbitrarily cut to shape. The ties binding us to the observations of others and to a consensus were also already evident in Herodotus. The well-travelled ethnographer and 'explorer' knew that alongside the Phasis, which flows from the Caucasus into the Black Sea, another view held that the Don also marked Europe's boundary at the Sea of Azov;[31] meanwhile, the ancient writer was unable to draw on his

---

[28]   See Michael Borgolte, 'Europäische Geschichten. Modelle und Aufgaben vergleichender Historiographie', in Marc Löwener (ed.), *Die 'Blüte' der Staaten des östlichen Europa im 14. Jahrhundert* (Wiesbaden: Harrassowitz 2004), pp. 303–28.

[29]   The following draws on Michael Borgolte, 'Türkei ante portas. Osman, Osman, gib uns deine Legionen zurück: Mit dem Beitritt zur Europäischen Union wäre die im frühen Mittelalter begonnene Westwanderung abgeschlossen', *Frankfurter Allgemeine Zeitung*, 21 February 2004, p. 39.

[30]   Herodotus IV.45 (the following quotation is also found here), see also IV.42, trans. Aubrey de Sélincourt, revised with introduction and notes by John Marincola, *Herodotus. The Histories* (London: Penguin, 2003), p. 254, see also p. 253. Quoted in Hagen Schulze and Ina Ulrike Paul (eds), *Europäische Geschichte. Quellen und Materialien* (Munich: Bayerischer Schulbuch-Verl., 1994), p. 25, see also p. 24.

[31]   Herodotus's (ca. 445 BC) work is called 'Histories', in other words, attempts to 'find out'. On the – contested – location of the Phasis, see *Der Kleine Pauly. Lexikon der Antike*, vol. 4 (Munich: DTV, 1979), col. 720, on the settlements of the Cimmerians (on the Black Sea) see *Der Kleine Pauly. Lexikon der Antike*, vol. 3 (Munich: DTV, 1979), col. 210.

own experience or eyewitness accounts by others to determine the reach of the continent in the west and north.[32]

In the present era, however, nothing seems as certain as Europe's western maritime boundaries, marked on one side by a line running from the North Sea to the Baltic, and on the other from the Mediterranean to the Black Sea.[33] Such certainties date back to the accounts of ancient geographers[34] or daring traders of later times.[35] Only in the east has the boundary remained approximate to this day. The tributaries to the Black Sea, which were sufficient for the ancient Greeks and subsequently the Middle Ages,[36] were too short in extension as soon as Russia laid claim to its place in Europe. A Swedish officer in the service of the empire therefore proposed shifting the boundary from the Don to the Ural, and this solution has become firmly fixed in Europeans' collective knowledge from the early nineteenth century on.[37] As contentious as the boundaries may be in particular cases, since then Asia has in any event been located behind this mountain range with its associated river of the same name; Vladivostok cannot claim to be part of Europe, any more than India or China.

Europe and its borders were correctly compared to a sea that ebbs and flows with the tides, mostly between west and east.[38] Particularly if one moves from geographical to historical discourse, authors make numerous proposals with

---

[32]   Herodotus III.115–16, Sélincourt, *Herodotus. The Histories*, p. 219.

[33]   Davies, *Europe: A History*, p. 48: 'In the north, the North-Baltic sea lane stretches 1,500 miles (2,500 km) from the Atlantic to Russia. In the south, the Mediterranean-Black Sea system stretches over 2,400 miles (4,000 km) from Gibraltar to the Caucasus.'

[34]   See Strabo's description of the Earth from around 7 BC, in Schulze and Paul (eds), *Europäische Geschichte*, pp. 33ff.

[35]   The quotation here is from the account of a journey by the Byzantine Laskaris Kananos from ca. 1400, Schulze and Paul (eds), *Europäische Geschichte*, p. 47.

[36]   See the testimony of Isidore of Seville (around 600), Schulze and Paul (eds), *Europäische Geschichte*, p. 39.

[37]   Davies, *Europe: A History*, p. 8: 'Neither the ancients nor the medievals had any close knowledge of the easterly reaches of the European Plain, several sections of which were not permanently settled until the eighteenth century. So it was not until 1730 that a Swedish officer in the Russian service called Strahlenberg suggested that Europe's boundary should be pushed back from the Don to the Ural Mountains and the Ural River [...]. By 1833, when Volger's *Handbuch der Geographie* was published, the idea of "Europe from the Atlantic to the Urals" had gained general acceptance.' On the situation of Russia around 1730, see Klaus Zernack, *Polen und Rußland* (Berlin: Propyläen, 1994), pp. 246ff.

[38]   Davies, *Europe: A History*, p. 9: 'tidal Europe', following W. H. Parker, 'Is Russia in Europe? The Geographical Viewpoint', in *An Historical Geography of Russia* (London: University of London Press, 1968), pp. 27–9.

respect to Europe as a unity and totality;[39] as we lack any objective facts to use as criteria, every verdict about what Europe might be is underpinned, alongside observations and conventions, by values, which only a limited number of people are ever willing to sign up to. The present is, of course, no different. As a rule, anyone holding forth on Europe today means the alliance of democratic states called the 'European Union'. People know that Europe and the EU are not identical, but consider it possible that they will one day be entirely congruent as a result of future enlargement of the confederation. When people outside of Europe say that they want 'in', this simply means that they aspire to join the European community of states. In the west, Europe is already equated with the EU, apart from three special cases,[40] and, of course, Baltic and west Slavic nations are to be united with peoples of Germanic and Latin origin through the mass accession of eastern European countries later this year.[41] Soon the question at issue will be how to classify Russia and the other eastern Slavic states,[42] and before that, as it seems at present, the EU will begin membership talks with Turkey.[43]

But the borders of the EU and the borders of Europe will probably never be identical, regardless of what decisions are ultimately made in the cases of Turkey and Russia. Were the EU to admit both states, it would itself lose the right to its name and identity. This is because a Europe extending to the Pacific Ocean or from the Aegean to Mount Ararat would fly in the face of every convention regarding its borders with Asia and would rob references to continents of their meaning. But if the Turks and Russians were rejected, then – it could be claimed – the EU would lag behind Europe as it has evolved historically and would give up part of European history. One argument might be that this history includes not only absolutist Russia under Peter the Great, but the first foundation of a Russian empire by Scandinavian Varangians and the conversion of the Rus' to Orthodox Christianity.[44] Turkey, too, one might go on to claim, is European, at

---

[39]   See for example the memorandum 'Paneuropa' by Richard Nicolas Coudenhove-Calergi from 1923, quotations in Schulze and Paul (eds), *Europäische Geschichte*, pp. 89–91.

[40]   Iceland, Norway, and Switzerland are not members of the EU.

[41]   Apart from Malta and Cyprus, on 1 May 2004 these should be: Estonia, Latvia, and Lithuania, Poland, Slovakia, Slovenia, Czech Republic, and Hungary. See *Der Fischer Weltalmanach 2004* (Frankfurt am Main: Fischer, 2003), col. 1117. See n. 1 above.

[42]   The prospect has been raised of Bulgaria and Romania acceding as early as 2007.

[43]   In December 2004, the European Council intends to decide whether the Union should open membership negotiations with Turkey.

[44]   See Janet Martin, *Medieval Russia, 980–1584* (Cambridge: Cambridge University Press, 1995).

least in so far as it represents, since the Kemalist revolution, a unique case of a Muslim people seeking to construct a western-style republic.[45]

It is thus quite possible to consider Europe as an imagined entity, but it cannot de defined arbitrarily; experience and consensus limit the scope for construction. But the conventions are insufficient for describing the continent geographically and historically as an indisputable whole. If we wish to take the history of European peoples into account, we must acknowledge the vagueness of the eastern boundary. From a historical perspective, Europe is indeed an imagined unity, but by no means a self-contained totality.

Of course, these insights also have consequences for how we understand diversity. If the discipline of history understands Europe in all its particular forms as a unity, the historian must remain aware that this unity is never perfect. He retains plausibility only in so far as he simultaneously draws attention to peculiarities that contradict his specific view of the continent. The principles of unity and diversity do not constitute a closed system: Europe is not a case of 'unity in diversity'. Rather, we must understand it as a system of unities featuring countless differences. Some modern-day intellectuals have already drawn conclusions in light of these findings. The French writer, Edgar Morin, has, for example, declared that imagining Europe means recognizing it as a complex which 'unifies within it the most tremendous differences without simply blending them together', and which 'links together contrasting elements in such a way that they are inseparable'.[46] On this view, we must abandon the idea of a homogeneous and clearly demarcated Europe; the important thing about European culture is not just its key ideas, but also the fact 'that all these ideas also have their opposites'. The 'principle of dialogue' is thus essential to Europe; the task for European historical research is to study the fruitful clash of differences, antagonisms, competition, and complementarities. The idea that the identity of Europe, in past and present, consists of its lack of identity has also been emphasized by Davies. All European countries differ from the others; even among the western states the differences

---

[45]   See Brigitte Moser and Michael W. Weithmann, *Die Türkei. Nation zwischen Europa und dem Nahen Osten* (Regensburg, Graz, Vienna, and Cologne: Pustet *et al.*, 2002), esp. pp. 79ff.

[46]   Edgar Morin, *Penser l'Europe* (Paris: Gallimard, 1987); trans. from the German edition: *Europa denken* (Frankfurt and New York: Campus, 1991), p. 19; see also Otto Gerhard Oexle, 'Stände und Gruppen. Über das Europäische in der europäischen Geschichte', in Michael Borgolte (ed.), *Das europäische Mittelalter im Spannungsbogen des Vergleichs. Zwanzig internationale Beiträge zu Praxis, Problemen und Perspektiven der historischen Komparatistik* (Berlin: Akademie, 2001), pp. 39–48, esp. p. 41.

dominate.[47] But, on this view, 'Europe', the idea of which first emerged during the Enlightenment, has never been completed. Lacking political unity, dissimilarity has always been one of its most stable characteristics.

Thus, after the theory-building debate within the contemporary discipline of history, we now know that Europe's diversity is not absorbed into Europe's unity, but that the diversity of phenomena within an imagined historical framework often manifests itself as divergence. We can go so far as to say that historical research has recently rediscovered the differences that mark European history.[48] We have thus learned a thing or two of relevance to the subject of this chapter, that is, how Europe became diverse, as we can expect the historian to pay increased attention to the particular. But the topic suggests something else as well: namely that we might fathom how Europe itself – the people of European history – discovered the diversity of its world. In line with the concerns of this anthology, this leads on to the further question of whether the discovery of diversity in the Middle Ages might not have something to do with the plurality of Europe's cultural values.

When you look at it more closely, it might be argued that the question around which this contribution revolves leads us astray. For there is no reality without diversity; diversity is 'something transhistorically general', a 'pure fact inherent to all natural and historical reality'.[49] In contrast, only through a feat of the intellect can unity be manufactured from the infinite wealth of phenomena, which are self-evident and which require no explanation in themselves. But it has already been established that the human being struggles to tolerate diversity and is reluctant to put up with disorder, to tolerate its impact, for any length of time. At most, it is claimed, these things are accepted by aesthetes and scholars on the fringes of society.[50] Our task can thus only be to seek out cases in which diversity as such has been acknowledged and to study how people come to grips with it both intellectually and in terms of everyday practicalities. Diversity also becomes historically significant whenever individual phenomena are perceived and evaluated in all their particularity with reference to something else. Understood in this way, diversity is abundance interpreted as heterogeneity. We cannot answer the question raised here, of how Europe became diverse, merely by looking back as historians; we also require the testimony of historical actors, their judgements and behaviour.

---

[47]   Davies, *Europe: A History*, p. 28. See also Michael Borgolte, 'Perspektiven europäischer Mittelalterhistorie an der Schwelle zum 21. Jahrhundert', in *Das europäische Mittelalter im Spannungsbogen des Vergleichs*, pp. 13–27, esp. pp. 25–6.

[48]   Borgolte, *Europa entdeckt seine Vielfalt*.

[49]   Borst, *Der Turmbau von Babel*, vol. 4, pp. 1964, 1973, see also pp. 2003, 1965: 'The diversity of the particular is an experience of reality and of the moment.'

[50]   Borst, *Der Turmbau von Babel*, vol. 4, pp. 1973, 1965.

European diversity seems first to have emerged, that is, to have become the subject of reflection, as a result of the 'barbarian' invasion of the Roman Empire. The response of a provincial Roman in the service of Pope Leo the Great is surely symptomatic. This writer had a hostile attitude towards the invading Sarmatians and Teutons, but when the Huns under Attila and the Vandals descended upon Italy, he pondered: 'When we observe differences and peculiarities in the times, among peoples, in families, in children, among those not yet born and twins, we have no doubt that this is one of the secrets which a just and merciful God did not wish us to know in this transitory world.'[51] The dramatic epochal change thus led to the perception of diversity in virtually all fields of life; this experience was obviously so overwhelming that rather than being understood and categorized, it was entrusted to the wisdom and providence of God.

We may assume that it was the diversity of kingdoms resulting from Germanic migration that forced people to think in terms of a multifarious order.[52] We name these states on the soil of the Roman Empire after the Visigoths and Vandals, Suebi, Burgundians, Ostrogoths, and Franks, but we need to be clear about the fact that these groups that made inroads into the Roman Empire were internally heterogeneous in origin, and that under the leadership of their kings new ethnogeneses occurred.[53] Only in exceptional cases can we draw connecting lines from these kingdoms to later times, but there is no doubt that they prefigured the typical European diversity of states up to the present. From the sixth and seventh centuries we must add the kingdoms of the Lombards in Italy and of the Bulgars and

---

[51]   Prosper Tiro, 'Libri duo de vocatione omnium gentium', II.30, in *Migne* PL 51, col. 716: 'ut cum in temporibus, in nationibus, in familiis, in parvulis, in nondum natis et geminis quaedam aut varie aut insigniter gesta noscuntur, non ambigamus ea ex illis esse quae justus et misericors Deus in hoc transituro saeculo noluit sciri'; here, see Borst, *Der Turmbau von Babel*, vol. 2.1 (Stuttgart: Hiersemann, 1958; reprinted Munich: DTV, 1995), pp. 418–19 (with translation). On the author and his work, see Domingo Ramos-Lissón, 'Art. Prosper Tiro v. Aquitanien', in *Lexikon für Theologie und Kirche*, vol. 8 (Freiburg, Basle, Rome, Vienna: Herder 1999), col. 644–5.

[52]   Apart from the texts cited above in n. 3, the most recent work here is by Patrick J. Geary, *The Myth of Nations: The Medieval Origins of Europe* (Princeton, NJ, and Oxford: Princeton University Press, 2002), pp. 99ff., 108ff. Hans-Werner Goetz, *Europa im frühen Mittelalter*, pp. 34ff.

[53]   In addition to the texts cited above in n. 52, see Walter Pohl, *Die Germanen* (Munich: Beck, 2000); Malcolm Todd, *The Early Germans* (Oxford: Blackwell, 2002); on later analogies, see Joachim Ehlers, 'Was sind und wie bilden sich Nationes im mittelal- terlichen Europa (10.–15. Jahrhundert)? Begriff und allgemeine Kennzeichen', in Almut Bues and Rex Rexheuser (eds), *Mittelalterliche nationes – neuzeitliche Nationen. Probleme der Nationenbildung in Europa* (Wiesbaden: Harrassowitz, 1995), pp. 7–26.

Serbs in the Balkans. In contrast to the west, where the empire had disappeared by 476, the Eastern Roman Empire, centred on the capital on the Bosporus founded by Constantine the Great, endured for centuries. Once Charlemagne had renewed the empire in the west and the east Frankish-German kings had succeeded him, there were two emperors in Europe. This was the beginning of the characteristic European polarity between the (evolving) nation states and the two versions of imperial rule, which were in principle universal empires, though how seriously they took this aim varied and they never had the opportunity to realize it.[54]

From what point in time did these European states constitute a region of diversity, a diversity that was not merely perceived near borders or during travel, trading journeys, and military campaigns, but was understood and appropriated as diversity? The difficult problem faced here by political traditionalists is apparent in the case of Byzantium, which considered itself a Roman empire and which saw its emperor as the ruler of the world, just like the ancient emperors.[55] Because the actual diversity of states could not be denied, the imperial chancery invented a strict protocol, according to which the βασιλεύς Ῥωμαίων in a family of kings and princes was ascribed the status of father, while the other Christian and non-Christian rulers were given a subordinate status in the graded system of relationships.[56] The Germanic kings could thus be sons to the emperor in Constantinople and brothers to each other. The medieval rulers also established real inter-familial links, whether through marriages or

---

[54]   See Goetz, *Europa im frühen Mittelalter*, passim; Borgolte, *Europa entdeckt seine Vielfalt*, pp. 24ff.; Matthias Becher, *Charlemagne* (New Haven, CT, London: Yale University Press, 2003); Bernd Schneidmüller and Stefan Weinfurter (eds), *Die deutschen Herrscher des Mittelalters. Historische Portraits von Heinrich I. bis Maximilian I. (919–1519)* (Munich: Beck, 2003); Ralph-Johannes Lilie, *Byzanz. Das zweite Rom* (Berlin: Siedler, 2003); John Haldon, *Byzantium: A History* (Stroud: Tempus, 2000).

[55]   Lilie, *Byzanz*; Haldon, *Byzantium*; Peter Schreiner, *Byzanz* (Munich: Oldenbourg, 1994); Lilie, 'Byzanz in Europa – Byzanz und Europa. Modelle der politischen und kulturellen Integration zwischen dem 6. und 15. Jahrhundert', in Evangelos Chrysos, Paschalis M. Kitromilides, and Constantine Svolopoulos (eds), *The Idea of European Community in History*, conference proceedings, vol. 1 (Athens: National and Capodistrian University, 2003), pp. 123–32.

[56]   Franz Dölger, 'Die "Familie der Könige" im Mittelalter', *Historisches Jahrbuch* 60 (1940), pp. 397–420, reprinted in Dölger, *Byzanz und die europäische Staatenwelt* (Ettal: Buch-Kunstverlag, 1953), pp. 34–69; Evangelos Chrysos, 'Perceptions of the International Community of States During the Middle Ages', in Karl Brunner and Brigitte Merta (eds), *Ethnogenese und Überlieferung* (Munich: VIÖG, 1994), pp. 293–307; Stefan Krautschick, 'Die Familie der Könige in Spätantike und Mittelalter', in Evangelos Chrysos and Andreas Schwarcz (eds), *Das Reich und die Barbaren* (Vienna and Cologne: Böhlau, 1989), pp. 109–42.

godparenthood.[57] This was, of course, not yet the recognition of a European system of autonomous states, and the question arises whether there was any such diversity, interpreted in this way, in the Middle Ages.

The problem first arose when the Ostrogoth king Theodoric conquered Italy in 493 and had to anchor his kingdom within the political system of Europe. Theodoric struggled with the emperor over his recognition as an independent ruler and, to safeguard his position, tried hard to establish a system of alliances with the other Germanic kingdoms. He and the women of his house entered into marital alliances with the Visigoths, Burgundians, Franks, and Vandals until 500, with other rulers and their kingdoms being added later.[58] Although Theodoric, as representative of the emperor in the East and as ruler of Italy and Rome, claimed for himself a position of pre-eminence, what we are seeing here is the first European system of equilibrium; at the level of states, diversity had been given the seal of approval. Had this political order lasted, European history would have turned out differently from the one we know. For Theodoric and almost all the other Germanic rulers were followers of so-called Arian Christianity; they were not members of the Roman Church, still headed by the emperor in Constantinople. The Arians merely formed national Churches, so that they lacked a supranational link as in the case of Catholicism and Orthodoxy.[59] As weak as the papacy's influence on the realms of Europe was for the time being, it nonetheless produced a unity of belief; it was the papacy that gave rise to the strongest factor in European integration in the high Middle Ages.[60] Had the Arian states and Theodoric's system prevailed for longer, then the national particularity of Europe would surely have been far more strongly developed than was possible under Catholic–Orthodox leadership. In fact, though, Theodoric lived to see the collapse of his policy of equilibrium; crucial to this development were the conquests of the Frankish king Clovis, who also adopted the religion of Rome and became an ally of the emperor.[61] Soon all the Arian *Völkerwanderung* states fell, while the Franks in Gaul formed a new empire.

---

[57]   See Arnold Angenendt, *Kaiserherrschaft und Königstaufe. Kaiser, Könige und Päpste als geistliche Patrone in der abendländischen Missionsgeschichte* (Berlin and New York: Gruyter, 1984).

[58]   Most recently Frank M. Ausbüttel, *Theoderich der Große* (Darmstadt: Primus, 2003), pp. 209ff.

[59]   Already tackled by Theodor Schieffer, *Winfrid-Bonifatius und die christliche Grundlegung Europas* (Freiburg im Breisgau: Herder, 1954; reprinted Darmstadt: Wissenschaftliche Buchgesellschaft, 1972), p. 40.

[60]   Borgolte, *Europa entdeckt seine Vielfalt*, esp. pp. 75ff.

' a recent treatment, see for example the contributions in the catalogue *Die Wegbereiter Europas. Vor 1500 Jahren: König Chlodwig und seine Erben*, 2 vols heim and Mainz: Reiss Museum, 1996).

Political and military alliances were also formed on numerous occasions in medieval Europe in later centuries, but medievalists have found scarcely any trace of a state system of equilibrium as in the modern period.[62] The difference is important. It is true that states co-existed for centuries and that an equilibrium often existed between them, but this was more tolerated than embraced. First

---

[62] Walther Kienast, 'Die Anfänge des europäischen Staatensystems im späteren Mittelalter', *Historische Zeitschrift* 153 (1936), pp. 229–71: since the collapse of the Hohenstaufen empire, around 1198, there has been a European system of states, but without a permanent system of embassies and, above all, without the principle of equilibrium; this first appears at the turn of the sixteenth century. Helmut G. Walter, 'Der westliche Mittelmeerraum in der zweiten Hälfte des 13. Jahrhunderts als politisches Gleichgewichtssystem', in Peter Moraw (ed.), *'Bündnissysteme' und 'Außenpolitik' im späteren Mittelalter* (Berlin: Duncker & Humblot, 1988), pp. 39–67: around 1300, while there was a system of equilibrium in Europe, it was not thought worth preserving, and was to be replaced by the hegemony of a state – with the French monarchy playing a particularly prominent role. Dieter Berg, *Deutschland und seine Nachbarn 1200–1500* (Munich: Oldenbourg, 1997), p. 48: from the twelfth century, 'above all in western Europe (Flanders) [there is evidence of] efforts to establish a "balance of forces" among the leading powers of Europe' (against Hans Fenske). But we still lack systematic studies of the system of foreign relations in Europe up to the late fifteenth century (see also Berg, *Deutschland und seine Nachbarn*, pp. 60–1 and passim). In the same vein as Kienast, see the recent work by Harald Kleinschmidt, *Geschichte der internationalen Beziehungen. Ein systemgeschichtlicher Abriß* (Stuttgart: Reclam, 1998), with chapters entitled: 'Der Kampf um das Gleichgewicht (1517–1648)', 'Die Festigung des Gleichgewichts (1648–1714)', and 'Die Erhaltung des Gleichgewichts (1714–1789)'. See also Heinz Schilling, *Die neue Zeit. Vom Christenheitseuropa zum Europa der Staaten. 1250 bis 1750* (Berlin: Siedler, 1999), p. 30: 'Renaissance Italy was also the place where a specific system of powers arose for the first time, consisting of the pentarchy of five independent, fundamentally equal states of similar strength, namely Milan, Venice, Florence, Naples and the Papal states. This was the birth of the European system of powers which is among the striking features of modern Europe.' In the work of John Locke (d. 1704), the 'balance formula' became 'a part of European cultural consciousness', the Peace of Utrecht of 1713 referred for the first time officially to a 'Balance of Europe', and according to David Hume (d. 1776), even ancient Greece had made use of the recipe of balance in its fragmented state: Fritz Wagner, 'Europa im Zeitalter des Absolutismus und der Aufklärung. Die Einheit der Epoche', in Wagner (ed.), *Europa im Zeitalter des Absolutismus und der Aufklärung*, Handbuch der europäischen Geschichte Europas, vol. 4 (Stuttgart: Propyläen, 1968), pp. 1–163, here p. 64–5. Martin Kintzinger, *Westbindungen im spätmittelalterlichen Europa. Auswärtige Politik zwischen dem Reich, Frankreich, Burgund und England in der Regierungszeit Kaiser Sigmunds* (Stuttgart: Thorbecke, 2000) takes us no further in terms of the question discussed here; Dieter Berg, Martin Kintzinger, and Pierre Monnet (eds), *Auswärtige Politik und internationale Beziehungen im Mittelalter (13. bis 16. Jahrhundert)* (Bochum: Winkler, 2002).

the empires and then the strong western European monarchies, above all France, disapproved of the state of equilibrium and strove to achieve hegemony or even universality.

Medieval Europeans, one might think, would have coped better with ethnic and linguistic diversity than with the plurality of states. For as we all know, Genesis offers us a story which establishes right from the outset a systematic connection between the origin and spread of peoples and languages. According to the biblical story, God scattered those who built the Tower of Babel, who were *one* people and who spoke *one* language, across the entire earth;[63] all new peoples are derived from Noah, who was blessed by God, and are ascribed to Noah's sons and grandsons in a 'table of peoples'. Here, then, we have only a limited number of ethnic groups, of which fourteen are descended from Noah's son Japheth, thirty from his brother Ham, and twenty-six from the third son Shem. We owe to Arno Borst, the Constance-based medievalist, the insight that this biblical narrative was the first and unrivalled example of religious historical thought, which achieved its world historical breakthrough with the Jews.[64] This historical thought is strictly monotheistic and at the same time universal in orientation; from the perspective of the Creator God, the entire world is imagined in terms of unity in diversity.

Borst has also devoted an excellent study in universal history to the consequences of this idea and to notions of the origins and diversity of languages and peoples. This empirically rich work offers a vast array of evidence relating to the perception and evaluation of the diversity of people, from the most ancient to the most recent of times.[65] We read, for instance, what a Rhenish Benedictine wrote in his handbook of canon law in 906.[66] The Church, argued the monk, is indeed spread across the entire world and everywhere the same in terms of the unity of the faith, but it is not uniform in its practices, 'just as the various peoples differ from one another with respect to their origin, their customs, their language and their laws'.[67] At around the same time, a writer dealing with

---

[63]   Genesis 11:1–10. See Borst, *Der Turmbau von Babel*, vol. 1 (Stuttgart: Hiersemann, 1957; reprinted Munich: DTV, 1995), p. 116.

[64]   Borst, *Der Turmbau von Babel*, vol. 1, p. 126, see also pp. 10–11 and 110; see Michael Borgolte, 'Europas Geschichten und Troia. Der Mythos im Mittelalter. Über die Zeit, als die Türken Verwandte der Lateiner und Griechen waren', in Archäologisches Landesmuseum Baden-Württemberg *et al.* (ed.), *Troia. Traum und Wirklichkeit* (Stuttgart: Theiss, 2001), pp. 190–203, here p. 200.

[65]   Borst, *Der Turmbau von Babel*, vols 1–4 (Stuttgart: Hiersemann, 1957–1963).
       Borst, *Der Turmbau von Babel*, vol. 1, p. 538.
       Reginonis Abbatis Prumiensis Chronicon cum continuatione Treverensi, rec. Fridericus Kurze, umenta Germaniae Historica, Scriptores rerum Germanicarum 50 (Hanover: Hahn,

the *Völkerwanderung* expressed an astonishingly down-to-earth view of Europe's differences: 'The third part of the Earth, my brothers, is called Europe; its highly diverse peoples differ in their customs, languages and names, and cults and religion clearly separate them from one another.'[68] Learned German clerics made further attempts to establish a hierarchical and functional order of states and peoples in the thirteenth century. On this view, there were four main states in Europe, 'namely the empire of the Greeks in the east and the kingdom of the Spaniards in the west, the Roman empire in the south and the empire of the Franks in the north, though this [is not meant to] deny the other states their sovereignty'.[69] In western Europe, special abilities and tasks are attributed to the Romans, French, and Germans:

> The fact that the Romans, as the oldest, received the papacy, the Teutons or Franks as the younger the empire, the French or Gauls as the particularly astute ones the study of the sciences, corresponds [...] perfectly to a meaningful and necessary order [...]. In these three, papacy, empire and study, as in the three powers of mind, body and spirit, the purpose of the holy Catholic church lives, grows and develops.[70]

The papacy was headquartered in Rome, study in Paris, 'but for the empire, as is known, according to the will of the Holy Spirit, four main seats have been

---

1890), pp. XIX–XX: 'Epistula Reginonis ad Hathonem Archiepiscopum missa', here p. XX: 'Nec non et illud sciendum, quod, sicut diversae nationes populorum inter se discrepant genere moribus lingua legibus, ita sancta universalis aecclesia toto orbe terrarum diffusa, quamvis in unitate fidei coniungatur, tamen consuetudinibus aecclesiasticis ab invicem differt.'

[68]   Karl Strecker (ed.), *Waltharius*, German trans. Peter Vossen (Berlin: Weidmann, 1947), p. 22: 'Tertia pars orbis, fratres, Europa vocatur, / Moribus ac linguis varias et nomine gentes / Distinguens, cultu, tam relligione sequestrans.' Trans. by Vossen modified in main text. See Borst, *Der Turmbau von Babel*, vol. 2.1, p. 566; Borgolte, 'Vor dem Ende der Nationalgeschichten?', pp. 569–70.

[69]   Alexander of Roes, 'Notitia Seculi, cap. 9' (from 1288), in *Die Schriften des Alexander von Roes*, ed. and trans. Herbert Grundmann and Hermann Heimpel, Monumenta Germaniae Historica. Deutsches Mittelalter, Kritische Studientexte 4 (Weimar: Böhlau, 1949), pp. 78 (Latin orig.), 79 (trans.). See Borgolte, 'Vor dem Ende der Nationalgeschichten?', p. 569.

[70]   'Memoriale' of Alexander of Roes from 1281, using a treatise of Master Jordanus of Osnabrück (attested as canon of the cathedral 1251 to 1283), in *Die Schriften des Alexander von Roes*, pp. 48–9 (Latin orig. with German trans.). See Borst, *Der Turmbau von Babel*, vol. 2.2 (Stuttgart: Hiersemann, 1959; reprinted Munich: DTV, 1995), pp. 824–5.

specified, namely Aachen, Arles, Milan and Rome'.[71] Finally, when Dante, the writer and philosopher of the late Middle Ages (1265–1321), contemplated the political order, he wished to entrust the protection of diversity to the world monarch: 'Necesse est multitudinem esse in humano genere' ('There must needs be a vast number of individual people in the human race').[72]

People certainly thought a lot about the plurality of languages and peoples in the Middle Ages, often with reference to the story of the Tower of Babel. Of those authors whom Borst evaluated, some big names are missing, while intellectuals of the second and third rank, on the other hand, have been paid a good deal of attention.[73] But this study in intellectual history from the 1950s tells us little about the reception and spread of thinking about plurality with respect to peoples and languages. In any case, it must be said that the testimony discussed above was scholarly literature, which failed to radically influence how the masses interpreted their world.

Without question, the perception of the vast majority of people in the Middle Ages was restricted to their familiar sphere of living; when people thought historically, they wrote the history of their own families, their own monastery, country, or empire.[74] These stories could co-exist, even if each group claimed for itself the same ancient origins as others. For example, on the model of Caesar and Rome, the Franks and French, the British and English, the Irish, Normans, and Danes, Icelanders, Poles, and Hungarians, the Belgians after 1500, and, according to one late medieval author, even the Germans traced their origins to the Trojans, and peoples were imitated in this regard by towns and aristocratic families.[75] Everybody wanted to be Trojans without, as a rule, taking any notice at all of the competing claims made by others. It was only with the humanists' verification of sources that questions were raised about the myth of Troy, and with it often the notion of derivation from one of the peoples of Babel. In the late Middle Ages, the historians also overcame the fixation on one's own history, discovering the history of others. A Florentine Minorite seems to have been the first. After the monk had returned to Europe from missionary work in the far east of Asia in the mid-fourteenth century and was staying at the court of Charles IV

---

[71]   Here, the (late) antique imperial residences of Arles, Milan, and Rome are combined with the place of coronation of the German kings, Aachen.

[72]   Dante Alighieri, *Monarchia*, Latin and English trans. and ed. Prue Shaw (Cambridge: Cambridge University Press, 1995), pp. 9–10, cap. I.3.8; see also Borst, *Der Turmbau von Babel*, vol. 2.2, p. 869.

[73]   As Borst himself puts it: *Der Turmbau von Babel*, vol. 1, pp. 11–12.

[74]   Borgolte, 'Perspektiven europäischer Mittelalterhistorie', p. 15; Borgolte, *Europa entdeckt seine Vielfalt*, pp. 11–22, 23.

[75]   Borgolte, 'Europas Geschichten und Troia', here esp. pp. 192ff.

in Prague, he felt prompted to produce an 'account of the land of Bohemia'. This is the first known history of another country by a western author for more than half a millennium.[76] Among the Italian humanists, it was, above all, Enea Silvio Piccolomini, later Pope Pius II (d. 1464), who subsequently composed histories of others, once again first and foremost a 'Historia Bohemica', as well as a famous 'Germania' and a contemporary history of Austria. The chroniclers of a kingdom or diocesan town had, of course, previously provided accounts of their neighbours' history, but the Other became a historiographical subject in its own right only in the late Middle Ages.

In terms of government and politics, ethnicity, language, and history, people were undoubtedly always aware of the difference between themselves and others, but it is doubtful that they really attempted to come to terms with the other, let alone embraced diversity itself. While we may be able to discern the first beginnings of such attitudes here and there, the discourses in question lay far beyond the experiential world of 'normal' people. And yet I believe that we can speak of the discovery of diversity in the Middle Ages, a discovery whose after-effects are still being felt within the value system of the present era. For large numbers of people undoubtedly experienced difference and diversity in one field which has been hinted at occasionally, but which must now take centre stage: the field of religion. Nothing has shaped the historical character of Europe as profoundly and distinguished it so clearly from its own pre-history as well as other parts of the world as the breakthrough of the monotheistic religions, with Christianity playing the leading role.[77] Paradoxically, it was the belief in one Creator God, the principle of absolute unity, that gave rise to diversity as structured variety. In order to explain this, we must contrast the religious world of the Middle Ages with that of earlier times.

Pre-Christian Antiquity was characterized by the worship of a plurality of gods.[78] Which gods this pantheon included was never laid down precisely, and the authorities merely demanded that citizens faithfully carry out the rituals; a profession of faith was not required. This *religio* featured almost no written documents, let alone theological tracts with explanations of dogma. For centuries,

---

[76]   Gerd Tellenbach, 'Eigene und fremde Geschichte. Eine Studie zur Geschichte der europäischen Historiographie, vorzüglich im 15. und 16. Jahrhundert', in Kaspar Elm, Eberhard Gönner, and Eugen Hillenbrand (eds), *Landesgeschichte und Geistesgeschichte. Festschrift für Otto Herding* (Stuttgart: Kohlhammer, 1977), pp. 295–316, esp. pp. 302ff.

[77]   See already Borgolte, 'Die Komposition Europas'.

[78]   See Louis Bruit Zaidman and Pauline Schmitt Pantel, *Die Religion der Griechen. Kult und Mythos* (Munich: Beck, 1994); Yves Lehmann (ed.), *Religions de l'Antiquité* (Paris: Presses Universitaires de France, 1999); Mary Beard, John North, and Simon Price, *Religions of Rome*, 2 vols (Cambridge: Cambridge University Press, 1998).

the Roman pantheon demonstrated its capacity to absorb new gods, which easily formed a group around the Capitoline triad with Jupiter at its head. If a general had a war to win, he could court the gods of the enemy by promising to build them a splendid temple in Rome itself if they abandoned their charges and defected. An *evocatio* of this kind was first applied to the goddess Juno, who was transposed to Rome from the Etruscan city of the Vçii in 396 BC and was housed in her own temple on the Aventine.[79] Later, the cult of the 'Great Mother' from Asia Minor was established by transferring the Black Stone from Pergamon to the Palatine (205/204 BC).[80] Since Caesar and Augustus, the emperors themselves were worshipped; this also applies to Aurelian, Probus, and Carus in the third century AD.[81] But ancient paganism was not absolutely tolerant.[82] Writings from the Augustan period present Octavian's victory over Cleopatra, for example, as a victory for the Roman gods over their Egyptian counterparts.[83] And centuries later, an emperor fought against Manichaeism from Persia, as he felt that the new *superstitio* called the traditional worship of the gods into question.[84]

Although the wellbeing of the state depended on the cult of the gods, when they conquered new territories the Romans never tried to systematically transplant their own deities and customs; rather, religion followed the soldiers and officials first to Italy and then the provinces.[85] The 'new' cults, which had penetrated the city of Rome from outside, were also disseminated from here. At the borders, the troops encountered 'barbarians', who also believed in many gods. North of the Alps, this meant the 'Celts' and the 'Teutons'.[86] Neither name refers to a major people, but to a plurality of tribes and groups, whose composition constantly fluctuated. All of these were non-literate peoples, so our conclusions about their religion and culture are inevitably tied to the Romans' perception. They interpreted the barbarian world on the basis of their experiences and named the foreign gods after their own. Caesar, for example, described the religions of the Gauls and Teutons with reference to the Roman deities of Mercury and

---

[79] Beard, North, and Price, *Religions of Rome*, vol. 1, pp. 34–5, pp. 132–4, and passim.

[80] Beard, North, and Price, *Religions of Rome*, vol. 1, pp. 96ff., 160 passim.

[81] See Beard, North, and Price, *Religions of Rome*, vol. 1, pp. 140ff., 166ff.; Yves Lehmann, 'La religion romaine traditionelle', in Lehmann (ed.), *Religions de l'Antiquité*, pp. 179–246, here pp. 223–4, 233ff.

[82] Beard, North, and Price, *Religions of Rome*, vol. 1, p. 212.

[83] Beard, North, and Price, *Religions of Rome*, vol. 1, p. 222.

[84] Beard, North, and Price, *Religions of Rome*, vol. 1, p. 242.

[85] Beard, North, and Price, *Religions of Rome*, vol. 1, pp. 313ff.

[86] See above nn. 53 and 88, and Bernhard Maier, *The Celts: A History from Earliest Times Present* (Edinburgh: Edinburgh University Press, 2003); Janine Fries-Knoblach, *Die 3000 Jahre europäischer Kultur und Geschichte* (Stuttgart: Kohlhammer, 2002).

Apollo, Mars, Jupiter, and Minerva, Sol, Vulcan, and Luna.[87] Much the same approach marks the work of Tacitus.[88] Researchers refer to the attribution of the Roman pantheon to the Germanic and Celtic gods as the *interpretatio Romana*, and we know that similar practices existed among the Sumerians.[89] But contemporary scholars doubt that the realm of the gods as found among the Celts and Teutons was from the outset highly self-contained and structured with only minor variations. Rather, the barbarian deities were probably only worshipped locally to begin with; it was surely contact with the Romans that triggered the development of a few supraregional cults.[90]

Recent research avoids labelling the religion of the Romans, Celts, and Teutons as 'polytheism'. We know that this is a hostile term of relatively recent vintage, first invented by Christian apologists.[91] Taking Christianity, as a supposedly higher form of religion, as the starting point, polytheism was understood as monotheism yet to be achieved or, alternatively, as the plural representation of the principle of a single God. Contemporary theology, on the other hand, makes an effort to acknowledge the inherent value of polytheism and to bring out its specific feats of cultural integration. On this view, so-called polytheism helped unite different groups with their local cults into larger units as the local deities were absorbed into regional or supraregional pantheons.[92] The transferral of the names of the Roman gods to the world of the Celts and Teutons indicates the feats of unification achievable by religions which see the cosmos as pervaded by the workings of a plurality of autonomous divine forces.[93]

---

[87] Caesar, *De Bello Gallico*, 6.17; 6.21.1.

[88] Tacitus, *Germania* 9. See Bernhard Maier, *Die Religion der Germanen. Götter, Mythen, Weltbild* (Munich: Beck, 2003); Rudolf Simek, *Religion und Mythologie der Germanen* (Darmstadt: Wissenschaftliche Buchgesellschaft, 2003).

[89] Jan Assmann, *Die Mosaische Unterscheidung oder der Preis des Monotheismus* (Munich and Vienna: Hanser, 2003), p. 32.

[90] See Bernhard Maier, *Die Religion der Kelten. Götter, Mythen, Weltbild* (Munich: Beck, 2001), p. 87.

[91] Assmann, *Die Mosaische Unterscheidung*, here esp. p. 49; Burkhard Gladigow, 'Polytheismus. Akzente, Perspektiven und Optionen der Forschung', *Zeitschrift für Religionswissenschaft* 5 (1997), pp. 59–77; Fritz Stolz, 'Wesen und Funktion von Monotheismus', *Evangelische Theologie* 61 (2001), pp. 172–89; Jürgen Werbick, 'Absolutistischer Eingottglaube? Befreiende Vielfalt des Polytheismus?', in Thomas Söding (ed.), *Ist der Glaube Feind der Freiheit? Die neue Debatte um den Monotheismus* (Freiburg im Breisgau: Herder, 2003), pp. 142–75.

[92] Gladigow, 'Polytheismus', pp. 61ff.

[93] Assmann would like to see the term 'polytheism' replaced by 'cosmotheism': *Die Mosaische Unterscheidung*, esp. pp. 61, 64.

That this is more than mere scholarly speculation is apparent in the life of the medieval saint Vladimir. Vladimir was ruler of Novgorod before he attained hegemony throughout the empire of the Rus', between the Baltic and the Black Sea, with the incorporation of Kiev in 980. Like other rulers of his time, he felt it his duty to unite his multiethnic empire, which, along with Varangians from Scandinavia and Slavs, also included Finns, Iranians, and Polans.[94] The key issue centred on the religious differences bound up with their different origins. Vladimir first attempted to produce a symbiosis of the different gods. The Russian Chronicle relates that he erected idols on the hill in Kiev: 'a Perun of wood, his head of silver and moustache of gold, and Hors and Dazbog and Stribog and Simargl and Mokosh'.[95] Human sacrifices are also said to have been made to these gods. Vladimir's uncle, Dobrynya of Novgorod, on the other hand, is said to have created just one devotional image above the river Volkhov, certainly that of Perun, the leading Slavic god. We do not know why Vladimir broke off his efforts to achieve political integration on the basis of a pagan pantheon a few years later. In any event, he and his people adopted the monotheistic faith of the Christians in 988.

As evident in the case of Rome or the Teutons, it is entirely possible to imagine the embracing of diversity on the basis of a polytheistic cult, but this was clearly no longer a possibility in Europe from the late tenth century. The last empire to feature a state of parity among its many religions seems to have been that of the Khazars on the Volga; until 965 a Khagan of the Jewish faith led a people consisting of followers of Islam, Christianity, and the ancient Turkish Tengri.[96] The monotheistic revelatory religions had, however, become so strong in Europe by this point that they laid claim to entire peoples.

On the other hand, the openness of the polytheistic pantheon, though it was not limitless, brought with it a considerable degree of indifference among the various cults. We might recall Nietzsche's excellent formulation: 'The ancient Greeks without normative theology: each individual has the right to make up his own stories and he can believe what he likes.'[97] But the Middle Ages saw the abandonment of ancient polytheism; instead, the breakthrough of monotheism

---

[94]   Martin, *Medieval Russia*, pp. 1ff.

[95]   *Die Nestorchronik. Die altrussische Chronik, zugeschrieben dem Mönch des Kiever Höhlenklosters Nestor, in der Redaktion des Abtes Sil'vestr aus dem Jahr 1116*, German trans. Ludolf Müller (Munich: Fink, 2001), p. 97 on the year 6488 (A D 980), paragraph 88.

[96]   Svetlana Alexandrovna Pletnyova, *Die Chasaren. Mittelalterliches Reich an Don und Wolga* (Leipzig: Koehler & Amelang, 1978).

[97]   Quoted in Hans Blumenberg, 'Wirklichkeitsbegriff und Wirkungspotential des Mythos', in Manfred Fuhrmann (ed.), *Terror und Spiel. Probleme der Mythenrezeption* (Munich: Fink, 1971), pp. 11–66, here p. 17.

was to be the key event in European history. It meant nothing less than the birth of Europe in the Middle Ages. Rather than worshipping the many gods in a pantheon or the particular god of one's own community, the emerging Europeans demanded belief in a single God, the creator of heaven and earth.[98] In contrast to myth, which told of many gods and indifferently tolerated a large number of co-existent gods, the universality of the Creator God meant that no-one could any longer remain indifferent to what his neighbours thought about God. There was no God of the Jews, Christians, or Muslims, but – insofar as people were consistent in matters of faith – just one single God for everyone.[99] Theology

---

[98] See Söding (ed.), *Ist der Glaube Feind der Freiheit?*; Jürgen Manemann (ed.), *Monotheismus*, Jahrbuch Politische Theologie 4 (Münster: LIT, 2003); Stolz, 'Wesen und Funktion von Monotheismus'; Fritz Stolz, *Einführung in den biblischen Monotheismus* (Darmstadt: Wissenschaftliche Buchgesellschaft, 1996); Peter Hayman, 'Monotheism – A Misused Word in Jewish Studies?', *Journal of Jewish Studies* 42 (1991), pp. 1–15.

[99] See Sura 29:46 (the message of the Koran with respect to the 'possessors of the book', that is, Jews and Christians): 'We believe in that which has been revealed to us and revealed to you, and our God and your God is one, and to Him do we submit'; see Rudi Paret, 'Toleranz und Intoleranz im Islam', *Saeculum* 21 (1970), pp. 344–65, here p. 349; Albrecht Noth, 'Möglichkeiten und Grenzen islamischer Toleranz', *Saeculum* 29 (1978), pp. 190–204, here p. 191 (which cites Sura 2:62). Things could, however, be quite different in practice. Following Granada's subjugation by the Catholic kings in 1492, the Christians courted the Muslim office-bearers: 'But the Christians were generally unsuccessful in this. A Muslim dignitary once remarked wittily in the presence of an envoy from the king of Castile, who was supposed to win over his "colleague", that he already had his hands full meeting all his obligations, more or less, to a single God. How was he supposed to cope with a triune God?': Alain Brissaud, *Islam und Christentum. Gemeinsamkeit und Konfrontation gestern und heute* (Berlin: Quintessenz, 1993), p. 238. I am aware that the statement above would require more discriminating formulation from a religious history perspective, see Stolz, 'Wesen und Funktion von Monotheismus', p. 174: 'Do the Christians have the same God as the Jews and the Muslims? This is a very simple question of identity. Who is the Muslim or Christian addressing during prayer for example? Is it the same God or a different one in each case? Is it perhaps possible to pray together? Historically, the question is easy to answer. Christianity developed out of Judaism, and the Muslim conception of God is derived from Judaism or Christianity. But the historical answer is, of course, insufficient. The Israelite's Yahweh ultimately stands in continuity with Baal and El, even though this was later denied. Does this mean that the Christian God is identical to El of Ugarit? Perhaps it does, but if so: is the Christian God identical to El of Ugarit in the same way as to the Yahweh of the Old Testament and the Allah of Muhammad? It is immediately apparent that this question cannot be settled historically; it must be posed as a systematic-theological problem, or more precisely, as a problem of religious theology.'

and dogma, which were based on the religious tradition of the book and were themselves codified in writing, were now also unavoidable.

The Egyptologist Jan Assmann, among others, has recently examined the caesura of monotheism, describing it as a turning point that was 'more fateful than any other political change in world history'.[100] It was not the distinction between one God and many gods that was crucial, but 'the distinction between true and false within the field of religion, between the true God and the false gods, the true teaching and the heresies, between knowledge and ignorance, belief and unbelief'.[101] In this sense, the monotheistic turn had fateful consequences. 'During its later historical reception', the 'Mosaic distinction' between 'true and false', fundamental to it, 'generated the distinction between Jews and heathens, Christians and heathens, Christians and Jews, Muslims and infidels, orthodox and heretics and manifested itself in an orgy of violence and bloodshed'.[102] The monotheistic religions were inevitably intolerant, that is, they had to have a clear sense of what they considered irreconcilable with their truths and what was acceptable.[103] In contrast, heresy was unknown to the pagan – or polytheistic – religions. Assmann's critique of monotheism is new only in the context of his Egyptological research and in the pointedness of his statements, but it is part of a wider trend. A quarter of a century ago the philosopher Odo Marquard spoke in 'praise of polytheism', while Hans Blumenberg investigated the sense of fascination with the myths fundamental to polytheism.[104]

Assmann, like other contemporary authors, suggests that monotheism, in its concern for unity, could lead only to division and not to the embracing of diversity. I reject this view. The profession of faith that belief in a single God demanded, and the religious differences and frictions it provoked, were certainly a nigh-on inexhaustible source of conflicts; but with its uncompromising approach,

---

[100]   Assmann, *Die Mosaische Unterscheidung*, p. 11. This essay strives to come to terms with critiques of Assmann's book *Moses the Egyptian. The Memory of Egypt in Western Monotheism* (Cambridge, MA, and London: Harvard University Press, 1997), falling back on the older exposition in an attempt to formulate his views more precisely.

[101]   Assmann, *Die Mosaische Unterscheidung*, pp. 12–13.

[102]   Assmann, *Die Mosaische Unterscheidung*, p. 22.

[103]   Assmann, *Die Mosaische Unterscheidung*, p. 26.

[104]   Odo Marquard, 'Lob des Polytheismus. Über Monomythie und Polymythie', in Hans Poser (ed.), *Philosophie und Mythos. Ein Kolloquium* (Berlin and New York: Gruyter, 1979), pp. 40–58; reprinted in Marquard, *Abschied vom Prinzipiellen. Philosophische Studien* (Stuttgart: Reclam, 1995), pp. 91–116; Hans Blumenberg, *Work on Myth* (Cambridge, MA, London: MIT Press, 1985). See Michael Borgolte, 'Historie und Mythos', in Mario Kramp (ed.), *Krönungen. Könige in Aachen – Geschichte und Mythos. Katalog der Ausstellung*, vol. 2 (Mainz: Zabern, 2000), pp. 839–46; Borgolte, 'Europas Geschichten und Troia'.

monotheism was also an invaluable school for the perception of the other, which could certainly lead to acceptance. As religion affected everybody and monotheism forced everyone to make a decision, everyone could come to know religious diversity. Even in cases where no clashes occurred between Christianity, Judaism, and Islam, and where they were not in competition, people were always concerned with the correct faith; schisms and heresies are the clearest manifestations of the potential for difference within the world of orthodox belief shared by Christians, Jews, and Muslims.[105] On the other hand, and this is often underestimated, religious differences by no means led inevitably to conflicts or murderous attempts to annihilate other groups. Europe's survival, but, above all, its culture, rests to this day upon the toleration of differences between groups.

Of the three monotheistic religions of Europe, Judaism and Christianity had already spread within the Roman Empire and beyond, while Islam arrived only in the seventh and eighth centuries. None of these religions has ever dominated Europe entirely, including Christianity. The followers of the law of Moses were the first to seek refuge in Europe;[106] a Jewish settlement existed in Rome before the birth of Christ.[107] Titus' destruction of the Second Temple in Jerusalem subsequently triggered Jewish emigration from their traditional areas of settlement in Palestine, Syria, Mesopotamia, and Egypt on a larger scale, which brought them over the course of time to Asia Minor and Greece as well as the western Mediterranean. In Europe, the 'Sephardic' (Spanish) Jewry formed a first centre of religion and culture, while there is evidence of Jewish settlements in southern French cities in the third century.[108] In the early Middle Ages, the Muslim conquests in Palestine and Spain triggered far-reaching shifts in settlement, and this happened repeatedly from then on. Jews were, however, by no means to be found everywhere in Europe; they reached England only from 1066,[109] while there were almost none in Norway,

[105] See the recent contribution by Irene Pieper, Michael Schimmelpfennig, and Joachim von Soosten (eds), *Häresien. Religionshermeneutische Studien zur Konstruktion von Norm und Abweichung* (Munich: Fink, 2003).

[106] On this topic and on what follows: Haim Hillel Ben-Sasson (ed.), *A History of the Jewish People* (London: Weidenfeld & Nicolson, 1976); Kenneth R. Stow, *Alienated Minority. The Jews of Medieval Latin Europe* (Cambridge, MA, and London: Harvard University Press, 1992).

[107] Beard, North, and Price, *Religions of Rome*, vol. 1, pp. 266–7.

[108] Michael Toch, *'Dunkle Jahrhunderte'. Gab es ein jüdisches Frühmittelalter?* (Trier: Kliomedia, 2001).

[109] Robert Bartlett, *England under the Norman and Angevin Kings, 1075–1225* (Oxford: Oxford University Press, 2000), pp. 346ff.; Paul R. Hyams, 'The Jews in Medieval England, 1066–1290', in Alfred Haverkamp and Hanna Vollrath (eds), *England and Germany in the High Middle Ages* (Oxford: Oxford University Press, 1996), pp. 173–92.

Sweden, Ireland, and Scotland.[110] With the exception of the realm of the Khazars, a semi-nomadic Turkic people living on the Dnieper, Don, and Volga, the Jews never managed to lead a realm. In the other parts of Europe where they lived together and formed communities, they were a small minority, dependent on the goodwill of the Christian or Muslim rulers or the religious leaders of other faiths. This is also why there are no dates in medieval history in which the Jews played a decisive role;[111] they felt that they were in exile,[112] and in Europe they were in fact always the objects of others' actions. In contrast to the other two religions, the congregations almost never grew as a result of conversion, let alone subjugation, but at most through immigration and biological self-reproduction.[113] The Jews' ritual practices, festivals, and strict laws separated them particularly from the Christians and Muslims among whom they lived,[114] but even among themselves

---

[110]   See the map of the Jewish diaspora in Ben-Sasson (ed.), *A History of the Jewish People*, p. 464.

[111]   See Robert Raphael Geis, 'Das Geschichtsbild des Talmud', *Saeculum* 6 (1955), pp. 119–24, here p. 123: 'The Jew no longer makes history, he suffers it.' In the same vein: Michael Borgolte, 'Zwischen Erfindung und Kanon. Zur Konstruktion der Fakten im europäischen Hochmittelalter', in Andreas Bihrer and Elisabeth Stein (eds), *Nova de veteribus. Mittel- und neulateinische Studien für Paul Gerhard Schmidt* (Munich: Saur, 2004), pp. 292–325, here p. 305.

[112]   Friedrich Battenberg, *Das europäische Zeitalter der Juden. Zur Entwicklung einer Minderheit in der nichtjüdischen Umwelt Europas*, vol. 1: *Von den Anfängen bis 1650* (Darmstadt: Primus, 1990), pp. 15–16; Haim Hillel Ben-Sasson, 'The Middle Ages', in Ben-Sasson (ed.), *A History of the Jewish People*, pp. 385–723, esp. pp. 393ff.; Borgolte, *Europa entdeckt seine Vielfalt*, pp. 246ff.

[113]   See Michael Toch, *Die Juden im mittelalterlichen Reich* (Munich: Oldenbourg, 1998, 2003), pp. 10–11; on settlements and expulsions in Germany (and neighbouring territories) see the recent work by Alfred Haverkamp (ed.), *Geschichte der Juden im Mittelalter von der Nordsee bis zu den Südalpen. Kommentiertes Kartenwerk*, 3 vols (Hanover: Hahnsche Buchhandlung, 2002), with maps and commentaries.

[114]   See Toch, *Die Juden im mittelalterlichen Reich*, pp. 34ff., 96ff.; David Jacoby, 'Les juifs de Byzance. Une communauté marginalisée', in Χρυςα Λ. Μαλτεζουμ (ed.), Οι ρεριδωριακοι στο Βυζαντιο (Athens: Hidryma Gulandrç-Chorn, 1993), pp. 103–54; Andrew Sharf, *Byzantine Jewry from Justinian to the Fourth Crusade* (London: Routledge, 1971); Steven B. Bowman, *The Jews of Byzantium, 1204–1453* (Tuscaloosa, AL: University of Alabama Press, 1985); Norman Roth, *Jews, Visigoths and Muslims in Medieval Spain: Cooperation and Conflict* (Leiden, New York, and Cologne: Brill, 1994); Eliyahu Ashtor, *The Jews of Muslim Spain*, 2 vols (Philadelphia, PA: Jewish Publication Society of America, 1993); Yitzhak Baer, *A History of the Jews in Christian Spain* (Philadelphia, PA: Jewish Publication Society, 1992); Marie de Menaca, *Histoire politique des Juifs d'Espagne au Moyen Age*, vols 1–3 (Nantes: University of Nantes, 1993–1996); Nora Berend, *At the Gate of Christendom:*

they formed only a loose-knit community; the congregations were not organized within any authoritative system, despite occasional attempts at centralization and the temporary dominance of certain houses of teaching.[115]

While the Jews were only ever a minority, Christians and Muslims could be a majority or minority within a society.[116] The Christianization of Europe had begun with the missionary journeys of the apostle Paul to Philippi, Thessalonica, and Corinth in Macedonia and Greece (49–51) and, advancing from the south and west, focused for centuries primarily on the conversion of polytheists.[117] The medieval culmination of this process was marked by the conversion of Lithuania in 1386,[118] while the invasion of the multi-religious and indifferent Mongols the century before had put a stop to the Christianization of Lapland, Cumania, and some of the peoples of the middle Volga region.[119] The incredibly long duration

---

Jews, Muslims and 'Pagans' in Medieval Hungary, c. 1000–c. 1300 (Cambridge: Cambridge University Press, 2001).

[115] See Ben-Sasson, 'The Middle Ages', pp. 421ff.

[116] On the following, see Borgolte, *Europa entdeckt seine Vielfalt*, pp. 261ff.

[117] On the Christian mission and the spread of Christianity, see the recent work by A. D. Lee, *Pagans and Christians in Late Antiquity: A Sourcebook* (London and New York: Routledge, 2000); Ramsay MacMullen, *Christianizing the Roman Empire (A.D. 100–400)* (New Haven, CT, and London: Yale University Press, 1984); Peter Brown, *Die Entstehung des christlichen Europa* (Munich: Beck, 1999); Richard Fletcher, *The Conversion of Europe: From Paganism to Christianity 371–1386 AD* (London: Fontana, 1997); F. Donald Logan, *A History of the Church in the Middle Ages* (London and New York: Routledge, 2002).

[118] Jūratė Kiaupienė, 'The Grand Duchy of Lithuania in the times of Vytautas and Jogila', in Zugmantas Kiaupa, Jūratė Kiaupienė, and Albinas Kuncevičius, *The History of Lithuania before 1795* (Vilnius: Lithuanian Institute of History, 2000), pp. 127–60; *La Cristianizzazione della Lituania* (Rome: Libr. Ed. Vaticana, 1986).

[119] Peter Jackson, 'The Mongols and Europe', in David Abulalfia (ed.), *The New Cambridge Medieval History*, vol. 5 (Cambridge: Cambridge University Press, 1999), pp. 703–19; Felicitas Schmieder, *Europa und die Fremden. Die Mongolen im Urteil des Abendlandes vom 13. bis in das 15. Jahrhundert* (Sigmaringen: Thorbecke, 1994); Ulrich Schmilewski (ed.), *Wahlstatt 1241. Beiträge zur Mongolenschlacht bei Liegnitz und zu ihren Nachwirkungen* (Würzburg: Korn, 1991); N. Pfeiffer, *Die ungarische Dominikanerprovinz von ihrer Gründung 1221 bis zur Tatarenverwüstung 1241–1242* (Zürich: Leemann, 1913); Heinrich Dörrie, 'Drei Texte zur Geschichte der Ungarn und Mongolen', in *Nachrichten der Akademie der Wissenschaften in Göttingen aus dem Jahre 1956, Philologisch-Historische Klasse* (Göttingen: Vandenhoeck & Ruprecht, 1956); Fred Singleton, *A Short History of Finland* (Cambridge: Cambridge University Press, 1998); Torsten Edgren and Lena Törnblom, *Finlands Historia*, vol. 1 (Esbo: Schildt, 1993); John H. Lind, 'Consequences of the Baltic Crusades in Target Areas: The Case of Karelia', in Alan V. Murray (ed.), *Crusade and Conversion on the Baltic Frontier, 1150–1350* (Aldershot: Ashgate, 2001), pp. 133–50.

of European missionary history points to substantial resistance everywhere, if not to a highly variable degree of engagement among the bishops and missionaries themselves.

The Church could never achieve a state of ultimate completion because it lacked the requisite unity. Even the post-apostolic Christian congregations feared nothing more than schism and heresy, without, from the outset, clearly separating the division in hierarchy and organization from dissent in matters of faith. Around 100, the Christians in Rome were already alarmed about the internal situation of the congregation in Corinth, which had long been famous for its spirit of brotherhood but was now at loggerheads to the point where a rival group had ruthlessly eliminated the old leadership.[120] The intense struggle over orthodox doctrine inspired the composition of the first tracts against heretics just a few decades later.[121] The most serious schism, at least as far as Europe is concerned, was the division into the Latin or Roman and the Greek Orthodox Church; embedded in the rivalries between two empires and the early Christian patriarchates, it was lastingly cemented in 1054.[122] Time and again, Christians fought passionately against discord in matters of faith or the Church, without, though, ever succeeding.

When the Muslims advanced towards Europe, they no longer had to deal with many polytheists, but only with Christians and Jews. Before the religious warriors crossed from North Africa to Gibraltar in 711, it is true, they had already conquered Damascus, Jerusalem, Antioch, and Egypt from their base in Arabia, but they had failed several times to capture Constantinople.[123] In western Europe, Arabs and Berbers rapidly succeeded in destroying the Christian empire of the Visigoths and in occupying almost all of Spain up to the Pyrenees;[124] shortly

---

[120]   Karl Baus, *From the Apostolic Community to Constantine*, History of the Church 1 (London: Burns & Oates, 1980), pp. 147, 152.

[121]   See Franz Dünzl, 'Art. Irenaeus v. Lyon', in *Lexikon für Theologie und Kirche*, vol. 5 (Freiburg, Basle, Rome, and Vienna: Herder, 1996), cols 583–5.

[122]   Most recently: Axel Bayer, *Spaltung der Christenheit. Das sogenannte Morgenländische Schisma von 1054* (Cologne, Weimar, and Vienna: Böhlau, 2002).

[123]   See Kettermann, *Atlas zur Geschichte des Islam*, pp. 19ff.; Lilie, *Byzanz*, pp. 75ff.; Walter E. Kaegi, *Byzantium and the Early Islamic Conquests* (Cambridge: Cambridge University Press, 1992).

[124]   Roger Collins, *The Arab Conquest of Spain, 710–797* (Oxford: Blackwell, 1989); 'Abdulwāhid Dhanūn Tāha, *The Muslim Conquest and Settlement of North Africa and Spain* (London and New York: Routledge, 1989); Rachel Arié, *España musulmana (siglos VIII–XV)* (Barcelona: Ed. Labor, 1993); Marie-Claude Gerbet, *L'Espagne au Moyen Age, VIIIe–XVe siècles* (Paris: Armand Colin, 1992); Bernard F. Reilly, *The Medieval Spains* (Cambridge: Cambridge University Press, 1993).

afterwards they occupied Sicily as well.[125] On the other hand, a cell of resistance against the foreign rulers emerged in Asturia, from which the Christians could begin the reconquest of their homeland. The *Reconquista* was to last for centuries, but the military victory of 1212, which forced the Muslims of Spain to retreat to Granada, was a breakthrough.[126] At around the same time, the Normans and ultimately Frederick II ousted the 'Saracens' from Sicily.[127] Islam, meanwhile, won important peoples and countries in the south-east during the late Middle Ages. The Volga Bulgars, who had adopted Islam and created an empire in the early tenth century, were subjugated by the Mongols; but the Khan of the Mongolian 'Golden Horde', to which most of the Christian Rus' now belonged, soon converted to Islam (1257–1266).[128] The Muslim sphere of influence was pushed beyond the Dnieper. The expansion and conquests by the Islamized Turks in Byzantium and in the Balkans from 1354 were even more far-reaching; with the fall of Constantinople in 1453, the Ottoman Empire finally took the place

---

[125]   Ferdinando Maurici, *Breve Storia degli Arabi in Sicilia* (Palermo: Flaccovio, 1995); Aziz Ahmad, *A History of Islamic Sicily* (Edinburgh: Edinburgh University Press, 1975); Bernd Rill, *Sizilien im Mittelalter* (Stuttgart and Zürich: Belser, 1995).

[126]   David Abulafia, 'The Nasrid Kingdom of Granada', in *The New Cambridge Medieval History*, vol. 5, pp. 636–43; see also Bernard F. Reilly, *The Contest of Christian and Muslim Spain, 1031–1157* (Oxford and Malden, MA: Blackwell, 1992); Ludwig Vones, *Geschichte der Iberischen Halbinsel im Mittelalter, 711–1480* (Sigmaringen: Thorbecke, 1993). But it is important to bear in mind that there were Muslim minorities in Spain under Christian rule, see L. P. Harvey, *Islamic Spain 1250 to 1500* (Chicago, IL, and London: University of Chicago Press, 1990).

[127]   Maurici, *Breve Storia degli Arabi in Sicilia*, esp. pp. 146–53; Ahmad, *A History of Islamic Sicily*, esp. pp. 82–7; Wolfgang Stürner, *Friedrich II.*, vol. 2 (Darmstadt: Primus, 2000), pp. 66–74; David Abulafia, 'The End of Muslim Sicily', in James M. Powell (ed.), *Muslims under Latin rule, 1100–1300* (Princeton, NJ: Princeton University Press, 1990), pp. 105–33; Abulafia, 'The Kingdom of Sicily under the Hohenstaufen and Angevins', in *The New Cambridge Medieval History*, vol. 5, pp. 497–521; Pierre Guichard, *Espagne et la Sicile musulmanes aux XIe et XIIe siècles* (Lyon: Presses Universitaires de Lyon, 1991); Hubert Houben, 'Neue Quellen zur Geschichte der Juden und Sarazenen im Königreich Sizilien (1275–1280)', *Quellen und Forschungen aus italienischen Archiven und Bibliotheken* 74 (1994), pp. 335–59, here esp. pp. 340ff.

[128]   Rudolf Kaschewsky, 'Die Religion der Mongolen', in Michael Weiers (ed.), *Die Mongolen. Beiträge zu ihrer Geschichte und Kultur* (Darmstadt: Wissenschaftliche Buchgesellschaft, 1986), pp. 87–123, here pp. 120–1; Jean Richard, 'La conversion de Berke et les débuts de l'islamisation de la Horde d'Or', in Richard, *Orient et Occident au Moyen Age: contacts et relations (XIIe–XVe s.)* (London: Variorum, 1976 [1967]), no. XXIX; Schmieder, *Europa und die Fremden*, pp. 35, 39.

of the Christian empire.[129] At the close of the Middle Ages, the lines separating Christian and Muslim settlements still ran through Europe, albeit in different places than before.

Although in principle the three monotheistic religions did not tolerate one another, their followers influenced one another in various ways. The Jews maintained the most defensive stance. This was by no means only because they considered themselves the chosen people with whom Yahweh had made his covenant; for into Roman Antiquity they had entertained the thought that other peoples might also come to share their faith in the one God of Israel as the creator of the world.[130] We do in fact have accounts of conversions of heathen Romans dating from the imperial period. But for the Jews, after their uprising failed in 70 and they were expelled from Jerusalem, the time of exile had finally begun, during which the preservation of their identity became far more important than any expansion through proselytizing. The number of converts from Christianity or Islam during the Middle Ages must have been negligible; we know of just a few names here and there.[131] Without the backing of their own state and constituting a small minority, the Jewish congregations were hardly in a position to contemplate a missionary offensive among majorities of a different faith. But Jewish activities were also limited by the fact that in Islam apostasy was punishable by death, and the same fate could also befall Christians.[132]

In contrast to the Jews and to the Muslims, Christians had a duty to spread their religion through the conversion of peoples. According to Matthew the Evangelist, after Jesus had risen from the dead he famously gave his eleven remaining disciples the task of spreading the word, promising them his support (Matthew 28:18–20):

---

[129] Suraiya Faroqhi, *Geschichte des osmanischen Reiches* (Munich: Beck, 2000); Josef Matuz, *Das Osmanische Reich. Grundlinien seiner Geschichte* (Darmstadt: Primus, 1990); Georges Castellan, *History of the Balkans: From Mohammed the Conqueror to Stalin* (Boulder, CO, and New York: Columbia University Press, 1992), pp. 33ff.; Edgar Hösch, *Geschichte der Balkanländer. Von der Frühzeit bis zur Gegenwart* (Munich: Beck, 2002), pp. 78ff.

[130] Menahem Stern, 'The Period of the Second Temple', in Ben-Sasson (ed.), *A History of the Jewish People*, pp. 185–303, esp. pp. 288–303; Beard, North, and Price, *Religions of Rome*, vol. 1, pp. 275–6.

[131] See Toch, *Die Juden im mittelalterlichen Reich*, pp. 125–6.

[132] On punishment by death for Muslim apostates, see Halm, *Der Islam*, p. 61. An example of the death sentence for Christian apostates: the Council of Oxford of 1222 condemned a deacon who had married a Jew as a proselyte to be burnt at the stake, see Wolfgang Giese, 'In Iudaismum lapsus est. Jüdische Proselytenmacherei im frühen und hohen Mittelalter (600–1300)', *Historisches Jahrbuch* 88 (1968), pp. 407–18, here pp. 411–12.

All authority in heaven and on earth has been given to me. Go therefore and make disciples of all nations, baptizing them in the name of the Father and of the Son and of the Holy Spirit, teaching them to observe all that I have commanded you. And behold, I am with you always, to the end of the age.

Researchers have discovered that a general command to spread the faith of this kind was unique among the world religions.[133] It was, however, only hesitantly implemented. It was not without conflicts that the insight spread among the first Christians that the Good News was not meant only for the Jews, but also for the heathen Romans, and much the same applies to the young Church's turn to the barbarians beyond the empire. But to convert these peoples required a different missionary method than had been deployed in Antiquity.[134] In the ancient world, conversion had generally begun with the individual. According to the teaching of the church father St Augustine, it was supposed to occur voluntarily and to be inwardly complete before baptism. Had the candidate been won over by a sermon, he had to pass the catechumenate before being baptized. Among the Teutons and the other peoples near the borders of the empire, the organized mission now took the place of individual conversion; this was aimed at collectives and began with the kings and nobility, in other words, the leaders of the peoples, tribes, and clans. From there, the process of change was intended to work its way 'downwards' through society. The mission left individuals little room to make their own decisions. Baptism, for which people were now prepared with a reduced amount of instruction, was considered the criterion of success for missionary work.

The Christians treated the Jews, who they often found had preceded them as they spread across Europe, differently than the heathens. Here again, a theological doctrine expounded by Augustine was fundamental to their approach.[135] According to this doctrine, the Jews were worthy of protection by the Church because their dispersion bore witness to the Passion of Christ for

---

[133]   Horst Bürkle, 'Art. Mission, I. Religionsgeschichtlich', in *Lexikon für Theologie und Kirche*, vol. 7 (Freiburg, Basle, Rome, and Vienna: Böhlau, 1998), cols 288–9.

[134]   On what follows, see Michael Borgolte, *Die mittelalterliche Kirche* (Munich: Oldenbourg, 1992), pp. 4ff.; recently: James Muldoon (ed.), *Varieties of Religious Conversion in the Middle Ages* (Gainesville, FL: University Press of Florida, 1997); Guyda Armstrong and Ian N. Wood (eds), *Christianizing Peoples and Converting Individuals* (Turnhout: Brepols, 2000); Arnold Angenendt, *Grundformen der Frömmigkeit im Mittelalter* (Munich: Oldenbourg, 2003), p. 3.

[135]   The following is gleaned from Borgolte, *Europa entdeckt seine Vielfalt*, pp. 247–8; Battenberg, *Das Europäische Zeitalter der Juden*, vol. 1, pp. 15–16.

which they, that is, their forefathers, were to blame. On the other hand, the Christians respected the followers of the Mosaic religion as keepers of the Old Law, who for this very reason pointed to God's New Covenant with humankind, which Christ had made possible. Finally, Paul's Epistle to the Romans predicted that the Jews would convert at the end of times. Christians' relationship to the Jews was thus always ambivalent. On the one hand they were considered participants in and witnesses to the *Heilsgeschichte*, on the other as deicides. In the Middle Ages, forced baptisms were prohibited under Church law; the killing of Jews was also decisively rejected, though not their expulsion.[136] Despite this, acts of violence against the Jews occurred everywhere they hoped to settle permanently in Europe. Even the temporal protection of Jews, which the Christian rulers had undertaken to provide, could not always prevent or put a stop to this.[137]

The Muslims also wished to fulfil their universal mission in a quite different way than the Jews and Christians. They divided – and still divide – the world into two segments, the 'House of Islam' and the 'House of War'.[138] Theoretically, the first part of the world, which is already under Muslim rule, is in a constant state of war with the yet-to-be-converted other part; following Mohammed's example, the war may be temporarily suspended if the enemy is too strong and one's own forces are insufficient. According to the teachings of the Koran, the heathens must accept Islam or be put to death, but this does not apply to the 'possessors of the book', primarily Jews and Christians. It is enough to spread Islamic rule, without the subject Christians or Jews themselves having to become Muslims. Treaties between Muslims and possessors of the book guaranteed them full possession of their religious institutions and worldly goods; they became 'charges' of the state, to which they paid a poll tax and land tax in return. The key legal basis for this relationship is laid down in Sura 9:29, according to which war must be waged against those who have received the Scripture

---

[136] Friedrich Lotter, '"Tod oder Taufe". Das Problem der Zwangstaufen während des Ersten Kreuzzugs', in Alfred Haverkamp (ed.), *Juden und Christen zur Zeit der Kreuzzüge* (Sigmaringen: Thorbecke, 1999), pp. 107–52; Rudolf Hiestand, 'Juden und Christen in der Kreuzzugspropaganda und bei den Kreuzzugspredigern', in Haverkamp (ed.), *Juden und Christen zur Zeit der Kreuzzüge*, pp. 153–208.

[137] See Battenberg, *Das Europäische Zeitalter der Juden*, vol. 1, pp. 17–18; Alexander Patschovsky, 'Das Rechtsverhältnis der Juden zum deutschen König (9.–14. Jahrhundert). Ein europäischer Vergleich', *Zeitschrift der Savigny-Stiftung für Rechtsgeschichte, Germanistische Abteilung* 110 (1993), pp. 331–71.

[138] On this and what follows, see Heribert Busse, *Die theologische Beziehungen des Islams zu Judentum und Christentum. Grundfragen des Dialogs im Koran und die gegenwärtige Situation* (Darmstadt: Wissenschaftliche Buchgesellschaft, 1988), pp. 142ff.

'until they pay the tax in acknowledgement of superiority and they are in a state of subjection'.[139] As the Koran is considered to be God's revelation, which cannot be altered in any way, the position of religious minorities, as far as the Christians, Jews, and other possessors of the book are concerned, was legally protected in a way unique in pre-modern societies;[140] however, the subjugated book possessors were inevitably 'second-class citizens', as it were, as they could achieve legal equality with Muslims only by converting to Islam.[141] The Muslim rulers, whether in early medieval Spain or the Turkish empire of the Ottomans from the fourteenth and fifteenth centuries on, were generally little interested in the mass conversion of the pre-existing Christian population, which nothing in their religion compelled them to pursue.[142] The tax revenue or tribute often held significantly more appeal. The Iberian peninsula and the Balkans were thus Islamicized only gradually, over centuries, though this process would never have been completed at the expense of the Christians.

It is thus by no means the case that the monotheism of Europe constantly drove the followers of the three religions to acts of violence against one another. The Jewish minority under Christian hegemony was protected by ecclesiastical principles and temporal law, and under Muslim rule both Christians and Jews enjoyed a privileged position sanctioned by the religious revelation itself. Without overlooking the social and political disadvantages which every outnumbered religious group nonetheless had to put up with, recent research has pointed to the long periods of symbiosis which for too long took second place to repression, persecution, expulsion, and murder in the perception of historians.[143] With respect to the relationship between Jews and Christians, they certainly refer to 'cultures of confrontation' and 'mutual exclusivity', but they also point to

---

[139] See also Tilman Nagel, *Der Koran. Einführung, Texte, Erläuterungen* (Munich: Beck, 2002), p. 148.

[140] Busse, *Die theologische Beziehungen des Islams zu Judentum und Christentum*, p. 145; Norman Daniel, *The Arabs and Medieval Europe* (London: Longman, 1975), p. 261.

[141] Albrecht Noth, 'Möglichkeiten und Grenzen islamischer Toleranz', *Saeculum* 29 (1978), pp. 190–204, here p. 197, n. 42.

[142] Busse, *Die theologischen Beziehungen des Islams zu Judentum und Christentum*, pp. 148ff.; Brissaud, *Islam und Christentum*, pp. 160–1, 211–12, 228, 247ff.; Hans Georg Majer, 'Aufstieg, Ende und Hinterlassenschaft einer Großmacht. Eine einleitende Skizze', in Majer (ed.), *Die Staaten Südosteuropas und die Osmanen* (Munich: Selbstverl. d. Südosteuropa-Ges., 1989), pp. 13–22; Castellan, *History of the Balkans*, pp. 109ff.; Richard W. Bulliet, *Conversion to Islam in the Medieval Period: An Essay in Quantitative History* (Cambridge, MA, and London: Harvard University Press, 1979).

[143] See, for example, Brissaud, *Islam und Christentum*, pp. 161, 345; Franco Cardini, *Europe and Islam* (Oxford: Blackwell, 2001).

the 'everyday cultural borrowings' between both religious communities.[144] A contemporary historian has explained what this means as follows:

> The sources offer a variety of evidence of normal neighbourly relations: from people living together in the same house through stays in other people's houses, participation in family celebrations, sometimes featuring mutual gift-giving, playing cards and games of chance together, to helping others as a matter of course in emergencies, such as fire, robbery and assault, which even justified infringement of the otherwise sacred peace of the Sabbath.[145]

To quote an account from the south-east of Europe, at the beginning of the eleventh century, the Jews of Byzantium are even said to have enjoyed freedoms which a Nestorian Christian from Persia considered nothing short of scandalous:

> The Romans tolerate a large number of Jews in their state. They give them protection, allow them openly to adhere to their religion and to build their synagogues [...] the Jews in their cities may say 'I am a Jew'. He may belong to his religion and say his prayers. No-one attacks him for this, prevents him from acting thus or puts obstacles in his way [...]. Just as in Egypt women, children and other unfit persons are allowed to enter the priest's sanctuary, so the Jews may enter the churches of the Romans.[146]

On the other hand, it was their different religious customs and regulations that divided the Christians as well as the Muslims from the Jews in everyday life. The laws governing the consumption of food limited or excluded the possibility of sitting down to eat with those of other faiths; mixed marriages and even sexual relations were prohibited on the Jewish side, etc. But it was precisely the daily alternation between closeness and distance which inevitably led to appreciation of difference and which facilitated the experience of a diversity of ways of life.

The same can be said of Muslims' relationship to Christians and Jews. It

---

[144]   Toch, *Die Juden im mittelalterlichen Reich*, pp. 120 ('mutual exclusivity' after Jakob Katz), 126–7 ('cultures of confrontation' after Amos Funkenstein), 138–9 ('everyday cultural borrowings'). See also Haverkamp (ed.), *Juden und Christen zur Zeit der Kreuzzüge*.

[145]   Toch, *Die Juden im mittelalterlichen Reich*, p. 40.

[146]   Account by Elîsha bar Sinhâya, quoted in Borgolte, *Europa entdeckt seine Vielfalt*, p. 251, after Andrew Sharf, *Byzantine Jewry from Justinian to the Fourth Crusade* (London: Routledge, 1971), p. 109.

has recently been shown how much Christians and Muslims in Spain depended on one another, regardless of which of the two held political power. Given that they were heavily outnumbered, the Saracens had to exercise the same degree of tolerance towards their new subjects after conquering the peninsula as did the Christians in the course of their *Reconquista* with respect to the Muslims.[147] Even under Christian rule the Muslims, the *Mudéjares*, composed their legal texts in Arabic and took the oath according to their faith:

> They built their own buildings and went about their business [...]. Many churches were built under their master builders, some of them financed by interest-free loans from the Jewish community. As late as the end of the 15th century, documents refer to Mudéjar musicians providing an instrumental accompaniment to the Catholic Corpus Christi procession and taking part in the banquet at the end.[148]

One scholar with an excellent knowledge of the situation has recently summarized the relations between Islam and Christianity during the Middle Ages as follows:

> [They] cannot be summed up as an uninterrupted succession of bloody conflicts and mutual contempt and humiliations. If you look at history across the centuries, the clashes between Christians and Muslims were neither more frequent nor more violent than the non-religious conflicts involving other antagonists or the real religious wars waged by both religious communities. Even in the case of the so-called Islamic-Christian confrontations, Muslims and Christians repeatedly entered into military alliances, showing that, at bottom, their motives for fighting were of a non-religious nature. [...] No-one talks about the crisis-free periods of tranquil, peaceful coexistence, yet these lasted for a long time and bore a good deal of fruit.[149]

However, every politically subordinate religious group was of legally inferior status, even when they made up the majority of the population, and ineradicable religious differences, often intensified by ethnic or biological separation, could break into violent conflict at any time. Recently, historians have become aware that, particularly in western Europe, in the realm of the Latin Church, a

---

[147]   Brissaud, *Islam und Christentum*, pp. 211–12; see also Robert I. Burns and Paul E. Chevedden, *Negotiating Cultures: Bilingual Surrender Treaties in Muslim Crusader Spain under James the Conqueror* (Leiden, Boston, and Cologne: Brill, 1999).

[148]   Brissaud, *Islam und Christentum*, pp. 234–5.

[149]   Brissaud, *Islam und Christentum*, p. 345.

previously unknown hostility towards Jews and Muslims, as well as heretics, took hold among Christians during the twelfth and thirteenth centuries.[150] We are talking about nothing less than the rise of a 'persecuting society'. One need only point to the pogroms against Jews and Muslims during the course of the first crusade.[151] Although the Muslim rulers of al-Andalus began to brutally repress and expel Christians and Jews at around the same time, the western Christians clearly surpassed them in repressing minorities of different faiths in terms of scale, systematic approach, and consistency. Other social 'deviants' such as homosexuals were also affected by these measures.[152] To explain this, scholars have pointed to the centralizing tendencies characteristic of the monarchies of the time and, above all, of the Roman Church itself. At the time, the papacy, with Rome as its base, was very keen to lead all of Latin Christendom to salvation and to enforce the same principles everywhere;[153] and from the thirteenth century at least, 'western Christendom [was] nothing less than obsessed with the idea of a necessary *reductio ad unum* in every field and on all levels. This is also mirrored within theology: it was most clerics' chief concern to trace everything back to unity while associating diversity with evil and heresy.'[154] The push to achieve societal uniformity with the tools of religion was also a promising approach to strengthening the European states under the leadership of the kings and a rational administration.

But despite all the oppression and persecution, Europe's monotheistic triad remained in place; even the Jews, who had been discriminated against, exploited, murdered, and driven away time and again from the high Middle Ages onwards,

---

[150]   See Borgolte, *Europa entdeckt seine Vielfalt*, pp. 261ff., 246ff.; Roger Ian Moore, *The Formation of a Persecuting Society: Power and Deviance in Western Europe, 950–1270* (Oxford and Malden, MA: Blackwell, 1998 [1987]).

[151]   Alongside the literature cited in n. 150 and Haverkamp (ed.), *Juden und Christen zur Zeit der Kreuzzüge*, see also Jonathan Riley Smith (ed.), *The Oxford Illustrated History of the Crusades* (Oxford: Oxford University Press, 1995); Steven Runciman, *A History of the Crusades* (Harmondsworth: Penguin, 1978), pp. 287–8; Battenberg, *Das Europäische Zeitalter der Juden*, vol. 1, pp. 61ff.; Cardini, *Europe and Islam*, pp. 70ff.

[152]   See Bernd-Ulrich Hergemöller, *Krötenkuß und schwarzer Kater. Ketzerei, Götzendienst und Unzucht in der inquisitorischen Phantasie des 13. Jahrhunderts* (Warendorf: Fahlbusch, 1996).

[153]   Borgolte, *Europa entdeckt seine Vielfalt*, pp. 75ff.; Colin Morris, *The Papal Monarchy: The Western Church from 1050 to 1250* (Oxford: Clarendon, 1989).

ıdré Vauchez, 'Der Kampf gegen Häresie und Abweichungen von der Norm sten', in Vauchez (ed.), *Machtfülle des Papsttums (1054–1274)*, Die Geschichte des ıntums 5 (Freiburg, Basle, and Vienna: Herder, 1994), pp. 886–911, here p. 889.

ultimately found a new exile in eastern Europe and the Turkish empire.[155] The
Ottomans, on the other hand, tolerated the Christians of the conquered Balkan
countries and forced them to convert, through the child-levy for instance, only
on a limited scale.[156] The thinkers of the three religions had by then already long
since begun to come to terms with the others; however, since the first study in
comparative religion, composed by the Muslim Ibn Hazm in Andalusia in the
eleventh century,[157] despite in-depth studies and frequently remarkable knowledge,
the authors always came to the conclusion that their own religion was superior
to the others.[158] They had at least recognized diversity as a problem. Tellingly,
the theologians of the high Middle Ages deployed the Latin words *diversitas*,
varietas, and *pluralitas* to capture the notion of religious difference and diversity.[159]
Admittedly, there is no question yet of tolerance in the modern sense; practical
'tolerance' of diversity was possible in the Middle Ages, but not theoretical

---

[155] Borgolte, *Europa entdeckt seine Vielfalt*, pp. 246ff.; Christian Lübke, '"... und es
kommen zu ihnen Mohammedaner, Juden und Türken ... ". Die mittelalterlichen
Grundlagen des Judentums im östlichen Europa', in Mariana Hausleitner and Monika
Katz (eds), *Juden und Antisemitismus im östlichen Europa* (Berlin: Harrassowitz, 1995),
pp. 39–57; Shmuel Ettinger, 'The Modern Period', in Ben-Sasson (ed.), *A History of the
Jewish People*, pp. 727–1096, esp. pp. 733ff.

[156] Majer, 'Aufstieg, Ende und Hinterlassenschaft einer Großmacht'; Castellan, *History
of the Balkans*, pp. 109ff.; *Ottoman Rule in Middle Europe and Balkan in the 16th and 17th
Centuries. Papers presented at the 9th Joint Conference of the Czechoslovak-Yugoslav Historical
Committee* (Prague: Academia, 1978), passim; Basilike D. Papoulia, *Ursprung und Wesen
der 'Knabenlese' im Osmanischen Reich* (Munich: Oldenbourg, 1963).

[157] See Borgolte, *Europa entdeckt seine Vielfalt*, pp. 265–6.

[158] On the writings of Yehuda ha-Levi from Toledo (d. 1150), see Borgolte, *Europa
entdeckt seine Vielfalt*, p. 183. On the work of the Christian Majorcan philosopher,
theologian, and writer Ramon Llull (d. ca. 1316), see for example: Ramon Lull, *Das Buch
vom Heiden und den drei Weisen*, trans. and ed. Theodor Pindl (Stuttgart: Reclam, 1998);
see Robert Pring-Mill, *Der Mikrokosmos Ramon Llulls. Eine Einführung in das mittelalterliche
Weltbild* (Stuttgart: Frommann Holzboog, 2000). Ora Limor (ed.), *Die Disputationen zu
Ceuta (1179) und Mallorca (1286). Zwei antijüdische Schriften aus dem mittelalterlichen Genua*
(Munich: Hahnsche Buchhandlung, 1994); Thomas E. Burman, *Religious Polemic and the
Intellectual History of the Mozarabs, c. 1050–1200* (Leiden: Brill, 1994). See also Bettina
Münzel, *Feinde, Nachbarn, Bündnispartner. 'Themen und Formen' der Darstellung christlich-
muslimischer Begegnungen in ausgewählten historiographischen Quellen des islamischen Spanien*
(Münster: Aschendorff, 1994).

[159] Klaus Schreiner and Gerhard Besier, 'Art. Toleranz', in *Geschichtliche Grundbegriffe.
Historisches Lexikon zur politisch-sozialen Sprache in Deutschland*, vol. 6 (Stuttgart: Klett-
Cotta, 1990), pp. 445–605, here p. 455 (K. Schreiner).

'approval' and 'recognition' of the alien religion.[160] From Augustine to Thomas Aquinas in the thirteenth century or Nicholas of Cusa in the fifteenth, Christian theologians have sought to establish the criteria for the tolerance of those of other faiths, often distinguishing precisely between Jews, heathens – Muslims, in other words – and heretics or apostates.[161] Without doubt, the history of tolerance, as it has unfolded in the west following the Reformation era, picked up the thread of the centuries-long symbiosis of Christians, Jews, and Muslims – as well as the differentiated treatment of Christian heretics – in the Middle Ages.

But it is not tolerance, one of our highest values, which I wish to elaborate here as the legacy of the Middle Ages, but diversity. Through the clashes between followers of different religions who believed in a single Creator God, my theory asserts, an awareness of difference and diversity developed which can never again be obscured or extinguished through reference to an enticing unity. The practice in this diversity through tolerance, but also through disputes, which sometimes resulted in murder, has laid the foundation that enables us to speak today of the cultural values of Europe in the plural.[162]

---

[160]   Schreiner and Besier, 'Art. Toleranz', pp. 446–7, 449 (K. Schreiner); p. 505 (G. Besier), on Goethe in the 'Maximen und Reflexionen' (Nos. 151, 146, 152, from 1809/29): '"Tolerance ought to be no more than a temporary state of mind; it must lead to recognition. To tolerate is to insult [...]. An idea cannot be liberal! It may be powerful, substantial, internally coherent, such that it carries out the divine mission of being productive. It is even less acceptable to call a concept liberal, for its task is quite different in nature [...]. The real liberality is recognition." These are the beginnings of the awareness of the distinction between formal and substantial tolerance; while the former is limited merely to leaving alien religious convictions untouched, the latter means positive recognition of other religions as a genuine and legitimate means of encountering the sacred.'

[161]   Schreiner and Besier, 'Art. Toleranz', pp. 452–61 (K. Schreiner). See also Alexander Patschovsky and Harald Zimmermann (eds), Toleranz im Mittelalter (Sigmaringen: Thorbecke, 1998).

[162]   On the topic of this essay, see also Michael Borgolte, Christen, Juden, Muselmanen. Die Erben der Antike und der Aufstieg des Abendlandes 300 bis 1400 n. chr. (Munich: Siedler, 2006).

Freedom, Slavery, and the Modern Construction of Rights

Orlando Patterson

I. Introduction

The end of the Cold War entailed not simply the political and ideological victory of the West over its Communist adversary, but the triumph of the West's most central and cherished value, freedom. Today we are living through one of the periodic explosive diffusions of this ideal as well as the related notion of human rights. According to Freedom House, the majority of the world's 5.4 billion people have declared themselves in favour of freedom. The world seems to be in anything but a festive mood as a result of the triumph of its master value. The former Soviet Union seems to lurch from one crisis to another, its people expressing increasing scepticism about the value of the ideal their leaders have embraced. Parts of eastern Europe have descended into the unspeakable nightmare of 'ethnic cleansing'. All this as a result of gaining more freedom.

Perhaps the most extraordinary recent development, however, has been the ideological counter-assault from several Near and Far Eastern states against the ideal of freedom itself, a movement that came to a head, taking the West completely by surprise, at the now notorious United Nations conference on human rights in Vienna early in 1993. Western delegates arrived at that conference expecting to stamp the final seal of triumph on freedom's behalf in a renewed universal Declaration of Human Rights. Instead, what they confronted was the Bangkok Declaration.

Produced by one of the strangest collections of international bedfellows the modern world has ever seen – communist China and Cuba, capitalist Indonesia, and anticommunist and fundamentalist Iran – the Bangkok Declaration defiantly called into question what most of us in the West had assumed was, by now, a foregone conclusion: that all peoples, even if they did not practise them, at least accepted freedom and fundamental human rights as laudable ideals.

It argued, in essence, first, that freedom and the notion of universal human rights are not and have never been universal, and have no root or sanction in the traditions of most countries of the world. And second, that if these ideals are to be taken seriously they must be expanded to include the idea of economic development as a basic human right, and, as such, an essential part of any acceptable conception of freedom.

II. On the Nature of Freedom

The Bangkok Declaration reminds us that perhaps the greatest danger to freedom at this, its seeming moment of triumph, lies in our tendency to take it too much for granted, and in our failure to explore rigorously just what it is, exactly what its roots are, and just where it might be heading. I will attempt here, in the very broadest outline, to tell the story (or to be more precise, I will give my account) of freedom.

Freedom is a triune concept that emerged with the rise of the West itself. From as early as the middle of the fifth century BC, the thing we call freedom emerged as a cultural chord composed of three notes: personal freedom, civic freedom, and sovereignal freedom. Personal freedom is the absence of constraint on our desire to do whatever it is we please; civic freedom is the capacity to participate in the governance of our community; sovereignal freedom is the capacity to do whatever we please, both in regard to ourselves – self-ownership, empowerment – and, more controversially today but emphatically true for most of the history of freedom and the West, in regard to others.

As a triune value, freedom achieves its conceptual coherence through the idea of power. We are free, personally, to the degree that we are released from the power of another, or not prevented by the power of another, to do what we want.

This is today the most fundamental meaning of the term; conceptually as well as historically, it may have been the most basic. For most of the history of the West, however, it has not been the dominant view, although often it has been the most popular. Only during the nineteenth century did this note of the chord become hegemonic, at which point, ironically, it ceased to be the most popular. We are free, sovereignally or positively, to the degree that we exercise power, over ourselves and others. We are free in the civic sense to the degree that we share in the collective power of the state that governs us. These most basic notes of freedom have always been chordally linked, constituting the most fundamental cultural triad of the West.

Apart from certain especially discordant times, people have always wanted negative freedom, personal freedom from those above them, in order better to exercise freedom over themselves (independence) and others; and they have always felt that having power in their most meaningful political order – whether this be village, borough, province, or state – the best guarantee for the other powers of freedom.

I have tried to show in *Freedom in the Making of Western Culture* that the social construction of freedom was made possible by the relation of slavery.[1] Slavery had to exist before people could even conceive of the idea of freedom as value, that is to say, find it meaningful and useful, an ideal to be striven for. Everywhere that slavery made its appearance, it became possible to conceive of the three notes of the chord of freedom and even, sometimes, to realize proto-historical versions of them. Thus, slavery immediately made possible something that had never existed before: the absolute, unprotected, unmediated power of life and death of one person over another. As Michael Mann has shown, the most distinctive feature of human society for most of the known history of mankind was the extraordinary resistance to the accumulation of personal power.[2] In other words, only with slavery did one person have the freedom to do absolutely as he or she pleased with another.

Slavery also immediately made possible, and stimulated the valorization of, the idea (so seemingly ridiculous to the pre-servile mind) that it is a good not to be under constraint: primordial personal or negative freedom. And only with the arrival of slaves did the idea of a class of people who are free become contradistinctively meaningful. All Gaul may have been divided into three parts, but until the Gauls took slaves, or were themselves made slaves, it would have made no sense whatsoever to call any part, however divided, free.

To conceive of something, to be able even to realize it in a sporadic way, and to desire it, however, is not to make a value of it. The shared valorization of an idea, wish, or practice only comes about when a special sociological context and a specific configuration of historical contingencies coexist. For most of human history, and for nearly all slave-holding non-Western peoples, neither the broader context nor the peculiar historical contingencies accounting for the social construction of freedom as value existed; I have attempted to explain why in my last work on the subject. The idea and proto-historical intimations of freedom remained simply that: the idea of freedom was never constructed as social value. Indeed, just the opposite happened. To the extent that the idea was conceived of in those societies that had small numbers of slaves, or even not insignificant numbers, as in the ancient Near East, it was condemned as a slave value, something desired only by the once-fallen, the debased, or the perverted.

---

[1]   Orlando Patterson, *Freedom*, vol. 1: *Freedom in the Making of Western Culture* (New York, 1991). What follows in this section is based on this work, and the reader should consult it for references. For my study of the nature, types, and comparative distribution of slavery, see *Slavery and Social Death: A Comparative Study* (Cambridge, MA, 1982).

[2]   Michael Mann, *The Sources of Social Power* (New York, 1986).

us in all non-Western cultures where it was found necessary to find a word for freedom, that word always had connotations of loss, unredeemable failure, nastiness, delinquency, debasement, and licentiousness. Only in the West did the word come to be cherished as the most precious in the language, next only to the sound of the name of God.

III. The Origins of Freedom in the Ancient and Medieval West

In *Freedom in the Making of Western Culture*, I have tried to demonstrate how this happened; how, at the end of the seventh century BC in Athens, a peculiar set of historical contingencies led to the emergence of large-scale slavery, and how in the struggle between the land-hungry small farmers and the slaveholding ruling class the demand for economic redistribution was met by political redistribution. Democracy was socially constructed out of this struggle and was directly related to the existence of a large class of slaves, a domestic enemy, which not only made ruling elite and emancipated small farmers independent of each other (the first such mutual independence in the history of post-acephalous polities), but solved the social problem it created by generating an internal bond between free masters and free native Athenians. The *demos* became a free *demos* vis-à-vis the unfree aliens, with a shared power vis-à-vis the powerless and dominated slaves.

While freedom became identified with the sharing of the power of the community, however, the primitive idea of freedom as power was also developed with respect not only to the slaves but to all foreign peoples, who were soon seen as being fit only to be slaves. The period of the Persian Wars was the decisive turning point in this development. The power, honour, and glory that had been an aristocratic monopoly were generalized to all free Athenian men after the triumphant victory over Persia. The naked concept of freedom as pure power over another was clothed with the fine armour of aristocratic *arete*. No one ever lost sight of what lay underneath; every Greek man knew and cherished the idea that to be 'truly free' was to be powerful and to pursue the *arete*, the dignity, independence, and self-possession of the noble life, and that achievement of these required, ideally, the enslavement or domination of other individuals and other peoples. They did not need Aristotle to justify such a view for them, quite apart from the fact that his theory of natural slavery was the most embarrassingly confused thing he ever wrote. Slavery, freedom, and empire, like father, bride, and groom, marched to the altar of Athena together.[3]

---

[3]   For the most accessible discussion of sovereignal or 'oligarthic' freedom among the Greeks, see Kurt A. Raaflaub, 'Democracy, Oligarchy, and the Concept of the "Free Citizen" in Late Fifth-Century Athens', *Political Theory* 11:4 (1983), pp. 517–44.

With the further expansion of slavery in the mining and urban economy of Athens, a large freedman and metic population emerged that was now predominantly male, highly skilled, and, most important of all, existed in a buoyant urban economy that provided all the space they needed to survive independently of their former masters (another first, in the history of stratified societies). These were the people who elaborated and elevated what was previously a value largely associated with Greek women: personal freedom. Hence, by the second half of the fifth century BC, the first chordal fusion of the three notes of freedom came about, and was given its immortal public expression in the funeral oration of Pericles.

All residents celebrated all three notes, but each note was ranked differently by the three main groups: citizen farmers and working-class urban Greek men cherished civic freedom above all; for the aristocratic elite, freedom primarily meant power, honour, and glory; and for the ex-slaves and other resident aliens, the primary note was personal freedom. From the very beginning, then, there was chordal unity in the expression of freedom – everyone recognized and valued, however grudgingly or enviously, all three notes, including the residents who were excluded from the experience of democracy – but there was an internal tension in its expression, reflective of the underlying class tensions in the society. The classic expression of both the chordal unison as well as the inherent tension in the triad of freedom was, of course, the funeral oration of Pericles.[4]

Classical republican and early imperial Rome marked the next critical moment in the history of freedom. With the demographic, economic, social, and cultural triumph of the freedman class at the heart of Europe's first world empire, freedom became the most cherished secular value in civilized Europe. With it came a new rendition of the chord. For a long time, historians of Rome have held that the civic or democratic note of freedom was a mere cultural echo, its political system dominated by a murderously competitive and oligarchic group of *nobiles* who controlled the Senate and the political process without regard to the masses. In a series of highly persuasive revisionist papers, however, Fergus Millar has shown us that this view, at least of classical republican Rome, is seriously flawed; that 'we cannot understand Roman politics if our view does not encompass, along with the power of individuals holding office and the collective power of the Senate as a body, the power of the people as represented, however imperfectly, in their assemblies'; that while not a democracy in the modern sense, there was a strong 'democratic element' in the legislative and legal processes and

---

[4]   For the most brilliant exposition of which, see Nicole Loraux, *The Invention of Athens: The Funeral Oration in the Classical City* (Cambridge, MA, 1986). See also, Patterson, *Freedom*, vol. 1, ch. 6.

in the enormous importance placed on oratory and persuasion of the people by the political elite.[5]

Even so, I am sure Millar would agree that in comparison with civic freedom, the other two notes were resounding: the negative, personal *libertas* of the freedman proletarian and middle classes, and the sovereignal freedom of the emperor. Both strongly complemented each other. The absolutely free emperor protected with his awesome power and patronage the negative freedom of the masses against the magisterial parasitism of the senatorial class; they, in turn, clothed his mightiness with all the dignity, the authority, the honour, glory, and virtue that he coveted, with their worship, which in the end was literally religious.

The third critical development came with the emergence of Christianity. Socially reconstructed by the freedmen at the most civilized urban centres of the empire – all large-scale slave systems – out of the primitive eschatological cult from the Jewish periphery, Christianity transposed to the spiritual level the value that was central to its urban congregation. It became the first, and only, world religion to make freedom – redemption, the purchasing out of spiritual slavery and the curse of Adamic death by the sacrifice of the Saviour's life – the ultimate religious goal. What Stoicism had only partially achieved on the intellectual level, what Gnosticism, with perhaps too strong a secular philosophic influence, had first attempted and then failed at in the young faith, Pauline Christianity brought to fulfilment on both the intellectual and the spiritual level: the sacralization of freedom, inscribed in the two great letters to the Galatians and the Romans. The former celebrates personal spiritual freedom, with a fervour and abandon not to be witnessed again until the first great evangelical movement in modern Protestantism; the latter puts the brakes on in an awesomely severe, seemingly conflicting, but ultimately highly complementary conception of spiritual liberty as the thing we ultimately find only in our surrender to the one true freedom: the absolute power of God. Note that this complementarity directly paralleled the secular relation between the absolute sovereignal freedom of the emperor and the personal *libertas* of this very same freedmen class.

---

[5]   Fergus Millar, 'The Political Character of the Classical Roman Republic, 200–151 BC', *The Journal of Roman Studies* 74 (1984), pp. 1–19; Millar, 'Politics, Persuasion and the People before the Social War (150–90)', *The Journal of Roman Studies* 76 (1986), pp. 1–11. Millar even speaks of the 'people' enjoying 'the three basic constitutional rights of direct voting on legislation […] of electing all the annual holders of political and military office; and of judging in the popular courts constituted by the *comitia centuriata* and *comitia tribute*.' I am sure, however, that he would want us to understand his use of the term 'rights' in the more general sense of collective powers, rather than in the more modern, Jeffersonian sense of subjective human rights.

With the triumph of Christianity in the ensuing medieval moment, freedom was fully institutionalized. What this meant was that the underlying social and historical factors that had initially generated it in Greece, and had accounted for its universalization in Rome, were no longer needed for its survival. By capturing the mind and soul of Europe, Christianity ensured that whatever culture it dominated and fashioned would be dominated and fashioned by the value of freedom. Freedom as autonomous, central value was now no longer determined by, or dependent on, any underlying social process or favourable contingencies. Instead, it became determinative; it created or moulded its own social space; it fashioned and was indeed axial to all other values and ways of culture. Europe became Christendom. And Christendom was relentlessly focused on one goal: redemption, freedom.

Since in the wholly organic rural world of Christendom all thought was Christian thought, even when men and women acted in what may have appeared to be primarily secular ways, even when they acted against the Church, their sole way of giving expression and lending meaning to their actions was by means of the only cultural vocabulary they knew, that of the Church that worshipped a god who had sent his son to free mankind. Political thought, as Ernst Kantorowicz showed long ago, was merely secularized theology; theories of kingly devotion were merely thinly disguised royal christologies.[6] The lord of the manor who protected and saved the body was only a mortal counterpart of the Lord who shepherded and saved the soul. Servile revolts were all religious revolts, attempting to give secular expression to antihegemonic interpretations of spiritual freedom. Ruling-class repressions were all imposed with godly righteousness, as the lords gave material expression to the hegemonic, sovereignal version of their god-given liberties.

All three elements of freedom cohered in a tightly rendered triad in the late medieval world. As in all other periods of the western past, people could recognize and even settle for one or another element, especially when they had no choice in the matter. Greater economic and political equality were certainly on the list of aims of the English rebels in 1381; as one of their leaders, John Ball, famously preached: 'Whan Adam dalf and Eve span, who was thanne a gentilman.' But they also knew that such equality was an apocalyptic dream. What preoccupied them most was their demand for the end to subjection to manorial dues: simple negative freedom. The hegemonic expression of freedom, however, was invariably chordal, and this comes out most clearly in the position of the burghers and the lords.

Liberty for the medieval lord was a bundle of three basic kinds of liberties:

---

6   Brost Kantorowicz, *The King's Two Bodies: A Study in Medieval Political Theology* (Princeton, NJ, 1957).

immunities, privileges, and representation. Immunities meant freedom from the restraint of the king in the management of the lord's affairs; privileges meant the power to do whatever he pleased within his domain, which in effect meant the capacity to impose taxes, demand labour services, and judge offenders against manorial law. Indeed, medieval lords saw nothing in the least bit odd about defending what they called 'liberty of gallows', which was the power to hang anyone found guilty of a capital crime in their domain. Finally, liberty meant to a lord, by the late Middle Ages and especially in England, the right to have some say in the most important aspect of government, that which affected him most directly, namely, the imposition of taxes, a right expressed through representation by one of his peers in the king's council, and later in Parliament.

IV. Freedom and Agrarian Capitalism: The British Case

For a long time the standard account of the rise of modern freedom was that it was a product of the bourgeois-led capitalist revolutions of Europe, especially in England and Holland. Capitalism was indeed the decisive new factor in the modern reconstruction of freedom. What is now at issue is who led this early, agrarian capitalist revolution and what were its ideological expressions. Understanding what happened requires a closer look at the old question of the development of the idea of possessive individualism, which according to C. B. Macpherson and his followers had fully emerged, along with the market, in seventeenth-century England, becoming the quintessence of bourgeois freedom. 'Its possessive quality', he writes,

> is found in its conception of the individual as essentially the proprietor
> of his own person or capacities, owing nothing to society for them
> [...] the relation of ownership having become for more and more men
> the critically important relation determining their actual freedom and
> prospect for realizing their full potential [...] the human essence is
> freedom from dependence on the wills of others, and freedom is a function
> of possession.[7]

My point of departure is J. G. A. Pocock's pregnant suggestion that there were several forms of possessive individualism, though perhaps not as many as he suggested.[8] There were, I believe, not one but two distinct forms of possessive

---

[7]   C. B. Macpherson, *The Political Theory of Possessive Individualism* (Oxford, 1962), p. 3.
[8]   J. G. A. Pocock, 'Authority and Property: The Question of Liberal Origins', in his *Virtue, Commerce and History* (Cambridge, 1985), p. 59.

individualism, which had their origins in two different sociohistorical sources. One form may be called bourgeois, the other honorific. Let us consider first the honorific version. The English gentry, like its European counterpart, developed the modern form of possessive individualism as part of its reconstruction of the traditional medieval value system in its successful attempt to meet the demands of the early modern world. The conventional wisdom contrasts the two sets of values – modern capitalistic possessive individualism with medieval honorific paternalism – but from what we now know about the behaviour associated with lordship in the Middle Ages, this simplistic contrast must be discarded. The medieval lord was a thoroughly acquisitive man, often brutally so, as Thomas Bisson and others have shown; he was fiercely protective of his independence, and he was also very possessive in precisely the sense defined by Macpherson. In the face of large-scale and significant levels of serfdom, self-possession had been the essence of freedom for all medieval persons, and the foundation of lordship was independence; this was the whole point of immunities and privileges.

There was a purely *in situ* economic source of this process. The enclosure movements and the aristocratic initiation of agrarian capitalism grew directly out of forces emerging from the late-medieval English past. However, these independently developed patterns were strongly influenced by, and rationalized in terms of, external ideas and models, especially those handed down from Renaissance Florence.[9] The 'end product of the Florentine experience', writes Pocock, 'was an impressive sociology of liberty, transmitted to the European Enlightenment and the English and American revolutions, which arose in reply to the challenge posed by the republic's commitment to existence in secular history'.[10] The essence of this tradition, he argues, was 'the citizen as necessarily involved in decision-making and power-relationships with other citizens in varying patterns of distribution'.[11] Furthermore, freedom was central to this tradition, although it was freedom conceived of as the expression of power – in other words, what we have called the sovereignal note of the chord of freedom: 'Freedom, civic virtue, and military discipline seem then to exist in a close relation to one another.'[12]

In like manner, *in situ* economic transformation of the mercantile order by the emerging British bourgeoisie was explained and rationalized in terms of an external model – in their case, the Dutch. Appleby has shown how, in their attempt to explain the crises and puzzles of the new capitalist economy, the

---

[9]   Joyce Oldhara Appleby, *Economic Thoughts and Ideology in Seventeenth-Century England* (Princeton, NJ, 1978), p. 247 n.

[10]   Pocock, *The Machiavellian Moment* (Princeton, NJ, 1975), p. 85.

[11]   Pocock, *The Machiavellian Moment*, p. 87.

[12]   Pocock, *The Machiavellian Moment*, p. 196.

English economic theorists and pragmatists of the seventeenth century muddled their way towards the idea of the market as an impersonal force emerging from the individual choices of ordinary persons rather than from an authority above, and towards the idea that 'private initiative and interests increased public good'.[13] In clarifying their thoughts they turned to that seventeenth-century version of the economic miracle, the Dutch,[14] who, in striking contrast with the aristocratic honorific elite, made a virtue of their 'unheroic qualities', and 'popularized the value of commercial virtues'.[15] The Dutch case also demonstrated the compatibility of an uncontrolled economy with stability. Further: 'Implanted and propagated as a part of this concept of commerce was a new vision of man's essential nature. What began as an explanation became a rationale for market practices. The uniform propensity to seek gain was turned into a constant in human behavior that permitted calculation and prediction.'[16]

We are now in a position to see not only how the two versions of possessive individualism differed in their relation to two of the notes of freedom, the sovereignal and the personal, but also how they were conceptually refigured from the broken chord of medieval freedom: the reconstructed idea of freedom as privilege and power was reinterpreted as the root note of positive sovereignal freedom in the aristocratic chord, whereas the idea of freedom as immunities from dues, monopolies, and constraints on trade and movement was reconstructed as the root in the bourgeois notion of negative personal freedom.

Property was the decisive instrument in the playing of both chords, but there was a critical difference in the honorific and bourgeois renditions: for the aristocrats it remained a fundamental tenet that property flowed from power and privilege – most obviously the privilege of birth and inheritance – while for the bourgeoisie it became an article of faith that power and privilege flowed from property, which was not acquired, unearned, by birth, but through thrift, hard work, and merit. For the aristocrat, freedom was power and that power was both the source and the guardian of property. It was natural, then, for him to see control of state power as an important precondition of both freedom and property. In response to the bourgeois rationale of merit, the aristocrats – all of them, not just the country set – countered with the notion of the aristocratic, civic ideal: power, both individually and collectively, was to be used for the good of the community, including the protection of the weak and poor. This defence of the poor was always partly opportunistic, but, as Isaac Kramnick notes, there was 'an element of principle here', however expedient, 'a lingering afterglow of

y, *Economic Thought and Ideology*, pp. 62–3.
y, *Economic Thought and Ideology*, ch. 4, passim.
y, *Economic Thought and Ideology*, p. 97.
y, *Economic Thought and Ideology*, p. 97.

the status model of society. [...] The gentry paid the revenue and looked after the poor; they could cede neither their privileges nor their duties.'[17]

In the struggle between the two forms of possessive individualism that occurred at the end of the seventeenth century, it was the landlords and manufacturers insisting on greater state intervention who won.[18] In advocating an alternate theory of balance of trade, they explicitly rejected the laissez-faire dogma of a harmony between private interests and public gain. John Brewer's 'fiscal-military' eighteenth-century state was the inevitable outward realization and expression of this inner aristocratic ideal. Or perhaps it was the other way around: the triumph of the fiscal-military state ensured the supremacy of the honorific version of possessive individualism and, with it, the hegemonic conception of freedom as power, and power as the guardian and generator of property.

What became of the bourgeois tradition of freedom during the eighteenth century? This is one of the least understood aspects of British history. Beyond the success of Royalist and later Whig control mechanisms, three factors may help account for the passivity of this tradition. First, the more middle-class and prosperous artisanal radicalism, when not completely cowed or diverted solely into money-making, was transformed into mild-mannered reformism – the commonwealthmen crowd. Second, a significant number of the radicals migrated, not only to America, but to the West Indies, where not a few became pirates, and the majority sustained a robust and cantankerous tradition of settler radicalism that was later to have important consequences for the history of freedom in Britain itself.[19] Third, proletarian militancy may have been diverted into increased criminality and political hooliganism that were then used to intimidate the radicals.

John Cannon, among others, has suggested that there was no challenge to the Whig hegemony because the bourgeoisie recognized fully the value of the political stability offered by aristocratic rule. That may have been so. But a part of the explanation must surely be the profound ambivalence and hypocrisy of bourgeois liberalism during the eighteenth century.[20] They could in one breath speak with passion about the equality of all mankind, and in another refer to the English masses as 'scum'. They shared John Trenchard and Thomas Gordon's conviction that 'Liberty is the divine Source of all human Happiness', yet, as Christopher

---

[17]   Isaac Kramnick, *Bolingbroke and His Circle* (Cambridge, MA, 1968), p. 55. See also, Appleby, *Economic Thought and Ideology*, ch. 6, passim.

[18]   Appleby, *Economic Thought and Ideology*, ch. 5, passim.

[19]   Christopher Hill, 'Radical Pirates?', in Margaret Jacob and James Jacob (eds), *The Origins of Anglo-American Radicalism* (London, 1984), pp. 19–34.

[20]   Kramnick, *Bolingbroke and His Circle*, ch. 8.

Hill notes, they more than any other group benefited from slavery and the slave trade, 'whose virtual monopoly was ultimately secured for English merchants thanks to the state power'.[21] Indeed, the nefarious involvement of the bourgeoisie with the slave trade brings into bold relief the relationship between bourgeois political passivity, economic greed, and neo-Puritan hypocrisy. Robin Blackburn, in his authoritative study of colonial slavery, has emphasized the importance of the Whig regime for the profitable alliance of colonial planters, metropolitan merchants, and manufacturing interests. The West Indian slaveholders and their allies had played an important role in the settlement of 1688–1689. With the striking exception of the Quakers, throughout the eighteenth century the 'slave trade and colonial slavery remained virtually unquestioned', and he adds:

> It was, after all, the privileges of the free-born *English* that were being celebrated. One of the earliest examples of the mobilization of a broad public opinion behind competing parliamentary factions had been a pamphlet war in the first decade of the eighteenth century concerning which ports could enjoy the custom of the slave-trading Royal Africa Company.[22]

Christopher Hill has also pointed out that former slaveowners brought back to England a contempt for labour that influenced intellectual attitudes. The Society for the Propagation of the Gospel invested profitably in West Indian slavery and forbade the conversion of their slaves: 'So the slave trade must have accentuated the Puritan tendency to hypocrisy, to double-thinking, which was to be so conspicuous among pious nineteenth-century factory-owners.'[23]

One other factor alleviated this situation: the common law. Although the law was undoubtedly used in a repressive manner, the fact remains that it imposed certain limits on the elite and its agents. As E. P. Thompson and his associates have shown, while the law was unequally and unfairly applied in the interest of the gentry, it nonetheless had its own inner, formal logic that, if it did not quite hoist those who applied it by their own petard, certainly set limits on their sovereignal freedom to do as they pleased.[24] Habeas Corpus was a reality, and every 'freeborn Englishman' knew about it. And while the situation may have

---

[21]   Christopher Hill, *Some Intellectual Consequences of the English Revolution* (Madison, WI, 1980), p. 37.

[22]   Robin Blackburn, *The Overthrow of Colonial Slavery: 1776–1848* (London, 1988), p. 79.

[23]   Blackburn, *The Overthrow of Colonial Slavery*, p. 79.

E. P. Thompson, *Whigs and Hunters: The Origin of the Black Act* (London, 1975), 58–69.

been worse than what prevailed during the last half of the seventeenth century, it was better than anything existing on the continent, as Hogarth discovered on his last trip to Calais. In *The Gates of Calais*, he showed that 'the best way to indicate English liberty was to paint French slavery'.[25]

To see in the Hogarthian crowd a society-wide 'reciprocity of gentry-crowd relations' might be going too far.[26] The occasional riots notwithstanding, what existed in the country was not the insubordinate freedom of the crowd with its contempt for law and authority, but an ingeniously executed paternalistic system in which 'the connections between property, power and authority [were] close and crucial', and where the Church, the state, and tradition reinforced the law 'in maintaining bonds of obedience and deference, in legitimizing the status quo, in constantly recreating the structure of authority which rose from property and in turn protected its interests'.[27]

V. Religion, Race, and Slavery in the American Reconstruction of Freedom

It was in colonial America and, to a remarkable degree, the horrendous slave societies of the British West Indies, that we find the next critical moment in the history of the Anglo-American construction of freedom.[28]

---

[25]   Derek Jarrett, *England in the Age of Hogarth* (London, 1974), pp. 20–1.

[26]   Thompson, 'Eighteenth-Century English Society', in Douglas Hay *et al.*, *Albion's Fata Tree: Crime and Society in Eighteenth-Century England* (London, 1975), pp. 158–65.

[27]   Hay, 'Property, Authority and the Criminal Law', in Hay *et al.*, *Albion's Fatal Tree*, p. 25.

[28]   For the following summary I draw mainly on the following general works and collections: Bernard Bailyn, *The Ideological Origins of the American Revolution* (Cambridge, MA, 1967); Bailyn, *The Origins of American Politics* (New York, 1968); Bailyn, *The Peopling of British North America* (New York, 1968); Hilary Beckles, *White Slavery and Black Servitude in Barbados, 1627–1715* (Knoxville, TN, 1989); Richard S. Dunn, *The Rise of the Planter Class in the English West Indies, 1624–1713* (Chapel Hill, NC, 1972); Richard S. Johnson, *Adjustment to Empire: The New England Colonies, 1675–1715* (New Brunswick, NJ, 1981); John J. McCusker and Russell R. Menard, *The Economy of British American, 1607–1789* (Chapel Hill, NC, 1991); Edmund S. Morgan, *Inventing the People: The Rise of Popular Sovereignty in England and America* (New York, 1988); Morgan (ed.), *Puritan Political Ideas* (Indianapolis, IN, 1965); Orlando Patterson, *The Sociology of Slavery: The Development of Negro Slave Society in Jamaica* (London, 1967); Clinton Rossiter, *Seedtime of the Republic: Origins of the American Tradition of Liberty* (New York, 1953); Francis N. Thorpe, for example, *The Federal and State Constitutions, Colonial Charters, and Other Organic Laws* (Washington, DC, 1909); Chilton Williamson, *American Suffrage: From Property to Democracy, 1760–1860* (Princeton, NJ, 1960).

Common to all the colonists was their claim that they continued to possess all the liberties of freeborn Englishmen. This was an essentially sovereignal conception of freedom, conceived of as a set of powers and immunities granted by a superior authority. As one would expect, the precise definition of these rights varied from one colony to another, but there were striking common demands. First among these was the early struggle for, and achievement of, various forms of representative government, all modelled on, or believed to have paralleled, the tripartite system of government in the mother country. In mimicking what they thought was parliamentary government in Britain, the colonists soon went well beyond what actually prevailed in the mother country. When the governors and crown resisted, the stage was set for the prolonged struggle between colonial assemblies and governors, a struggle that was decisive in the modern history of freedom. Thus, the early insistence on the selection of public treasurers, on the right to examine the accounts of the governor, and the general demand to have an important say in the selection of officials, all went well beyond contemporary practice in Britain. In these matters, the Caribbean islands, especially Jamaica and Barbados, were often more precocious than their mainland North American counterpart.

Far removed from the centre of power, local politics soon came to be seen as matters that should be the sole concern of the locals themselves, a view with which the isolated governors found it expedient to go along, however grudgingly. This, in turn, reinforced commitment to the view that government was legitimate only with the consent of the governed.

Who constituted the governed, or the people? In Britain, radicals such as the Levellers had lost out badly in their attempt to expand the size of the electorate, in spite of their willingness to exclude servants. The Levellers also lost the battle to implement fundamental laws, or 'agreements', to protect the people from their leaders. It was in the New World English colonies that the first major resolution of both these problems took place. By the late seventeenth century the majority of free adult males in colonial British America had the right to vote – somewhere between 50 and 80 per cent – and, as such, were counted among 'the people'. This was the first time that majorities of free males had such political powers since the final collapse of ancient Athenian democracy.

The role of charters and fundamental legal codes achieved pragmatically what the Levellers had ideologically failed to do in England with their agreements. All new colonies were legally established through written charters, which in effect were like proto-constitutions. It certainly promoted the unprecedented idea that a political community should be established on the basis of certain clearly defined legal principles. It was a short step from the colonial charter of Massachusetts to the Fundamental Order of Connecticut and the even more remarkable charter for Rhode Island secured by Roger Williams.

This was further reinforced by the commissions and secret instructions that were given to each new governor by the colonial authorities in Britain: authority, even that of the highest in the colony, was strictly defined and could be contested if there was the slightest suspicion – and there often was – that there had been departure from them.

The major problem facing the colonists everywhere was the shortage of labour, and everywhere the problem was solved in the same manner: reliance on two forms of unfree labor – white indentured servants and black slaves. There is no need to retell the now well-known story of how these two statuses were initially closely assimilated, then separated as slavery became identified with blacks. The story that is often not told is the one of greater interest to us, namely the extraordinary way in which one of the pivotal constructions of modern free societies – the idea of free labour – was partly invented in the colonies of the New World. As Robert Steinfeld has recently shown, it was the juxtaposition of slavery and indentured labour that, by bringing out the inherently servile nature of the latter, forced the issue of defining in a legally clear way just what constituted free labour.[29]

The acceptance and institutionalization of religious toleration, for the first time in the history of the world, was another major first for the British New World colonial societies. Many factors account for this development. Although the British tradition of an established Church was transferred to all the colonies except Maryland, in nearly all of them there were, from the start, many dissenting sects among the populace, however great the degree of, and desire for, religious uniformity among the elites. When the persecution of these sects in the early period, especially in Puritan New England, proved a failure, they were eventually accepted as the only path to domestic peace, a development that would take place decades later in Europe.

In a few cases, toleration emerged as a matter of principle, most notably in the Quaker colony of Pennsylvania and, largely under the fabulous influence of Roger Williams, in Rhode Island. In most cases, toleration emerged under force of circumstances, only grudgingly accepted in principle, which became true of most of the mainland colonies by the early eighteenth century: in Maryland, the Catholic elite found it in its own interest to pass an act of toleration; in the Carolinas and Georgia, mercantile economic policies and the proximity of the Spanish border made toleration, even of Jews, prudent. And in the case of the West Indies, toleration emerged largely as a result of religious indifference or corruption. Whatever the reason, it was in America and the West Indies that the principle of religious toleration, with its implicit right to religious freedom,

---

[29]   Robert Steinfeld, *The Invention of Free Labor: The Employment Relation in English and American Law and Culture, 1350–1870* (Chapel Hill, NC, 1991).

was first practised. It need hardly be added that religious liberty and toleration had immediate implications for political liberty and for freedom of expression. Religious views elicit the most extreme passions, and when a people finds it possible to tolerate the dissenting beliefs of others, it is easy and natural to accept their political and other intellectual differences.

Having emphasized the similarities in the social construction of freedom among the British colonial societies, I now turn to the important ways in which they differed. Differences were caused partly by differing regional origins and consequently differing views of freedom brought over to the New World, and partly by the kind of physical and socioeconomic environment that emerged, partly by the demographic and ethnic mix of the different colonies, and, not least of all, by the kind of labour regime on which they depended, especially the degree and kind of slavery.

Although his emphasis on English cultural survival and regional provenance may at times appear excessive, David Hackett Fischer, in his recent historical ethnography of early America,[30] has persuasively demonstrated the importance of these factors. The predominantly East Anglian origins of the New England colonists partly account for much that was distinctive in the material culture, stratificatory system, and religious as well as secular beliefs of the Puritans.

Central to the Puritan conception of liberty was the age-old Western distinction between inner and outer freedom. As their most brilliant theorist, John Wise, stated explicitly: 'Internally as to his Mind, and Externally as to his Person.' All life was suffused with moral purpose and graced by God's will and demands. The covenant with God immediately implied a covenant among members of the community.

The constant inner struggle, even though it was one the believer could never win, nonetheless generated an extraordinary degree of self-preoccupation that was as much secular as it was religious. It is in this struggle that we find the origins of America's almost obsessive individualism. Sacvan Bercovitch has brilliantly explored this source:

It is an involuted manifestation of that spirit, to be sure, a sort of narcissistic *Liebestod*, constantly reenacted because incapable of fulfillment: the individual affirming his identity by turning against his power of self-affirmation. But to affirm and to turn against are both aspects of self-involvement. We can see in retrospect how the very intensity of that self-involvement – mobilizing as it did all the resources of the ego in what

---

[30]   David Hackett Fischer, *Albion's Seed: Four British Folkways to America* (New York, 1989).

amounted to an internal Armageddon – had to break loose into the world at large.[31]

Break loose it did, although what it generated was perhaps too sweepingly described by Bercovitch as 'the American self'. Rather, it was that part of the American national character that David Riesman has called the 'inner-directed' personality: freedom as individualistic self-realization.

The upper-middle-class cavaliers from south-western England who colonized the Old South had an entirely different vision, one rooted in their royalist sympathies, Anglican faith, honorific individualism, and sovereignal chord of freedom. It was a vision that glorified continuity, indeed romanticized the English past which they imagined themselves to be perfecting.

With the introduction of large-scale African slavery, a system emerged that, ironically, while it reinforced the British aristocratic heritage of sovereignal freedom, also laid the foundations for the most radical democracy the modern world had known. Although he never mentions the ancient parallels, making them all the more telling, Edmund Morgan's seminal study of colonial Virginia portrays one of the great instances of history repeating itself – in broad sociological and cultural terms, of course, which is the only way history repeats itself. Morgan begins with the bold assertion that 'the rise of liberty and equality in America had been accompanied by the rise of slavery. That two such seemingly contradictory developments were taking place simultaneously [...] is the central paradox of American history.'[32]

In order to prevent any insurrectionary union of white servants and slaves, racism was deliberately reinforced through legal enactments and strong social sanctions aimed at separating the groups. With the growth of this 'screen of racial contempt', there was a general raising of the status of the lower-class whites. 'Partly because of slavery', Morgan writes, 'they were allowed not only to prosper but also to acquire social, psychological and political advantages that turned the thrust of exploitation away from them and aligned them with their exploiters.'[33]

The growth of popular government, and of a strong local legislature increasingly opposed to the rule of the colonial governors, were all of a piece with this association. The Virginian barons had no fear that the populace would vote in people who would then turn against them. On the contrary, they encouraged populist politics and it was the 'union of freedom and slavery' that made this possible. By the second quarter of the eighteenth century, the basic pattern of

[31]   Fischer, *Albion's Seed*, p. 20.

[32]   Edmund Morgan, *American Slavery, American Freedom* (New York, 1975), p. 75.

[33]   Morgan, *American Slavery, American Freedom*, p. 344.

Southern freedom and democracy and the ingredients that supported it were well in place: a large slave labour force isolated by racism and strong solidarity among all classes of whites who felt a commonality of interests with the dominant slave-holding elite.

What emerged from this by no means unique system, in terms of Western history, was first the seemingly paradoxical phenomenon of a conservative ruling class eagerly taking the reins of revolution. Second was the strong conviction that there was no inconsistency between liberty and slavery. As William J. Cooper notes, indeed, 'the white southern celebration of liberty always included the freedom to preserve black slavery'.[34] In the end, even those elite whites who had misgivings about this paired commitment came around to the view that 'slaves were property, and the right to hold property was an integral part of liberty'.[35]

Let me hasten to add that there were other important traditions, or chords, of freedom interplaying with this dominant counterpoint, although space restraints prevent me from exploring them.[36] There were the middle colonies that, under Quaker influence, developed a chord strongly biased towards a more egalitarian and principled notion of personal freedom and toleration. Because all inner 'lamb's wars' found immediate expression in outer behaviour, it came about that the Quakers were the first Christian group to come to a principled realization that slavery was not just evil, but an abomination to be abolished. The Quakers were not the first to discuss, in theory, the evils of slavery, but as David Brion Davis has pointed out, 'genuine abolitionism, as distinct from isolated protests against human bondage, originated in the great Quaker revival' of the late eighteenth century.[37]

There were also the whites of the back country and borderlands of the south and middle colonies – the region that produced the likes of Patrick Henry and Andrew Jackson – which developed a version of pure, negative personal freedom so hostile to all authority that it bordered on the anarchic.[38] And there were, of course, the black slaves, who in their fear, trembling, and outrage, experienced the pristine rediscovery of freedom in its most elementary form: the stark, primal desire simply to be removed from the power of another. Both of these elemental sources of freedom were to greatly influence America and the development of its notion of freedom and rights. The borderlands, in spite of primitivism, have

---

[34]   William J. Cooper, *Liberty and Slavery: Southern Politics to 1868* (New York, 1983), p. 39.

[35]   Cooper, *Liberty and Slavery*, p. 35.

[36]   On which see Fischer, *Albion's Seed*.

[37]   David Brion Davis, *Slavery and Human Progress* (New York, 1984), p. 136.

[38]   On which see Fischer, *Albion's Seed*, pp. 772–82.

contributed a disproportionate number of the nation's presidents. And African Americans have not only been the cause and the agents of the civil war over slavery and all that it entailed for the reconstruction of freedom, but the major agents of the modern resurgence of rights in American society.

Nonetheless, the most striking thing to note about the colonial period is that, in spite of many important differences, the chords of freedom constructed in the two dominant regions – New England and the Upper South – were both essentially similar in their sovereignal focus, and, up to the end of the revolutionary era, highly complementary, even in their differences. In both, power and authority were the essence of freedom, the one religious and inner-directed, the other secular and outer-directed.

Sooner or later these two intensely individualistic reconstructions of freedom in the American continent had to come together. That fateful bonding happened in the great fraternal slaughter of the common father in the American Revolution.

It was the freest and most powerful of these Southern aristocrats who, in leading the colonies to independence from Britain, became the founding fathers of the new nation. Torn from its Southern context in the common war of independence, the aristocratic ideal of freedom as an inherited quality of the individual person – the honorific version of possessive individualism – fused with the borrowed European notion of natural rights to fashion the distinctly American conception of the individual as a bearer of inalienable rights. Forced to accommodate to the Northern notion that all men were equal, covenanted children of God, this honorific ideal of freedom was dramatically transformed and democratized, generating the belief that all men are, legally and politically, created equal. Inherited privileges and powers of birth for a few became inalienable rights for many through the simple replacement of the earthly aristocratic father by the law-giving, godly creator.

One critical element in this extraordinary cultural fusion was the use of the language and ideology of rights, resulting in the popularization of such talk, previously the preserve of philosophers, for the first time in history.

VI. The Universalization of the Rhetoric of Rights

From early medieval times, as far back as the laws of Alfred in the late ninth century, the term 'right' was being used in common law and usage to mean, generally, 'a justifiable claim, on legal and moral grounds, to have or obtain something, or to act in a certain way'. This general meaning, understandable to a ninth-century English lawyer, is exactly the sense in which we use the term today, as when a black American speaks of his civil rights, or an illegally arrested person claims his Miranda rights.

A right is, then, a legally enforceable claim to something, on someone or some group. In common law it is the same thing as a property. In general usage during the Middle Ages, and indeed right up to the end of the eighteenth century, the term occupied the same semantic field as the nearly synonymous terms 'powers' and 'liberties', which in the positive sense were often referred to as 'privileges', and in the more negative sense as 'immunities'.

What confused the issue were the attempts by philosophers and theologians, and, later, political theorists and practitioners, to theorize, specify, and justify a special category of fundamental or essential rights. Behind all the various attempts to do so was the scholastic tradition of natural law. The theological foundation for this tradition was shattered by Protestantism and philosophical scepticism, resulting in Protestant and secular versions of natural law and rights. The Protestant tradition emphasized duty, infinite obligations, as the central feature of godly natural law, with rights being correlatively derived from them. The most fundamental of these rights was the right to do the good, for one's soul and for others in one's community.

While its communitarian emphasis and the austerity of its demands were new, the basic idea of the close identification of rights and duties goes back to the earliest Middle Ages. Indeed, what Protestant natural law theology and philosophy had done was to de-emphasize the traditional legal conception of rights as claims and powers and entitlements, and to replace this with a strong emphasis on the most important traditional, non-legal, Christian meanings of the term 'right'. First, 'that which is proper for or incumbent on one to do; one's duty'.[39] Second, 'right' in the sense of being under an obligation to act rightly according to the moral code, to do good deeds, to act with moral rectitude – these are meanings that can be traced back to the ninth century, and were common during the period of middle English. And third, 'right' in the sense of doing that which is just and equitable; the virtue of justice; doing justice and seeing justice done; to be fair; and especially when done 'in the light of nature', which is to say, with 'right and resoun' or with 'godright and resoun'.[40]

We already find this view of rights highly developed in Luther's treatise on Christian liberty. However, it was to culminate, via Calvin and Geneva, in practical terms in the American Puritan tradition of ordered liberty, briefly discussed above.

On the secular side, the development of rights theory and rights rhetoric took a decisive turn in the attempt by Hugo Grotius and Thomas Hobbes to answer Renaissance scepticism with theories of minimal natural rights, premised on secular conceptions of human nature and contractarian notions of society and government. While both men were important in the intellectual history of ideas,

---

[39]   The Oxford English Dictionary traces this usage back to Alfred.
[40]   The Middle English Dictionary.

they had little impact on the dramatic development of rights rhetoric during the eighteenth century. As Knud Haakonssen reminds us, both were dismissed as dangerous radicals, and the typical reaction to Hobbes during the seventeenth and eighteenth centuries was one of 'horror and incomprehension'.[41] For this reason and others, I am sceptical of Ian Shapiro's claim that the rhetoric of rights 'became central to the Western liberal tradition around the time of the English Civil War', and even more so of his assertion that Hobbes played a 'central role in articulating much of the vocabulary and underlying grammar of the modern liberal rights tradition'.[42]

Of far greater sociohistorical significance were John Locke's contributions to this tradition.[43] It is no easy matter, however, to specify just what the nature of Locke's influence was, beyond the assertion that he greatly legitimized rights talk and the notion of the social contract made in the state of nature. Ian Shapiro presents the extreme, traditional view in summarizing Locke's ideological consequences: that, like Hobbes, he promoted the view of the individual as an autonomous subject of all legitimate rights, and radically departed from the Christian tradition in separating rights from obligations; that he redefined rights in substantively negative terms; that by giving priority to rights of property and inheritance, he sanctioned intergenerational inequality; that by making toleration rather than participation central to his notion of the just state, he originated the 'paradigmatic, conservative liberal view of "genuine freedom" as freedom from politics'.

This reading of Locke contradicts those of major modern Locke scholars, several of whom insist that there was a strongly communitarian and Christian emphasis in his writings.[44] Furthermore, Locke's influence was extremely limited in his native England during the eighteenth century, and in America, where it was much stronger, it has been shown repeatedly that, whether or not he was the originator of possessive individualism, this was definitely not how he was interpreted by colonial or revolutionary Americans. As John M. Murrin observes of the most celebrated of eighteenth-century Lockeans: 'Jefferson, in a word, was not a nineteenth-century liberal, much less a possessive individualist. He did indeed take his Lockean rights seriously, but he located them within a

---

[41]   Knud Haakonssen, 'From Natural Law to the Rights of Man: A European Perspective on American Debates', in K. Haakonssen and M. J. Lacey (eds), *A Culture of Rights* (New York, 1991), p. 31.

[42]   Ian Shapiro, *The Evolution of Rights in Liberal Theory* (Cambridge, 1986), pp. 4, 23.

[43]   See Pocock, 'Authority and Property'.

[44]   See, in particular, J. Dunn, *The Political Thought of John Locke* (Cambridge, 1969); J. Tully, *A Discourse on Property: John Locke and His Adversaries* (Cambridge, 1980).

context of personal sacrifice for the public good.'[45] The other major influence on eighteenth-century rights rhetoric was, of course, Samuel Pufendorf. A good part of his success, however, was due to his return to traditional Christian notions of rights and duties. Rights are derived from the moral domain of God-given natural laws, the most fundamental of which was to be sociable.[46] Rights are the benefits we derive correlatively from the duties God imposes on all of us. In more practical terms, rights are 'powers' over ourselves, over others, over property belonging to us, and over property belonging to others. The most fundamental of these rights or powers, however, is the ownership or power over, or property in, oneself; in other words, liberty, the antithesis of slavery. What we have here is a complete return, in thinly disguised eighteenth-century jargon, to the late medieval conception of rights as claims or powers, only now interpreted within the Protestant moral framework.

It is these intellectual sources that combined with the idea of rights implicit in evangelical Christianity, and with a strong dose of common law,[47] to give Americans of the revolutionary era the vocabulary they needed to justify their revolt and then to craft and justify the federal constitution.

When the revolutionary era began with the Stamp Act crisis of the mid-1760s, Americans were all convinced that what were being threatened were their 'liberties' as descendants of 'freeborn Englishmen'. Increasingly, however, the defence of these liberties – largely understood in traditional common-law terms – was expressed in terms of rights language. It is no easy matter deciphering just why Americans became attached to this manner of expressing their political claims. We know that there was almost no reference in colonial America to the language of rights during the seventeenth century, and only occasional references to it, in mainly educational circles, during the first part of the eighteenth. By whatever means, however, attached they were, and it is generally agreed that by the time the revolutionary war broke out the language of rights was pervasive.

It is also the consensus among historians of the period that Americans became increasingly confused about just what it was they were talking about when they boldly claimed their rights. Actually, the situation got worse as the revolution unfolded. In the beginning, most people were simply using the term 'right' in

---

[45]   John M. Murrin, 'Can Liberals Be Patriots?', in Robert P. Davidow, *Natural Rights and Natural Law: The Legacy of George Mason* (Washington, DC, 1986), p. 53.

[46]   I follow Haakonssen's excellent survey in what follows, in 'From Natural Law', pp. 27–30.

[47]   For John Phillip Reid, this is the all-important source of ideological change during this period. See his *Concept of Liberty by the Age of the American Revolution* (Chicago, IL, 1988); and *The Constitutional History of the American Revolution* (Madison, WI, 1987).

its old, clear-cut, common-law sense of a legally guaranteed claim on something; that is, a power or privilege or liberty.

A statement John Adams made in 1765 not only supports this, but hints at the source of the impending confusion. He complained that Americans were failing to grasp the notion of rights, because 'we have been afraid to think. [...] We have felt a reluctance to examine into the grounds of our privileges and the extent to which we have an indisputable right to demand them.'[48]

It is obvious from this statement that Adams had a clear, common-law grasp of what rights meant; his complaint was really about the intellectual 'grounds', the philosophical justification, for these claims or privileges. Now, it may be wondered, why would so sensible and pragmatic a person as Adams waste his time on such inscrutable philosophical matters? It is all the more puzzling when we consider that Americans, as Richard Hofstadter demonstrated long ago, have always been a notoriously pragmatic and anti-intellectual people, especially during colonial times.[49] Why on earth, then, did this most anti-intellectual of peoples end up waging what was arguably the most intellectualized revolutionary war?

The answer is simple. Precisely because, up to the revolution, they had held to a common-law view of their liberties, claims, powers, or privileges and firmly believed that the moral and legal basis for such claims were the laws and traditions of Britain to which they had a birthright, their rebellious break with Britain immediately created a crisis in the grounds on which they based their claims. In rebelliously demanding and pursuing their liberties, they had undercut the legitimacy of these claims, which was the link to Britain and its traditional liberties. To solve their problem they turned to philosophy and theology, along with other traditions such as British oppositional rhetoric, which, however, were not directly relevant to the problem of explaining rights language and were, indeed, counter to this development.

What they found, to their relief and further confusion, were the language and ideology of rights – more particularly, the ideology of the state of nature, of natural rights, and of the right to rebellion against arbitrary and unjust authority. The more religious found the natural rights tradition of Protestantism, filtered through the evangelical theology of Jonathan Edwards and John Wesley and others; the more philosophical, especially those, such as Madison, who had gone to Princeton, found what they wanted in Scottish moral sense philosophy and the works of Pufendorf; all turned to Locke, whether they read him or not.

What emerged during the last quarter of the eighteenth century was the most extraordinary intrusion of philosophy into politics that the world had ever seen.

---

[48]   Cited in James H. Hutson, 'The Bill of Rights and the American Revolutionary Experience', in Haakonssen and Lacey (eds), *A Culture of Rights*, p. 65.

[49]   Richard Hofstadter, *Anti-Intellectualism in American Life* (New York, 1963).

Americans came seriously to believe that Britain's arbitrary acts had provoked their Lockean right to rebellion. Rebellion, in turn, had reduced them to the state of nature, and, as such, had returned them to a condition of complete natural rights. Understandably, everyone was eager to depart once more from this pristine condition, which meant that they had to form a new social compact in which they would surrender some rights to government, the formation of which would guarantee all the more those rights which they had reserved. It is these reserved rights, as they came to be called, that were spelled out in the many bills of rights enacted by the various states, the first and most important of which being the Virginian Bill of Rights. This bill, authored by the Virginian slaveholder George Mason, was the model not only for most of the other states of the young confederation, but for the French Declaration of the Rights of Man.[50] Mason's bill is pure Locke, as were the bills written for most of the other states and, of course, Jefferson's Declaration of Independence.

Contractarian ideology, however, presented its own set of problems, the details of which we cannot enter into here, except to note the most important for our story, namely the enormous conflict waged between the Federalists and the Antifederalists over the need for a Bill of Rights in the Federal Constitution. The Antifederalists insisted on such a bill as an essential guardian against arbitrary federal rule. The Federalists argued against the need for such a bill. These bills already existed in the constitutions of the states where they rightfully belonged, since it was in the formation of these states that individuals left the state of nature in their social compact with each other. The federal government was not emerging from such a state of nature, nor was it a compact of individuals, but a compact of collectivities, of already existing sovereign states that had happily rescued their individual members from the state of nature.

In the end a Bill of Rights was attached to the Constitution, but almost no one was happy with it. The Federalists cynically agreed to it as the only way of getting the Federal Constitution ratified, and its author, the remarkably resourceful James Madison, had been among its strongest critics, although he did in the end come around to a lukewarm support of it, especially after his observation of the behaviour of the new state legislatures convinced him that minority interests needed as much protection from the tyranny of corrupt majorities as the ruled, in general, needed constitutional protection from their rulers.

The Antifederalists felt that they had wasted their time, especially those for

---

[50]   For an itemized comparison of the Virginian bill and the French declaration, see Robert Palmer, *The Age of Democratic Revolution* (Princeton, NJ, 1959), appendix. See, more generally, Leslie Lispon, 'European Responses to the American Revolution', in Richard L. Park (ed.), *The American Revolution Abroad* (Philadelphia, PA, 1976), pp. 22–42.

whom the debate over the Bill of Rights had simply been a tactic in their fight against ratification. As Leonard Levy observes:

> The history of the framing and ratification of the Bill of Rights indicates slight passion on the part of anyone to enshrine personal liberties in the fundamental laws of the land. [...] Our precious Bill of Rights [...] resulted from the reluctant necessity of certain Federalists to capitalize on a cause that had been originated, in vain, by the Antifederalists for ulterior purposes.[51]

So a strange thing happened in the history of rights. Immediately after the triumph of rights rhetoric in the enactment of the American Bill of Rights, the Bill and the whole tradition of rhetoric surrounding it quickly sank to insignificance. Indeed, several states had not even bothered to ratify it, Massachusetts and Connecticut eventually getting around to it only in 1937!

The first of two near-lethal legal blows to the Bill's effectiveness came in 1833 when the Marshall court, in *Barron v. Baltimore*, unanimously ruled that the Bill of Rights was a constraint on the federal government only, and not applicable to the individual states in their relations with individual citizens. So the situation remained until 1868 when the Fourteenth Amendment – making all persons of all races born in the United States citizens – seemed for a brief moment to revive the relevance of the Bill of Rights by making it applicable to the states. Such hopes were soon dashed, however, when the intent of the Fourteenth Amendment was completely perverted in the Slaughterhouse cases of 1873, where the dogma of dual citizenship was declared. Individuals whose 'privileges and immunities' (and it is remarkable that the author of the bill had reverted to these medieval terms rather than the simple term 'rights') were protected in their capacity as federal citizens did not necessarily share such protection as state citizens who 'depend upon different characteristics or circumstances in the individual'.[52]

---

[51] Leonard W. Levy, 'Bill of Rights', in Paul Murphy (ed.), *The Historical Background of the Bill of Rights* (New York, 1990), p. 331.

[52] See Henry J. Abraham, *Freedom and the Court: Civil Rights and Liberties in the United States*, fifth edition (New York, 1988), ch. 3. Ironically, the Slaughterhouse case, brought by New Orleans butchers against a 'carpetbag' Louisiana legislature for granting a monopoly in the slaughtering of livestock to a single New Orleans firm, initially reaffirmed the states' right to regulate commerce and restrict laissez-faire. It reflected the argument of the plaintiffs that the privileges and immunities clause of the Fourteenth Amendment protected their occupational rights against the state and, as such, upheld the doctrine that the Bill of Rights was inapplicable to individuals in their relations with their states. The main effect of this decision was, however, to legitimize

In other words, a black ex-slave or a brutally exploited white worker was protected in his or her status as a federal citizen, but could still be brutalized with impunity under state law. Since people lived in states and not on federal property, and since nearly all the legal occasions on which an ordinary person would be likely to seek redress were under state jurisdiction, this amounted to another reactionary shutting out of the Bill of Rights. Indeed, it would not be until after the Second World War that the Supreme Court was to give life and meaning to the Bill of Rights, initiating the era of rights rhetoric through which we are now living.

Why did America, after struggling so hard to promote and then enact the world's first Bill of Rights, proceed immediately to spurn it? For two reasons. First, because the language and ideology of rights, having served their purpose in the war of independence and in the struggle to form a strong, centralized federal government, were recognized by the essentially conservative men who had made the revolution – especially the Northern Federalist entrepreneurs – as a dangerous tool in an emerging mass democracy. And second, because with one in five Americans being slaves, concentrated in the large-scale slave system of the South where they were the major form of property, keeping alive the language and law of rights was a constant invitation to legal mischief on the part of black slaves and their radical white supporters. There were, in fact, innumerable petitions by enslaved blacks to declare their condition an infringement of the Bill of Rights. More important, the Bill was a constant source of embarrassment for the slaveholders who were its greatest advocates. That acute embarrassment was already evident in the hypocrisies, blatant self-contradictions, and unbecoming prevarications of the revolution's greatest hero, Thomas Jefferson.[53]

---

the enactment of racial discrimination by the states and to continue to make the Bill of Rights a useless tool in the struggle against racism. From this decision onward to the end of the 1920s, the Court used the 'due process' and 'equal protection' clauses of the Fourteenth Amendment – which had been clearly enacted to protect the rights of African-Americans, in particular, and individuals in general – primarily as a protection for business interests against further state regulation and welfare legislation. The Fourteenth Amendment became a virtual Magna Carta of 'entrepreneurial liberty'. At the same time, writes Robert G. McCloskey, 'the question of Negro rights and with it the question of civil rights in general, had been relegated to a minor almost negligible place among the Court's concerns'. See McCloskey, *The American Supreme Court* (Chicago, IL, 1960), p. 134, and, more generally, ch. 5–6.

[53]   For one of the best treatments of Jefferson's untenable moral stances on the subject of slavery and abolition, see Charles L. Griswold, Jr, 'Rights and Wrongs: Jefferson, Slavery, and Philosophical Quandaries', in Haakonssen and Lacey (eds), *A Culture of Rights*, pp. 144–214.

Once the language and law of rights were abandoned, Americans went back to the more familiar language of freedom. It is the term 'liberty' that became the catchword, once again, of the nineteenth century. Upon doing so, however, something new became clear: the extraordinary unity of views that had seemed to emerge during the revolutionary era in the glorious rhetoric of rights was largely a function of the revolutionary situation. Everyone could agree on the rights and liberties of Americans against the authoritarian British. But with the common enemy out of the way and the problem of the union settled, the fundamentally different notes of freedom to which different groups of Americans adhered became painfully evident. These divisions were to lead irrevocably to one of the most brutal civil wars of all time.

What were they? First, there was the rise of civic freedom, of mass democracy, which increasingly alarmed the elites of both the North and the South. It was one thing to declare, in the heat of revolution, that all men are created equal; in the sober light of the morning after, it was dangerous talk. The problem is that it had been carved in the stone of the Constitution. Nothing comes through more clearly in the writings of most of the founding fathers and the first generation after the revolution than the dangers of too much democracy. We are 'all born to equal rights', warned John Adams in 1814, 'but to very different fortunes; to very different success and influence in life'. He was not always that tactful in his view of democracy, which he once denounced as 'the most ignoble, unjust and detestable form of government'. This is one subject with which he and his mortal enemy, Alexander Hamilton (who once called the masses 'swine'), could agree. The Virginian Edmund Randolph spoke for the great majority of the elite when he stated simply, 'We have suffered from an excess of democracy.'

There, however, agreement ended among the elite. The alternatives to too much democracy that Northern industrialist and Southern plantocrat offered were two radically different notes of freedom. The conflation of the honorific, other-directed sovereignal freedom of the aristocratic, slaveholding South, and of the conscience-driven, inner-directed sovereignal freedom of the bourgeois North which had achieved its apotheosis in the heroic revolutionary personality, collapsed right after life returned to normal. For the rapidly emerging capitalists of the urban-industrial North, a purely negative, personal conception of freedom became the order of the day, one in keeping with similar developments in the England of the industrial revolution. Possessive individualism had indeed finally become the hegemonic note of freedom, no longer simply the conceit of obscure philosophers and economic theorists.

The South, however, not only continued to hold on to the old agrarian capitalist version of possessive individualism, with its emphasis on honour and on freedom as power over others, but began to expand this system as never before under the twin impact of the massively increased demand for cotton in

Britain and the technical revolution of the cotton gin. As they did so, the shame and embarrassment that revolutionary slaveholders had felt about their peculiar 'species of property' gave way to a brash celebration of sovereignal freedom. Indeed, the most brilliant social theorist of nineteenth-century America, George Fitzhugh, not only wrote two powerful treatises in defence of sovereignal freedom, drawing freely on its ancient heritage, but in the process launched an extraordinary attack on the evils of industrial capitalism and of its revered negative conception of liberty in ways that often anticipated Marx.[54] Slavery, he audaciously argued, was the ideal social system, for if there were always to be power and the rule of the virtuous, it were best that people be dominated by people rather than be enslaved to capital. Industrial capitalism he condemned as a form of 'moral cannibalism' in which free labour had no liberties. Drawing parallels between ancient Athenian slavery and democracy and his own beloved South, he wrote: 'We need never have white slaves in the South, because we have black ones. Our citizens, like those of Rome and Athens, are a privileged class.' But even black slaves had their place and their traditional rights, including their 'property rights' in their masters, based on their expectations that their masters would perform their duty and honourably meet their obligations as good masters and protectors. They were certainly better off than the masterless white slaves of the capitalist world, enslaved to the merciless impersonality of capital. 'Free society asserts the right of a few to the earth', he wrote, 'slavery maintains that it belongs, in different degrees, to all [...] capital is a cruel master.'

The leaders of the new liberal ideology in both America and Britain viewed such ideas with increasing horror. Indeed, all forms of slavery, however mild, came to be seen in liberal Europe as the ultimate evil. The works of David Brion Davis have laid bare the extraordinary social and ideological meaning of the drive towards abolitionism. Up to the eighteenth century, moralists and philosophers of freedom, including Locke, had found ways of accommodating the strains and contradictions between slavery and Christianity. Nonetheless, as he points out, 'since the concept of slavery carried a penumbra of association involving sin, punishment, obedience, self-surrender, and deliverance, the strains were related to central antinomies in the structure of Western thought'.[55] During the late eighteenth century and the early nineteenth, exactly paralleling the rise of the industrial bourgeoisie and evangelical Christianity, an extraordinary moral reversal took place in Western bourgeois culture in both Europe and America,

---

[54]   'Cannibals All'; and 'Sociology for the South', both reprinted in Harvey Wish (ed.), *Ante Bellum Writings of George Fitzbugh and Hinton Rowan Helper on Slavery* (New York, 1960).

[55]   David Brion Davis, *The Problem of Slavery in the Age of Revolution, 1770–1823* (Ithaca, NY, 1975), p. 263.

in which slavery came to stand 'as the central metaphor for all the forces that debased the human spirit'.[56]

By the turn of the century, the involvement with slavery was as much metaphorical as real: 'In the United States a series of compromises on slavery became the fulcrum of an uneasy balance of power; in Britain the triumph of the anti-slave trade movement signalled a redefinition of national interests; in France anti-slavery and anti-colonialism became ideological weapons in the contest for revolutionary leadership.'[57] In the ensuing struggles to abolish the slave trade and slavery, religion, politics, and economics fused to create the most intense passions and indelible impressions, for what was at stake was the redefinition of what was central to the Western system of values, its hegemonic notion of freedom.

New World slavery, for the dissenting Protestants of Britain and the United States, was Christianity's 'fortunate fall', providing it with 'an epic stage for vindicating itself as the most liberal and progressive force in human history'.[58] Under the banner of 'practical benevolence', the struggle became a unifying force for all the evangelicals in their attack on the worldliness of the established churches. The struggle was also an agent of secular redemption that challenged both the new paganism of the Enlightenment and the heartlessness of the new industrial order. It was also a response to the revolutionary fever that had swept the Atlantic world.

On the secular front, slavery came to be seen by enlightened liberal thought as the embodiment of all that was most irrational and restraining, the antithesis of material and moral progress. But, as Davis shows, the belief in the idea of progress that swept late eighteenth- and nineteenth-century Europe worked both ways. If history was the gradual unfolding of man's perfection through either the providential hand of God or the secular emergence of the world spirit, demonstrated most clearly in the passing of serfdom and feudalism, there would be no need for direct human intervention. Gradually all things would get better. This argument won strong support from the new or, one should say, renewed science of economics. For Adam Smith, slavery was inherently irrational and inefficient; it had no place in a modern capitalist economy. Left to its own fate, it would surely wither away. The same conclusion was drawn years later for the American case by the liberal economist John Elliot Cairnes in his classic study *The Slave Power*. The gradualist theory of progress, the abolitionists soon discovered, was their most dangerous intellectual enemy.[59]

Hence the shift to an immediatist strategy by the abolitionists, led by Garrison.

---

[56]   Davis, *The Problem of Slavery in the Age of Revolution*, p. 263.

[57]   Davis, *The Problem of Slavery in the Age of Revolution*, p. 86.

[58]   Davis, *Slavery and Human Progress*, pp. 129–53.

[59]   Davis, *Slavery and Human Progress*, pp. 104–16.

In the end, of course, it took one of the bloodiest civil wars in the history of the world to settle the dispute. It used to be thought by Marxist as well as by many bourgeois historians that the root of the conflict lay in the irreconcilable economic systems of the North and the South: the one a rapidly expanding, progressive industrial capitalist system, the other a backward, paternalistic, anticapitalist throwback to the agrarian past.[60] We now know from recent cliometric studies that this interpretation was seriously flawed. The antebellum South was capitalistic through and through, and its central business, the slave plantation, typically more profitable than the average Northern firm.[61] Pragmatic Northerners were also keenly aware of the backward and forward economic linkages between the cotton plantations and their textile and shipping industries.

The radical abolitionists such as Garrison, Tappan, and Birney were among the few who saw that economic forces alone would never lead to the erosion of slavery. This realization coincided with a growing sense of social and political crisis in Jacksonian America during the early 1830s. On the one hand, there was the intransigence of the Southern slavocracy, reflected in the nullification crisis of 1831. On the other hand, there were alarming indications of black militancy throughout the Anglo-American New World: the published call for armed resistance by the ex-slave activist David Watkins, the Nat Turner revolt in Virginia, and the even bloodier island-wide revolt of Sam Sharp in Jamaica, itself an important factor in the British Parliament's decision to abolish slavery the following year.

The result of all this was the decision of the radical abolitionists to shift to an immediatist strategy, expressed in the Anti-Slavery Society's Declaration of Sentiments. This declaration appealed directly to the values of the revolutionary era, especially the Bill of Rights, in its demand that every person, regardless of race, must be 'secure in his right to his own body – to the products of his own labor – to the protections of the law – and to the common advantages of society'.[62]

Ironically, as scholars of this period have noted, while such sentiments were

---

[60]   For the last serious Marxist interpretation in this vein, over-laden with a highly functionalist theory of paternalism, see Eugena Genovese, *The Political Economy of Slavery* (New York, 1965).

[61]   Robert W. Fogel, *Without Consent or Contract: The Rise and Fall of American Slavery* (New York, 1988). It remains controversial whether plantation farming was more efficient than 'free' Northern family farming; but this is a rather tedious technical matter, having to do more with definitions and methodological issues in agricultural economics than with real issues concerning real people in real time.

[62]   Cited in James Brewer Stewart, *Holy Warriors: The Abolitionists and American Slavery* (New York, 1976), p. 52.

perfectly in tune with the Jacksonian attacks on the inequities of the post-revolutionary economic order – inequities of which the much-quoted Alexis de Tocqueville was so exquisitely innocent in his celebration of American equality[63] – there could be no alliance with this populist movement, since it was racist to the core. As James Brewer Stewart points out, the Jacksonians made it clear that they were dismantling monopolies so as to 'restore economic freedom to the common people, citizens could now invest as they wished – in a slave or a candy store, it made no difference'.[64]

What, then, eventually induced the Northern middle and working classes to become involved in the whole debate over slavery and, in the end, to participate in so drastic a thing as a civil war over it? The reasons largely centred on differing conceptions of their most vital interests. As in Europe, concern for the black slaves themselves was secondary. As Foner has shown, the critical issues were the free soil and free labour ideology and the critical role of the western territories in both the dreams and the realities of the middle-class and working people of the North.[65] For middle- and upper-class Northerners, what was of central concern was not the dehumanization of blacks but the fear of what they came to call the Slave Power spreading to the west, and ultimately to the North, as well as the monopolization of the government by the Southern plantocracy. For the working class, who saw the west as the escape route from the hopelessness of the urban slums, the spread of slavery threatened their one remaining dream.

Ironically, racism prompted both Northerners and Southerners to go to war. For the North, the west had to be kept safe and open for free white men and women, and Republicans played upon fears of miscegenation in their attacks on slavery. In the South the same fears were being exploited by the Southern slaveholders in their attack on abolitionism. In the end, even so radical a defender of black freedom as Frederick Douglass came to pragmatic acceptance of one of the saddest imperatives of American political life: 'the power to free the slaves lay in the rough-and-tumble of racist free-soil politics, not in the salons of Beacon Hill Garrisonians'.[66]

Thus, in America, as in Europe, emancipationists triumphed in the ideological war only when they were able to persuade people that their own liberty and spiritual salvation were at stake. Even so, there was a profound ideological issue in this realpolitik of abolitionism. It focused on one of the most ancient notes

---

[63]   On some of the factors that may account for Tocqueville's monumental blind spot, see William J. Murphy, Jr, 'Alexis de Tocqueville in New York: The Formulation of the Egalitarian Thesis', *New York Historical Society Quarterly* 61 (1977), pp. 69–79.

[64]   Stewart, *Holy Warriors*, p. 53.

[65]   Eric Foner, *Free Soil, Free Labor, Free Men* (New York, 1970).

[66]   Stewart, *Holy Warriors*, p. 146.

of the chord of freedom: the idea that one is most free when one can do as one pleases with others; freedom as the exercise of power or domination over others. We have seen that from the seventeenth century, men and women had begun to have real qualms about such a notion. It was in the American Civil War that the West had its first cataclysmic assault on this age-old Western idea. The speeches of Lincoln, and in particular the debate between the defender of slavery, Stephen A. Douglas, and Lincoln during the senatorial campaign of 1858, reveal in the full glare of history the final assault on the sovereignal notion of freedom in its naked form in the Anglo-American world:

'That is the real issue', Lincoln declared.

It is the eternal struggle between these two principles – right and wrong – throughout the world. They are the two principles that have stood face to face from the beginning of time; and will ever continue to struggle. The one is the common right of humanity and the other the divine right of kings.[67]

Actually, Lincoln posed the issue even more cogently in one of his most brilliant speeches, given six years later:

The world has never had a good definition of the word liberty, and the American people, just now, are much in want of one. We all declare for liberty; but in using the same word we do not all mean the same thing. With some the word liberty may mean for each man to do as he pleases with himself, and the product of his labor; while with others the same word may mean for some men to do as they please with other men, and the product of other men's labor. Here are two, not only different, but incompatible things, called by the same name – liberty.[68]

The significance of the American Civil War for the history of freedom as a value and idea can now be summed up as follows: It marked the final removal of the ancient notion of freedom as *direct* personal power over others from the semantic field of freedom. Such an idea now rapidly approached the semantic status of an obscenity.

But this did not mean that power itself was dissociated from freedom. Quite the contrary. The exercise of such power, however, had to be mediated through

---

[67]   'Lincoln's Reply, from the Seventh Debate, Alton, Illinois, Oct. 15, 1858', in Paul M. Angle (ed.), *The Complete Lincoln-Douglas Debates of 1858* (Chicago, IL, 1991), p. 393.
[68]   Lincoln, Address at 'Sanitary Fair', Baltimore, Maryland, 18 April 1864, in Marlo Cuomo and Harold Holzer (eds), *Lincoln on Democracy* (New York, 1990), p. 321.

control over property. Hence the sacred status that property came to acquire after this, a status reinforced by the demonization of slavery. It was during America's gilded age after emancipation that a US federal judge shamelessly, indeed proudly, announced that 'of the three fundamental principles which underlie government, and for which government exists, the protection of life, liberty, and property, the chief of these is property'.[69]

And it was during the late nineteenth century, too, that all Western peoples had learned from the Anglo-Americans the art of using the emancipation of black slaves to achieve the religious end of collective redemption, the moral purpose of reinforcing liberty, the political goal of justifying imperial expansion to protect the 'child-races' – the Belgians began their brutal colonization of the Congo as a self-righteous antislavery crusade! – and the capitalist requirements of free or cheap labour.

Later developments, during the nineteenth century and the first half of the twentieth, reveal a continuing disregard for the language and rhetoric of rights in both America and Europe. In Europe, rights ideology suffered an even more final demise than in America. The French Declaration of the Rights of Man went the way of the Revolution. It is significant that French workers during the insurrectionary period of the 1840s rarely appealed to the rhetoric of rights. Instead, as William Sewell has shown, in making their demands they turned to the *ancien régime* corporatist rhetoric of claims and liberties in a moral community that was hierarchical and that jealously guarded its privileges. The July Revolution may have seen the emergence of class consciousness, but 'it was by developing a corporate vocabulary that workers found their own voice'; it did not take the workers who manned the barricades of the July Revolution with cries of 'Vive la Liberté!' long to discover that their conception of liberty was fundamentally different from that of their liberal government. More to the point, no one, on the Right or the Left, appealed to any notion of the rights of mankind.[70]

The same pattern prevailed in liberal England, during the formative years of the working classes as well as the later period of effective collective action. This is hardly surprising, since the British had never taken to the language and philosophy of rights, in spite of Britain being its philosophical home. As Alan Ryan has recently pointed out, in continental Europe the rationalistic notion has always prevailed that citizens have only those rights granted them in authoritative legal codes; and contempt for the language and philosophy of rights is the one thing that the Right and the Left of the British political spectrum shared. Burke's polemic against the French Revolution and its infernal declaration of rights finds

---

[69]   332 U.S. 46 (1947), cited in Bernard Schwartz, *The Great Rights of Mankind: A History of the American Bill of Rights* (Madison, WI, 1992), p. 209.
[70]   W. H. Sewell, *Work and Revolution in France* (Cambridge, 1980).

its counterpart in Bentham's celebrated dismissal of rights as 'nonsense on stilts'. In spite of strong current pressures to enact a code of rights, it is still the case among the 'unmetaphysical British' that 'alongside this practical attachment to individual liberty, there has been widespread skepticism of any attempt to found politics on a constitution embodying natural rights, whether these are understood as the dictates of reason, the laws of God, or rules inscribed in hearts'.[71]

The growth of the welfare state in continental Europe and Britain was wholly expressed and justified in terms of the language and notes of freedom. As T. H. Marshall observed in his classic lectures of 1949, the growth of the welfare state entailed an expansion of the domain of civic freedom or citizenship from the political to the social, and although Marshall himself resorted to the language of rights towards the end of his lectures, it is clear that he was introducing, if not a foreign concept, then what was certainly an orphaned British one, to clarify his ideas. Neither the British Labour Unions demanding greater security, nor the famous White Paper on Personal Income of 1948 responding to these claims, used the language of rights. The paper instead spoke of 'certain traditional and customary relationships' that had to be changed.[72]

As is well known, Britain, although a signatory to both, has refused to enact into British law either the United Nations Declaration of Human Rights of 1948 or the even more pertinent European Convention on Human Rights of 1951. It is significant that, in the present heated debate over the future of the welfare state in Britain, the issues are posed entirely in terms of the relationship between freedom and the welfare state. No one, either on the Right or the Left, poses the issues in terms of rights, in spite of Ronald Dworkin's repeated appeals to his British colleagues to take rights seriously. This is extraordinary, in light of the American rights-drenched approach to the issue.[73] Maurice Cranston notwithstanding, the philosopher Alasdair MacIntyre seems to speak for most British intellectuals when he writes that 'there are no such rights, and the belief in them is one with the belief in witches and unicorns'.[74]

---

[71]   Alan Ryan, 'The British, the Americans and Rights', in Haakonssen and Lacey (eds), *A Culture of Rights*, p. 375.

[72]   T. H. Marshall and Tom Bottomore, *Citizenship and Social Class* (London, 1992), pp. 3–51.

[73]   See, for example, the lively debate between Robert E. Goodin and Roy Van Den Brink-Budgen in which the terms 'rights' is conspicuous for its absence: Goodin, 'Freedom and the Welfare State: Theoretical Foundations', *Journal of Social Policy* 11.2 (1982), pp. 149–86; Brink-Budgen, 'Freedom and the Welfare State: A Multi-Dimensional Problem', *Journal of Social Policy* 13.1 (1984), pp. 21–39.

[74]   Alasdair MacIntyre, *After Virtue: A Study in Moral Theory* (South Bend, IN, 1982), p. 67.

America has taken a radically different path. There, of course, there was much greater resistance to the growth and legitimization of the welfare state, and vicious state hostility to the organization of labour. In this resistance, the forces of reaction found an all-too-willing ally in the US Supreme Court, which, as Henry Abraham correctly argues, pursued right up to the Second World War a 'double standard' of justice, in which political freedom, meaning essentially individual freedom against the state in defence of property, was vigorously protected at the expense of economic freedom and security.[75] In spite of the powerful struggle of capital and the legal system against the growth of economic freedom, however, America did not lag as far behind Europe as had originally been thought. This is the main finding of the recent work of Theda Skocpol, who shows that veterans and women were able to tap into American nationalistic, pro-military, and materialist values to extract from the state a surprisingly high level of welfare support.[76] The culmination of this ad hoc, resisted, but grudgingly conceded, welfare process was the reforms of Franklin D. Roosevelt.

When in January 1941 he made the classic call to world peace and order based on the four freedoms, he still avoided the language of rights, although this would have been the perfect occasion to invoke them. It is all the more remarkable, then, that in 1944 we find Roosevelt issuing his 'Economic Bill of Rights', phrasing his call for an expansion of freedoms to the domain of economic security in terms of a set of basic economic 'rights'. In those four years a rhetorical revolution had taken place. The language and rhetoric of rights, now called 'human rights', were back with great force in the vocabulary of politics.

By that time the language of rights had entered its new golden age. The factors accounting for this dramatic turn of events are beyond the scope of this essay. I merely list here the generally accepted reasons for this change. Foremost among them was the formation of the United Nations, which not only had written into its charter the promotion of 'human rights', but immediately undertook as one of its first major tasks the setting up of a commission to issue a Universal Declaration of Human Rights. The main reason for such urgency on the matter of rights was, of course, the Nazi horror, which, as slavery had done previously, imprinted upon the consciousness of Europe the need to protect that which was essentially human by the thoroughness of its barbaric denial of all things human. Even so English a statesman as Churchill felt moved to urge the UN to 'enthrone' human rights. The shift from talk about *natural* rights to talk about *human* rights partly reflected the changed intellectual climate in which it was no longer felt necessary to derive rights from a god, especially the Christian

---

[75]   Abraham, *Freedom and the Court*, esp. ch. 2.

[76]   Theda Skocpol, *Protecting Soldiers and Mothers: The Political Origins of Social Policy in the U.S.* (Cambridge, MA, 1992).

God, or reason, or innate moral sense, or nature. But it also partly reflected the final ebbing of slavery as the contradistinctive leviathan in the conceptualization of freedom and rights.

The quintessence of slavery was its violation of nature, of what is most seemingly natural in the human condition – being a taken-for-granted part of the community in which one is born; owning, being in possession of, one's most intimate carnal, social, and spiritual self. The slave is not, strictly, dehumanized. Rather, he or she is denaturalized, denativized, natally alienated, deprived of all claims to citizenship; and he or she is depersonalized, deprived of all claims to selfhood and independent identity. Slaves are perversely but nonetheless humanly claimed in an embrace of social death with their owner, who wants them to be very much alive, to possess them physically and personally, to use them, to use them up, parasitically, for his or her own carnal ends, contradistinctively, to define the owner's own identity, his or her own most cherished personal value and social status. Hegel and Kojeve were just plain wrong – although brilliantly and instructively so: there was no existential dilemma for the master, who always knew that, for the slave to be most useful, he or she had to be kept human; kept inferior, and apart to be sure, the ultimate human other, essential for the definition, the conception, the very construction of the owner's own human identity and his or her cherished natural rights. It is noteworthy that no master class has ever denied its slaves human agency in, or even diminished responsibility for, their crimes, which is what one expects of the truly dehumanized; to the contrary, in all slaveries, the slave pays a greater price for his or her misdeeds.

With the Nazis things were a lot simpler, because we are reduced here to bestiality. Nature is not violated, for to make war and to kill are natural. There is here no complex, symbolically laden process of denativization and parasitic resocialization, no 'othering', no embrace of death. There is simply physical death and carnage on a scale that is humanly incomprehensible for reasons that defy all human, moral sense. And there is a cold, calculated hatred of the other that is inhuman because so lacking in the natural passions of war-making as the world had previously known it. Nazism brought into question not the natural, but the human. The efficient, moral bestiality of Europe's most civilized nation threatened to undermine all confidence in the fundamental difference between being human and being a mere beast with a more complex head. It was this threat that led even Churchill to call for the enthronement of 'human' rights.

Other factors played a role in the sudden shift back to the language of rights. There were the post-war decolonization movements, all of which drew upon the Western language of rights, especially the right to national self-determination, in their ideological struggle against the imperial powers, a strategy that obliged the United States to support them out of its respect for its own proud tradition as the first new nation.

In addition, the Cold War played its role. As the leader of the 'free world', the United States found the rhetoric of rights a powerful weapon with which to beat its Communist adversaries, in spite of its own contradictory record of support for authoritarian regimes in Latin America and other parts of the world.

The Cold War, however, was to influence the resurgence of rights rhetoric even more powerfully on the domestic front in America. It provided one important opening for oppressed minorities in their struggle for equal political and social rights. It is no accident that the minority group that led this struggle were African Americans who succeeded, finally, in persuading the Supreme Court to take the long-moribund Bill of Rights seriously. In doing so, the modern history of rights had come full circle. Hobbes and Locke, it will be recalled, had initiated the modern world's reconception of freedom in terms of fundamental natural rights. The fundamental right for both was the right not to be enslaved. Neither, however, had the courage or the means to practise or even to encourage what they preached for real living slaves. It was the descendants of the very slaves in whose ancestors Locke had financially speculated with such extravagant contradiction who finally gave meaning to Locke's celebrated definition of freedom in the second treatise on government, a discourse which, it will be recalled, was written under the chapter entitled not 'Of Freedom', as one might have expected, but, as this wisest, if most contradictory, of dead, white, English males correctly figured, under the title 'Of Slavery'.

6

The Value of Introspection

Kurt Flasch

> Noli foras ire, in interiore homine habitat veritas.
> Do not go outward. Truth dwells in the interior of man.
> St Augustine, *De vera religione*[1]

With this striking exhortation, Augustine summed up introspection as a
constitutive element of the old European system of merit. At the same time, in an
anxious, nothing less than beseeching, peremptory tone, it reminds us that human
beings have a tendency to throw themselves outwards, to live amid diversions,
to fail to appreciate themselves. It is not only with the emergence of industrial-
technological civilization that introspection comes under threat; it faces inherent
threats. Before Augustine, Neoplatonic and Stoic philosophers reminded us of the
same thing: it is we who forget our inner world, plunge into the external world,
and lose ourselves in hustle and bustle. Augustine's lamentation culminates in the
famous passage in the tenth book of the *Confessions*, which Petrarch is supposed
to have opened at the summit of the Mont Ventoux: 'This question moves me
to great astonishment. Amazement grips me. People are moved to wonder by
mountain peaks, by vast waves of the sea, by broad waterfalls on rivers, by the all-
embracing extent of the ocean, by the revolutions of the stars. But in themselves
they are uninterested.'[2]

Old Europe rejected the escape into the external and discovered introspection
as a value; it heaped praise on it – in the words of Novalis: 'The mysterious path
leads inwards.'[3] It urged people to engage in a kind of self-examination, which

---

[1] St Augustine, *De Vera Religione*, Corpus Christianorum 32, ed. Klaus-Detlef Daur
(Turnhout: Brepols, 1962), p. 79.

[2] St Augustine, *Confessions*, ed. Henry Chadwick (Oxford: Oxford University Press,
1989), p. 187, X.15.

[3] Novalis, *Schriften*, ed. P. Kluckhohn and R. Samuel, vol. 2 (Darmstadt: Kohlhammer,
1965), p. 419.

was of ancient, Socratic origin, was intermittently allied with Christianity, but which was detachable from, and was in fact detached from, its Christian goal. This discovery of the value of introspection became part of European identity; as such, it has been described on many occasions. A complementary achievement of European thought is less well known: it thought about the value of introspection and did not hide away the doubts which its culture of the inner being also throws up; it articulated the problems which its discovery entailed. It also discovered the ambivalence of introspection, the need to supplement it with other things. European philosophy not only prompted people to explore themselves and produce 'confessions'; it was a process of reflection on introspection. I intend to present some of the stages of these reflections, supplementing the important studies by Charles Taylor on the sources of the self and Jan Assmann on the invention of the inner world from the perspective of a reader of medieval books.[4]

But first I would like to explain why I consider such a look back across the history of philosophy useful, if not indispensible.

It is possible to identify locations other than philosophy in which European introspection has stood apart from the 'noise of world history'. Examples of this are: the history of the diary and of the still life, the history of meditative rather than merely ritual piety, the emergence of conscience and an awareness of guilt, the history of lyric poetry, the development of the division between public and private, the development of the study and of the private library (*St Jerome in his Study*). Without implying that these phenomena are non-essential, today I remain within the framework of my profession, the history of thought. It has the advantage, to put it explicitly, of having developed the specifically European project of introspection; it accompanied its history, making people conscious not only of its greatness but also its wretchedness. It understood its danger: the menacing lack of substance, almost meaninglessness.

Today, it is not just the 'noise of world history' that makes it hard to engage in intimate reflection, but that of motorbikes and the culture industry, planes and information flows. In this situation of excessive stimulation, friends of introspection risk reacting in an abstract or one-sided way. The philosophical founding fathers of the culture of introspection produced not only apologias, but analyses. The following remarks draw on their works, which both laid the foundations for introspection and critiqued it.

---

[4]   Charles Taylor, *Sources of the Self: The Making of the Modern Identity* (Cambridge: Cambridge University Press, 1989); Jan Assmann (ed.), *Die Erfindung des inneren Menschen. Studien zur religiösen Anthropologie* (Gütersloh: Mohn, 1993).

I

Let's begin with Socrates. In the *Apology* 29d–30b, Plato has him relate how, when he meets one of his judges on the street, he addresses him as follows:

> 'Best of men, you who are an Athenian, from the city that is greatest and best reputed for wisdom and strength, are you not ashamed that you care for having as much money as possible, and reputation, and honour, but that you neither care nor think about prudence (*phronesis*), and truth (*aletheia*), and how your soul (*psyche*) will be the best possible?' And if one of you disputes it and asserts that he does care, I will not immediately let him go, nor will I go away, but I will speak to him, and examine and test him. [...] For I go about and do nothing but persuade you, both younger and older, not to care about bodies and money before you care just as vehemently about how your soul will be the best possible. I say: 'Not from money does virtue come, but from virtue comes money and all of the other good things for human beings in both private and public life.'[5]

This is a forceful call for people to make the journey inwards. Socrates rejects a life in which one's thoughts are directed only towards pleasure, money, or status. The soul, he tells us, comes first. We find ourselves here at the origin of the concept of care of one's soul, but much depends on removing from the concept of the 'soul' its non-ancient, Christian, not to mention sentimental patina. The text itself shows the need for these corrections. Care of the soul, Socrates tells us, reveals the greatest love for the polis and ultimately brings more money into the city. For the *chremata* grow out of the *arete*, and not the other way around. Socrates' care of the soul consists in scrutinizing the convictions that guide one's life. He shows that the usual set of priorities is wrong and that the prosperity of the polis depends on correcting it. 'Soul' is the location of insights and of the right or wrong way of living in the city as community. The move inwards, that is, towards truth and *phronesis*, is Socrates' life's work, it is what the god of Delphi instructs one to do, but it leads back to the polis.

Augustine's dictum, with which I began, already belongs to a different world: the reference to the polis has not so much disappeared as been extended to the whole of the sensory and intelligible world. To evaluate the sensory world, this is the function of the 'inner person'; the 'inner person', here, in early Augustine, as yet without added Pauline emphasis, is the location of criteria for evaluating the

---

[5]   *Plato's Apology of Socrates*, an interpretation with a new translation by Thomas G. West (Ithaca, NY, and London: Cornell University Press, 1979), p. 36.

sensory world. Here alone lies the truth, that is, the unchanging norm applied to external things; only here do we find the totality of ideas upon which we call, in order to be able to evaluate our perceptions when we have them – not in isolation from them. From an Augustinian perspective, we might say: only the inner world, concentration on that which cannot be seen, yields the insight that we are dealing with the same concept when we find the number 3 in different sign systems or languages. Augustine uses mathematical and ethical norms as examples to explain how he imagines the inner process of establishing the truth. It goes something like this: we possess the definition of the circle; only because of this can we assess the extent to which the circle we have drawn corresponds to this concept, what the drawing, which is always imprecise, is worth. We know we should not lie, even if lies are a common feature of everyday life and thus, as it were, 'normal'. Augustine's inner world is the location of criteria, the benchmark for correcting everyday depravity.

There is more to this: Augustine's inner world is the turning point of our evaluations. It is the intellectual and intentional authority to break free of the maelstrom of things, the splendour of the perceived. It is the ability to say no, to come back to oneself and to experience for the first time what it means to be more than a mere thing among things. Later generations called this the *Icherfahrung* and protested in its name against the everyday consciousness of which Fichte says: people would sooner believe themselves a piece of lava on the moon than a self. It would be Augustinian to state: they submit all too readily to the external world and its fascination; they fail to understand that they merely set themselves up for disappointment; they would rather take their concept of 'reality' from trees than from themselves and thus fail to appreciate their status. Their concept of reality is oriented towards the external, natural world; as a result they grasp neither what they are, nor what they experience, and they lack the foundation for the rational knowledge of God, which is mind. In early Augustine, 'inner world' and 'soul' are not primarily the awareness of sin or examination of one's conscience. At issue here is not individual error or original sin; these motifs took centre stage in Augustine's writings only from 397, determining the Christian concept of the soul until the thirteenth-century reception of Aristotle; the Reformers took them up again after centuries of intellectual muddle; pietism popularized them. In Augustine's early work, the turn inwards did not mean individual psychology, but rather the active understanding of universal norms. According to Augustine, it is only within the inner realm that we obtain an intellectualized concept of reality, and thus of the 'inner person', and finally, on this basis, of God.

We tend to think of the Middle Ages as a period of intensive introspection and a culture of the soul. And in the shape of the monasteries there were in fact institutions that were supposed to be detached from utility and violence in order that they could devote themselves to the purification of souls and the appreciation of the inner world. There were written guides to help one determine one's progress on the precisely graduated inward path, and thus on the stairway to heaven; there were individual and monastic exercises to further this goal. In theory, the monasteries were the institutionalized form of the inward turn, that is, the realization of sins, of penance, and of contemplation. There were good reasons why things were different in reality; these were not based solely on the corruption of human beings or the temptations of Satan. Rather than investigating this further, I would like to present a document of monastic meditation, a voice from the inner world of the fourteenth century. Not that all monks or all theologians and philosophers thought in the same way as Meister Eckhart. Not that Eckhart merely repeated Augustine's theory of introspection. He was an original thinker and insisted that he was saying something rare and unheard, *rara* and *inaudita*. But let us listen to the man himself talking about the inner and the outer, contemplation and action.

The sisters Mary and Martha (Luke 10:38–42) were considered the embodiment of the two ways of life: Mary of the turn inwards, Martha of external work. The way Eckhart interpreted this is apparent in his German Sermon 86; I reproduce it here in slightly abbreviated translation.

II

Meister Eckhart, Sermon 86[6]
INTRAVIT JESUS IN QUODDAM CASTELLUM, etc.

St Luke writes in his gospel that our Lord Jesus Christ entered a little town where a woman named Martha received him. She had a sister named Mary who sat at the feet of our Lord and listened to his words; but Martha hurried about, serving our dear Lord. Three things caused Mary to sit at the feet of Christ. The first was that God's goodness had embraced her soul. The second was ineffable longing: she longed for she knew not what, and she wanted she knew not what. The third was the sweet consolation and delight she drew from the eternal words which flowed from the mouth of Christ.

Martha, too, was drawn by three things which caused her to go about and wait on our dear Christ. The first was her respected age and a ground very rich in experience. This made her think that no one could do the

---

[6]   Bernard McGinn, *Meister Eckhart: Teacher and Preacher* (New York, Mahwah, NJ, and Toronto: Paulist, 1986), pp. 338–44.

work as well as she. The second was a mature power of reflection which enabled her to accomplish external works with the perfection that love demands. The third was the great dignity of her dear guest.

Now Martha says, 'Lord, tell her to help me'. Martha did not say this out of spite. Rather, she said it out of endearment; that is what motivated her. We might call it affection or playful chiding. Why? Note what follows. She realized that Mary had been overwhelmed by a desire for the complete fulfilment of her soul. Martha knew Mary better than Mary Martha, for Martha had lived long and well; and living gives the most valuable kind of knowledge. Life knows better than pleasure or light what one can get under God in this life, and in some ways life gives us a purer knowledge than what eternal light can bestow. Eternal light gives us knowledge of self *and* God, but not knowledge of self apart from God. Seeing oneself alone makes it easier to recognize what is like or unlike. St Paul and pagan masters confirm this. St Paul saw in an ecstasy God *and* himself in God in the manner of the spirit, but he did not discern clearly in God through images each individual virtue. This was the case because he had not exercised them in actions. The masters achieved such lofty knowledge through the practice of virtue that they knew each individual virtue more distinctly than Paul or any saint in his first rapture.

This was the case with Martha. When she says, 'Lord, tell her to help me', it was as though she were saying: 'My sister thinks she can do what she pleases while she sits by you filled with consolation. Let her find out whether this is true, and tell her to get up and leave you'. This last remark was said with tender regard, but this could not be gathered from the words themselves. Mary was too full of longing. She longed for she knew not what, and wanted she knew not what. We harbour the suspicion that dear Mary was sitting there more for enjoyment than for spiritual profit. Therefore Martha said, 'Lord, tell her to get up', because she feared that she would remain stuck in this pleasant feeling and would progress no further. Then Christ answered her, saying, 'Martha, Martha, you are careful, you are worried about many things. One is necessary. Mary has chosen the best part, which can never be taken from her'. Christ did not speak these words to Martha to chasten her. Rather, he responded by giving her the comforting message that it would turn out for Mary as she desired.

Why did Christ say, 'Martha, Martha', calling her name twice? He wanted to indicate that Martha possessed completely everything of temporal and eternal value that a creature should have. When he said 'Martha' the first time, he indicated her perfection in temporal works. With his second calling out, 'Martha', he affirmed that she lacked nothing of all that is necessary for eternal happiness. Hence he said, 'You are careful', by which he meant: You stand in the midst of things, but they do not reside in you; and those are careful who go about unimpeded in all their daily pursuits. Those people are unimpeded who perform all their daily works properly according to the image of eternal light, and such people stand in the midst of things, but not *in* things. They stand very near and yet do not have less of it than if they stood up above, at the rim of eternity. 'Very near', I say, because all creatures act as means. There are two kinds of means. One kind (without which I cannot come to God) is work and activity in time, and this does not lessen eternal happiness. By *work* I mean when one practises externally works of virtue, but *activity* is when one practises them internally with full rational consciousness. The other kind of means is to be rid of this. We have been put into time for the purpose of coming nearer to and becoming more like God through rational activity in time. This is what St Paul meant when he said, 'Redeem time, for the days are evil'. One 'redeems the time' by ascending continually by means of the mind to God, not according to different images; rather, by means of living intellectual truth. And 'the days are evil' means that day implies night. If there were no night, there would not be day nor would one use the word. It would all be one light, and this is what St Paul means because a life of light is insufficient if there can still be enough darkness to cast a veil and a shadow over eternal happiness for a noble spirit. This is what Christ meant when he said, 'Continue to walk while you have light'. He who works in light ascends to God free and stripped of all means. His light is his activity and his activity is his light.

This is how it was with dear Martha. Thus he said to her, 'One thing is necessary', not two. You and I, once embraced by the eternal light, are one; and this two that is one is a flaming spirit standing above all things (yet under God) on the rim of eternity. It is two because it does not see God without something mediating. Its knowing and its being, or its knowing and the image that it knows, will never become one. They do not see God, for there God is only seen spiritually, free of all images. One becomes two, two is one; light and spirit, these two are one in the embrace of eternal light.

But now back to our explanation of how dear Martha, and, together with her, all of God's friends are *near* care but not *in* care. Here a work done in time is as valuable as any joining of self to God, for this [work in time] joins us as closely as the most sublime thing that can happen to us, except for seeing God in his pure nature. Hence he says, 'You are near things and near care', and he means that she certainly was worried and concerned in her lower senses because she was not pampered by the

sweetness of the spirit. She was near things, not in things; she stood apart,
[...]

Our works should have three qualities: One should work orderly,
with discrimination, and with contemplation. I call that 'orderly' which
at all points answers the highest. I call that done 'with discrimination'
when one at the time knows of nothing better [to do]. And I call that
done 'with contemplation' when one feels in the good works the gratifying
presence of living truth. Wherever these three things are, they join [us to
God] as closely and are as useful as all the joys of Mary Magdalene in the
wilderness.

Now Christ says, 'You are bothered by many things', not about one
thing. This means that when she is in a purely simple state performing
no activities and is focussing her attention on the rim of eternity, she is
bothered when something acts as an [interfering] means, so that she cannot
remain there above in consolation. A person is bothered by something who
descends and stands in the midst of concern. But Martha stood in lordly,
well-founded virtue with a free spirit unimpeded by anything. Hence she
wished for her sister to be put in this same state because she saw that she
was not standing firmly. It was a splendid ground out of which she wished
that she [Mary] might be established in all that is necessary for eternal
happiness. This is why Christ said, 'One thing is necessary'. What is the
one thing necessary? It is the One that is God. That is necessary for all
creatures. If God were to withdraw all that is his, all creatures would
turn into nothing. If God were to withdraw what is his from the soul of
Christ, where their Spirit is united to the eternal Person, Christ would
remain a mere creature. Thus this One is certainly necessary. Martha was
afraid her sister would remain clinging to consolation and sweetness, and
she wished her to become as she herself was. This is why Christ said, 'She
has chosen the best part', as if to say, 'Cheer up, Martha; this will leave
her. The most sublime thing that can happen to a creature shall happen
to her: She shall become as happy as you.'

Now Christ says, 'You are bothered by many cares'. Martha was so
grounded in being that her activity did not hinder her. Work and activity
led her to eternal happiness. Granted, her happiness was somewhat
impaired by mediation; but her noble nature, her constant striving, and
the aforementioned virtue stood her well. Mary was a Martha before she
became a Mary, for when she sat at the feet of our Lord, she was not Mary.
She was, of course, Mary in name but not in her being because she was
sitting there in joy and sweetness but had just begun to be schooled and
to learn about life. But Martha was very steadfast in her being and hence
she said, 'Lord, tell her to get up', as if to say, 'Lord, I would wish that

she were not sitting there just for the pleasure of it. I would like her to learn life so that she might possess it in being. Tell her to get up, so that she might become perfect'. Her name was not really Mary as she sat at Christ's feet. This is what I call Mary: a well-disciplined body obedient to a wise soul. Obedience is when the will satisfactorily carries out what insight commands.

III

In this sermon, Eckhart grapples with the medieval, particularly the monastic, culture of introspection in an original way. Rather than rejecting it, he takes it further. He sees it as a first step rather than an end in itself. It is essential, but not the highest value. This surprises us for several reasons: first, because he reverses the order of precedence, which the Gospel according to Luke (10:38–42) – in the view of Bible researchers, including modern ones – clearly establishes between Mary and Martha. Did not the early Christians use the story of Mary and Martha to say that meditation and the teachings of Christ took precedence over activity in the outer world? Eckhart approaches the two women as symbolic figures, as was commonly done, but explains the Gospel in such a way that Martha signifies the *higher* stage of perfection. Second, Eckhart surprises by contradicting a long tradition of religious, especially monastic, literature; this saw Martha as exemplifying the worldly, Mary the more highly valued secluded life. Previously, Mary had vouched for the pre-eminence of the contemplative life or the path inwards. Third, we would surely have expected something different than the prioritizing of the active life from an author who was and is still described as a 'mystic' in line with a stubborn miscategorization. But let's forget about the superficial labels and have a look at what Eckhart actually said.

How does he characterize Mary? The Jesus of the Gospel according to Luke assures her that she has chosen the best part. Eckhart illustrates his own concepts of status through the figure from the parable. With gentle irony, he places Mary under suspicion of sitting at Jesus' feet more out of pure pleasure than because of 'spiritual profit'. 'Spiritual profit', this is not run-of-the-mill practicality, utility, but rather progress in reasonableness. She listens, ponders, revels in the spiritual pleasure. She was not captivated solely by a thirst for knowledge or even curiosity; intense feelings were at play: 'she longed for she knew not what, and she wanted she knew not what'. Eckhart repeats this sentence twice, thus giving it particular emphasis. He makes out of Mary the figure of vagueness, whose inclinations are good but who lacks substance; a figure, we might almost say, that embodies 'idolization'. She has yet to work out what to do with her life. This is possible only through the setting of limits, committing, renouncing, negating one possibility in favour of another. She allows no 'thing' to come between her and her highest impulses. She is an example of pure remaining-within-oneself. She enjoys her introspection and closeness to God, and thus keeps life at arm's length.

Eckhart goes even further in distancing himself from the otherwise much lauded sister. He has Martha say that Mary certainly thinks she *can* do everything she *wants* while she sits amid consolation. 'Let her find out whether this is true, and tell her to get up and leave you.' Mary is well-meaning, yet to experience opposition. She feels no sense of lack, and thus sees no reason to act. She feels no conflict, has no need to make a choice. She has drawn her existence tight around a point of security, and it feels good. She does not put herself to the test, and thus overestimates herself. She has not translated her good intentions into practice, has not carried them out body and soul. But that, Eckhart explains through a peculiar etymology, is the meaning of the name 'Maria' – 'a well-disciplined body obedient to a wise soul', Mary avoids constant practice and drills. She does not yet live up to her name. She is not yet the 'real' Mary. The praise which Jesus bestows on her relates, Eckhart tells us, to what she will become. Mary will become like Martha, that is, she will get beyond the stage of pure introspection.

But where will she get to? What is the goal? The goal is not, for example, that she consciously decides to interrupt her contemplation in order to bring a beggar a bowl of soup. This would, in fact, be right and would correspond to a distinctly Eckhartian imperative, but this is not at issue here. She should (according to this text; a thinker does not always say the same thing) not *do* something, but *be* something else. She must gain a new awareness, both inwardly and outwardly. She will look upon her sublime inner state differently, relate to the world differently.

Eckhart declares: she will become like Martha. Martha has not steered clear of 'things'. She has tied them to her innermost self and has linked her innermost self with things in such a way that they have ceased to be merely external. She has brought 'things' and their constraints into line with her highest goals. She has left behind the notion of the *vita contemplativa* and *vita activa* as alternatives. She is a role model of a third way. She has exposed herself to life, she has taken herself to it. In doing so, she has grasped something which we can only ever learn by going outside of ourselves. Eckhart writes odd things about the experience of living: living provides the best understanding. To live is itself to understand; living makes us think more than do pleasure and light, in a better, purer way indeed than the eternal light could. In Augustine, the eternal light of truth burns only within. This is where it burns for Eckhart as well. The eternal light, the truth, reveals itself and opens the way to the rational understanding of God. Life reveals itself – without God. It consists, as it were, of 'things', of 'godless things'. It looks at itself, shows differences more sharply; without it, everything looks the same. Paul was in seventh heaven – this prevented him from seeing clearly enough the perfections of a good person. The pagan ethicists – we might think of Aristotle's *Nicomachean Ethics* and Seneca's *Epistulae morales* – practised the virtues, saw them in life itself, and understood them more exactly than the apostle transported heavenwards. They tell us more about them.

This idea of Eckhart's is difficult. It is hard to find any parallels in the medieval philosophical literature. There is probably no sermon that stands the Gospel according to Luke so clearly on its head, albeit Albertus Magnus' explanation of this section prepared the ground for an enhanced evaluation of Martha.[7] Kurt Ruh and others disputed Eckhart's authorship: the constant praise for Martha at the expense of Mary contradicts the text of the Gospel too openly. The fact that Eckhart prefers the pagan philosophers to the enraptured Paul as ethical guide also seems out of place. But the most astonishing thing is the concept of life: the eternal light, the truth, points to itself and thereby to God, but life points to itself without God and is considered here the higher source of insight. Life is self-referential performance, life is practice. Life is leaving-oneself-behind and coming-back-to-oneself. The goal of life is inherent within it; it is teleologically in life itself. This is a good Aristotelian idea. Here, 'life' is surely not to be read in a primarily biological sense, but as reality in its entirety, which encompasses God and the world, and in this sense exists without a specifically revealed God.

Martha's pre-eminence is due to the fact that she lives in this life. She thus achieves the 'mature power of reflection which enabled her to accomplish external works with the perfection that love demands'. The truly wise life consists not in contemplative pleasure, but in arranging activities in the outer world in line with the best that we know, the best that love demands. She goes out into the world of things, she is among things, but these things are not within her; rather than repressing her individual inner life, they give it expression. She is in close proximity to the things of the external world, these things play a mediating role between her and the best that love demands, but she is also, as we learn, up above, at the rim of eternity. Does this refer to the highest celestial sphere? As found in much the same way in the work of Eckhart's contemporary Dante? However this may be, the crucial thing is the shift in thinking that gets us to realize that our temporal impact matches the extent to which we merge into God. She who merely loses herself in her inner world cannot 'stand firmly'. 'Things' cause her much worry; as there are things lying around all over the place, she lives in permanent conflict, and her life shrinks to a state of narrow isolation. Martha steps towards them, arranges them in line with her own way of living, and, free of anxiety, stands *among* them, not *in* them.

---

[7]   Albertus Magnus, *Opera*, ed. Auguste Borgnet, vol. 23 (Paris: Vives, 1894), pp. 87–9.

Eckhart's stress on the factor of time is also remarkable. He makes Martha older and concludes: she has lived for a long time and lived rightly – this produces understanding. She knows Mary better than Mary knows Martha. She fears that Mary might evade the test of time. Eckhart endows time with tremendous significance, as if rejecting the momentary immersion in eternity. He states that he understands 'with discrimination' to mean that one knows no better at the moment. The temporal position of the person seeking to establish how to act with discrimination partly determines the outcome. Time and living as the basis of understanding – this thesis, put forward in the twentieth century from Dilthey onwards, can be heard here from afar. When Jesus talks about Mary, he trusts in the effects of time. Humorously, he comforts Martha: 'Cheer up, Martha; [she has chosen the best part] this will leave her.' She is still at school, but she will learn how to live. 'To learn to live', to possess life in being, not merely in terms of personal characteristics; this is what it is to become perfect.

Eckhart pushes this idea further in a different direction: 'One thing is necessary'. He who lives in a state of aloneness, he is a glowing spirit, the one *in* things and *above* things. He is *among* things, but these things do not live *in* him, weighing him down. In him, duality becomes unity. For others, understanding and being are different, or, Eckhart puts it more precisely, as we never know being directly, but only through images, for these others, knowing and images known are different. He who enters into unity sees God without images; knowing and images known, knowing and being become one. That is Martha: the exemplar not only of the active life, but of wisdom entered into unity, which no longer makes a distinction between things and the best that love demands. Martha exemplifies practised virtue that has stood the test of time, a free soul, free because in those things which Mary saw as distracting and kept her distance from, Martha has found herself in the best, in unity, free of all worry. In Martha, the metaphysics of the One goes beyond the distinction between *vita activa* and *contemplativa*.

IV

There is no undifferentiated problem of the inner and the outer; there are merely historical and intellectual processes which we tie together into a unified 'problem' later on. Lutheran professional ethics and Calvinist economic ethics have created a new set of circumstances; they have upgraded the outer world. This has, in turn, triggered a new flight inward; Angelus Silesius switched religion because Protestantism had lost the 'ars mystica or the art of becoming one with God'. Pietism returned to Augustine's motto: God and the soul. Nothing else? *Nihil omnino!*, but it was forced to innovate – first because of its confrontation with the Protestant orthodoxy, second, and above all, because of its individualization of the concept of the soul. Now – rather like the practices of the Jesuits – the examination of one's conscience, the monitoring of souls and sins, was on the agenda. This modernization, almost against the will of those involved, reached a critical stage around 1800.

When Goethe extended the *Theatralische Sendung* into *Wilhelm Meister's Apprenticeship* between 1794 and 1796, he created a panorama of divergent ways of life. This is a colourful work, diversified in form, but the sixth book is devoted entirely to the confessions of a beautiful soul. Here, the scrupulous self-examination of the hat-maker, her fear of leaving the precious inner world, has found its most masterly literary expression, which is not lacking in sympathy for this highly sensitive and intelligent woman who observes how she changes when she goes out to the world of things. She finds that she clothes herself 'in the garb of foolishness', and she laments that it is not just a matter of a mask that she wears on the surface; 'rather, the foolishness immediately penetrated me to the core'.[8] The outer tends to overwhelm the inner. It is better to remain within.

In his *Phenomenology of the Spirit*, Hegel systematized Goethe's attempt to come to terms with the pietist culture of introspection. The beautiful soul appears in the last major section, under the heading 'The spirit', in other words at a later, more significant, esteemed place. The European spirit, because it has begun to withdraw within itself, has the tendency to drop out of the outer world. This is not a random aberration; there is something of the nature of the spirit here. Hegel, though, makes it clear that, due to its nature, the spirit cannot remain like this. What Eckhart showed through the figure of Martha, a woman, what Goethe described through the *sfumato* of individualizing tangibility and rendered understandable with reference to the development of a young woman, Hegel set out in powerful terms:

> Here, then, we see self-consciousness withdrawn into its innermost being, for which all externality as such has vanished – withdrawn into the contemplation of the 'I' = 'I', in which this 'I' is the whole of essentiality and existence. It is submerged in this notion of itself, for it has been driven to the limit of its extremes.[9]

To withdraw into its innermost being – this is the life of the spirit, but it cannot endure in this extreme form and with a plan to remain within; this state of affairs must come undone. Should the spirit be purged until it reaches this state of stylized purity (Mary at the feet of the Master), consciousness takes on its

---

[8]   Johann Wolfgang von Goethe, *Werke*, vol. 7 (Zurich: Artemis, 1949), p. 407.

[9]   This quotation and the following quotations are from Hegel, *Phenomenology of Spirit*, trans. A. V. Miller with analysis and foreword by J. N. Findlay (Oxford: Clarendon Press, 1979), pp. 398–400.

most impoverished form; it has lost all worldly substance; it is nothing more than self-consciousness and beatitude, yet as consciousness, it is, of course, also consciousness of the world. 'This will leave her' – consciousness, withered to mere self-consciousness, will not last. The inner that takes shape through opposition to the outer must disappear. It never attains reality; it remains – like Mary – within itself, attending to itself. Objects do not become 'a negative of the actual self' for it. They do not cut into it and do not, therefore, unlock it. 'It lacks the power to externalize itself, the power to make itself into a thing and to endure being.' This is Mary, who refrains from going out to the world of things and is unable to coordinate them with the best that love demands.

Hegel goes on:

> It lives in dread of besmirching the splendour of its inner being by action and an existence; and, in order to preserve the purity of its heart, it flees from contact with the actual world, and persists in its self-willed impotence to renounce itself, [a self] which is reduced to the extreme of ultimate abstraction.

It renounces everything in order to avoid having to renounce itself. If it produces objects for itself, these are illusory entities, proxies, empty in themselves – Goethe referred to the 'mask'. For him, they merely generate an awareness of emptiness. Goethe wrote: 'The folly penetrated me to the core.' This sought-after state of remaining-within-oneself Hegel calls 'an unhappy, so-called "beautiful soul"', and predicts 'its light dies away within it, and it vanishes like a shapeless vapour that dissolves into thin air'.

I conclude here. I can well imagine people saying: I'd be happy to have such problems; the problems we face are far removed from the critique of the beautiful soul. But it is worth considering: anyone speaking of the value of introspection would do well to bear in mind its origins, particularly at a time when it is in such great danger. It has almost been made to disappear entirely; it has retreated into the zeal of penniless poets and the pre-planned ten-minute meditations of one successful business magnate or another. It's a good idea to know what it was, which movements and counter-movements it sparked off. It did not fall into Europe's lap from outside, but was the product of the hard labour of abstraction. You don't play with introspection. It entails a certain inherent radicalness, which enables it to keep itself apart from life. Its founding fathers – Socrates and Plato, Plotinus and Augustine, Eckhart and Goethe – moderated it and constructed counterweights. Anyone contemplating the value of introspection today should pay attention to this largely ignored process.

7

Rationality – A Specifically European Characteristic?

Wolfgang Schluchter

1. Preliminary Remarks

Reformulating the topic

The title of my discussion comes with a question mark. I suspect that the conference organizers chose it deliberately. Is not rationality, understood at a first approximation as the ability to think in a reasoned and consistent fashion (theoretical rationality) and to act in accordance with certain rules in a reasoned and consistent fashion (practical rationality) what we ascribe to the human being qua human being? Is not the human being the *animal rationale*, the creature that reasons, as, for example, Immanuel Kant thought? Further, have not processes of rationalization occurred in a number of civilizations, above all in those which we call, with Karl Jaspers, axial age civilizations, or better, axial civilizations, and which Shmuel N. Eisenstadt has dealt with so impressively?[1] Questions after questions, which already give us reason to reconsider the title of this article: instead of 'Rationality – a specifically European characteristic?' perhaps 'Europe – a specific rationality?' This title does, in fact, seem better suited to what I have in mind here. But the question mark stays. For we do not yet know whether we can uphold what this implies.

---

[1] Eisenstadt took up the idea of axial age civilizations, first expressed by Alfred Weber, then developed further by Karl Jaspers, and made it the object of a comprehensive comparative endeavour. See, for example, the volumes edited by him: *The Origins and Diversity of Axial Age Civilizations* (Albany, NY: State University of New York Press, 1987) and *Kulturen der Achsenzeit. Ihre institutionelle und kulturelle Dynamik* (Frankfurt am Main: Suhrkamp, 1992). We should, however, refer to axial civilizations rather than axial age civilizations. Islam, for example, is an axial civilization but not an axial *age* civilization.

Our exploration may come to an end without the question mark giving way to an exclamation mark.

Before answering the question of whether there is a specifically European rationality, it is helpful to consider two issues first. One is methodological, one conceptual. Methodologically, we must distinguish clearly between the origin and spread of a cultural phenomenon on the one hand, and its validity on the other. When we explore origin and spread, we remain on the empirical and historical level; we seek out causal attributions that tally with the facts. When we explore the validity of a cultural phenomenon, we switch to the normative level and inquire into its justification. We may elucidate this distinction with regard to the cultural phenomenon of capitalism. We distinguish between the universal meaning of capitalism and its general validity. Capitalism may possess universal meaning, it may be relevant to all of us. But this does not necessarily imply that it is of general validity. Most likely, no-one will dispute that the globalized capitalist economy exercises a significant influence on all our lives, that we must therefore have an interest in fathoming how it functions and ascertaining its cultural preconditions and consequences, and thus that it represents a cultural phenomenon of universal significance in this sense. But there are many who would dispute that this cultural phenomenon is also of general validity. On the contrary, they see in the globalized capitalist economy a power that is threatening the survival of mankind.

The fact that these two levels, the empirical-historical and the normative, are linked but must be kept apart analytically clarifies another issue. A cultural phenomenon may initially emerge in a particular civilization, spread from there, and finally achieve universal significance, but it may also gain general validity. A good example is the emergence and spread of human rights, to which we nowadays ascribe not only universal significance, but also general validity. Human rights initially emerged in a particular civilization, the European, and were first institutionalized in the United States and France as rights. They no doubt started out as a project bound to a specific civilization, a project whose roots, as we know since Georg Jellinek's famous work on the origins of human rights, lie deep in the history of Latin Christianity.[2] But this culturally specific project turned into a project of general validity. This, at least, is *our* view. We should emphasize: *our* view, for this claim is not uncontested. A considerable number of members of other civilizations regard this claim as part of Western cultural imperialism. However this may be, against the background of these considerations we can reformulate our title even more precisely: 'Europe – bearer of a specific rationality of universal significance *and* general validity?'

---

[2]   See Georg Jellinek, *The Declaration of the Rights of Man and of Citizens: A Contribution to Modern Constitutional History* (Westport CT: Hyperion Press, 1979 [1895]).

Europe: an unstable historical entity

Our modified title contains two terms which must be clarified before we go any further. What does Europe mean here? What does rationality mean? Let's first examine the concept of Europe. It quickly becomes apparent that this word does not refer to a fixed historical entity. Geographically, Europe never had clearly defined eastern borders; religiously, Europe remained divided between Latin Christianity, Orthodox Christianity, and Islam; linguistically, Europe was never confined to the Romanic and Germanic languages; and politically, the demarcation between Europe, Russia, and the Ottoman Empire, for instance, shifted too.

Thus, when we refer to Europe, we refer to a fluid construct. And yet, from a historical perspective at least, the outlines of this construct seem fairly stable from relatively early on. In his study on the historical foundations of Europe, the historian Ferdinand Seibt states:

> It is possible to make out all the contemporary 'Western' European nation states on the political map around the turn of the first millennium. They were either clearly delineated or were beginning to emerge: Britain, France, Germany, Poland, Bohemia, Hungary, Croatia; in addition, the protrusion of Italy in several segments and Scandinavia and the Baltic countries, which as yet lacked clear borders. Spain, highly distinctive, gradually emancipated itself over centuries from Arab rule. Or to reverse our perspective: the present era has reached, in the form of nation states, the degree of consolidation seen in form of kingdoms at the turn of the millennium.[3]

To sum up: Europe was not and is not an entity fixed for all time, but rather a historical construct always devised and put into effect anew by participants and observers. When we refer to Europe in this article, we mean *western* Europe as a changeable construct, nonetheless relatively stable in its outlines. So let's ask: Was this western Europe the bearer of a specific rationality? If it was, is this rationality merely of universal significance or also of general validity?

Rationality: an unstable concept

What does rationality or rationalism mean? Just as Europe is not a fixed historical entity, neither is rationality or rationalism a fixed concept. It is no accident that Max Weber, the great theorist and historian of rationality and rationalism, in his

---

[3]   Ferdinand Seibt, *Die Begründung Europas. Ein Zwischenbericht über die letzten tausend Jahre* (Frankfurt am Main: Fischer, 2002), p. 21.

study of the link between ascetic Protestantism and the new spirit of capitalism published 100 years ago, which I will examine in more detail shortly, delivered this warning:

> In fact, one may – this simple proposition, which is often forgotten should be placed at the beginning of every study which essays to deal with rationalism – rationalize life from fundamentally different basic points of view and in very different directions. Rationalism is an historical concept which covers a whole world of different things.[4]

How can we conceptualize this world of different things? In my view, Max Weber had much to say about this as well. He proposed three pairs of concepts with respect to rationality and rationalism: value and instrumental rationality, material and formal rationality, and theoretical and practical rationality. What is the significance of these distinctions, and how are they best related to one another?

Whenever we use these paired concepts in a Weberian sense, we are operating on the empirical and historical level. Here, Weber's view involves a multi-level model. The first pair of concepts, value and instrumental rationality, describes the orientations which actors in given situations may have among others: are they oriented towards the idea of success, that is, ultimately instrumentally rational, or towards the idea of validity, and thus ultimately value rational? The second pair of concepts, formal and material rationality, is concerned with the problem of how actions are coordinated, or more precisely, the coordination of the action orientations of at least two actors. Here, the focus may be on the 'how' or the 'what' of this coordination. If we are concerned with the 'how', the crucial point is the way in which the coordination is carried out (formal rationality), if we are concerned with the 'what', it is the content of the coordination that matters (material rationality). There is a third consideration, however. Orientation and coordination are anchored in supra-individual contexts of meaning, worldviews (*Weltbilder*) in Weber's terminology, which feature both a cognitive and an evaluative side. If the cognitive stands centre-stage, we refer to theoretical rationality, if the evaluative is our focus, to practical rationality. Such world views consist of ideas and ideals, which must be subjectively acquired by the individual. Orders and organizations, or to put it more generally, institutions play a key mediating role here. It is no accident that Weber refers to the 'tremendous confusion of interdependent influences

---

[4]   Max Weber, *The Protestant Ethic and the Spirit of Capitalism* (London and New York: Routledge, 2002), p. 38.

between the material basis, the forms of social and political organization and [...] ideas', and he explores the affinities that exist between these 'levels'.[5] In what follows, we shall adhere to this conceptual framework and the methodological recommendations associated with it.

Our question is thus: has western Europe, as delineated earlier, become the bearer of a specific rationality of universal significance *and* general validity with respect to action orientations, the coordination of action and worldviews? This is the question posed by Max Weber, to which I now turn.

2. Max Weber's Question

The uniqueness of modern European civilization

Max Weber does, in fact, urge us to 'explain genetically the *distinctiveness* of Occidental rationalism, and within it that of modern Occidental rationalism',[6] and he connects this plea with the question of why in China and India 'the scientific, the artistic, the political, or the economic development [did not] enter upon that path of *rationalization* which is peculiar to the Occident?'[7] Thus, he thought that the 'modern European cultural world', as he puts it elsewhere, was characterized by a rationalism of a specific kind, which he initially identified as economic rationalism, as '*bourgeois* capitalism with its rational organization of *free labour*'.[8] However, in the course of his development he extended this rationalism to the entire 'modern European cultural world', to western science, with its linkage of conceptual work, mathematical foundation, and laboratory experiments; to western music with its counterpoint and harmony, formation of the tone material on the basis of three triads with the harmonic third, its chromatics and enharmonics, interpreted not in terms of equal distance, but of harmony; to western painting with its linear and aerial perspective; as well as to the western constitutional state with statutory law and a professional bureaucracy

---

[5]   Weber, *The Protestant Ethic*, p. 49, and the famous formulation: 'Not ideas, but material and ideal interests, directly govern men's conduct. Yet very frequently the "world views" that have been created by "ideas" have determined as switchmen the tracks along which action has been pushed by the dynamic of interest. "From what" and "for what" one wished to be redeemed and, let us not forget, "could be" redeemed, depended upon one's world view' (translation slightly altered). See Max Weber, 'The Social Psychology of the World Religions', in H. H. Gerth and C. Wright Mills (eds), *From Max Weber: Essays in Sociology* (New York: Oxford University Press, 1946), p. 280.

[6]   Weber, *The Protestant Ethic*, p. xxxix (translation slightly altered).

[7]   Weber, *The Protestant Ethic*, p. xxxviii.

[8]   Weber, *The Protestant Ethic*, p. xxxvii.

oriented towards it.[9] According to Max Weber, it was not only in the inherently rational value spheres and life orders, but also in the inherently non-rational or a-rational ones that a thoroughly rational approach prevailed. This produced a constellation that did not emerge elsewhere. For him, this applies in particular to the trinity of industrial capitalism, the modern state, which successfully lays claim to a monopoly of legitimate physical force, and modern science, which 'has brought about the disenchantment of the world and its transformation into a causal mechanism'.[10]

As Weber sees it, a peculiar rationalism is at work in Europe which manifests itself differently in the various value spheres and life orders, but which has a common core, a core that may be of universal significance *and* general validity.

Normative or heuristic Eurocentrism?

It thus comes as no surprise that Max Weber opens his unfinished 'collected essays in the sociology of religion' (*Gesammelte Aufsätze zur Religionssoziologie*) with a provocative statement which seems Eurocentric to many:

> The son of modern European civilization, studying any problem of universal history, is bound to ask himself to what combination of circumstances the fact should be attributed that in Western civilization, and in Western civilization only, cultural phenomena have appeared which (as we like to think) lie in a line of development having *universal* significance and validity.[11]

He goes on to list these cultural phenomena, most of which I have mentioned already. Among these, Weber views modern industrial capitalism as the 'most fateful' force. But according to him, this capitalism will operate rationally only if it is embedded in a rational legal system and a rational administration as well as supported by modern science based on rational concepts and on experiments. Today, following the dissolution of the bipolar world order, which inhibited its global spread, modern industrial capitalism seems to be more fateful than ever.

Was Max Weber Eurocentric? Certainly, but in what sense? In order to answer this question, we must read this opening statement very carefully. We then notice the warning signs he erected. For 'a product of modern European civilization', seeing things in this manner is, above all, *inevitable*. And *we* like to

---

[9] See Weber, *The Protestant Ethic*, pp. xxviii–xxx.

[10] Gerth and Wright Mills (eds), *From Max Weber*, p. 350 (translation slightly altered).

[11] Weber, *The Protestant Ethic*, pp. xxviii (translation slightly altered).

think that European cultural phenomena are not only of universal significance, but also of general validity. Indeed, Weber would be the last to claim that modern European civilization is the pinnacle of human development. He does not hide his scepticism about the consequences of this cultural development. What he says here means that our hermeneutic point of departure makes this way of seeing necessary for us. We can disrupt this reflexively, but we cannot simply leapfrog it. Yet this hermeneutic tie does not compel us to assume the superiority of western civilization vis-à-vis other civilizations. The centrism practised by Weber thus remains heuristic. It remains such because, as a researcher, he limits himself to the issues of origins and spread.

Let us turn now to Weber's analysis of the emergence of western civilization. In so doing, I shall include consideration of other analyses, particularly those by his brother Alfred and his colleague Ernst Troeltsch. I will discuss, first, external conditions, if you will, decisive institutional developments important to the rise and spread of modern European civilization, then internal, mental conditions. Finally, I will return to the issue of the type of rationalism specific to the west. But whether we are considering the external or internal conditions, the multi-level model, the triad of action orientation, action coordination, and worldviews – we might also say the triad of action, order, and culture – always plays a crucial role, even when these components are not discussed individually.

3. Causes of the 'Unfolding of a Dynamic Historical Process Unique in World History' (Ferdinand Seibt)

Structural tensions and their resolution

It is widely acknowledged that Europe lagged behind other civilizations, the Chinese, the Indian, and the Arab, as late as the turn of the first millennium, but that then, step by step, a dynamic set in which, at least for some time, made it the most developed region in the world. How can we explain this phenomenon? What were the key events that set the course for this, as Ferdinand Seibt puts it, unique and dynamic historical process?

First, let's be clear that the Europe to which we have been referring, in which, from a rather backward starting point, that dynamic process unique in world history unfolded, is not the Europe that we know from ancient mythology. As Ferdinand Seibt remarks, Zeus did not carry the virgin Europa off to Paris or London, but to Crete, and for a long time the inhabitants of western Europe did not describe themselves as Europeans, but as belonging to (Catholic) Christianity or the Latin west. Ernst Troeltsch, in his great study of the social teachings of the Christian Churches and groups, refers to the relatively unified western Christian culture of the Middle Ages led by the Church,[12] followed, as a result of the Reformation, by a period of denominationalism with its bloody religious conflicts, out of which modern European-American civilization ultimately emerged.[13] Europe is thus not a term that would have been used descriptively by participants or observers before the Enlightenment. It is itself part of that process of political-cultural construction and reconstruction to which I have referred.

Second, let's also be clear that despite all the continuities, there are also ruptures between Middle Eastern and Mediterranean Antiquity with its pagan and Judeo-Christian cultural phenomena (Alfred Weber calls them secondary cultures of the first stage), and the medieval, Church-led unified Christian culture (Alfred Weber calls this a secondary culture of the second stage) out of which the modern European cultural world developed. This was clearly perceived, prominently, by the young Max Weber, who was well versed in ancient and medieval legal and agrarian history. An early lecture includes the following observation on the decline of ancient civilization and on its long-term effects. The text is – I'm sure you will agree – of literary quality. With the fall of the Roman Empire, Weber begins his remarks, 'the economic development of the ancient world had come full circle'. The intellectual work, which was once part and parcel of it, he tells us, seems entirely wiped out. For as a consequence of the return to a barter economy, 'the marble pomp of the ancient cities [has] disappeared, so too all the intellectual achievements and values of these cities seem sunk in darkness: their art, their literature, their science and their sophisticated commercial law. Meanwhile, on the manors of the possessores and

---

[12]   Ernst Troeltsch, *The Social Teaching of the Christian Churches* (London: Allen & Unwin, 1931), esp. ch. 2.

[13]   Troeltsch endeavours to determine more precisely the character of the modern world, of modern Euro-American culture, and this he does by contrasting it with the Church-based, unified Christian culture of the Middle Ages. The latter is a culture of authority, is considered infallible and is intolerant of the other; the former, meanwhile, is relative and characterized by tolerance of the other. It has, of course, also lost its homogeneity. It is based on the idea of an autonomous, rational individual, a life lived in accordance with one's own internal motivations and an optimism featuring an implicit faith in progress; it developed out of the unified Christian culture initially continued by the Reformation, though it then went on to destroy this unified culture. See Ernst Troeltsch, 'Die Bedeutung des Protestantismus für die Entstehung der modernen Welt', in Ernst Troeltsch, *Kritische Gesamtausgabe*, vol. 8 (Berlin and New York: Gruyter, 2001), esp. ch. 1. For Troeltsch, modern culture encompasses 'the broadest array of endeavours, but it nonetheless bears a certain coherent character' (Troeltsch, *Kritische Gesamtausgabe*, vol. 8, p. 208). He later applied his proposed cultural synthesis to Europe, to some extent to shared European culture.

seigneurs', Weber continues, 'the songs of the troubadours were not yet heard.'
And he goes on:

> It is impossible not to feel a certain sadness as we view this spectacle – a
> great civilization apparently approaches the heights of perfection, then
> loses its economic basis and crumbles away. Yet what did this mighty
> process really involve?
>
> What we have described was a transformation of the fundamental
> structures of society, a transformation which was necessary and which
> must be interpreted as a tremendous process of recovery. For the great
> masses of unfree people regained family life and private property, and they
> themselves were elevated from the status of 'speaking tools' to the plane
> of humanity. Ascendant Christianity now surrounded their family life with
> firm moral guarantees; indeed even the laws of the Later Empire for the
> protection of peasants' rights acknowledged the unity of the unfree family
> to an unprecedented degree.
>
> It is of course also true that at the same time a part of the free
> population sank to a position equivalent to serfdom, and the civilized
> aristocracy of Antiquity was barbarized. Furthermore, the barter economy
> now became dominant. It had always formed the infrastructure of ancient
> civilization, but the expansion of unfree labour had for a time relegated
> it to a subordinate position, although the more slave property caused
> differentiation in wealth the more it in turn grew. However, when the
> political centre of the Empire shifted from the coastal areas to the interior,
> and slave supplies dried up, then the barter economy imposed its pressures
> towards feudalism on the once commercialized superstructure of the
> ancient world.
>
> Thus the framework of ancient civilization weakened and then
> collapsed, and the intellectual life of Western Europe sank into a long
> darkness. Yet its fall was like that of Antaeus, who drew new strength
> from Mother Earth each time he returned to it. Certainly, if one of the
> classic authors could have awoken from a manuscript in a monastery and
> looked out at the world of Carolingian times, he would have found it
> strange indeed. An odour of dung from the courtyard would have assailed
> his nostrils.
>
> But of course no Greek or Roman authors appeared. They slept in
> hibernation, as did all civilization, in an economic world that had once
> again become rural in character. Nor were the classics remembered
> when the troubadours and tournaments of feudal society appeared. It
> was only when the medieval *city* developed out of free division of labour
> and commercial exchange, when the transition to a barter economy

made possible the development of burgher freedoms, and when the bonds imposed by outer and inner feudal authorities were cast off, that – like Antaeus – the classical giants regained a new power, and the cultural heritage of Antiquity revived in the light of modern bourgeois civilization.[14]

Undoubtedly, the old prejudice that the period between the fall of the Roman Empire and Merovingian and Carolingian rule was 'dark' is implied in these remarks. But more importantly: for Weber, there was the legacy of ancient culture, symbolized by the names of Jerusalem, Athens, and Rome, by the culture of beauty, sublimity, and expediency in the Hegelian sense, which had to be appropriated anew under radically different economic and political conditions. Two processes had changed the early medieval point of departure vis-à-vis Antiquity: firstly, the shift in the focal point of social, political, and cultural life from the coasts to the interior, and secondly, in conjunction with this, from the city to the countryside. The ruralization of culture – this above all marks the break with Middle Eastern and Mediterranean Antiquity. This was not primarily a culture of the interior and of the countryside, but of the coasts and the cities. However, at least for western Europe, Roman law and the 'Roman Catholic Church resting on the Roman concept of office' ensured continuity.[15] The later division between the Western and the Eastern Church reinforced this development characteristic of western Europe.

If one follows Max Weber's brother Alfred, there were four tensions in particular within this new framework. These grew out of the clash of the ancient legacy with the young peoples of the *Völkerwanderung* era, which had not yet achieved the status of developed cultures. A tension existed between:

1. The vitality of these young forces and a Christianity, in the shape of the organized Church, influenced by Augustine and oriented towards ethical action.

2. The increased autonomy of local centres of domination and the universal pretensions of the papacy and reviving empire.

3. The scattered country manors and the resurgent urban centres.

---

[14] Max Weber, 'The Social Causes of the Decline of Ancient Civilization', in *The Agrarian Sociology of Ancient Civilizations* (London: NLB, 1976), p. 409. Weber's key thesis: 'The fall of the Roman Empire was not due to external factors such as the numerical superiority of its enemies or the incapacity of its leaders.' He continues: 'the barbarian invasions simply concluded a development which had begun long before.' Weber, 'The Social Causes of the Decline of Ancient Civilization', p. 389.

[15] See Max Weber, *Ancient Judaism* (New York: The Free Press, 1952), p. 6.

4. The universal Latin culture embodied by the Church, a culture which also moulded science, and the linguistic and cultural independence of the indigenous and immigrant groups. To put it differently: the tension between a universal Latin culture and local cultures capable of producing their own literature, cultures which, far from disappearing, developed further and ultimately encouraged the formation of nation states, not least through the ongoing exchange with the *koine*.[16]

Alfred Weber thus sees Antiquity as a whole, its pagan and Judeo-Christian components, as a universalizing 'authoritarian template',[17] which had to be appropriated by the young forces and merged with their own parochial cultures. Not least, the fact that these tensions had to be resolved anew again and again, without being eliminated, explains something about the dynamics of the new development referred to above.

Incidentally, Max Weber had a similar view. Though he was denied the chance to write a coherent text on this subject due to his early death (in his *Aufsätze zur Religionssoziologie*, planned to comprise four volumes, the fourth was to deal with western Christianity), his manuscripts handed down to us, collectively entitled *Economy and Society*, contain a sufficient number of statements that support this view. He cites four medieval 'revolutions', more in the sense of structural history than the history of events, in order to render comprehensible the special developmental path trodden by western Europe, as he put it, and its dynamic: the papal, the scientific, the urban, and the feudal revolution. Following the division of the Western and Eastern Churches, the papal revolution driven forward by Gregory VII and the Investiture controversy certainly helped strengthen the Church-led unified Christian culture, but it also led to a complementary dualism of hierocratic and political power, although it did not entirely prevent attempts to resolve the relationship between religion and politics in favour of either party (caesaropapism or theocracy). But it laid the ground for the institutional separation of religion and politics established much later.[18] While the scientific revolution, associated with the founding of universities in Bologna, Paris, and Oxford, prioritized a theology influenced by Platonic ideas, it

---

[16]   See Alfred Weber, *Kulturgeschichte als Kultursoziologie*, Alfred Weber-Gesamtausgabe, vol. 1 (Marburg: Metropolis, 1997), particularly ch. 5 A.

[17]   Alfred Weber, *Kulturgeschichte als Kultursoziologie*, p. 302.

[18]   On this and the following, apart from Ernst Troeltsch's *Social Teaching*, see esp. Harold J. Berman, *Law and Revolution: The Formation of the Western Legal Tradition* (Cambridge, MA: Harvard University Press, 1983), esp. Part I: 'The Papal Revolution and the Canon Law.' As a supplement to my remarks here, see my efforts in Wolfgang Schluchter, *Religion und Lebensführung*, vol. 2 (Frankfurt am Main: Suhrkamp, 1988), ch. 10.

also promoted, not least through the profound reception of Aristotelianism, the 'scientification' of all fields and, via the idea of the corporation, an idea promoted by teachers and students, the autonomy of research gradually emancipating itself from theology.[19] The urban revolution, which also created the setting for the universities, promoted citizens' political-legal autonomy and autocephaly vis-à-vis the territorial authorities and, supported by the community of the Eucharist, also made possible the beginnings of democracy. Finally, the feudal revolution, 'rex et regnum', as Weber put it, led to the sociation (*Vergesellschaftung*) of individualized feudal relationships and thus set the course for state formation based on the model of social contracts, at the end of which the state as a political institution 'with a rational, written constitution, rationally ordained law, and an administration bound to rational rules or laws, administered by

---

[19]   For reflections on the development of science anchored in the comparative analysis of culture, see the excellent book by Toby E. Huff, *The Rise of Early Modern Science: Islam, China, and the West* (Cambridge: Cambridge University Press, 2003 [1993]); among other things, he deals with the role of Arab science and the Islamic world in the development of science as a whole, without whose mediation the comprehensive reception of Aristotle in the West could not have taken place. He also examines the difference between the madrasa and the university as organization. See esp. ch. 5. The development of the western university as an autonomous corporation was closely bound up with the development of the city. See, for example, Franco Cardini and M. T. Fumagalli Beonio-Brocchieri, *Universitäten im Mittelalter. Die europäischen Stätten des Wissens* (Munich: Südwest, 2000), which states on p. 29: 'The university grew out of the radical change in population structure that occurred between the 11th and 13th century, in transportation, and in the urban and economic sphere. The university is closely linked with the city and the street, with the mobility of the lower clergy and its role as social and cultural link between priests and laity, with the commercialization of knowledge and the development of the independent professions, with the theological debate, which was closely linked with heretical movements, which had a socially explosive effect and represented a challenge demanding a response: through a dialectic process, propaganda and through suppression of these disturbances.' The western science, of such importance later on, as the foundation of the three universities mentioned here shows, 'began' as a western European phenomenon, and it required from scholars a willingness to be mobile, in fact, to be more or less homeless. With the famous *authentica habita* from 1158, Emperor Frederick Barbarossa created a scholarly privilege for Bologna, which protected the scholars from attacks by the town dwellers and strengthened the autonomy of the university as corporation. Cardini and Fumagalli Beonio-Brocchieri, *Universitäten im Mittelalter*, p. 68. A further sixteen universities were founded in the thirteenth century. The network grew – with no 'German' involvement at the beginning. See also Rainer A. Müller, *Geschichte der Universität. Von der mittelalterlichen Universität zur deutschen Hochschule* (Munich: Nikol, 1990), pp. 31ff.

trained officials' emerged.[20] In addition, at the turn of the millennium an agrarian revolution caused a revival in the money and market economy and an increase in population. This development was probably stimulated primarily by monks. With mouldboard ploughs, the three-field system, the formation of humus, the draining of marshes, and massive clearances, it was not only the material basis of social, political, and cultural life that was bettered; the climate changed as well. Ferdinand Seibt tells us:

> More than half the northern Alpine forest in the low mountain regions [*Mittelgebirgen*] and in the eastern forest regions were cleared, which certainly improved the dank climate. Agricultural production increased several times over. All hands were no longer needed for sowing and harvesting, and a portion of the rural population was released from working in the fields.[21]

But we should not overlook the fact that the emerging Church-led unified Christian culture with its internal institutional differentiation also tightened the criteria of inclusion and exclusion. The key terms here are, on the one hand, Inquisition, persecution of witches, pogroms of Jews, and, on the other, crusades and *Reconquista*. The crusades in particular had a dynamizing effect. In a work entitled 'The beginnings of modern capitalism' (*Die Anfänge des modernen Kapitalismus*), based on a speech, even Max Weber's older colleague Lujo Brentano, supposedly correcting Max Weber's approach, claimed:

> The beginnings of modern capitalism thus lie in trade, money lending and the waging of war; as a consequence of the military expeditions of the crusaders, organized on a capitalist basis, the capitalist economic order also penetrated the commerce and agriculture of Italy and other countries with flourishing urban centres.[22]

However, for Weber, all of this, including the four medieval 'revolutions' imputed to him here, was, as it were, merely the curtain-raiser. The main performance was still to come. It pertained to the rise of the modern professional man, the man with a vocation, with a calling. His question was: how did a conduct of life (*Lebensführung*) develop which initially supplied industrial capitalism with

---

[20]   Weber, *The Protestant Ethic*, p. xxxi.

[21]   Ferdinand Seibt, *Die Begründung Europas*, p. 24. Another important factor is that the barbarian invasions had now been repulsed.

[22]   See Lujo Brentano, *Die Anfänge des modernen Kapitalismus* (Munich: Akademie der Wissenschaften, 1916), p. 48.

the entrepreneurs and workers suited to its needs, but which came to include other occupational groups as well, such as officials and scientists, a conduct of life characterized by a rationalism of self-control and, above all, mastery of the world? It is a theoretical and, above all, practical rationalism that Weber thought had been invented in western Europe. And from here it had spread, to North America and beyond.

Mental tensions and their resolution

If we wish to understand this thesis, often called the Weber thesis, we must leave the eleventh, twelfth, and thirteenth centuries and turn to the sixteenth and seventeenth centuries, that is, the phase in western Europe's development in which, as different churches and sects emerged, the Church-led unified Christian culture gradually disintegrated. As early as 1904/1905, Weber published his soon-famous study 'The Protestant Ethic and the "Spirit" of Capitalism' to demonstrate the contribution of certain currents within Protestantism in the post-Reformation period to the development of the modern world, in much the same way as Ernst Troeltsch tried to do from a theological perspective, someone with whom Weber, to deploy Friedrich Wilhelm Graf's felicitous formulation, enjoyed a 'friendship of experts', particularly during this period. It is fair to say that Weber's later comparative studies on the economic ethics of the world religions are also grouped around this original thesis. Their purpose is to demonstrate that the rational conduct of life, privileging control of the self and mastery of the world, is a cultural phenomenon which arose only in western Europe in the post-Reformation era, spreading from there.

What is the kernel of this thesis? It is that the rational conduct of life, on the basis of the idea of a vocation, was born out of the spirit of Christian asceticism. In the post-Reformation period, this spirit influenced certain groups of people, particularly petit bourgeois urban classes eager to climb the social ladder. The crucial point: in much the same way as Georg Jellinek with respect to human rights, Weber tries to show in the case of the bourgeois way of life that religious factors played a role in its development, and thus that religion and rationalism did not, as 'enlightened' critics of religion since the encyclopaedists had always claimed, inevitably obstruct one another or remain mutually indifferent; that each may promote the other, that a certain religion under certain conditions is thus capable of triggering a process of rationalization of universal significance and possibly of general validity. But there is an immediate qualification: not everything characteristic of Western, particularly modern Western, rationalism is of Christian or even Protestant origin. There are other 'plastic elements' of modern European culture of different origin, humanist rationalism for example, developed in the Renaissance period, but also philosophical and scientific empiricism, the technologies bound up with the development of natural sciences in general, which also advanced through revolutionary leaps forward and in the third phase of which we find ourselves today, a phase defined by the technology of automation, information, the atomic and cell nucleus. The ground was laid for all these achievements as early as the Middle Ages, with the institutionalization of research in universities, and for long periods Europe remained the spearhead of science. Of course, modern science is not confined to Europe any more, but has conquered the world.[23]

Having outlined the difference between ancient coastal culture and medieval inland culture, having identified some institutional innovations that occurred mainly from the eleventh to thirteenth centuries, we now conclude by asking: how did this modern professional man, the man with a vocation, a calling, come about, a being Weber claims is characterized by a specific rationalism? In other words, we must take a closer look at the Weber thesis. What is his explanatory model?

As we have said, Weber's key concern was to explain the development of 'the most fateful force in our modern life', modern industrial capitalism.[24] He was *not* primarily concerned to explain the emergence of modern science and the modern state. But even in the case of modern industrial capitalism, his explanatory pretensions remained limited. He did not want to explain the emergence of modern industrial capitalism as such. Capitalism (and we are always referring here to the modern rather than the ancient or medieval version, which Weber also analysed in detail), like all social formations, has to be analysed in terms of 'form' and 'spirit'. The 'form' is external; in this case, this pertains to the economic order (market economy) and to economic organizations (commercial firms and households). The 'spirit' is internal, and has to be distinguished from the 'form'. 'Form' and 'spirit' are two 'sides' of capitalism, and they may 'very well occur separately'. For 'the capitalist form of an enterprise and the spirit in which it is run generally stand in some sort of adequate relationship to each other, but not in one of necessary dependence'.[25]

---

[23]   On the three technological revolutions, of which the second, the rise of the machine, chemistry, and electricity, is closely bound up with European culture, see Heinrich Popitz, *Epochen der Technikgeschichte* (Tübingen: Mohr, 1989), pp. 10ff. Popitz recognizes that the techniques of agriculture, the use of fire (ceramics and metallurgy), and urban development (large-scale construction) already partly determined the character of the ancient civilizations. First of all came tools, of which there is evidence for 500,000 BC. Modern science has, of course, long been more than a purely European project. It is a project of mankind, an example of a project of universal significance and general validity. Even as a European project, it was never self-sufficient. It developed under the influence of Greek and Arab thinkers, not least in terms of the reception of Aristotle.

[24]   Weber, *The Protestant Ethic*, p. xxxi.

[25]   Weber, *The Protestant Ethic*, pp. 27–8.

Weber never claimed in his study on the Protestant ethic that he had established a causal relationship between ascetic Protestantism and the 'form' of modern industrial capitalism. In his view, even the connection between ascetic Protestantism and the 'spirit' of capitalism is not direct. Rather, it was an unintended consequence of intentional religious action, exclusively meant to cater to the believer's desire to be among those who are saved. It was thus based on value orientations. This is important in light of the fact that the economists of Weber's time, like those of the present, saw this 'spirit' as triggered by the rational calculation of utility, in other words by an instrumentally rational orientation.

Weber first arranges the currents of post-Reformation religion in line with whether they nurtured the spirit of Christian asceticism. In his view, this applied neither to lay Catholicism nor Lutheranism, but to Catholic monasticism and the Protestant sects, including Calvinism as a kind of sect-Church (the invisible Church within the visible Church). Schematically, Weber's arrangement of the various religious currents may be presented as follows:

Figure 7.1   *Currents within Western Christianity*

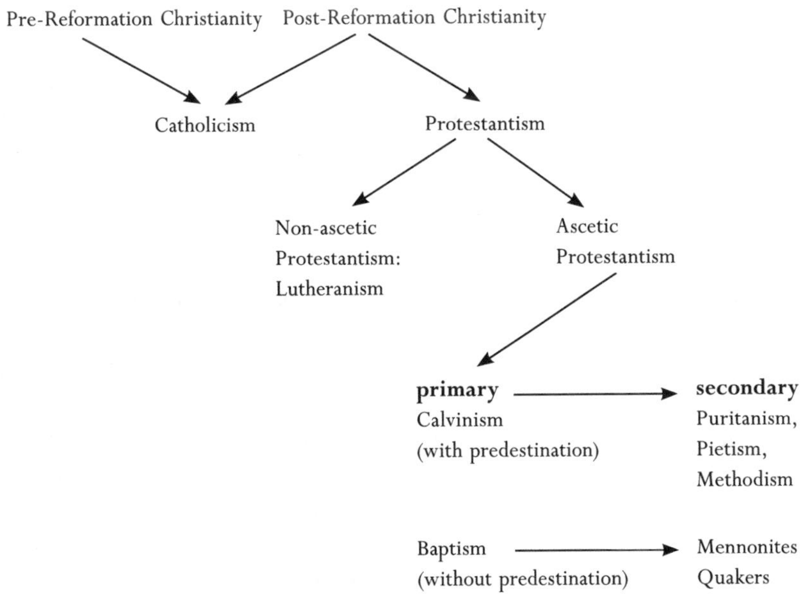

The strands of ascetic Protestantism, as Weber expressly underlines, differed greatly. As a group, they differed not only from Catholicism, but also from Lutheranism. They tended to associate the idea of redemption with the God of the Old rather than of the New Testament, and had to prove themselves in this world (rather than merely reconcile themselves to their circumstances), by seeing themselves as the tool (rather than the vessel) of God. Adding an additional degree of intensity, in some, though by no means in all currents, the theodicy of predestination, the doctrine of the eternal selection of those who will be saved, held sway. This gave rise to a religious worldview that came into conflict with believers' desire for salvation (*certitudo salutis*). They wanted to know what their prospects of salvation were. But the religious world view initially blocked all routes to such knowledge. For the unshakable principle applies: God is absolutely free in His decisions, unfathomable in His will and, above all, cannot be influenced by human action in His decisions. This gave rise to a feeling of extreme insecurity among the faithful. They thus pressed for a way out of this situation, which initially seemed hopeless. Pastoral care ultimately complied with this desire: success in one's occupation was interpreted as a *sign* that one was chosen, though not as the cause of it. The original construction was thus retained, but believers' need for certainty was satisfied as well. An educational approach took hold that radically changed the attitude towards work. Work, and, above all, successful work, received a religious foundation. How one behaved in one's occupation on a daily basis was suddenly of relevance to salvation.

I cannot discuss in detail here the complex explanatory model used by Weber in his study. The most important points can be gleaned from the following schema, which also deploys the multi-level model mentioned above. The crucial point is that the connection between the religious ethic of ascetic Protestantism (context of meaning I) and the 'spirit' of rational capitalism (context of meaning II), which also initially featured an ethical foundation, is not a direct one. It is 'ruptured' by institutional factors on the one hand, and by the subjective appropriation of the basic tenets of the faith by the faithful and their response to it on the other.

As in his analysis of the shift from ancient coastal culture to medieval inland culture, Weber also sees continuity and ruptures in his analysis of the shift from religious to secular inner-worldly asceticism. The link made by ascetic Protestantism between religiously motivated asceticism and one's *worldly* occupation is something new, for previously the only connection made was with one's *spiritual* (not inner-worldly, but other-worldly) vocation. However, the fact that religiously motivated asceticism became culturally significant in the first place, that it may even be understood as work-related asceticism, is not primarily an achievement of ascetic Protestantism. It is an achievement of western monasticism, which it attained long before the Reformation. This encouraged major cultural achievements, not least the agricultural revolution mentioned earlier. Monastic asceticism, however, remained a special morality embedded in a religiously motivated rational conduct of life centred on the overcoming of the world. To a certain extent, it led the faithful out of the world. Protestant asceticism, however, led them into the world and thus to a religiously motivated

Figure 7.2   *The Protestant ethic and the 'spirit' of capitalism*

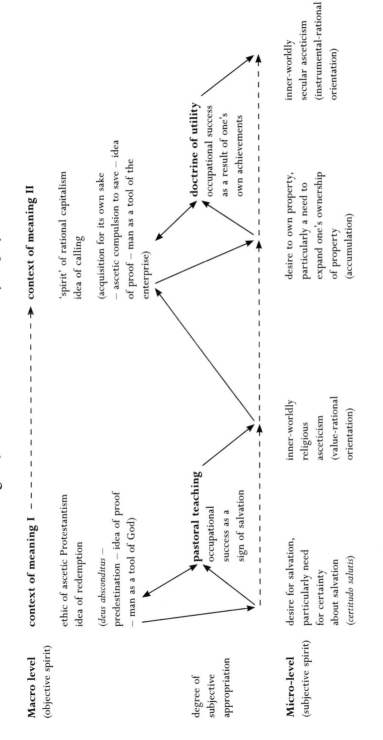

Macro level
(objective spirit)

context of meaning I – – – – – – – – – – – – – – –► **context of meaning II**

ethic of ascetic Protestantism
idea of redemption

(*deus absconditus* –
predestination – idea of proof
– man as a tool of God)

'spirit' of rational capitalism
idea of calling

(acquisition for its own sake
– ascetic compulsion to save – idea
of proof – man as a tool of the
enterprise)

pastoral teaching
occupational
success as a
sign of salvation

doctrine of utility
occupational success
as a result of one's
own achievements

degree of
subjective
appropriation

Micro-level
(subjective spirit)

desire for salvation,
particularly need
for certainty
about salvation
(*certitudo salutis*)

inner-worldly
religious
asceticism
(value-rational
orientation)

desire to own property,
particularly a need to
expand one's ownership
of property
(accumulation)

inner-worldly
secular asceticism
(instrumental-rational
orientation)

Figure 7.3   *Comparison of types of Christian asceticism*

Catholic asceticism	Protestant asceticism
Monastic asceticism	Lay asceticism
Purity through celibacy	*Purity* through and within marriage
Poverty through the renunciation of worldly possessions	*Poverty* through the renunciation of pleasure-loving resting upon worldly possessions
Distance from the world through silence, prayer and work for the glory of God	*Distance* from the world through ceaseless work in one's occupation for the glory of God

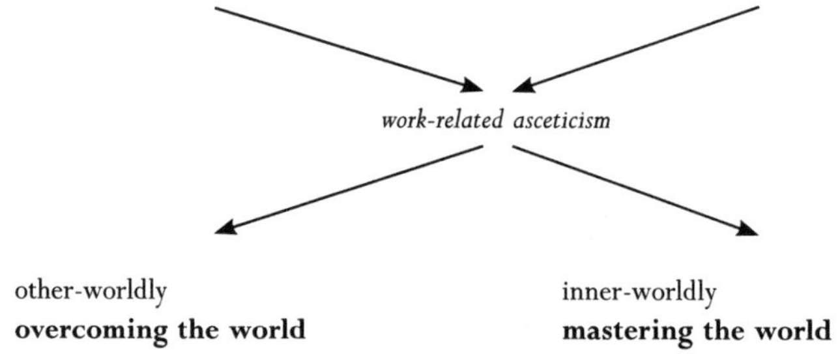

work-related asceticism

other-worldly	inner-worldly
overcoming the world	**mastering the world**

rational conduct of life that privileged the mastering of the world, which was then open to secularization.

Finally, though, Weber goes one step further. He not only sees a continuity between ascetic Protestantism and monastic asceticism and thus between ascetic Protestantism and medieval as well as ancient Christianity – Christian asceticism, he notes, 'had a definitely *rational* character in its highest Occidental forms as early as the Middle Ages, and in several forms even in Antiquity'.[26] He also sees a connection that stretches back much further, namely to ancient Judaism. Here, however, the focus is not so much on asceticism as on morally correct action. In the everyday morality of ancient Judaism, inculcated by the Levites and Prophets, Weber saw a prelude to the 'later official workaday ethic of the Christian West'.[27] Ascetic Protestantism realizes this everyday ethics in a more consistent and therefore more rational way. In the revised version of his study on Protestantism, Weber thus inserted a passage that linked ascetic Protestantism with ancient Judaism: 'That great historic process in the development of religions, the *disenchantment* of the world, which had begun with the old Hebrew

---

[26]   Weber, *The Protestant Ethic*, p. 72.

[27]   Weber, *Ancient Judaism*, p. 296 (translation slightly altered).

prophets and, in conjunction with Hellenistic scientific thought, had repudiated all *magical* means to salvation as superstition and sin, came here to its logical conclusion.'[28]

Ultimately, then, Weber saw many bridges between Antiquity, the Middle Ages, and the early modern period. These consist of institutional inventions and spiritual content. But the contribution of ascetic Protestantism is, nevertheless, independent and indispensable to understanding the modern European cultural world. For in terms of its cultural significance, the ethically based occupational sphere extends far beyond the economy. It forms the basis for a theoretical and, above all, practical rationalism, whose flipside is a moral individualism.

3. Closing Remarks: The Fate of the Idea of Calling

Even in his own day, however, Weber saw the erosion of the ethical foundations of the idea of vocation, of calling. For him, the secularization of this idea was followed by its functional application to the external conditions of work, and it thus ultimately lost its old meaning. Moreover, the rationalism centred on the mastery of the world was never without competition as people wondered how to live their lives. The desire for mediation, for reconciliation, always stood opposed to its strict dualism of *ratio* and nature, not only within its own culture, but beyond it. At the end of his study on Protestantism, as mentioned earlier, Weber also made some highly sceptical observations. For in his view, capitalism, at least its victorious variant resting upon 'mechanical foundations', no longer required the ethically grounded notion of calling: 'No one knows who will live in this cage in the future, or whether at the end of this tremendous development entirely new prophets will arise, or there will be a great rebirth of old ideas and ideals, or, if neither, mechanical petrification.'[29] What else does this mean but that the 'modern European cultural world' also has its dark sides, that, particularly on the basis of the associated cultural phenomena, we are faced with a future that is literally questionable.

We are thus left with a question mark after all. A specific process of rationalization is undoubtedly associated with the modern European cultural world, whose outcome is a theoretical and, above all, practical rationalism of world mastery. Its origins lie in that religious world, and it was from there that it spread around the world. It became universally significant, but is it also generally valid? In light of the history of violence that accompanied this process of rationalization, there is good reason to doubt that it is. Max Weber did so as well.

---

[28] Weber, *The Protestant Ethic*, p. 61.
[29] Weber, *The Protestant Ethic*, p. 182.

Bibliography

Berman, Harold J., *Law and Revolution: The Formation of the Western Legal Tradition* (Cambridge, MA: Harvard University Press, 1983).

Brentano, Lujo, *Die Anfänge des modernen Kapitalismus* (Munich: Akademie der Wissenschaften, 1916).

Cardini, Franco, and M. T. Fumagalli Beonio-Brocchieri, *Universitäten im Mittelalter. Die europäischen Stätten des Wissens* (Munich: Südwest, 2000).

Eisenstadt, Shmuel N., *The Origins and Diversity of Axial Age Civilizations* (Albany, NY: State University of New York Press, 1987).

—, *Kulturen der Achsenzeit. Ihre institutionelle und kulturelle Dynamik* (Frankfurt am Main: Suhrkamp, 1992).

Gerth, H. H., and C. Wright Mills, *From Max Weber: Essays in Sociology* (New York: Oxford University Press, 1946).

Huff, Toby E., *The Rise of Early Modern Science: Islam, China, and the West*, second edition (Cambridge: Cambridge University Press, 2003 [1993]).

Jellinek, Georg, *The Declaration of the Rights of Man and of Citizens: A Contribution to Modern Constitutional History* (Westport, CT: Hyperion Press, 1979 [1895]).

Müller, Rainer A., *Geschichte der Universität. Von der mittelalterlichen Universität zur deutschen Hochschule* (Munich: Nikol, 1990).

Popitz, Heinrich, *Epochen der Technikgeschichte* (Tübingen: Mohr, 1989).

Schluchter, Wolfgang, *Religion und Lebensführung*, vol. 2 (Frankfurt am Main: Suhrkamp, 1988).

Seibt, Ferdinand, *Die Begründung Europas. Ein Zwischenbericht über die letzten tausend Jahre* (Frankfurt am Main: Fischer, 2002).

Troeltsch, Ernst, *The Social Teaching of the Christian Churches* (London: Allen & Unwin, 1931).

—, 'Die Bedeutung des Protestantismus für die Entstehung der modernen Welt', in Troeltsch, *Kritische Gesamtausgabe*, vol. 8 (Berlin and New York: Gruyter, 2001).

Weber, Alfred, 'Kulturgeschichte als Kultursoziologie', in Eberhard Demm (ed.), *Alfred Weber-Gesamtausgabe*, vol. 1 (Marburg: Metropolis, 1997).

Weber, Max, *Gesammelte Aufsätze zur Religionssoziologie*, vol. 1 (Tübingen: Mohr, 1920).

—, *Gesammelte Aufsätze zur Religionssoziologie*, vol. 3 (Tübingen: Mohr, 1920).

—, *Ancient Judaism* (New York: The Free Press, 1952).

—, 'The Social Causes of the Decline of Ancient Civilization', in *The Agrarian Sociology of Ancient Civilizations* (London: NLB, 1976).

—, *The Protestant Ethic and the Spirit of Capitalism* (London and New York: Routledge, 2002).

8

The Affirmation of Ordinary Life

Wolfgang Reinhard

I

When I consider all the unsolicited emails I receive every day, it seems to me that there are two main values for our contemporaries, money and sex, both quite everyday things. Now the world does not, of course, consist solely of spam, but on a somewhat higher level, in the case of professional and economic success measured in monetary terms, and in the case of love, we are in fact dealing with core values of Western culture and society. But they are so normal and everyday that they are scarcely perceived as values that function as guides to action.

However, that such values are nonetheless at play and that they are in fact of key importance becomes immediately clear if we subject our culture and society to the contrast of a longitudinal analysis drawing on history and a cross-sectional one anchored in cultural anthropology. It then emerges that while the everyday production and reproduction of the human being certainly played and continues to play an important role everywhere, these things were not and are not imbued with values in the same way as they are for us. We are clearly dealing with a special characteristic of our culture's value system, a fundamental difference from others, and one with far-reaching consequences.

Someone who has managed to guide a product to market dominance or who has created a successful firm can be rightly and uninhibitedly proud of having achieved something of value.

Someone like myself, a university professor, who has built up a modest scholarly reputation and some very modest family assets, can also claim to have achieved something regarded as valuable in our society.

A person who becomes unemployed while still young feels, in line with our system of values, rightly unhappy, that his life is meaningless; he may even feel like a victim of discrimination, a failure.

In the European Middle Ages, the situation with regard to the evaluation of such facts was very different. To be an enterprising merchant, to carry out one's occupation with ambition and industriousness, to have work was, of course, normal and necessary. But it was not a means of advancing within the world of values characteristic of the culture of the day.

To this end, a successful merchant would have had to found a monastery, a charitable hospital, or sponsor a work of art, which therefore occurred often enough; an official would have to have won a war for his monarch and married his daughter (as in fairytales); a worker had no need to suffer as a result of unemployment and poverty, because these were religiously transfigured. If he was unmarried, he could have entered a mendicant order and become a saint; with respect to values, this was, in fact, to surpass everyone else.

In dealing with values, the key point is thus not so much the reality of life as such, but rather the meaning which people endow it with. For people have, of course, always engaged in economic activity, worked, and loved, albeit in differing ways. This should be made clear from the outset. But the fact that, at some point, these activities were no longer regarded merely as unavoidable necessities but as extremely valuable, as also applies at present, is anything but self-evident. Such a value-shift naturally had consequences for the way in which these activities were carried out and thus for culture and society. We shall be considering this as well.

But first the task at hand requires me to explain, in terms of the topic formulated by the philosopher Charles Taylor,[1] how and why the evaluation of ordinary life, of the productive and reproductive activities carried out by human beings, changed so fundamentally between the fourteenth and seventeenth centuries in southern, central, and western Europe. However, I will have to be content if I can do reasonable justice to the *how*, for the learned continue to argue over the *why*, not only because of their notorious quarrelsomeness, but because it is a far from simple task to explain in terms of logical necessity a fact as complicated as macro-social value change. Here, the humanities have a harder time of it than the natural sciences. They often have to content themselves with the conclusion that a good description is still the best explanation we have to offer.

2

In this spirit, I turn first to the initial context within which this value shift began, the background against which the processes I intend to describe truly stand out. In terms of world history and cultural comparison, value systems differed from our own everywhere; this was hinted at already in our brief look at the European Middle Ages.

---

[1]   In Charles Taylor, *Sources of the Self: The Making of the Modern Identity* (Cambridge: Cambridge University Press, 1989).

Let's begin with the field of human economic activities. Here, it is a good idea to distinguish economy in the sense of money and the market, particularly on a large scale, major production and global trade, from physical labour in agriculture and small-scale commerce. This is because, first, the money economy is a far more recent phenomenon than physical labour, which has been a feature of human life from the very outset, and because there is by no means a consensus as to whether markets in the modern sense have always and everywhere existed. Second, physical labour and the money economy were for this reason long assigned to separate groups of people. In the class and caste societies of East Asia, India, and the European Middle Ages, peasants, artisans, and merchants were separate social groups of differing social status; it was hard to move from one to the other, something which was certainly looked upon with disapproval.

This brings us to a significant difference between the pre-modern and modern value system. In all pre-modern societies, the forms of life most highly valued within society as a whole and those components of culture considered values in themselves were the property of the higher groups and classes of the society. Work was not among them. The ancient Greeks and Romans and the elites of other advanced civilizations were, of course, aware of the necessity of human labour and were certainly capable of valuing its results, but it would never have occurred to them to view it, in all its everyday banality, as a form of self-realization that makes life meaningful. It was not the bourgeois principle, *work ennobles*, that held sway at the time, but the notion that *work makes you mean*. In many European countries, a nobleman who had got it into his head to do the work of a peasant or artisan or to run a shop would automatically have lost his class affiliation, becoming a common man (a *gemeiner Mann*, as it was put in sixteenth-century Germany, *gemein* meaning both 'common' and 'mean').

The Middle Ages were all too well aware that God had condemned Man to work as punishment for the Fall, while women had to suffer pregnancy and birth (Genesis 3:16–19). In Middle High German, the word *arebeit* cropped up rather rarely, for it meant toil and misery, as in the *Nibelungenlied* for example. The French *travail* and its English counterpart of the same spelling are even supposedly derived from the late Latin *tripalium*; this was an instrument of torture. In line with this, work was defined by a French dictionary simply as demanding and tiring activity as late as 1724. While the principle *ora et labora*, pray and work, applied in the Benedictine monasteries, even there, work was not the substance of life, but penance. But it did attain a certain spiritual worth, a certain value, in this way.

The apostle Paul censured idleness and propagated the famous principle: 'if anyone is not willing to work, let him not eat' (2 Thessalonians 3:10), but this still did not mean that he was praising work. For Jesus, son of a carpenter, is never described as working. He seems to have lived as something of a dropout, had a higher opinion of the contemplative Mary than the busy Martha (Luke 10:38) and praised the birds of the sky and the lilies of the field, which neither toil nor spin, and yet which, thanks to the heavenly Father, are better clothed than Solomon in all his magnificence (Matthew 6:25).

In line with this, the leading theologian of the high Middle Ages, Thomas Aquinas, has a highly prosaic rather than ideal notion of work. In his opinion, it serves four very concrete aims: first, making a living (note, not yet to increase family property; this motif appears only with the recognition of social mobility towards the end of the Middle Ages). Second, the avoidance of idleness, the well-known source of many vices. Third, along the same lines, the curbing of the desires of the flesh, because work weakens the lustfulness of the body. Fourth, acquisition of the means necessary to alms-giving (*Summa Theologiae* 2 II, q. 187, a. 3).

On the other hand, for him the highest value of all, namely eternal bliss in the beyond, consisted in the *visio beatifica*, in the ceaseless contemplation of God, a kind of eternal contemplative state of leisure. The medieval writer Dante Alighieri had no trouble imagining what this might involve in his *Divine Comedy*. This system of values corresponded perfectly to that of European culture at the time and, with appropriate modification, that of most pre-modern advanced civilizations, including not least that of the ancient Greeks and Romans, whose intellectual world, of course, had a decisive impact on European history, including Christianity. And as I have outlined, the various social orders, the various types of social stratification, faithfully mirrored this system of values.

The first estate of old European society was the clergy. They, above all the monks in the monasteries, were supposed to have leisure time at their disposal to pray, meditate, as well as for intellectual activity, to write and copy books, from which modern scholarship was ultimately derived, a field which until recently was also informed by the principle of creative leisure. The second estate, the nobility, was originally the warrior class, destined to win honour through bravery. However, corporative honour, detached from martial activity and having become an end in itself as the second highest value in the west, could become sterile and morally problematic. It is no accident that *superbia*, pride or arrogance, was considered the worst of sins in the high Middle Ages.

In India, analogously, the performers of sacrifice, the Brahmans, were the highest caste, the warriors and rulers the second, each featuring activities to match. The highest value of all, occupying the place of the *visio beatifica* in the life beyond found in Christianity, but rather similar structurally, was the foregoing of all activity, even mental engagement, and the extinguishing of the self, becoming one with the world soul or reaching Nirvana. In Japan, the Buddhist monks had to take second place behind the Samurai warrior caste as the first estate, while in China a non-religious and highly prosaic form of leisure stood at the pinnacle of the system of values, the erudition of the Confucian elite, from which the officials who governed the empire were recruited. Though there was no similarly developed hierarchy of classes, among the Greeks and, in their wake, the Romans, scholarly *theoria*, reflection upon God and the world, was also placed highest within the value system. But for ancient men, at least in classical times, before their monarchs had deprived them of their rights, the good life included a second value, political activity, the highly demanding participation in the life of the polis, the polity. Both required a great deal of leisure, a great deal of free time, such that, economically speaking, the classical citizen of the polis could be no more than a part-time worker.

In each case, others did the heavy work, primarily the slaves in classical Antiquity, in other settings the peasants and urban underclasses. In this respect it is revealing that the peasants in China and Japan, however unfavourable their lot may have been in practice, were placed immediately behind the elite in the theory of the social value hierarchy. In ancient China, in contrast to the west and Japan, warriors were not particularly highly valued as a class. And merchants, however rich they might be, were the lowest, most despised social class in China and Japan.

In the west, too, trade and commerce had a poor reputation, which was by no means of purely Christian origin, but which can once again be traced back to Antiquity, and to Aristotle in particular. First, transactions beyond immediate household needs tended to be seen as immoral; anyone carrying them out was automatically suspected of enriching himself unjustly by charging extortionate prices. Second, this was bound up with the fact that most of the goods being sold were luxuries not directly necessary to life (it was not worth trading in cheaper ones), and their sale consequently had both the whiff of sinful temptation and of the irresponsible waste of scarce resources. And, third, as far as lending money at interest was concerned, it was not clear why money should multiply in this way without its original owner having done anything, quite apart from biblical prohibitions. In this regard it is noteworthy that strict Muslims still reject the charging of interest and have constructed an alternative banking system in some Islamic countries.

On the whole, while work and the market economy were accepted as unavoidable in pre-modern times, they were nearly always seen as necessary evils, and were far from being endowed with any kind of value. And where this did occur in nascent form, as in the monastic principle of *ora et labora*, these values were of a different origin, related not to this activity itself, but to a higher purpose quite alien to it, penance in the case of monks.

Many Greek citizens of the polis, to give another example, were not content to become rich through production and trade and merely to enjoy life. Rather, a conduct very much informed by market economics in terms of income contrasted with what would seem to us absurd squandering of resources in terms of expenditure. People would spend vast sums on public institutions in their own city, such as buildings, which would otherwise never have come into being, with the sole purpose of obtaining an inscription in their honour or even having a statue dedicated to them as their fellow citizens expressed their gratitude following a vote by all members of the commonwealth. Once again we are confronted with honour as the highest or second-highest value, entirely alien to economics. Anthropology has taught us that such behaviour is by no means out of the ordinary. The so-called *potlatch* found among the Indians of America's north-west coast was particularly famous. These were absolute orgies of gift-giving and the destruction of valuable goods with the sole purpose of enhancing one's standing and humiliating rivals unable to afford such things. On a more limited scale, such conduct was also a matter of course for the European aristocracy, including many monarchs. While the money was often already acquired by fairly modern means, it was spent with unbridled generosity in order to practise the monarchical and aristocratic virtue of *liberalitas*, munificence, and thus obtain honour.

In much the same way as work and economics, love as such was not imbued with value but served other, higher values. I repeat: sexuality in all its unusual varieties has, of course, always existed, there have always been lovers, husbands, and wives who love each other, and there has always been parental love for children, regardless of cultural differences in detail. But none of that constituted a value as such; it was either a mere means to an end or, at most, a more or less tolerated practice without significance in itself. The aim of reproduction and a key value, towards which everything within this sphere was geared, was the family, its maintenance and future survival. As intimated earlier, work and economic activity were also carried out with the family in mind; profit became suspicious the moment it exceeded that which was necessary to the upkeep of the family, the so-called domestic economy.

History and anthropology are replete with accounts of different family and household forms. But in the overwhelming majority of cases, the families in question are male-dominated. The gendered division of labour, common across the world, which has lost its validity only in modern times, and which allocated household 'domestic policy' to the woman and 'foreign policy' to the man, with the latter including not least politics in the true sense of the word and military activities, by no means led in principle and everywhere to the complete repression and disempowerment of women as a result of patriarchy, as radical feminists would have us believe. In pre-modern Europe at least, the housewife could certainly attain the important position of second-in-command. But there is no doubt that men dominated there as well.

But this means that the re-evaluation of love as a relationship in the spirit of partnership, based on reciprocity, presupposes a certain degree of emancipation of women. This was more difficult than achieving a re-evaluation of the economic activities of men. For this reason, the re-evaluation of love met with greater resistance and took longer; I therefore have less to say about it for the fourteenth to seventeenth centuries.

It is said that love, as a phenomenon imbued with value, was invented in the twelfth century, in two settings: as a mystical relation with God, featuring very concrete sexual symbolism in the monasteries, and as a cult of the woman transfigured in a literary sense by the minnesingers and the troubadours; in both cases, this process of invention was bound up with a certain emancipation of women. It is immediately apparent, however, that we are dealing here with exceptional elite behaviour and that there can be absolutely no question of a re-evaluation of the everyday love life.

On the contrary, the normal husband was in no way expected to love his wife in a passionate way. Passion was considered fornication and, if applicable, was reserved for extra-marital relations, but rather than valuable, these were considered reprehensible. It is anything but accidental that legal and accepted sexual intercourse bore the lovely name 'the conjugal duty'. Even a contemporary as 'enlightened' as the French sceptic Michel de Montaigne, towards the end of the sixteenth century, remained explicitly attached to this view of things, and he was not alone in this.

3

My observations so far were intended to show that from a historical perspective, the affirmation of ordinary life, the high value placed on everyday production and reproduction, is anything but self-evident. Not this affirmation but its opposite, a quite different world of values, which I have briefly described, was the norm. Thus, strictly speaking, it is *our* evaluation that requires explanation rather than that of others, for the latter is to some extent 'normal', while the affirmation of ordinary life, with its profound consequences, is the exception.

You may be astonished to hear that we tend to look for the roots of this phenomenon in the development of the Judeo-Christian tradition between the fourteenth and seventeenth centuries, and not so much in the simultaneous revival of classical Antiquity, which is associated with humanism and the Renaissance. But in light of what has been said about the theory- and leisure-oriented culture of Antiquity, it should be clear why the decisive impetus could not come from there. Incidentally, this is true also because, once again, humanism and Renaissance were highly elite phenomena, whose achievements could not smoothly gain general status. In contrast, at the time, Christianity was still of concern to everyone because it was taken for granted. Everyone was affected by its processes of change, which are generally described as late medieval Church reform, Reformation, and Counter-Reformation, though these traditional terms no longer correspond precisely to the current state of scholarly debate. But this is of no concern to us here.

The Christian roots of this revolution in values only *appear* to clash with the well-known fact that we are dealing here with values that have long been entirely secular. In fact, the modern evaluation of work and sexuality in its further developed secular form is only now being imported back into the Churches. But the apparent contradiction vanishes when we realize that history tends to proceed in dialectical rather than linear fashion. This means that things secular and things Christian may be derived from sources other than secular and Christian ones, respectively, that through unintended side-effects of human action something may arise that is alien, even opposed, to the original intention. In the opinion of the sociologist Max Weber, Calvinists longing for certainty about their eternal salvation brought about capitalism, though they had not the slightest intention of doing so.

We require the trope of dialectic in order to understand why, paradoxically, it was none other than the sublime Judeo-Christian notion of God that ultimately caused the re-evaluation of everyday life and thus our modern-day secular system of values. Incidentally, Judeo-Christian means that while the foundations were laid by Judaism, they were not conveyed to Europe directly from this source, but chiefly through Christianity. The Judeo-Christian God is, in essence, transcendent, that is, He is not part of the world, but is to be found beyond it, and He created it out of nothing, separate from Himself. While the world of other religions is populated and inhabited by divine beings or is even itself God, the Judeo-Christian world has a certain autonomy, is only indirectly subject to God, and may ultimately even be conceived as godless, as is the case today. The world loses its magic, as Max Weber wrote. Among other things, this means that the world may follow its own laws and develop its own worldly values, which are initially still under indirect divine rule, but which certainly entail a tendency towards the gaining of total independence. In abstract terms, this is precisely the process with which we are concerned here.

Naturally, the question immediately arises as to why the worldly affirmation of ordinary life needed to take hold if it was already in place from the outset. According to the philosopher Charles Taylor, this is due to the way the original Christian message was overlaid with Greek thought, in other words Greek values, after the expectation, fundamental to the early Christians, that the world was about to end and Christ set to return had been disappointed. We are already familiar with one Greek value, the high estimation of the theoretical worldview

l concurrent disdain for the everyday, active practice of living. The other
isists in the veiled return of the idea that God is present in the world, as a

result of the penetration of the Neo-Platonic idea of a complicated hierarchy of semi-divine beings present everywhere, the angels, or the Stoic idea of God as a kind of world soul. This also means that the affirmation of ordinary life was, from the outset, present in nascent form in the Christian Gospel and had only to be developed.

4

I begin with the best researched field, that of economics, first with work and the related transition from the traditional ideal of contemplative leisure to the positive evaluation of an active life.

St Augustine and other Church Fathers of late Antiquity still very much thought of human labour as a joyful extension of divine creation, and by no means merely as miserable toil due to divine damnation. But this perspective receded when, with the corporative distinction between clergy and laity, the contemplative life of the clergy, above all, monks, was valorized, and the active life of the laity correspondingly devalued. Medieval theology was a theology of the clergy and those in holy orders; it scarcely concerned itself with the laity. Those who complied with the so-called 'evangelical counsels' of poverty, chastity, and obedience and even lived apart from the wicked world in a monastery, automatically found themselves in a state of perfection. To put it rather maliciously, the theologians, who enjoyed interpretive sovereignty over Christian teaching, exercised it to the advantage of their own class. It thus takes a bit of effort to unearth the simple and concurrently existing theological affirmation that the calling to eternal salvation applies to all, though it might be easier for those in orders thanks to their particular way of life. But if the common people, who have to do some work, faithfully carry it out, then it, too, is in the service of God; because they, too, are called to eternal salvation (*per vocationem*), it is their divinely legitimized occupation. 'Useful and honest work is also pleasing to God', preached Berthold of Regensburg as early as the thirteenth century.

It is thus by no means the case that, in emphasizing this idea, the Reformers, particularly Martin Luther, were the first to consecrate professional work, and by re-evaluating everyday labour in this way created the modern concept of occupation, as some have claimed. They were merely propagating a teaching that had long existed. In fact, in a certain respect they immediately withdrew again this affirmation of everyday life due to the radical nature of their theology. For work is a cross which a Christian must bear in obedience to his faith, though this cannot contribute anything to his salvation. God alone is the cause, the human being no more than His marionette. This clear-cut teaching stood in contrast with the rather nebulous teaching of the old Church, according to which God is indeed the first cause (*causa prima*), but the human being is at least the second cause (*causa secunda*) and as such, by dint of his free will, may contribute to his own salvation and that of the world. While no-one was quite sure how this worked in concrete terms, as a trope it was nonetheless fundamental to the re-evaluation of professional work.

The Reformation, however, contributed crucially to this re-evaluation in a different way, namely through the theological and subsequently practical elimination of the clerical class in general, and the monastic class in particular. Justification through faith alone, mediated by direct access to the Scriptures, rendered the entire ecclesiastical apparatus of salvation and its extensive personnel superfluous. As the Reformers saw things, monastic life also wrongly appealed to the evangelical counsels, it was in reality anything but pleasing to God. The old teaching that any activity performed well was an occupation pleasing to God could at last gain the upper hand.

The polemical offensive against the idle monks and clerics brought about a re-evaluation of the manual labour carried out by peasants and artisans. While this was a temporary development, for in the Protestant churches as well the pastors soon re-emerged as the leading group, not required to perform manual labour, it coincided with the growing self-awareness of the working population and thus had a significant impact. For alongside the traditional work of the peasants new forms of work had developed in the cities, industrial, but also commercial and intellectual. Alongside the various servants in noble, urban, and rural households, there were now journeymen and apprentices plus the members of artisan families who helped the artisan with his work; there was the new wage labour, which lacked an educational element and any prospect of advancing up the occupational ladder; and finally, there was rural outwork, above all in the textiles industry.

The typical contempt for and mockery of the peasant changed into the notion that the manual labour of the peasant rather than the idleness of the monk was the most perfect way of life. In line with this, Luther's colleague in Wittenberg, Professor Andreas Karlstadt, gave up his chair and became a peasant. The shrewd peasant was a standard Protestant character in the pamphlets of the Reformation era. The Swiss in particular contrasted peasant virtues with aristocratic vices. The peasant movement, which was to reach its peak in the Peasants' War of 1525, targeted not only the clerics, but also the nobility. But the bourgeois critique of the aristocracy also pulled no punches, particularly in its digs at idleness and the high value placed on manual labour:

> When Adam ploughed and Eve spun
> wherever was the nobleman?

In the fable of the lazy cricket and the industrious ant, the ant addresses the cricket from time to time as 'Junker', that is, a nobleman. Those deploying this fable to critical ends could, after all, refer to the Bible, which states in the Book of Proverbs (6:6–11):

> Go to the ant, O sluggard; consider her ways, and be wise.
> Without having any chief, officer, or ruler,
> she prepares her bread in summer
> and gathers her food in harvest.
> How long will you lie there, O sluggard [...] ?
> Poverty will come upon you like a robber

The Peasants' War passed, but the re-evaluation of manual labour proved so enduring that it could constantly be referred back to, as occurred in a book on agriculture from 1596. I would like to present you with an illustration from it here (Fig 1).[2] For this is a very special example of the affirmation of everyday life which takes a subject of ancient mythology, something quite out of the ordinary that has practically nothing to do with rural labour, reinterprets it as the symbol of and thus uses it to re-evaluate such labour. At least in Germany, something like this would have been scarcely conceivable 100 years earlier.

What we are dealing with here is a representation of the god Mithras, found in much the same form in countless cult centres, so-called Mithraea, all over Europe. For the cult of Mithras enjoyed such popularity, particularly among the Roman military of late Antiquity, that people even speculated about whether it may have been the most dangerous rival to Christianity as future religion of the empire. Be that as it may, the originally Persian god was transformed into a sun god in the Roman Empire and worshipped as cosmic bringer of salvation. In this role, he is depicted by the standard representation which we see here, the details of which are by no means entirely clear because of the secret nature of this religion. In the upper left we have the sun god, in the upper right the moon goddess on her chariot, and between them seven altars, which may be intended to embody the three phases of day and the four phases of the moon. The two torch-bearers to the left represent the day (above) and the night (below), reflected in how they are holding their torches. The main image, as ever, shows the god Mithras, kneeling on a bull, grasping its mouth and killing it with a stab to the neck, causing much blood to flow. A dog, a lion, and a snake are also involved, a scorpion is pinching the poor animal's genitals, while a bird, presumably a raven, looks down on the scene. The mythological significance of the various animals is not entirely understood.

---

[2]   Borrowed from Konrad Wiedemann, *Arbeit und Bürgertum. Die Entwicklung des Arbeitsbegriffs in der Literatur Deutschlands an der Wende der Neuzeit* (Heidelberg: Winter, 1979), p. 298.

DESIGNATIO PICTVRÆ, OFFICIVM BONI
COLONI EXPRIMENTIS.

But in any case, our concern is solely with how our author chooses to interpret this material in the legend below. For him, it symbolically expresses the activity which it is the good farmer's duty to carry out (*officium boni coloni exprimentis*). Mithras mutates into the best and most diligent peasant (K = *terrae colonus, optimus et diligens agricola*), the bull (L) represents the earth that is to be cultivated, the sword (M) our topic, namely the work done by the peasant, the blood (N) the fertilization of the earth which this brings about, while the various animals are intended to embody primarily positive qualities of the splendid farmer, the raven care, the dog love and loyalty, the snake foresight, etc. There is no doubt about our author's high regard for peasant labour.

Alongside peasant labour, the work of the artisan, and indeed his entire way of life, was also re-evaluated, in the writings of the Nuremberger Hans Sachs for example. Alongside the noble concept of honour, there was now a specific German artisans' honour. This entailed diligence and sound work, thrift, moderation in eating and drinking, and a strict sexual morality. The unmarried were, for example, discriminated against in a way that was not common elsewhere. Artisans were, of course, already diligent and their lives were no more dissolute than those of others. But now an explicit system of values was established. Thanks to Lyndal Roper, we now know that this late medieval petit bourgeois value system was legitimated and validated by the Reformation.[3]

The link made by Max Weber in 1904/1905 between Calvinism and a capitalism of a more haut bourgeois character in his famous essay *The Protestant Ethic and the Spirit of Capitalism* is, of course, better known. According to Calvin, God could control the world directly, but He wishes, very much in line with my earlier remarks on God's transcendence, to use people as His instruments. This is the value of work, even if the human being, as in the writings of Luther, remains a mere marionette of God. For according to the inexorable doctrine of predestination, who is to be saved and who damned has been decided for all eternity. While the decision has been made and it thus makes no difference what the believer does, if he leads a virtuous life and does good works, this may be an indication that he is among the elect. In this respect, it made sense for Calvinists to keep an exact record of the everyday doings of their own lives, for this creation of a written record of their rationally controlled way of life was nothing other than the means of providing themselves with religious reassurance.

It was not Calvin himself but his epigones, who lacked the self-confident piety of the Reformer, who made use of this idea in order to obtain by force certainty – in an inner-worldly sense – about their status as elect, by means of a rationally organized, virtuous way of life. For the special virtuousness of the monastic flight

---

[3]   Lyndal Roper, *The Holy Household: Women and Morals in Reformation Augsburg* (Oxford Clarendon, 1989).

from the world had been abolished. Because the success of this inner-worldly version of an ascetic lifestyle was gauged, according to Weber, primarily in terms of economic success, this liberated the entrepreneurial acquisition of goods from the traditional agonies of conscience mentioned earlier, not in order to enjoy such goods, but only to engage in further self-denying accumulation. On this view, when the religious impulse receded and finally disappeared, because it had become a habit that shaped people's behaviour, all that remained was the capitalist spirit as a compulsion to acquire for its own sake. In Weber's own words: 'the Puritan *wished* to pursue a profession – we *have to* do so'.

Now this idea of Weber's is certainly inherently logical and thus still very welcome to some capitalists of Calvinist origin as a historical justification of their activities. But unfortunately it is empirically unsustainable. First, it has been shown that Weber misinterpreted the theoretical texts on which he based his argument. Second, most Calvinists were very far from identifying the success of their inner-worldly asceticism with economic success. The opposite is true. In the supposedly highly Calvinist Netherlands, bankers who lent money at interest were sometimes excluded from Communion as sinners, which would generally have provoked merriment in Catholic Italy.

We can still follow Weber as far as the theological foundation of a rational and industrious way of life is concerned, but no longer with respect to the foundation of capitalism, which is not, of course, identical with it. In cases where Protestants *ceteris paribus* (as the economists say) have nonetheless proved economically superior to Catholics, this was probably an unintended side-effect of their particularly pronounced affirmation of an ascetic working life, linked with the habit of providing for themselves in matters of eternal salvation, which could easily be carried over to temporal existence. Such links may be demonstrated.

Above all, though, it is possible to show that there was a concurrent Catholic affirmation of ordinary life, a highly prominent one in fact, whose roots, remarkably enough, lie in theological attempts made within the old Church to accommodate the concerns of the Reformers. Its most potent expression is surely aphorism No. 251 in the moral *oráculo manual* ('oracular manual') produced by the Spanish Jesuit Baltasar Gracián in 1647, which states: 'One must deploy human means as if there were no divine means, and [at the same time] divine means as if there were no human means (*Hanse de procurar los medios humanos como se no hubiese divinos, y los divinos como se no hubiese humanos*).' This is underpinned by the theological model of so-called double justification, realized first by means of God's undeserved mercy and then in good works carried out in a state of grace. A certain kinship with the thought of Calvin is unmistakable here. In line with this, the Council of Trent rejected this teaching, but it clearly endured for at least another century. Significantly, what we are seeing here is the practice of keeping a record of one's own works that we met earlier among the Calvinists.

This is a Catholic theology of living in the world, as taught already in a different way, in a form both orthodox and pragmatic, by François de Sales in 1609 in his *Introduction to a Devoute Life* for lay people. His target group was primarily distinguished lay people, including aristocratic ladies, but his teaching was more widely applicable. He, too, takes on the false notion that one can be truly pious only as a priest, monk, or nun, just like the Reformers, but as the Catholic bishop he was, he is, of course, less radical. In his own words:

> [W]hen it [devotion] goes contrary to our lawful vocation, then without doubt it is false. [...] True devotion [...] does no injury to any vocation or employment, but on the contrary it adorns and beautifies it. [...] The care of the family is rendered more peaceable, the love of the husband and wife more sincere, the service to the prince more faithful and every type of employment more pleasant and agreeable. [...] All these things are the will of God [...]. Of the virtues, we must give preference to those which correspond to the duties of our vocation [... for every] vocation demands its own special virtues. [...] Let us leave sublimity to the sublime souls; we [...] ought to be blissfully happy if we work [in the service of God] in the kitchen or bakery, if we are allowed to be his lackeys, porters and servants. The great opportunities to serve God are rare; there is never any lack of small ones. But he who is faithful over a little, the Saviour tells us [in the Parable of the Talents, Matthew 25:21], will be placed above much. Thus, do everything in the name of God [Collosians 3:17] and it will be done well. Whether you are eating or drinking [1 Corinthians 10:31], resting or cooking: if you do your work well, you will be of much use before God, if you do everything because God asks it of you.[4]

However, whether Lutheran, Reformed, or Catholic, everywhere the new value of work lies not in work itself, the content of which is thus fundamentally irrelevant (this is where Max Weber went wrong), but in the insight that God's will is done through work. Italian humanists had already gone further than this from the late fifteenth century on by declaring human creativity, and thus the content of work itself, a continuation of God's creation. The best-known voice here is that of Giovanni Pico della Mirandola, whose treatise *Oration on the Dignity of Man* (*De hominis dignitate*) from 1487, with its grandiose optimism, stands in conscious contrast to the anthropological pessimism that characterized not only

---

[4]   Francis of Sales (François de Sales), *Philothea. Einführung in das religiöse Leben* (*Introduction à la vie dévote*) (Eichstätt and Vienna: Franz-Sales-Verlag, 1981). Trans. based in part on Francis of Sales, *An Introduction to a Devoute Life* (London: Scolar, 1976), pp. 40–1.

the religious tradition of the Middle Ages, but also the theology of the Reformers. Medieval treatises were called *On the Misery of Man* (*De miseria hominis*). Pico even went so far as to declare the human being, made in the image of God the Creator, not only the creator of the world, but even the creator of himself – the modern principle of self-realization through activity is now with us. Such ideas may have caused offence among theologians of various backgrounds, but this by no means makes them un-Christian and purely secular in the sense in which this concept was understood in the early Renaissance. They were of good Christian rather than ancient origin. Hints to this effect are even found in the work of Calvin.

On a practical level, this resulted in praise for technology as a means by which the human being, through his work, could harness nature in the service of the good life. The architect Leon Battista Alberti expressed something similar as early as 1450. In this spirit, the Alsatian Johann Fischart declared his boundless faith in the power of human labour in 1576, when he produced the rather clumsy poem:

> For there is nothing hard or sharp
> That cannot be subjugated by work
> Nothing is so awkward
> That it cannot be resolved through work
> That which idleness considers impossible
> Is easily overcome through work.[5]

Though he was a Protestant, Fischart went further in his faith in work and technology than all his contemporaries. Among others things, he no longer referred to God when praising work.

Because work was no longer cross and suffering as it had been for the Reformers, but rather a joyful and creative activity, it was also possible for the ancient and taken-for-granted link between work and poverty to dissolve; to put it very simplistically, until then, only those who had needed to work did so. This development was, of course, fostered by the fact that work had long been more than just manual labour. The self-evident allocation of work to specific classes came undone, as did the associated self-evident notion that the good life could only be a life of leisure, a pious life one of contemplation. We have already seen that François de Sales grappled with this idea in the early seventeenth century.

In the fifteenth century Antonino Pierozzi, an influential preacher of the

---

[5]   'Dann nichts ist also schwer und scharff / Das nicht die arbeit unterwarf / Nichts mag kaum sein so ungelegen / Welchs nicht die arbeit bringt zuwegen / Was die Faulheit halt für unmüglich / Das überwind die Arbeit füglich.'

Dominican order and archbishop in the Florence of the Medici, had already tussled, successfully, with the problem of how an active working life could be justified theologically with respect to the contemplative ideal that had applied hitherto. In Florence, a focal point of big industry and early capitalism, he clearly had no other option. He, too, of course fell back initially on the proverbial ant mentioned in the Bible. But he came up with other ideas, first promulgating a mixed way of life on the model of Jesus Christ, who famously withdrew into solitude on many occasions in order to pray, but then went back to running around, as Antoninus literally states (discurrebat), in order to pray, heal the sick, make loaves multiply, and so on. For him, this is because the process by which the Son of God became human was nothing other than God's becoming active in the world. In his exegesis of the psalm verse 'Man goes out to his work and to his labour until the evening' (Psalm 104:23) he interprets human labour as follows: 'man realizes himself in relation to his work and to that which he has produced by the end of the day, that is, by the evening of his life'.[6]

It says a great deal about the changed attitude to activity that the most important new order produced by the Catholic Church as it came to terms with the new era, the Society of Jesus, was from the very beginning geared towards an active life in the world in contrast to the ancient tradition of monastic life. The Jesuits were characterized by intensive spiritual and psychological moulding and strict discipline, and no longer by life-long affiliation to a community in one place with an unchanging daily routine regulated down to the fine details. The Church leaders granted the Jesuits this degree of freedom to engage in activity in the world with reservations, and it was denied implacably to all women who tried to establish analogous female orders without seclusion. Once again, for women the affirmation of everyday life required more lead time. Nonetheless, the Catholic Church played its part in re-evaluating the working individual active in the everyday life of the world.

The dissolution of the corporative order began earliest in England; a market for the wage labour of independent individuals not only developed, but was also perceived as such. It is thus no accident, in light of the re-evaluation of human labour that had already occurred, that a modern concept of work was formed in this milieu by John Locke in 1690 within the context of the economic boom of the late seventeenth century. He combined it with the second key concept of modern economics, property. The person is now seen as an autonomous individual and is thus considered initially to be the owner of himself. In consequence, his labour and its results, which he achieves by processing the raw materials provided by nature, are also indisputably his property and not at the disposal of third

---

[6]   Peter Francis Howard, *Beyond the Written Word: Preaching and Theology in the Florence of Archbishop Antoninus, 1427–1459* (Florence: Olschki, 1995), p. 245.

parties. Labour became one's inalienable personal property and the foundation of an independent existence based on work – an anthropological revolution in economics.

Before long, it was even possible to read in a 'devotional book for the female sex':[7]

> You have created all of us to live a life of service to the community, O God, a life of work and blissful happiness [...] industriousness is one of the main reasons You called me into existence[!] and gave me my rational life. Activity is the only true life[!].

For the new concept of work produced by the Enlightenment, which ultimately made the dignity of every individual dependent on doing appropriate work for which he himself was responsible, came at just the right moment for the aspiring bourgeoisie. Thanks to the re-evaluation of everyday life, it was now possible to counter the ongoing arrogance of the aristocratic disdain for work with a contempt for aristocratic idleness, a contempt legitimized by one's own work. In line with this, in the 'Song of the Bell' (*Lied von der Glocke*) Friedrich Schiller wrote:

> Work's the burgher's decoration,
> Labour's prize is to be blest;
> Honour kings by royal station,
> Busy hands us honour best.[8]

5

We have said almost nothing so far about monetary activities, particularly large-scale, long-distance trade and financial transactions. We were in fact forced to cut the link which Max Weber established between theology and capitalism as unfounded. From a historical perspective, it was far more difficult to affirm these activities than work and inner-worldly activity generally. This is not only because there was no place for trade and financial transactions in the value systems of the advanced civilizations in general, but also because of Europe's particular prehistory, in which Greeks and Christians had equally little time for such things. When Martin Luther praises manual labour, he is polemicizing not only against the idleness of the monks, but also against the merchants' profits,

---

[7]   J. G. Marezoll, *Andachtsbuch für das weibliche Geschlecht* (Leipzig, 1798), quoted in Wiedemann, *Arbeit und Bürgertum*, p. 30.

[8]   'Arbeit ist des Bürger Zierde, / Segen ist der Mühe Preis; / Ehrt den König seine Würde, / Ehret uns der Hände Fleiß.'

obtained without effort on their part, whom he, very traditionally, suspected of practising usury.

Yet large trading and banking firms of a capitalist character already existed in thirteenth-century Italy. Long-distance trade and financial transactions set the tone for a long time to come; only in the eighteenth and nineteenth centuries did goods production become the key factor in economic development. They were, of course, accepted as an aspect of reality, but retained unambiguously negative associations from the perspective of the value system. The leading high medieval theologian Thomas Aquinas treated such transactions as sins against justice (*Summa Theologiae* 2 II, q. 118; 1 II, q. 77, a. 4, q. 78), applying the key term *avaritia* ('avarice'; the alternative German translation *Geiz* also means 'avarice' in Old German). For in place of the aristocratic *superbia*, pride or arrogance, bourgeois *avaritia*, avarice, had now attained the status of society's key vice.

The avaricious pursuit of profit is a sin because it offends against due moderation, which allows only that which is necessary to a life befitting one's place in the social hierarchy. This moderation is necessary because one person cannot have a surplus without another suffering from want. The idea of economic growth was as yet unknown; goods were seen as a cake of unvarying extent which must be divided up. According to Thomas, trade that serves to provide people with necessities and ensure one's own subsistence through moderate profit is allowed, while trade involving the limitless pursuit of profit and speculation is as sinful as the charging of interest. For the correct use of money consists in spending it to acquire goods necessary to life.

Scholastic casuistry found many routes to reconciling early capitalist practice with these strict principles, at least to some extent. The papacy itself was a financial power, which successfully developed a highly modern system of public credit. But rather than affirmation, all of this was toleration. The same applied within the Church of Rome into the twentieth century. And we have seen already that the Reformers, too, were anything but protagonists of modern capitalism. Even according to Max Weber, they became such *despite* their real intentions. In this regard, Christianity offered little toehold for the affirmation of ordinary life; the impetus had to come from the worldly realm, while attempts were made to latch it to the affirmation of the working world that I have dealt with here.

In 1428 in Florence, the centre of early capitalism, the humanist Poggio Bracciolini wrote a *Dialogue against Avarice* (*Dialogus contra avaritiam*). This features a defence of avarice, which is dutifully rejected, yet the reader comes away with the impression, as so often in the humanists' dialogues, that the author's sympathies lie on the opposing side. Avarice is natural, useful, and necessary because it causes individuals to provide themselves with the goods necessary to life. Everyone, particularly the great figures of history, wants to obtain more than he needs (this is the classical definition of avarice according to Augustine); almost no-one strives to advance the common good. But it is only this surplus that allows alms-giving, sociability, works of art, the beautification of cities, and the maintenance of the polity.

The first to *openly* defend commercial capitalism was the Augsburg humanist Conrad Peutinger, at a time when the business of the large firms of Augsburg – he was married to Margarete Welser – was threatened by the project of an anti-monopoly law cleverly launched by Ausgburg's competitors from Nuremberg in 1530. Provisions were made for a ban on certain transactions, an upper limit on company assets, and regular public supervision. Explicit reference was made to the fact that, instead of a large firm, twenty to thirty smaller merchants could make a living. Peutinger disputes the accusations levelled against the large firms, before launching a counter-attack by claiming that their risky activities and high capital expenditure contribute significantly to general prosperity and tax revenue, in other words to the common good. Their business must therefore remain unhindered, for who would wish to expose themselves to risk if there was no prospect of profit?

Still, he went on to safeguard the pursuit of profit against the accusation of contemptible self-interest by referring to its value to the commonweal. But as early as 1564, Leonhard Fronsperger, a military writer by trade, did without this obligatory act in his little book *In Praise of Self-interest* (*Von dem Lob deß Eigen Nutzen*) and simply claims that there is no such thing as public interest, that the whole world, marriage and family, economy and science, is kept in motion by self-interest: self-interest creates and works in such a way that nothing on earth is lacking. Even religion is based on self-interest, namely the hope of making it to heaven. Self-interest comes up against its limits only with respect to the interests of other people, in other words their self-interest.

Admittedly, his was an isolated voice to begin with. The final reversal of the ancient value system, the affirmation of the everyday economic pursuit of profit, first occurred in the eighteenth century. In his allegorical *Fable of the Bees* of 1714,[9] a certain Bernard Mandeville depicted a beehive in which vanity and luxury, corruption and other vices held sway, which the bees were always as one in accepting whatever other conflicts might exist, for its result was a state of general prosperity. When a miracle caused honesty to spread through the hive, the consequences were catastrophic:

> As pride and luxury decrease,
> So by degrees they leave the seas.

---

[9]   Bernard Mandeville, *The Fable of the Bees, or Private Vices, Publick Benefits* (Harmondsworth: Penguin, 1970).

> Not merchants now; but companies
> Remove whole manufacturies
> All arts and crafts neglected lie;
> Content the bane of industry,
> Makes 'em admire their homely store,
> And neither seek, nor covet more.

The outcome was impoverishment, decline, political powerlessness. Thus, the only just conclusion can be that:

> Fraud, luxury, and pride must live
> Whilst we the benefits receive.

In fact, at around the same time that work, as stated earlier, lost its seemingly natural association with poverty, people also abandoned the time-honoured contempt for luxury. The demand for superfluous things was no longer considered a waste, but was identified as a stimulus for trade and commerce and thus as a source of national welfare.

After the so-called physiocrats had declared production, albeit the agricultural variety for the time being, the source of national welfare for the first time in the eighteenth century, Adam Smith provided modern economic behaviour with a theoretical foundation in his 1776 book *The Wealth of Nations*. This behaviour is based on the fact that while everyone perceives his own interests, the necessity of the division of labour and of goods exchange, in line with the laws of supply and demand, as if by 'an invisible hand', bring about general welfare and national prosperity. 'It is not from the benevolence of the butcher, the brewer, or the baker that we expect our dinner, but from their regard to their own interest', declares perhaps the most famous sentence in the book. Of course, according to Smith, the rich, who employ thousands, thus serve their own greed, but in this way they unintentionally promote the wellbeing of their workers and of the national economy as a whole.

Everyday economic life had thus finally been affirmed, legitimized, and, under certain conditions, had even become an element in the value system. For Smith by no means claimed to have discovered morality-free economic laws, let alone declared immoral action a new morality à la Mandeville. On the contrary, as the moral philosopher he was, building on his *Theory of Moral Sentiments* from 1759, he was eager to demonstrate that, on closer inspection, the supposed amorality of economic life in Mandeville's beehive amounts to the interplay of the well-ordered nature of the world and the human being, guided by his moral sense and – all too readily overlooked – corrected by state legislation.

6

The general affirmation of love took longest; for the reasons mentioned above, it hardly got beyond the first steps between the fourteenth and seventeenth centuries, during which the emphasis of the present account lies. The evaluation of sexuality in particular remained restrictive, and it was very far from being regarded as a value. Realistic acceptance and a fair number of concessions to human weakness were for long the highest of sentiments in this regard. To some extent, the potential for a partnership-based relationship between man and woman, which was certainly present in the Judeo-Christian tradition and even in medieval theology, is only today being truly acknowledged.

For alongside the story of the creation of the woman from the rib of the man (Genesis 2:21–2), providing material for countless male jokes, the Book of Genesis also contains another version of the creation of human beings, which states, in succinct and egalitarian fashion: 'male and female he created them' (Genesis 1:27).

Above all, though, medieval theologians and canon lawyers came to the conclusion, improbable though it was for the time, that according to the Bible a legally valid sacramental and thus indissoluble marriage comes into being exclusively by means of sexual intercourse to which both partners have freely consented; strictly speaking, neither family nor the Church had any say in the matter. This was an unintended but consequential blow to the pre-modern social system, in which a person was not allowed to live, let alone marry, in line with his own aspirations, but solely in the service of the family (as may be gleaned once again from the free spirit Michel de Montaigne). The result was countless contested secret marriages and serious familial conflicts – since Shakespeare the Romeo-and-Juliet, or more recently, since Gene A. Brucker, the Giovanni-and-Lusanna syndrome.[10]

The Churches then rowed backwards. At the Council of Trent, the Catholic Church introduced the formal obligation that a valid marriage could in future be contracted only before a priest and two witnesses. The Protestant Churches declared marriage a temporal business and thus subjugated it de facto to the authority of parents and the authorities. Revealingly, the fact that this made divorce possible was an achievement only in theory, for empirical investigations have shown that all Protestant authorities long remained extremely reluctant with respect to divorces.

But what emerged during the time of the Reformation was at least a limited re-evaluation of the conjugal partnership vis-à-vis the dominant goal of marriage,

---

[10]   Gene A. Brucker, *Giovanni and Lusanna: Love and Marriage in Renaissance Florence* (London: Weidenfeld, 1986).

namely the production of offspring. Within this framework, while sexual desire, viewed with suspicion until then even within marriage, could not be regarded as a value, it could at least be legitimized. The Protestant vicarage, featuring the everyday presence of Christian family life, which at least aspired to exemplary status but was also entirely normal, may have contributed to strengthening the perspective privileging partnership, despite the notoriously high number of children. There is no lack of relevant studies on Luther, Calvin, and, above all, on the Puritan family.

But even this development was not a Protestant monopoly, as is often assumed, despite the increased emphasis on celibacy in the Catholic camp. From the research carried out by Louis Châtelier, we know that in none other than the societies for the worship of the Virgin Mary spread across Europe by the Jesuits, the Marian congregations, a family ideal based on partnership was propagated which was closer to the modern family than to the conventional patriarchy.[11]

And even François de Sales, whom we met earlier, wrote things which may seem rather strange from a modern point of view, but which must be considered nothing less than revolutionary against the background of traditional ideas of sexuality. 'It is [indeed] unseemly, but not a sin, to demand conjugal intercourse on communion day, but it is not unseemly, but even meritorious, to provide it when asked.' For the 'legitimate mutual satisfaction of married spouses' is not only right, it is in fact a duty; abstinence is, strictly speaking, permissible only with the partner's consent. For 'within the lawful marriage' – though nowhere else – 'there is space for sexual desire; its sanctity is capable of compensating for the spiritual lapse caused by sexual pleasure'. The key thing is to remain in control of oneself. This is conjugal chastity, which is more difficult than the much vaunted retention of virginity, which is by no means explicitly granted the typical higher status here. Apart from this, his work makes no mention of the concept of 'children as a blessing', an idée fixe in all Catholic utterances on this subject until recently.

There were, of course, alternative practices to the Churches' teachings on marriage, but these did not revolve around values. There were, of course, alternative values, which can be found in works of literature, but these long remained elite exceptions. The Churches set the tone for everyday life and they at least produced a fair number of promising innovations, which partnership-based love could pick up on later as a core value of everyday life.

---

[11]   Louis Châtelier, *The Europe of the Devout: The Catholic Reformation and the Formation a New Society* (Cambridge: Cambridge University Press, 1989).

7

We have traced the development from the more or less reluctant acceptance of work, trade and commerce, and sexuality to the affirmation of these significant components of ordinary life. Let us pause for a moment and attempt to find a common denominator for these three processes, which appear to have little to do with one another at first glance. And let's examine whether this perhaps provides some kind of answer to the question of *why* this far-reaching shift of values occurred.

I assert that values always correspond to the needs of social groups, which is not to say that they are no more than group ideology; things are not that simple. But we would do well to ask who exactly had an interest in looking upon their own everyday action as valuable. Posing the question like this, the answer is obvious. At issue was the emancipation of the laity from the clerics. For this entails typical lay activities becoming valuable, activities which were irrelevant to the lives of the clerics and thus at best tolerated, if not denigrated by them: working, earning money, making love.

In the early and high Middle Ages, education was a Church monopoly. In modern jargon, the Church was the discursive hegemon, that is, all spheres of thought, natural science and morality, political theory and economic theory, were approached theologically or were even part of theology. There was simply no other option. This gave rise, once again expressed in modern jargon, to the clerics' interpretive sovereignty over reality, with the consequence that the system of values tallied with the world of values characteristic of clerical society. This was not a clerical ruse; there was quite simply no other possibility. The aristocratic system of values, geared towards honour, certainly existed alongside this. But this often came into conflict with that of the Church and came off worse because it was too group-specific, was unable to offer a comprehensive interpretation of the world, and, moreover, could not be articulated broadly enough, as long as most aristocrats, as an alternative elite to the clergy, were, like the rest of society, illiterate.

This changed with the rise of the cities. A lay elite with its own lay education now developed. Radiating out from Italy, humanism and Renaissance contributed substantially to this. These lay people were capable of thinking about their lives and articulating their need to orient their action towards their own values instead of seeing it sneered at or at best ignored. The processes described above thus played themselves out primarily in the old European urban belt between central Italy and the Low Countries. But it should be sufficiently clear by now that this emancipation of the laity was not, as was thought earlier, a first wave of modern secularization with an anti-Christian tenor. On the contrary, I hope to have shown that the creative thinking about values entailed in this emancipation was quite often able to draw on Judeo-Christian precedents, which had been suppressed by Greek spiritualism within the worldview of the clergy.

New values are never entirely new. Creative thinking about values has its roots in the needs of life and, to satisfy them, initially makes use of the available raw material, that is, ideas which may well have existed previously but which lay fallow. Something new is then crafted which may in turn have an effect on reality. People emit thoughts and actions, externalize them, as the sociologists say; they then lie around objectively, as it were, waiting for other people to take them up afresh, to internalize them, at which point everything can begin again anew. The overall phenomenon is thus not a simple linear relationship of cause and effect, nor a linear sequence with a beginning and end, but rather a circular, or better, spiral-like process, because the circle never closes, but proceeds to a new level. Additional external influences (input) may also be felt along the way or branchings-off occur, which often culminate in dead ends.

From this point of view it is not terribly surprising that the rebellion of the laity, as I choose, rather provocatively, to put it here, occurred with help from the ranks of clerical society. There were enough priests who recognized the new needs of the laity and were prepared, or even saw it as their duty, to respond. If we take a look at the five most important Reformers during one of the peaks of the rebellion, the Reformation, we obtain a not untypical profile: two members of religious orders, the Augustinian Luther and the Dominican Butzer, a lay priest, Zwingli, two laymen, namely a humanist philologist, Melanchthon, and a lawyer and humanist, Calvin. But even in the old Church there were enough people who could see the signs of the times and responded to the needs of the laity, not least the Jesuits.

8

However, the common denominator was not merely the discovery of values anchored in everyday life. Rather, almost necessarily a new way of thinking emerged in the wake of this discovery, if it did not in fact precede it; while it may not have brought it about, it certainly made it easier. This way of thinking moulds our relationship to reality to this day. This brings me to the still current consequences of the affirmation of ordinary life. Though it means overstepping the bounds of my area of academic responsibility as a historian and stepping onto the black ice of philosophy, literature, and sociology, I nonetheless consider it appropriate to make a few more remarks.

This way of thinking, new then but which we take for granted today, rests on nothing other than a shift of emphasis from the grandiose to the everyday, in other words, from the general to the particular or from the abstract to the concrete. The ancient Greeks, in whose footsteps medieval thought trod, which applies also to a large portion of its modern counterpart, were not only great researchers and thinkers, but also achieved a whole slew of technological advances. Yet they never crossed over the crucial threshold to experimental natural science and technology, which characterizes modernity more than anything else. I assert that this was not because they were incapable of doing so, but because they did not wish to. They, too, were certainly interested in everything in the world, but always from a systematic perspective. *Theoria* meant an overall view, not individual analysis. A single observation was correct if it fit into the system. This could lead to misinterpretations on a grand scale, as regards, for example, the anatomical and physiological difference between men and women.

This did not immediately change, and did so less in the wake of than as a consequence of the re-evaluation of the everyday described here, but it did change. A science took hold which was interested in the concrete. From then on, correctness was determined by empirical verification through controlled observation, that is, observation open to scrutiny or experiment. Most Greeks would have considered that procedure below their dignity as thinkers. Around 1600, when the affirmation of ordinary life that we are dealing with here was already well advanced, Francis Bacon formulated the programme of this science of the everyday. The classical striving for an overall view was declared a vain endeavour in a dual sense: it was now considered both presumptuous and futile. What would count in future was to investigate how concrete things function individually, not least with respect to how such knowledge could benefit humanity. This brought us to the threshold of natural science and technology.

While many philosophers made it their ambition to formulate grandiose systems until into the nineteenth century, even Hegel realized that the general is only ever manifest as the particular, to simplify, that *the* human being as such does not exist, but only the qualities shared by men and women, Germans and French, etc. But revealingly, this insight had already cropped up in the work of Spanish thinkers of the sixteenth and seventeenth centuries, who in fact worked within the tradition of the great medieval systematic theologian, Thomas Aquinas. In light of practice, the Dominican Francisco de Vitoria had ripped up the monumental systems characteristic of papal or imperial claims to world domination and raised the specific, individual state to the status of the epitome of politics. Incidentally, this made him the father of international law. And in the philosophical-theological system of Francisco Suarez a few centuries later, we may observe how he takes up the thought of Thomas Aquinas, but nonetheless no longer declares the universal *whatness* (*quidditas*) of things the primary object of human knowledge, but rather their individual *thisness* (*haecceitas*). This is certainly not yet modern empirical knowledge, but it is an attempt to do greater justice to the clearly pressing problem of the knowledge of the concrete.

9

In the wake of this turn to the concrete, the specific, individual person could also be interesting and valuable; to overstate things a little, the affirmation of ordinary life culminated in the affirmation of the normal person as a whole in all his everyday reality; this meant, not least, in his working and loving.

The contemporary relevance of this particular interest is expressed not only in such peculiar phenomena as talk shows and *Big Brother*, but also, for example, in the tendency of contemporary history, known as microhistory, to concern itself with the painstaking reconstruction of the normal, everyday world of normal people, with the history of a Bavarian village, with poachers in Salzburg, or, to take a recent example, with the life of a nineteenth-century French worker, a downright non-person in fact, selected randomly from the records of an archive.

History is thus moving closer to literature, which has since the eighteenth century produced novels which are 'modern' in the sense that they no longer, like their predecessors and traditional epic literature since Homer, wish to depict outstanding and exceptional individuals and exceptional events. By traditional standards, their 'heroes' and now 'heroines' are nothing of the kind, for they love and suffer in very unheroic, everyday ways.

The equivalent may be said of the genres of biography and autobiography, which had previously been located thematically between the *Vita Caroli Magni*, the life of Charlemagne, by Einhard and the *Confessiones* of Augustine. That is, either the person under consideration had to be someone of significance, or alternatively the work must relate a religiously edifying story, such as an account of one's own conversion.

In connection with such lives of saints, it is interesting to observe that the social composition of the saints of the Catholic Church also follows the trend that we have identified. Until well into the nineteenth century, the heavens remained populated chiefly by priests and nuns as well as a fair number of royal personages and other prominent earthly figures. Exceptions were made at most for martyrs. The need to affirm everyday life was expressed only very late in the tendency to beatify normal men and women who had died a natural death.

Yet this interest in the normal individual is ultimately based on the values of the Judeo-Christian tradition. It would have been inconceivable without the theory of the individual person morally responsible in light of his conscience, who possesses an immortal soul and whom God has very personally and individually assigned to eternal salvation or perhaps, according to Calvin, marked out for eternal damnation. This not only created the potential for a religiously grounded personal identity but, beyond this, facilitated the practice, unique in world history, of making this identity the object of iterative reflection, not just thinking _bout one's own individuality, but also about how this individuality is possible in the first place. Such ideas most likely never entered the heads of members of other cultures.

The basic Christian motif of the individual salvation of unique personalities, which was a novel development, makes personal life histories interesting in the first place – the religious *Confessiones* of Augustine are a prerequisite for the latest thing in this regard, Anthony Giddens' secular reflexive project of the self, according to which we are never finished, but must work our whole lives not only on new chapters, but even on new editions, in other words new overall interpretations, of our biography. The *Confessions* of Jean-Jacques Rousseau took over the mediating role. Originally, human subjectivity was experienced as imperfect, as dependent on its Creator, yet, in contrast, it also perceived the qualities of unchanging identity as predicates of His divine perfection: autonomy, immutability, eternalness, omniscience, creativity:

> To the extent that the human being strove to achieve his autonomy and began to ground his true self in his own identity, rather than looking for it in the external You of God the Creator, the aesthetic experience usurped the predicates of divine identity and converted them into the norms of an experience of the self, manifest in a literary sense in the forms and pretensions of the modern autobiography.[12]

Rousseau asserted the immutability of his autonomous self that knows or at least wishes to know everything about itself and which becomes immortal through the process of remembering. Finally, the human being became the creator of his own identity; for Goethe, the world and other human beings were merely the raw materials out of which the genius formed his unique personality, in order to make a work of art out of his own life. However, the *niveau* has sunk since then, for what was once a highly elite achievement is possible for everyone in the plural society, that is, the philosophical way of life has become trivial.

The Reformation reinforced this aspect of Christianity in particular because it eliminated the Church apparatus of salvation, thus leaving the individual person to take care of himself in a quite new way and making him fully and entirely responsible for his own salvation. Thus, the Protestant was and is especially dependent on observing, interpreting, and justifying himself. He is in a way the born autobiographer. And because salvation is conveyed to him through the Scriptures, he is accustomed to living according to the text; it is also because of

---

[12]   Hans Robert Jauss in Odo Marquard and Karlheinz Stierle (eds), *Identität* (Munich: Fink, 1979), p. 709.

this that he tends to produce new texts about his personal history. All of you are presumably familiar with a relevant genre. I am referring to the ubiquitous annual 'round robins' on personal or family activities which many contemporaries tend to send at Christmas or New Year. Calvin kept the tendency towards egocentrism inherent in this view of things in check by maintaining a cool distance and diverting it to the external life story. As far as he himself is concerned, we know almost nothing about his inner religious life and only a little about his calling as a Reformer. We have already seen how the Calvinists tried to attain certainty about salvation through an exemplary life in terms of outward appearances.

Luther, instead, consistently treated his inner experience as an arena of salvation and therefore told us a great deal about it. As a result, there are few early modern individuals about whom as much is known as Martin Luther. But because, for him and the Lutheran type that he moulded, it is only the inner action that is important, the external is devalued, and may even be omitted. If need be, an external signal of one's beliefs is sufficient to show that one has the correct feelings. As a behavioural pattern characteristic of normal people, this culminated in the renowned German inwardness, bound up with what has recently been termed the German *Betroffenheitskultur* or culture of contrition.

10

But this has already brought us to the present, which I want to take another look at in order to see where the affirmation of ordinary life has led us. While the subject of the revelation, Luther struggling with his God, has now degenerated into the revelation of the subject, to the triviality of everyday self-exposure on television, our empirical interaction with the details of the everyday world furnishes us with one scientific and technological triumph after the other. The affirmation of love within the sexual partnership has been consistently realized, at the expense of the family, which formerly suppressed it. To some degree, finance no longer even requires the real foundation of goods to function as splendidly as never before thanks to new technology. Work has probably become the highest value of all for the majority of westerners, for having it or not having it determines one's existence or non-existence in a moral and, often enough, physical sense.

It seems to me, in contrast to the time of its emergence, that the affirmation of ordinary life has become an entirely independent phenomenon, detached more or less from any connection with other values. While the transcendent God, as I explained at the outset, had left the world alone in its autonomy, He nonetheless retained an indirect control and a kind of right of veto, mediated through the service rendered by human beings. Even Francis Bacon saw his new empirical science as being not only at the service of human utility, but also as designed to ascertain God's intentions for the world more precisely than ever before.

But, of course, God is dead and other attempts to draw on higher values seem not to have amounted to much. Little has come of the moral feelings and ties to the commonweal discussed by Adam Smith. The market economy has not only detached itself from all ties, but is even emerging today as a yardstick for non-economic spheres. It pervades our language; whether we are talking about love or sport, science or religion, we use economic categories. That is, economics is now the discursive hegemon as theology was in the Middle Ages. We used to believe in God, now we believe in the market. And we have no other option.

9

Inner Nature and Social Normativity: The Idea of Self-Realization

Christoph Menke

Two hundred years ago, at the spring fair of 1804, Friedrich Wilmans of Frankfurt am Main published Hölderlin's translation of the two tragedies by Sophocles, under whose dual star all modern thinking about the subject, his status as self-responsible and autonomous citizen, his volition and his fate, stands: *Oedipus Rex* and *Antigone*. It is Antigone whom the chorus describes as follows: 'You alone among mortals live according to your own law.' Her path thus takes her 'down into the realm of the dead'.[1] The chorus means this partly as a rebuke: to obey her own and only her own laws is Antigone's hubris, which can only lead to death. When Creon asks Antigone how she can dare to break his law, to act in breach of his, Creon's, prohibition on burying the traitor Polynices, she refers to what '*my* Zeus', that is, her God, tells her: '*My* Zeus did not dictate that law'.[2] In other words: my God, my source of authority and guide to action, has not imposed this prohibition, your prohibition, upon me. The emphasis, in the response of Hölderlin's Antigone, is very much on this possessive pronoun ('*my* Zeus'); it is the only word in the entire text which Hölderlin's translation highlights by applying italics. What Hölderlin emphasizes about Antigone is that she is prepared to obey only her own God. The fact that there is one God and that His laws hold sway means that He exists for her, indeed *within* her – perhaps even through her? When her sister Ismene considers the possibility of acting in the same way, helping Antigone bury their brother and dying with her, Hölderlin has Antigone say: 'Don't die in common' (p. 87). That is, do not do as I do solely because you think that *one* must act (and die) in this way; act and die not in a

---

[1]   Sophocles, *Antigone*, v.821–4; this rendering based on the translation by W. Schadewaldt, in Sophocles, *Tragödien* (Düsseldorf and Zurich: Artemis, 2002).

[2]   Sophocles, *Antigone*, trans. by David Constantine after F. Hölderlin's translation, in *Hölderlin's Sophocles* (Tarset: Bloodaxe, 2001), p. 84.

general, but in an individual way. This is also why Hölderlin's interest in the first quotation above, in which the chorus rebukes Antigone for her autonomy, lies less in the law than in the life. Schadewaldt's more literal translation goes: 'You alone among mortals live according to your *own law*' (my emphasis). Hölderlin meanwhile translates these two lines as 'Living *the life of your own* among mortals unique, you go down into the world of the dead' (p. 96, my emphasis). The self-determination of Hölderlin's Antigone relates not only to the law, but to life. For her, freedom is not limited to making laws herself, her own laws. For her freedom means something more, something different: the fulfilment and realization of her own life. The chain of her actions and omissions, her wanting and suffering, must add up to a life which expresses what she herself and in truth is.

Antigone's decision to live her own life ends in death, a death to which she is condemned by Creon, representative of the community. This is the risk which Antigone takes: those who live their own lives may come into conflict with the community, which interprets this, and punishes it, as a wanton crime. But this conflict remains superficial for Antigone; it fails to disturb, in fact it further enhances, the image of wonderful fulfilment which Antigone's life offers. From the outset, though, modern thinking about the subject was alarmed by a question sparked off by the experience of the other figure whose tragedy Hölderlin translated: the question of whether the flipside of the beautiful image of fulfilment, offered by the living of a life fully one's own, is not terror. For does not Oedipus also live his own life – but one which ultimately requires him to condemn and damn himself? Oedipus, too, makes full use of the first person pronoun: 'But then *I* came, Oedipus the ignorant, and silenced her [the Sphinx], having attained the answer through my wit alone, rather than relying on birds'[3] – while all the others, especially the seer with his skill and his knowledge, were unable to solve the riddle of the Sphinx and save the city. Oedipus's acts are his own; he lives in line with his own volition. But far from beautiful self-fulfilment, this culminates in profound inner division and a terrible damning of the self. In the end, he says 'I' in a very different sense: I, Oedipus, damn myself for what I have done and how I have lived. Oedipus, too, lives his own life – but one for which he is forced to condemn himself. First, he does terrible things while 'living his own life'; he murders his father and commits incest with his mother. Then, judging his own life according to his own laws, he imposes a further terrible fate upon himself; he

---

[3]   Sophocles, *Oedipus Rex*, v.396–8; this rendering based on the translation by W. Schadewaldt. On the preceding remarks on (Hölderlin's) *Antigone*, see Christoph Menke, *Tragödie im Sittlichen. Gerechtigkeit und Freiheit nach Hegel* (Frankfurt am Main: Suhrkamp, 1996), ch. 3 and 4; on the following remarks on *Oedipus Rex*, see Christoph Menke, *Die Gegenwart der Tragödie. Versuch über Urteil und Spiel* (Frankfurt am Main: Suhrkamp, 2005), part 1.

damns himself to a ghostly state of vegetation outside of society and culture. By living his own life, Oedipus becomes an intolerable monster in his own eyes.

Just as Oedipus and Antigone share an affinity, the two conflicting experiences with life, with the living of one's own life, which have become attached to these figures, also belong together. Antigone has become the Romantic heroine of an 'authentic' life, a life of 'self-realization', whose enemies are external enemies, the conventions of society and the authorities of tradition. Attached to Oedipus meanwhile are all the post-Romantic, 'modern' doubts as to whether a threatening Other reigns within one's own unique self, such that, far from realizing itself, it must battle with, if not damn, itself. The understanding of self-realization that I wish to outline in what follows is intended to be such that, rather than being exposed to this doubt, it includes it; not as an external doubt about self-realization, but a doubt *within* all self-realization properly understood. But first I shall attempt to define self-realization, properly understood. This I shall do in two steps. The first step develops the fundamentals of a correct understanding of self-realization, beginning with a critique of the ego-model of the inner core (I). The second step is intended to elaborate this further by outlining a two-stage model of self-realization (II). Only then do I conclude by returning to the ambivalence of self-realization (III).

I. The Critique of the Inner Core: The Present and Prehistory of Authenticity

I

Hölderlin's Antigone establishes (or reflects) a new form of subjectivity: a subject that not only wishes to obey its own laws, but which wishes to live its own life. To act in accordance with one's own laws is the modern idea of autonomy. On this view, that person is free who is subject to no laws laid down by others, but only those which he has imposed upon himself (or might have done). According to the modern idea of autonomy, it is of this that the freedom of the subject *consists*: in the act of making a law for oneself – and then obeying it in everything one wants and does. By shifting focus from the right to make one's own laws to the right to live one's own life, Hölderlin's Antigone expresses the objection raised by the Romantic theorists of authenticity to the modern concept of freedom as autonomy. This Romantic objection is not opposed to the idea of subjective freedom, but endows it with a different, radicalized form: what matters is not whether I am the creator or author of the law which I obey, but *how* I live while adhering to this law – what my life is actually like under or in accordance with this law.

When Immanuel Kant introduced the concept of autonomy, he explained it by stating that the subject becomes the *Glied*, in other words, the *member* of a 'kingdom of ends'. Every subject is in the position of a 'head' of this kingdom, that is, he is sovereign in the sense that 'as legislating, he is not subject to the will of any other being'. But this is an inadequate, negative definition of his freedom. For the (autonomous) subject is not only the (sovereign) head, but also a 'member' in the 'kingdom of ends', because 'while legislating its universal laws, he is also subject to these laws'.[4] This is understood by the Romantic critics of autonomy and theorists of authenticity, none more than Schiller in his letters published as *On the Aesthetic Education of Man*, in such a way that while autonomy does indeed make me the author of the law, it changes nothing about my relationship *to* this self-established law; it remains a relationship of subjugation – albeit self-subjugation. I am subjugated by myself, I live in a state of self-imposed subjugation. *This* is where the ideal of authenticity or self-realization begins. It does not reject the normative content of self-imposed law; it rejects its form. It rejects an understanding of subjective freedom as the faculty first of constructing and then obeying a law.[5] For obeying a law, regardless of its origins, means subjugation to a law. Freedom on the other hand, understood in the Romantic sense, is aimed at a relationship of expression or correspondence: between what I do and what I am. According to the Romantic critique of the imposing of laws upon oneself, to be free means to lead a life which is my 'own' or of which I am the author because it expresses or I realize within it who I truly or really am. And this relationship of correspondence or expression should, in fact, can only manifest if one eschews the detour involved in the drawing up and adherence to a law.

2

As familiar as this Romantic idea sounds, the idea that one can understand what a subject does and how he lives in this way and that one would wish to act and live in a way that expresses or realizes oneself, it is doubtful that this idea can be understood in any clear and comprehensible way in the first place. How can this authentic 'self' (to which one's actions and life are meant to 'correspond') exist, what does it consist of and how are we supposed to know of it? Further: what is meant by a relationship of 'expression' or 'correspondence' if it is supposed to be a relationship without laws, that is, without rules and thus criteria? These doubts are fuelled by the common ideologies of self-realization and authenticity; they combine conceptual confusion with politically and ethically fatal consequences.

---

[4]   Immanuel Kant, *Groundwork for the Metaphysics of Morals*, trans. Arnulf Zweig and ed. Thomas E. Hill and Arnulf Zweig (Oxford: Oxford University Press, 2002), 4:433, p. 233.

[5]   Therefore, as Scheler objected, it does not help to think in terms of an 'individual law' (Simmel) rather than a general one; see Hans Joas, *The Genesis of Values* (Chicago, IL: University of Chicago Press 2000), pp. 166–7.

'Self-realization' and 'authenticity', as expressions intended to refer to the ideals of a radically individualized way of life, have been in circulation only for a few decades.[6] They emerged in connection with the youth and student movements of the 1960s; with their subsequent depoliticization into a culture of individualistic hedonism during the 1970s, they rapidly developed into a vocabulary used on a massive scale. In a negative sense, the appeal to self-realization and authenticity is intended to express the claim to a life which is *not* absorbed by fulfilling role expectations, fitting in with behavioural conventions, or implementing traditionally defined life-plans. In a positive sense, the appeal to self-realization and authenticity is concerned, as Michel Foucault stated with respect to what he called the 'California cult of the self', to 'discover one's true self, to separate it from that which might obscure or alienate it, to decipher its truth thanks to psychological or psychoanalytic science, which is supposed to be able to tell you what your true self is'.[7] On this view, the idea of an authentic life is linked with the notion that of all the definitions which apply to a self (and are thus 'true' in the common sense of the term), there are some which apply to it to a different degree or even in a different way (and which constitute its 'truth' in a deeper sense). In his account of the so-called 'self-realization milieu', Gerhard Schulze has described this notion as the ego-model of the 'inner core':

> Although unclear and intangible, in the view characteristic of the self-realization milieu, the inner core is a concrete reality. It 'exists' with the same clarity as the body, and it is seen as just as crucial to one's existence. [...] A key component of this ego-model is a kind of psychological doctrine of predestination which states that the inner core is programmed for a very specific, but at the same time hard to define developmental path, like a genetic disposition.[8]

---

[6]   The expression 'authenticity' begins its career with the French translation of Heidegger's *Eigentlichkeit* as *authenticité*; see K. Röttgers and R. Fabian, 'Authentisch', in *Historisches Wörterbuch der Philosophie* (Basle: Schwabe, 1971), vol. 1, no. 692. Among other things, Hegel refers to the connection between conviction and action as *Selbstverwirklichung* or 'self-realization'; see G. Gerhardt, 'Selbstverwirklichung, Selbstaktualisierung', in *Historisches Wörterbuch der Philosophie*, vol. 9, no. 556. The term has attained its common meaning of individual self-realization via an existentializing reception of Marx.

[7]   M. Foucault, 'On the Genealogy of Ethics: An Overview of Work in Progress', in H. L. Dreyfus and P. Rabinow, *Michel Foucault. Beyond Structuralism and Hermeneutics* (Chicago, IL: University of Chicago Press, 1982), p. 245.

[8]   Gerhard Schulze, *Die Erlebnisgesellschaft. Kultursoziologie der Gegenwart* (Frankfurt am Main and New York: Campus, 1992), p. 314.

The inner core is thus not only an extant and ascertainable truth about the self, it also has the power to characterize, indeed determine, the actions taken and the life lived by the self.

One can respond to this (for a time) very widespread 'ego-model' in two ways. Cultural sociologists such as Gerhard Schulze have persuasively argued that there is a link between the turn against convention and towards one's own truth and a new phase of the capitalist economy marked by 'post-industrial' forms of production and an unprecedented expansion and acceleration of mass consumption. This confronts the individual with much confusion, making it ever more urgent to find a source of orientation and to create order, a problem which, however, the individual can now resolve himself. The ideas of self-realization and authenticity are 'attempts to establish order in a situation in which the loss of order is a constant threat' by developing an 'inward-looking semantics' which hopes, there inside the self, by appealing to the idea of an inner core, to rediscover the stability which external tradition and convention can no longer offer.[9] A functional perspective of this kind could also explain why the 1970s model of authentic self-realization seems increasingly superseded by a model of self-redesign, as flexible as it is permanent, since the 1990s. This would suggest that forms of subjectivity may arise which are able to deal with the threat of loss of order resulting from de-traditionalization and increased contingency in ways other than by searching for stability in a fixed and fixable ego-core.

However, the pathologies entailed in this more flexible ego may be no less serious than those produced by the model of the fixed inner core.[10] This points to the second perspective from which one may view the ego-model of authentic self-realization. If the sociology of culture approach is concerned to produce a functional explanation, as a strategy for resolving an intensifying social and economic problem of achieving order, cultural critics focus on the disintegrative, the generally destructive consequences of the appeal to an ego-core for culture and society. Their critique assails the ideals of self-realization and authenticity for two seemingly contradictory failings. The first objection, raised by Michel Foucault and inspired by Nietzsche's concept of decadence, relates to ego-weakness: a self that orients itself by reference to its pre-given ego-core, ignores (täuscht sich!) that its reference to itself is a 'creative practice'.[11] It seeks security and stability by grounding its evaluations in mere statements about how and what it already is. Thus, the 'authentic' self does not care about itself – that is, not in a real, active sense. The other criticism, which relates to

---

[9]   Schulze, Die Erlebnisgesellschaft, pp. 72, 249ff.

[10]   See Richard Sennett, The Corrosion of Character: The Personal Consequences of Work in the New Capitalism (New York and London: Norton, 1998).

[11]   Foucault, 'On the Genealogy of Ethics', p. 237.

excessive concern with the ego or self, contradicts this and is largely inspired by conservative analyses of the modern age; it has been made by the likes of Alasdair MacIntyre. It asserts that a self that believes it can find the guiding principle of its action in the characteristics of its inner core fails to grasp the unavoidably social context in which all self-understanding occurs.[12] It thinks it can find something in itself that is free of all social and culture superimposition, something all its own. This is why the authentic self no longer cares about the society and culture to which it belongs, but only about itself. The idea of an inner *core* generates a passive stance; one accepts oneself for what one is. The idea of an *inner* core produces narcissism; each individual is interested only in who she actually is.

Both perspectives on self-realization and authenticity, the functional explanation and the cultural critique, know their target — yet they misjudge it at the same time. What 'self-realization' and 'authenticity' mean cannot be captured by the ego-model of the inner core, through which they were interpreted, first within the counter-culture of the 1960s, then in the mass culture of the 1970s and 1980s. This not only means that 'self-realization' and 'authenticity' must be understood differently than in the ego-model of the inner core. It also means that it is impossible to understand the ego-model of the inner core itself correctly if one fails to grasp that it is a *mis*understanding of what 'self-realization' and 'authenticity' are all about. This is the thesis through which Charles Taylor re-opened the debate on the 'ethics of authenticity' ten years ago, against both a purely cultural sociological explanation and a pure cultural critique: the passivist-narcissist model of the inner core, which often equates the ideas of self-realization and authenticity, whether for purposes of explanation or evaluation, is a 'debased and discredited' form of a 'higher moral ideal'.[13]

Taylor's new perspective on self-realization and authenticity, first of all, helps highlight the fact that behind and opposed to the (hopefully) short-lived ego-model of the inner core lie ideas that have been around for a very long time. They belong, as Taylor has already shown, at the centre of what he calls 'the making of the modern identity';[14] I shall comment on this briefly in a moment. Taylor's new perspective on self-realization and authenticity makes it possible, second, to apply a different critique to the ego-model of the inner core than with respect

[12]   Alasdair MacIntyre, *After Virtue: A Study in Moral Theory* (London: Duckworth, 1981), ch. 15.

[13]   Charles Taylor, *The Ethics of Authenticity* (Cambridge, MA, and London: Harvard University Press, 1992), pp. 17, 72.

[14]   Charles Taylor, *Sources of the Self: The Making of the Modern Identity* (Cambridge: Cambridge University Press, 1989).

to its consequences.[15] Here, the ego-model of the inner core appears as a wrong answer, but to a correct question.

The nature of this question which the ego-model of the inner core answers wrongly (because it understands it wrongly in the first place) is apparent if one takes seriously the problem of practical orientation to which this model, both understandably and despairingly, tries to find a solution. On this view, each person experiences herself as a self which might do and have all kinds of things and wishes to do and to have more things still. How are we to choose from this wealth of possibilities and wants? The thesis with which the model of the inner core begins states that, in a situation like this, if only we pay proper attention to ourselves, we make a discovery: that we want some things more than others. And indeed, 'more' not only in a relative sense, but in a (quasi-) absolute sense. We want some things so much more that, if we cannot acquire or do them, we have no interest in getting or doing anything else. That which we want more has for us a 'categorical' status; we want it 'unconditionally' in the sense that this wanting constitutes the conditions for everything else we want.[16]

If one has followed (and can follow) up to now how the ego-model of the inner core sees the problem at hand, then the next step which this model takes to solve the problem makes the model itself problematic. Which of my wants have such unconditional status for me is a matter of mere observation for the ego-model of the inner core: I find within myself and ascertain which wants are unconditional for me (or which form the 'core' of my ego; my 'real' wants). The fact that this is a matter of mere observation for the ego-model of the inner core does not mean that it considers this observation straightforward. On the contrary, it is easy to get it wrong, and, above all, to be led astray, believing wants to be unconditional which are in fact not. Because of this, one must, for example, produce the circumstances suited to making such a genuine observation (which may include helpful guidance). But if, however I may have gone about it, I have come to the conclusion that this is for me an unconditional want, then the

---

[15]   It would, of course, be quite wrong to reduce the cited criticisms made by Foucault and MacIntyre to such an external, outcome-oriented critique. Quite the contrary, in the spirit of the argument outlined in what follows, their objections to the objectivism and solipsism of the ego-model of the inner core may be understood in such a way that they are criticizing the reduction of normativity to nature in this model; see especially MacIntyre's critique of emotivism in *After Virtue*, ch. 2 and 3.

[16]   Bernard Williams, 'Persons, Character and Morality', in Williams, *Moral Luck* (Cambridge: Cambridge University Press, 1981), p. 11. On the structure of the choice between desires, see Charles Taylor, 'What is Human Agency?', in Taylor, *Human Agency and Language. Philosophical Papers 1* (Cambridge: Cambridge University Press, 1985), pp. 15–44.

ego-model of the inner core understands this to mean that I have established its unconditional nature like a fact; to be unconditional is a quality which wants have and which one may recognize or fail to recognize, which one may establish or be wrong about. If one looks around for a model of such qualities of wants, one finds the notion of the strength (or weakness) of wants common in utilitarian thought. The ego-model of the inner core thus secretly places the unconditionality of wants on the same level. The self, in search of its core, registers the strength of its wants. The idea of an inner core is thus as follows: in order to know what I ought to do, I need to find out which are my real wants, and this means those wants about which I can ascertain through certain procedures that they are the ones that move me most. The 'ethic' of a model of the inner core is thus: pursue your strongest wants.

If this is the answer of the ego-model of the inner core, then it is now possible to indicate its flaws. The question is the practical one of what I want to do or how I wish to live. This question is normative in nature, concerned with which way of acting or living is right or good for me. A first attempt at an answer might be to act or live in such a way that I realize my unconditional or categorical wants. As the ego-model of the inner core sees things, this means acting in line with the wants which I have established as those which move me most. But this fails entirely to answer the question of what I want to do or how I want to live. For the strength of a want may indeed be able to explain why I have in fact done something. But the fact that a want is strong cannot explain why I wish to try and realize it – why it is right or good for me to do so.[17] The self which refers to its inner core merely observes the strength or weakness of its wants and, through this relationship of self-objectification, becomes incapable of doing the very thing it set out to achieve: answering the practical question of what it wishes to do or how it wishes to live. It sways disoriented within the stream of its constantly changing observations of whatever its strongest want is at a given moment.

With respect to the idea of authenticity or self-realization, it is possible to formulate this objection to the ego-model of the inner core in a more general way as follows. The idea of authenticity or self-realization characterizes a life that is my 'own' as free or good: a life which expresses or which corresponds to who I truly or really am. The ego-model of the inner core declares who I truly or really am to be the object of an observation and thus a fact, the fact of how strong wants are. This also objectifies, or naturalizes, the nature of the expression or correspondence (the relationship between what I truly am and my actions). It becomes a relationship of cause and effect. As we have seen, as a consequence the ego-model of the inner core fails to answer the practical question. Conversely,

---

[17]   Or: to want something does not mean to desire it most strongly; rather, it means evaluating it as good.

this means that the nature of the 'expression' or 'correspondence' in the context of the idea of authenticity or self-realization must be understood differently: not as a relationship of cause and effect, but as one based on normative evaluation. The judgment on authenticity takes the form: 'This is the way of acting that truly fits who I am.' The ego-model of the inner core translates this judgment into the observation: 'This is the way of acting which the want I have registered as my strongest leads me to.' In terms of its normative content, however, the judgment of authenticity states: 'This is the way of acting appropriate to me; or which, when measured against who I truly am, is right.' This shows the true nature of the mistake made by the ego-model of the inner core. By declaring who I truly am to be the object of an objective observation, it can no longer explain what role it plays in the normative, evaluative judgment of authenticity. Who I truly am is not a fact that I observe but a criterion according to which I judge.

3

It would be quite wrong to understand this critique of the model of the inner core to mean that one can or must do without a concept of 'inner nature' in order to define self-realization or authenticity. Rather, the ideal of self-realization or authenticity *is* that of a life as the 'expression' of that in which the 'nature' of an individual consists.[18] The problems which the ego-model of the inner core comes up against, however, show how the relationship to the inner nature of the individual should *not* be thought of (as the observation of a fact, which may have an impact as an underlying cause), and how we must think of it: as a normative relationship to the standard of evaluation. Thus, the inner nature of the individual can be the point of reference for determining how to act or live if it is not merely ascribed causal power[19] (the power of the 'strong' want to produce an action), but normative power; the power to make demands of one's own life. It is not a question of normativity rather than nature, but of the normativity *of one's* (inner) nature. The task of any discussion of the ideal of self-realization or authenticity consists in becoming clear about this idea: that the inner nature of the individual can and indeed must be a standard for evaluating and leading her life.

But this seems a paradox: how can the inner nature of an individual be a normative yardstick for evaluating what he does and how he lives if 'nature', including the inner variety, is nothing more than an ordering of things and events, of facts? We can take a first step towards resolving this seeming paradox if we look more closely at *how* in fact, in what context and in what way, the question about the inherent, inner nature of the self arises. Here, one of Charles Taylor's remarks about the prehistory of self-realization or authenticity is revealing.

---

[18]   Taylor, *Sources of the Self*, pp. 368ff. 'The Expressivist Turn'.
[19]   The German *Kraft* is translated throughout as 'power'.

Taylor[20] certainly underlines that the ideal of authenticity or self-realization is of recent vintage: it became possible to refer to authenticity or self-realization only with the emergence of the idea of an inner criterion, in line with which an individual can evaluate and lead his life. And this occurred in emphatic fashion only with the Romantic critique of the idea of subjective freedom as the imposing of laws upon oneself. But at the same time, Taylor places the Romantic concept of authenticity or self-realization within a tradition stretching far back into the past, all the way to the patristics. He calls this the tradition of 'Augustinian spirituality', which experienced 'an immense flowering [...] across all confessional differences' in formative phases of the modern period, in the sixteenth and seventeenth century.[21] This connection with Augustine relates to this 'radically reflexive' 'turn to the self' (pp. 130–1). In relation to God and the good, Augustine's *Confessions* adopt the 'first-person standpoint'. The idea set in motion by this Taylor refers to as one of an 'ethic of the whole will'. Augustine's *Confessions* formulate a perspective 'which makes commitment crucial: no way of life is truly good, no matter how much it may be in line with nature, unless it is endorsed with the whole will.' (p. 185) Crucial to wanting the good, so Augustine tells us, is to overcome weakness of will, which is a 'morbid condition of the mind'. Thus, what is crucial is the *manner* in which a self wants the good: it must want it in a 'complete' way (*ex toto*); or: the will must commit in 'wholehearted' fashion to the good that it wants.[22] We must want the good with all our hearts, or, conversely, have taken the good into our hearts entirely, have made it inhere within us.

---

[20]   See *Sources of the Self*, pp. 111ff., 362ff.; *The Ethics of Authenticity*, p. 25.

[21]   *Sources of the Self*, p. 141. Taylor's ideas need to be supplemented by the history, related by Schneewind, of the 'invention of autonomy': J. B. Schneewind, *The Invention of Autonomy: A History of Modern Moral Philosophy* (Cambridge: Cambridge University Press, 1998). Schneewind demonstrates that the question which has stimulated and defined the history of modern moral philosophy since the Renaissance is that of the relationship between law and self, compliance with the law and 'self-governance'. Schneewind, however, finishes his account of this history with Kant's concept of autonomy (see ch. 23 in particular). On the problems, indeed 'paradoxes' of this Kantian solution, which his critics, particularly Hegel, have pointed out, see Terry Pinkard, *German Philosophy 1760–1860: The Legacy of Idealism* (Cambridge: Cambridge University Press, 2002), pp. 59–60, 224ff.); Robert Pippin, 'Über Selbstgesetzgebung', *Deutsche Zeitschrift für Philosophie* 51.6 (2003), pp. 905–26.

[22]   Augustine, *Confessions* (Oxford: Oxford University Press, 1992), VIII.9, pp. 147–8. This idea is taken up by Harry Frankfurt; see 'Identification and Wholeheartedness', in *The Importance of What We Care About* (Cambridge: Cambridge University Press, 1988), pp. 175–6.

One of Taylor's theses on the development of the ideal of authenticity or self-realization is that it should be understood as a perpetuation of this 'ethic of the whole will'. On this view, to realize or express in my wanting and acting that which constitutes my inner nature is a new way of explaining what it means to want and to do something 'wholly'. The 'ethic of the whole will' refers, as we have seen, to the manner of wanting, not its content; it refers to *how* one ought to want or do something – not *what*. If it is true, as Taylor suggests, that the ideal of authenticity or self-realization may be understood as a late variant of this 'ethic of the whole will', then this also applies to the idea of a realization or expression of one's inner nature. In line with this, to express my inner nature is not an alternative definition of what I want, but of *how* I want, whatever it is that I want. The ideals of 'self-realization' and 'authenticity' entail no definitions of the content of wants, action, and life; 'self-realization' and 'authenticity' are not goals or ends, but refer to the way in which a person has and pursues goals or ends. They encourage me to have and pursue goals or ends in such a way that I want them with all my being. And this means that in having or pursuing these goals or ends, whatever they consist of, my inner nature is simultaneously expressed or realized.[23]

That the ideal of self-realization or authenticity refers to the manner, not the goals or ends, of wanting means, conversely, that it is impossible to pursue self-realization or authenticity directly. If 'self-realization' or 'authenticity' are definitions of the 'how' of wanting, then I can reach them only by wanting something, something specific and different. This refers back to the critique of the ego-model of the inner core described earlier. This was a dual critique. The first objection (from Foucault) was that this model leads to passivism and theoreticism because it treats the inner core like an observable fact. This critique inspired the suggestion that we understand the inherent, inner nature of the self, which is to be realized or expressed in one's life, not as a fact but normatively, as a yardstick. The second objection (from MacIntyre) was that the ego-model of the inner core leads to narcissism, to an unrestrained turn to and concern only with oneself. It is now apparent how profound a misunderstanding of 'self-realization' or 'authenticity' this narcissism is linked with. The ego-model of the inner core confuses the manner of wanting with the content of wants. Its mistake is to believe that one can turn the how of wanting directly into the what of wanting; in other words, one can want, which here means want in an authentic way, without

---

[23]   This fits with the definition of authenticity provided by Dieter Thomä, following Joseph Raz's definition of 'integrity' (*The Morality of Freedom*, Oxford: Oxford University Press, 1986, pp. 381–5) as the kind and intensity of 'personal commitment' with respect to a thing (of mine); see D. Thomä, *Erzähle dich selbst. Lebensgeschichte als philosophisches Problem* (Munich: Beck, 1998), p. 29.

pursuing specific goals or ends. This makes the ego of the inner core 'worldless': it believes it can want *itself*, without wanting *something*.

But given that there is substance to my wanting, I am no longer all that it contains. For everything which I may want, all the goals and ends, are (co-) determined by the culture and society of which I am part. Any way in which I wish to act is thus determined by a mostly informal set of mostly implicit rules that enjoy social recognition; a way of acting embodies socially given and defined norms. Thus, through the substance of its wanting, the self is always related to a social world of rules, norms, and standards. The question of which way of acting is particular to the self, of how this self must act in order to realize itself or express its nature – these are questions that relate not to a relationship of 'inner' correspondence, but to the relationship of the self *to* a social world, or more precisely, to the norms and rules which make up a social world. If the ideal of authenticity or self-realization relates to the how rather than the what of wanting; and if the what of wanting is always socially and culturally standardized, then the ideal of authenticity or self-realization does not encourage us to want the inherent or inner nature of the self *instead of* the socially determined normative substance – this was the narcissistic view of 'self-realization' or 'authenticity' in the ego-model of the inner core. Rather, the ideal of authenticity or self-realization demands that the self, *with reference to* the socially determined normative substance, expresses or realizes its own, inner nature. Its narcissism thus expresses a second aspect of the blindness to normativity which dominates the ego-model of the inner core: it is blind to the fact that the judgment of authenticity is a judgment about the relationship between the individual (and his inner nature) *and* social norms. Authenticity or self-realization is not remotely possible other than with reference *to* social norms, even, perhaps especially, when it is directed against social norms.[24] And it is only through this relationship to social norms that the inner nature of the individual can take on normative power, that is, counteracting normative force.

---

[24]   See Michael Theunissen, *Selbstverwirklichung und Allgemeinheit. Zur Kritik des gegenwärtigen Bewußtseins* (Berlin and New York: Gruyter, 1982). Theunissen, however, interprets this irreducible reference to 'generality' (which he emphasizes against a reduced understanding of self-realization) in such a way that self-realization must therefore be understood (with Hegel) as a 'general life' (*Selbstverwirklichung und Allgemeinheit*, pp. 12–13, 16ff.). But the relationship to generality can take various forms; one of these is irony, which Hegel (in light of Antigone) identifies as a constitutive factor in individual self-determination and self-realization in *The Phenomenology of Spirit*; see Menke, *Tragödie im Sittlichen*, ch. 4. On the relationship between generality and self-realization in Hegel, see Axel Honneth, *Suffering from Indeterminacy: An Attempt at a Reactualization of Hegel's Philosophy of Right* (Assen: Van Gorcum, 2000).

II. A Concept of Self-Realization: Subjective Abilities and Natural Powers

I

The ideal of self-realization or authenticity sees the action and life of a subject as the expression or realization of its own, inner nature. The critique of the way in which the ego-model of the inner core understands this led to two theses: the fact that an action is an *expression* (or realization) of the inner nature of a subject means, first, that the inner nature of the self becomes a criterion for evaluating his actions. The fact that an *action* (or way of acting) is the expression of the inner nature of a subject means, second, that the subject is in a relationship with the socially given and determined norms of action. Thus, in the ideal of self-realization or authenticity, the subject is regarded not just from a simple, but from a dual normative perspective. Let us reverse the order found in our discussion so far: in his action, the subject relates, first, to the world of socially determined norms and, second, to the normative demands of his inner nature. According to the ideal of self-realization or authenticity, this is the situation of the subject: it is subject to the dual demands of its social world *and* its inner nature.[25]

This idea still runs the risk of misunderstanding, and this is often linked with the notion of 'authenticity' or 'self-realization'. This notion projects the social normativity to which the judgment of authenticity relates into the 'world', outside of the subject, in order to confront it with its 'inner' nature in a comparative and evaluative way. Here, the judgment of authenticity seems to refer to a relationship between internal and external. But this is wrong because the subject itself, in its 'inner being', is constituted through its relation to social normativity. The social form which it thus acquires is no less an inner determination of the subject than its ('inner') nature. In this sense, very different from that found in the ego-model of the inner core, the notion of 'authenticity' or 'self-realization' does in fact refer to a relationship *within* the subject: to the relationship between its social form and its inner, inherent nature.

This thesis, which I shall explain in more detail in what follows, may be formulated at the outset by distinguishing between and linking various meanings of the expression 'self-realization'.[26]

---

[25]   The thesis of the ideal of self-realization outlined in what follows states that although this coexistence (of social world and inner nature) must be understood in terms of a successive movement (from inner nature to social world), it continues to exist at the same time as an antagonism.

[26]   I understand the concept of self-realization in such a way that it is opposed to the

We may speak of 'self-realization', first and basically, with respect to socially determined norms: a norm (or rule) exists only inasmuch as it is realized through application to specific cases. The norm does not exist prior to, but in its application; its reality is its realization. The norm is its sequential, concrete expression in specific events, in which it nonetheless retains its own identity, indeed, exists only as 'itself'. In this sense, the realization of the norm is its *self*-realization. But this it is also in the further sense that the norm can only be realized as itself, can only retain its identity amid the wealth of its various applications, if it becomes a self: if the norm (as Hegel stated of the true) as a substance is also a subject. The norm exists only *through* the self, indeed, normativity exists only *as* subjectivity.

This is the fundamental but only the first level of the conceptual content of 'self-realization'. On a second level, this expression means that the subject, by realizing the socially determined normative demand, also realizes *itself* at the same time. The subject is thus not merely, as in the first step to defining the concept of self-realization, the agent of the norm's realization; beyond this, the subject is also itself part of the normative content, which he must realize. Realization of the self – this genitive is understood subjectively on the first level, as realization carried out by the self. In addition, on the second level, this genitive acquires its objective meaning: that it is the self, which is being realized (by itself). Self-realization means, first, that the self is that which realizes the law, and, second, that the self is also itself being realized. To put

---

paradigm of self-legislation in *both* of its stages. The objection raised to the concept of 'self-legislation' by the concept of 'self-realization' is that it adopts a one-sided or abstract perspective. The idea of self-legislation regards the relationship between law and subject solely from the perspective of the drawing up of the law. It thus reduces the problem of 'extraneousness' in the relationship between law and subject to the question of the origin of the law: the heteronomy of the subject, brought about by the law, must *and can* be overcome solely by the subject becoming the origin, the 'author' of the law. The ideal of self-realization is anchored in the experience that this does not do away with the 'extraneousness' within the relationship between law and subject: a self-imposed law may weigh upon the subject with particular force as something alien because the subject is in fact in the role of 'subject' in the literal and political sense of the word even with respect to the law he has imposed upon himself: his is the role of the subjugated or underling. The problem of 'extraneousness' in the relationship between law and subject cannot therefore be limited to the question of which authority creates the law. It must also consider how the law is applied. This perspective is concerned with the *reality* of the law. As against the modern idea of self-legislation, the Romantic ideal of self-realization thus brings about a change of perspective: from production to application and thus from the content to the reality of the law.

it differently: the self is first the agent and second the (normative part-) content of realization.

These two levels in the conceptual content of 'self-realization' can also be understood as two sequential steps within the historical process of subjectification – within the history of experience or consciousness in which the idea of the subject has developed. In the first step, the subject gains self-awareness such that it depends on him whether the socially determined norms exist in the first place; the subject discovers that his wants and action are the only instantiations of the socially defined norms. In the second step, which requires and radicalizes the first, the subject also gains the self-awareness that in every action in which he realizes the socially determined norms he also realizes himself; that his actions, which comply with socially determined norms, express and develop at the same time who he himself is. In the ideal of self-realization or authenticity, this second experience becomes an explicit demand.

These two steps in the model of subjectification understood as self-realization are explained in more detail in what follows by taking a sidelong glance at the eighteenth-century theory of the subject. In the eighteenth century there was a break with the manner in which the rationalism of the seventeenth century had thought about the 'ego'. The rationalist ego is defined by its transparent relationship with itself, by the certainty of its self-consciousness. The subject of the eighteenth century, meanwhile, is a practical subject: a subject of abilities and activities. The key discourse for this new concept of the subject is the developing philosophical discipline of aesthetics. It forms the background and prerequisite without which the Romantic ideal of authentic self-realization, as an expression of inner nature, cannot be formulated.

2

The question of the reality or realization of norms is the question of how one gets from ought to action. The answer provided by the subject theories of the nineteenth century is that one gets from ought to action via ability: that which one ought to do must become that which one is able to do in order that it become a reality. To put this idea in a somewhat more detailed way: when we enquire into the realization of a norm, this assumes that the norm itself or 'as such' is not yet a reality. But the norm tells us what ought to be a reality; the norm is the as-yet unrealized: it initially does no more than make a claim to (its) reality. But this claim to reality is directed not at reality, but at the doings and actions of subjects. For subjects to be able to realize norms, the subjects must *be able to* realize these norms.[27] The norm may be the not-yet real not only in the sense of

---

[27]   Here, 'able to' is used in two different ways. In the first case it has a logical meaning, and in the second a practical one.

that which ought to be, it must also be (or become) the not-yet real in the sense of the possible. And indeed, in the sense of that possible for the subjects themselves, their faculties or abilities. The norm cannot remain a mere normative claim, it must, in order to become real, become a subjective ability. The realization of the norm requires the internalization, the appropriation of the law by the subject: the norm is (and remains) unreal as long as it is only a demand made of the subject and vis-à-vis the subject. The norm becomes real only when it becomes 'inherent to' the subject (when it becomes his own). In the terminology of the eighteenth century, this means when the normative demand made of the subject becomes an inherent 'power'.

We misunderstand this basic idea through which the subject theory of the 'aesthetic' eighteenth century contrasts with the rationalistic model of the ego if we take it to mean that there is already a subject in existence which then, by appropriating the normative demand, acquires powers and faculties (in addition). Rather, the subject first *arises* through this process of gaining powers, of acquiring faculties. Or: the being of the subject consists in (nothing but) the having of powers and faculties to realize norms.[28] (In the same way, we misunderstand the basic idea of the aesthetic theory of the subject if we take it to mean that there is already a norm or an ought prior to its realization through subjective action. Rather, a norm can become an ought for a subject – an individual subject – only if it is already being realized by subjects, that is, if the norm already *is* a subject.) The associated model of subjectivity states that being a subject consists not primarily in knowing oneself, but in being able to do something. Subjectivity is not initially a theoretical relationship, that is, it is not definable as self-awareness, but rather a practical relationship. Indeed, subjectivity's practical relationship with itself consists in being able to manage itself: self-government or self-management is the basic definition of subjectivity. Here, being able to manage oneself means nothing other than possessing the capacity to act; having the potential or the power to bring about changes in the world. This begins with seemingly minor things: the 'power' of the infant,

---

[28]   *Anima mea est vis* is the key definition of the concept of subject introduced by Baumgarten; A. G. Baumgarten, *Metaphysik*, § 505, after Baumgarten, *Texte zur Grundlage der Ästhetik*, ed. H. R. Schweizer (Hamburg: Meiner, 1983), p. 2. For a more detailed treatment, see Christoph Menke, 'Wahrnehmung, Tätigkeit, Selbstreflexion. Zu Genese und Dialektik der Ästhetik', in A. Kern and R. Sonderegger (eds), *Falsche Gegensätze. Zeitgenössische Positionen zur philosophischen Ästhetik* (Frankfurt am Main: Suhrkamp, 2002), pp. 19–48. On the following, see Christoph Menke, 'Zweierlei Übung. Zum Verhältnis von sozialer Disziplinierung und ästhetischer Existenz', in A. Honneth and M. Saar (eds), *Michel Foucault. Zwischenbilanz einer Rezeption. Frankfurter Foucault-Konferenz 2001* (Frankfurt am Main: Suhrkamp, 2003), pp. 283–99.

acquired with much effort, to use his hand in such a way that he succeeds in moving something from here to there. And it culminates in major things: the power or the ability of the politician to conduct herself in such a way, in her actions and, above all, speech, that others follow her; the power or ability of the artist to conduct himself in such a way in his imagining and depicting (which includes opting 'not to conduct himself' when the time is right) that a work emerges which others look at and admire.

It is this practical understanding of subjectivity which explains why education, practice, and discipline (and disciplining) became a key topic in the thought of the eighteenth century. The capacity to conduct oneself, which constitutes subjectivity, is not something one has already, but something that must be acquired. But the capacity to conduct oneself cannot be acquired in the abstract or as such; rather, the capacity for self-conduct is acquired in such a way that the capacity to engage in certain ways of acting or practices is acquired. In the concept of capacity, faculty, power – or whatever terminology one may use here – both these aspects are linked with one another from the outset; the ability to conduct oneself is acquired as the ability to carry out tasks. Here, we should not understand the ability to carry out a task in a purely instrumental sense, as the successful bringing about of external changes. This is in fact the exception. Rather, the basic definition of the ability to carry out a task is the ability to master and carry out a way of acting or practice. A way of acting or practice is defined by its particular standard of success. What a particular way of acting or practice is, what constitutes making a chair, playing football, giving a lecture, can be indicated only by stating what it means to do it correctly or well. Behaviours or practices are not subject to external criteria of success; rather, the criteria of success, and the reference to them, are immanent to behaviours or practices. To be able to carry out a behaviour or practice thus also means the capacity to have it succeed. Or: to be able to do something always means to be able to do something good – the capacity to bring about the good of a behaviour or practice.

This practical definition of the subject and its ability, its capacities, now casts new light on the connection between the two steps which make up the concept of self-realization. In the first step, 'self-realization' means that *one oneself* realizes a normative demand. The second more radical step states that the subject, by realizing the normative demand itself, realizes *itself* at the same time. It now becomes apparent that the second step is in a certain sense already entailed in the first step: if one understands correctly what it means that the realization of a norm can occur only through a subject, then every instance of the realization of a norm, correctly understood, is always also the self-realization of a subject. The argument for this is the theory of ability outlined above. On this view, a norm becomes reality only by becoming an (inherent) ability of the subject, that is, *the subject's* faculty or capacity.[29] This is apparent in the connection between the normative demand immanent to a practice, and the subjective ability which makes it possible for a practice to succeed. Ability is the ability to have something succeed – to be able to conduct oneself in accordance with the normative demand inherent to a practice. But at the same time, it is precisely this practical self-relationship that defines subjectivity. The bringing about of the good of a practice, or: the fulfilment of a normative demand, and the putting into effect of one's own faculties, which means both conducting oneself and carrying out a task, is one and the same thing. *All* action is at once the fulfilment of a normative demand *and* 'self-realization' – because it is possible only as such.

3

The result of the revised 'practical' version of the concept of subject, as a subject of powers and faculties, consists in making self-realization a basic definition of subjectivity itself. Every action undertaken by a subject to which normative demands apply must thus be understood as its self-realization, that is, as the realization of one of its abilities or faculties.[30] This result, as convincing as it may be with respect to the definition of the (acting) subject, is, however, disappointing with regard to the ideal of self-realization. For with this ontological understanding of self-realization, as a definition of the reality of subjectivity, the demand for 'self-realization' appears to lose its normatively exacting sense. If every action is already self-realization, the *ideal* of self-realization becomes empty – a mere tautology.

---

[29]   This is my attempt to counter Dieter Thomä's objection to the notion of self-realization. His objection is that reference to 'self-realization' assumes that the self is previously a (mere) possibility. Thomä calls this the 'conceptual misfortune' of any notion of self-realization (D. Thomä, *Vom Glück in der Moderne*, Frankfurt am Main: Suhrkamp, 2003), p. 275. My explanation attempts to identify the fundamental (and correct) insight of the notion of self-realization in this very fact: by realizing a norm, the subject makes a reality of that which makes up his potential, his faculties.

[30]   Here, the proposed definition corresponds to Charles Taylor's programmatic title, which suggests that we understand 'action as expression'; see 'Action as Expression', in C. Diamond and J. Teichmann (eds), *Intention and Intentionality. Essays in Honour of G. E. M. Anscombe* (Ithaca, NY, and New York: Cornell University Press, 1979), pp. 73–89. My difference from Taylor lies in the fact that he understands that which is expressed through action as meaning rather than power. The reason for this is apparent in Taylor's contribution to the Ricœur festschrift; see 'Force et sens', in G. B. Madison (ed.), *Sens et existence. En hommage à Paul Ricœur* (Paris: Seuil, 1975), pp. 124–37. Here, Taylor understands power solely in the sense of causal efficacy (see pp. 124, 131) – rather than as faculty or capacity.

But it only seems this way. In reality, the reverse is true: the ontological definition of subjectivity as self-realization, far from robbing the ideal of self-realization of its normative sense, makes its normative use meaningful in the first place. To put it historically, the revised 'practical' version of the concept of subject, as a subject of powers or faculties, above all in the aesthetic theories of the eighteenth century, is the prerequisite for the 'Romantic' proclamation of the ideal of self-realization at the end of that century. Detaching this ideal from this prerequisite gives rise to the 'debased and discredited' versions to which Charles Taylor has referred: 'self-realization' becomes the pigheaded insistence upon the natural definition of a self, but one which for this very reason lacks all normative power. On the other hand, if one sees the Romantic ideal of self-realization against the background of the revised practical version of subjectivity, first the problem and then the solution to which it points become apparent.

Subjective abilities, this is the thesis of the revised practical version of subjectivity, are acquired normative demands. Becoming a subject consists in the process of internalization through which demands become abilities; here, a subject develops that knows how to conduct itself (and in this sense also knows *about* itself). But this process of subjectification is at once a process of socialization. For the ability to conduct oneself, constitutive of the subject, is nothing other than the ability to carry out behaviours or practices defined by their normativity, by their immanent standard of success. But as normative phenomena, behaviours or practices are also fundamentally social; they are always social in nature. This does not mean that, once we have mastered them, we always carry them out with others. In the case of activities such as hammering in a nail and going for a walk, this is obviously not so. Practices are 'social' in a different sense: because their immanent standards of success exist as social realities. What success means for a specific practice is not laid down by the individual, but is socially prescribed. To learn to carry out a practice or behaviour thus means to learn how *one* does them. As a rule, learning situations therefore require an other, whose function it is to embody the social 'one' (and who is thus a *de facto* third party). He, the teacher or referee for example, speaks for or *as* the social 'one', whose standards of success we attempt, through learning, to make our own – such, that is, that we are able to satisfy them. Thus, subjectification as the attainment of abilities of self-conduct means becoming a representative of the social 'one' oneself through learning and practice.

The fact that subjectification, socialization, and becoming a subject means becoming 'one' is unavoidable; for without learning how to carry out a socially defined practice, it is impossible to acquire the abilities involved in conducting oneself. But if subjectification only means socialization or socialization to the exclusion of all else, it is, as Michel Foucault reformulates Heidegger's critique of the 'one' ('critique' in the sense of restriction rather than rejection), a process of disciplining. As is well known, Foucault talks of 'disciplining' or 'disciplinary power' with reference to the early modern societies of the seventeenth and eighteenth centuries. However, one may also understand these concepts, defined in terms of the history of power, in such a way that Foucault is using them to point to a problem of the new *concept* of the subject, which developed during this period (and under these social conditions). Foucault characterizes the motif of this critique as 'the paradox of the relations of capacity and power'. This means that 'the relations between the growth of capabilities and the growth of autonomy are not as simple as the eighteenth century may have believed'.[31] Subjectification, as an increase in ability or power, always means an increase in freedom: only when one is able to do something is one free to do it or not do it. But at the same time, this freedom to do or not do is attained only in as much as the subject learns to satisfy the socially defined criteria of success that characterize practices. In Foucault's account of disciplinary power, the subject gains the capacity to comply with a 'system of gradations of normality' (or, to use Wittgenstein's term for such processes, is 'trained' to do so). Here, the meaning of the acquisition through practice of the capacity to act or power over oneself consists in being normal or being able to function. A process of subjectification, which is only socialization or socialization to the exclusion of all else, is a process of 'normalization'.

With this criticism, Michel Foucault, though he certainly did not see things in this way, reformulates the feeling of unease with which the ideal of self-realization or the ethics of authenticity begins. Negatively, this unease includes the fact that it is insufficient to understand the process of acquiring normative demands, through which subjectivity develops, solely in the manner elucidated so far. As yet, 'acquisition' meant merely that normative demands on the subject become its own abilities. The critique of disciplining as normalization shows that this is not enough. However, with the attempt to grasp exactly *what* is missing here, the difficulties of an ethics of self-realization already begin, and these become glaring in its 'debased' forms. Rather than the various ways in which it is expressed, let us therefore look at its leading intuition. An initial way of expressing this intuition might be as follows: what matters is not just that I acquire normative demands or make them my own in such a way that I learn how to carry them out, but *which* normative demands. They must be normative demands that I can accept or affirm. But this fails to take us much further. For I can surely accept or affirm many of the normative demands which constitute the criteria of success of social practices: I can affirm their existence as social practices. The affirmation at which

---

[31]   M. Foucault, 'Was ist Aufklärung?', in E. Erdmann *et al.* (eds), *Ethos der Moderne. Foucaults Kritik der Aufklärung* (Frankfurt am Main and New York: Campus, 1990), pp. 50–1 (I assume that Foucault understands 'autonomy' here in the unspecific sense of 'subjective freedom'.)

the ideal of self-realization aims must therefore be of a different, more specific kind: an affirmation not only by me, but *for* me. The intuition which stands at the beginning of the ethics of authenticity thus means that the process of making socially given normative demands one's own must itself again be subjected to a – further, stronger – normative demand, geared not towards the success of the specific social practice, but towards the individual life. This is what it means when Hölderlin's chorus tells us that Antigone wishes to live her 'own life'.

There are two different ways in which we can try (and which have, of course, been tried) to spell out this further or stronger normative demand on individuality, to which the process of making socially normative demands one's own is subject. The first approach wishes to understand it as a demand for the *linkage* of all, or at least the majority of and most important, activities, which an individual has learnt to carry out. Here, 'individuality' is an idea of wholeness, of the integration of the subject's many activities and abilities into a meaningful context (often understood as the narrative context of a life story). The alternative to this explanation consists in understanding the nature of the self's relationship *to* the specific behaviour or practice, which it has learned to execute, differently. According to this second explanatory approach, that it is a behaviour through the performance of which the individual 'realizes himself' or experiences the behaviour as 'authentic', means that this behaviour is his 'own' in another, more exacting sense than in the fundamental sense that he has the means or ability to realize its socially defined normative demands: it means that the behaviour *fits* him. And in contrast to the first explanatory approach, this does not mean that the behaviour corresponds to his other behaviours (such that they interconnect meaningfully), but that the behaviour corresponds to *him* – to that which he himself *is*.

4

But this way of putting things again throws up the question which the ego-model of the inner core could answer only in such a way that it failed to grasp its real meaning as a normative question (regarding the normative relationship of correspondence between self and action). In contrast to the ego-model of the inner core, we can at least now ask the question properly: as a question about how the self relates to the socially defined normativity of behaviours, which it has learnt how to comply with or practise. To be more precise, the question is *whether* the self can relate *to* the socially defined normativity of behaviours, which it has learned how to comply with or practise, in the first place; for the subject arises only *through* this process of acquisition through learning and thus consists *of* the abilities acquired within it. A 'social' subject of this kind can no doubt decide against individual practices that it is able to carry out, and can understand and lay down specific criteria of success differently than the community ('one') does. But these are critical operations carried out within the execution of social practices, while participating in social practices. The question of whether a behaviour can be my 'own', meanwhile, does not assume the social character of the subject, but is directed at this character in an evaluative way.

Thus, for such evaluation to be possible, the definition of the self must not be equated with its social character. That is, it must have a 'natural' definition. Yet the critique of the ego-model of the inner core has shown that an evaluation in the name of natural definitions is internally inconsistent (or circular). Natural definitions as such cannot be the source of normative demands – let alone demands against which the socially acquired abilities of conducting the self and carrying out tasks might be measured. But a subject which has acquired these abilities, and is in this sense a social subject, may make normative claims *for* its natural definitions: as a social subject it may become aware of its natural definitions and pay attention to its relationship to its social character in explanatory and evaluative fashion.

It was by developing this new way of looking at the self that Herder moved decisively beyond the theory of becoming a social subject reconstructed so far and into an ethics of self-realization. Herder calls this way of looking at the self 'anthropology' and understands it as a different way of describing the 'birth', origins, and development of the subject. Here, on the one hand, Herder takes up the concept of practical-social subjectivity through which the aesthetics of the eighteenth century breaks with the rationalism of the seventeenth, while opposing the equation of subjectification and socialization through which aesthetics risks becoming a mere ideology of disciplining.[32] One passage, with which Herder concludes a lengthy reflection on the learning of language, shows this in exemplary fashion:

> For the most part this '*birth of our reason*' is so indecent to the wise men of our world that they quite fail to recognize it and revere their reason as a congenital, eternal, utterly independent, infallible oracle. Doubtless these wise men never walked in children's smocks, never learned to speak as their nursemaids spoke, or perhaps have no limited 'circle of sensation', no *mother- and human-tongue*, at all. They speak like the gods, that is, they *think purely* and cognize ethereally – wherefore, then, also nothing but sayings of the gods and of reason are able to come from their lips. Everything is for them innate, implanted, the spark of infallible reason stolen from heaven without a Prometheus. Let them talk and pray to their idol-words; they

---

[32] On the critique of (eighteenth-century) aesthetics as an ideology of aesthetics in the work of Foucault and Eagleton, see Christoph Menke, 'Die Disziplin der Ästhetik. Eine Lektüre von *Überwachen und Strafen*', in G. Koch, S. Sasse, and L. Schwarte (eds), *Kunst als Strafe. Zur Ästhetik der Disziplinierung* (Munich: Fink, 2003), pp. 109–21.

know not what they do. The more deeply someone has climbed down into himself, into the structure and origin of his noblest thoughts, then the more he will cover his eyes and feet and say: 'What I am, I have become. I have grown like a tree; the seed was there, but air, earth, and all the elements, which I did not deposit about myself, had to contribute in order to form the seed, the fruit, the tree.'[33]

'What I am, I have become' – this is the principle of an anthropological reflection which Herder conceives in historical fashion, or more precisely, as a genealogy. On this view, everything that makes up the human being as a subject must be understood as the result of his development and learning. For only a perspective which recognizes the 'genesis' of the subject out of his 'ground' is capable of understanding the composition of the subject and his abilities. This programme is aimed at the 'wise men of our world', that is, the rationalist philosophers. They talk as if their reason was 'stolen from heaven without a Prometheus' (that is, without mediation or assistance). Therefore, 'they know not what they do'. Because they are mistaken about the origins and development of reason, they are mistaken also about its presence and its limits; because they fail to appreciate the beginnings of reason in the 'limited "circle of sensation"', they wrongly see the achievements of reason as 'infallible oracle', as a source of pure, error-free certainty – the 'sayings of the gods'.

Against rationalism's tendency to forget about development, Herder's anthropological genealogy of subjective abilities reminds us, first, that we would be and have nothing without others' help. As they see themselves, the rationalist philosophers 'never walked in children's smocks, never learned to speak as their nursemaids spoke, or perhaps have no limited "circle of sensation", no *mother- and human-tongue*, at all'. Here, Herder again reformulates the insight that the process of becoming a subject can occur only through socialization, by means of teaching and practice (p. 212):

This teaching, this sense of an alien which imprints itself in us, gives our thinking its whole shape and direction. Regardless of all seeing and hearing and inflow from outside, we would grope about in deep night and blindness if instruction had not early on thought *for us* and, so to speak, imprinted in us ready-made thought-formulas.

But according to Herder's account, the acquisition and internalization of the

---

[33]   J. G. Herder, 'On the Cognition and Sensation of the Human Soul', in Herder, *Philosophical Writings* (Cambridge: Cambridge University Press, 2002), p. 212.

standards and forms of social practice is just one side of the development of the subject. The other side is expression – the expression and further development of a pre-existing ground. Without doubt, there is a need for 'external media', which 'spell out for [us] certain properties and sides of things' (p. 211); this is evident to anyone who 'has noticed children, how they learn to speak and think' (p. 211). But these are 'media' precisely in the sense that something is expressed in or through them. This is also apparent through observation of a child, which, 'just as it brings with it the form of its body and face, also brings with it the traits of its inner manner of thinking and sensing' (p. 235); it brings something with it or has been given something as a 'gift' (pp. 232–3), which constitutes its 'individual human nature' (p. 235). The idea outlined by Herder here is that of a subject which can think and say nothing (specific), indeed, which can feel and perceive nothing (specific) without external 'help'; but which at the same time, if it were not already busy interpreting and making connections in some vague way through its 'energy of the soul', would neither be in need of nor capable of accepting such external direction and guidance. Herder's anti-rationalist genealogy not only leaves behind the finished subject to return to the processes of socialization through which it acquired its abilities; in Herder's genealogical perspective, the prehistory, the 'dark ground', which takes us behind the processes of subjecti-fication-as-socialization, also comes into focus.

This is the new understanding of subjectivity that Herder outlines through his critical analysis of the practical-social concept of the subject. All acquisition of abilities occurs as the development of powers already at work; powers of one kind or another must always already be at work within the individual for it to be possible for the development of abilities to begin. These powers are present or given within the individual. This applies, first, to their status: they precede the process of subjectification-as-socialization; they are, in this sense, natural powers. This applies also to their content: through the powers of the soul already at play from the outset, individual human beings differ from one another;[34] in this sense, they are individual powers. To be more precise, all social acquisition of subjective abilities thus occurs as the development of naturally given and individually specific powers. Without this gift or template, there can be no formation of subjectivity; without a nature, particular to each human being, capable of development or education, there could be no social capacity for normativity.

---

[34] 'The deepest basis of our existence is individual, both in sensations and in thoughts' (Herder, 'On the Cognition and Sensation of the Human Soul', p. 217). '[I]t is, I think, the most flat-footed opinion that ever entered a superficial head that all human souls are alike, that they all come into the world as flat, empty tablets. No two grains of sand are like each other, let alone such rich germs and abysses of forces as two human souls – or I have no grasp at all of the term "human soul"' (p. 236).

The 'genealogical' reference to natural and individual powers as the 'ground' of subjectification has, first, an objective-explanatory purpose in Herder's anthropology: the aim is to understand clearly upon which preconditions all processes of becoming a subject rest. But the 'genealogical' reference is not limited to this; rather, the natural-individual powers identified as the 'ground' themselves attain normative power through this reference, a power which, for example, Herder expresses in the following demand: 'If genius and character are only *living human nature*, nothing more and nothing less,[35] then observe this, nourish the inner source, train the activity and elasticity of the soul, but only *as it wants* to be trained' (p. 236). With this 'they' – to develop the natural-individual powers as *they* 'wish' to be developed – these powers themselves become a yardstick for evaluating processes of subjectification. More precisely, they are declared or made a yardstick for evaluating processes of subjectification. For to state that the natural-individual powers themselves 'want' something is only an abbreviated way of talking about a more complex, two-stage process. That the natural-individual powers of a subject 'want' something means that they (like all powers not subject to external impediment) strive to manifest themselves in a particular way. But this striving of natural powers is not a normative demand. On the contrary, normativity means negativity vis-à-vis the mere striving of natural powers. The natural is no criterion. But it can be made into one. And indeed by none other than the subject, by making the striving of its natural powers the content of its wants. Only a subject that is more than merely its nature can claim to be true to its nature; one can only wish to become – only *wish* and only *become* – what one is as a result of one's nature. Thus, that the natural-individual powers themselves 'want' something (not only strive to be developed) is, normatively understood, not an observation about these powers, but about the subject which possesses them. It tells us something about what the subject wants: a subject which – in Herder's sense – reflects upon itself anthropologically and genealogically wants its socially acquired subjective abilities to take on a form in which using them may also be considered the development and further development of its natural-individual powers. A subject that wants this is a subject concerned with its own self-realization.

---

[35]   This refers back to the critical, ironic remarks which Herder previously made about the cult of the 'genius' and with which he counters Klopstock's definition: 'The modest German, says *Klopstock*, thankfully calls it *giftedness*, and I have no further concept or explanation of it. *Genius* and *character* are – "the individual *human nature* [Herder's footnote: *Genius, ingenium, indoles, vis animae, character* have this meaning in all languages] that God has given to someone", neither more nor less.' Herder, 'On the Cognition and Sensation of the Human Soul', pp. 232–3.

5

That the negativity of the subject (vis-à-vis nature) is a prerequisite for the normativity of nature (the nature of the individual) sounds like a paradox, but isn't. Rather, it is a description of how, in the ideal of self-realization or authenticity, the individual's natural powers attain normative power, that is, become a criterion for evaluations and demands. For this can occur only with reference to socially constituted subjectivity. The form this reference takes is the subject's recalling of his 'natural' prehistory. I have interpreted Herder's genealogical perspective as an example of such recalling. In this interpretation, for Herder, the genealogical perspective does not primarily have the objective meaning of a philosophical examination of the human being's natural endowments, but is an aspect of the way individuals look at *themselves*. The genealogical return to natural powers performed by Herder indicates the historical dimension of individual self-consciousness. This also has consequences for that which appears as 'nature' in such genealogical self-reflection.

Jean Starobinski's account of the 'genetic' method practised by Rousseau in his autobiographical writings, particularly the *Confessions*, is illuminating here. This method takes us 'back to [...] the source': 'The goal is to demonstrate continuity of evolution ("the *thread* of my hidden dispositions"); but in so doing Rousseau also wants to record the discrete "impressions" that impinged on his soul "for the first time".' [36] This return does not lead us to any 'absolute' beginnings. But they may be treated as absolute in autobiographical writing: as origins out of which that which followed developed and thus must be understood. They *are* the origin or beginning *of* a particular development. Herder's concept of nature, which he uses genealogically, can also be understood in light of this genetics. Here, 'nature', or natural power, is not substantially distinct from history. Rather, 'nature' and 'history' indicate a functional distinction made from the perspective of the self-reflective individual. In narrating her history, the individual treats something *as* the 'dark' ground, on the basis of whose unfolding that which followed developed; she reflects upon her history by referring back to something which both precedes this history and which unfolds through it. What Herder's genealogical model calls 'nature' is that which, to the self reflecting upon its history in this position, seems the underlying or preceding condition.

---

[36] Jean Starobinski, *Jean-Jacques Rousseau: Transparency and Obstruction*, trans. Arthur Goldhammer (Chicago, IL, and London: University of Chicago Press, 1988), p. 192. Here, Starobinski quotes the following passage from the *Confessions*: 'The earliest traces engraved in my mind have remained there, and those that have impressed themselves upon me since then have combined with rather than enfaced their predecessors. There is a definite sequence of emotions and ideas, and those that come first modify those that come later; one must know this sequence in order to judge properly. I always try to bring out the initial causes in order to explain the sequence of effects' (p. 193).

This determines the structure of the judgment we make when we evaluate a life (or a piece of one) as authentic or as self-realization. It is a judgment of a relationship: the relationship between the natural powers of an individual and that which she is capable of doing through her socially acquired capacities to act; a judgment, that is, of the relationship between nature and history, between nature and culture. It is thus a judgment of a relationship that has an impact both within the self – the relationship between its natural powers and socially acquired abilities constitutes the self – and between individual and society. For one side of this relationship, that of history or its culture, is the form of the subject, which it has attained through its socialization, that is, through its internalization of the normativity of social practices. In judging authenticity or self-realization, this social form of the subject is evaluated with respect to the natural powers of the individual. Thus, what is *not* evaluated here – this was the mistake made by the ego-model of the inner core criticized at the beginning – is whether an act or a life corresponds directly to (or is the expression of) the natural powers of an individual. Such direct correspondence could pertain only if natural powers were already capacities to act. But natural powers become capacities to act only through socialization, that is, by breaking with the immediacy of natural powers. The ideal of self-realization or authenticity is anchored in the insight into this rupture at the centre of the subject. Every capacity to act is non-natural in the sense that it is socially acquired; subjectification is socialization. But this is not a solution; on the contrary, it puts into words the problem to which the ideal of self-realization or authenticity wishes to provide a solution (and which, in its debased and discredited form, it anxiously avoids): the problem of the 'alienation' of nature and culture which emerges within the subject. To resolve this problem cannot mean searching for behaviours that are natural or in line with nature (for as *behaviours* they are always subjective or social). Rather than level it out, a solution must assume and take for granted the difference between nature and culture whose aggravated form, alienation, it wishes to combat.[37]

---

[37]   One way of avoiding this difference within the subject, between nature and culture, consists in wishing to realize natural powers directly, without the detour of its manifestation in capacities to act, that is, socialization through internalization of norms; this is, once again, the ideology of the inner core. But the other way of avoiding this difference consists in the contrary assertion that the natural powers are absorbed completely, without leaving a trace, into the capacities for social action whose basis and prerequisite they constitute. If we wish to avoid both these forms of avoiding difference (and thus break out of the unreflected opposition between ethics of quasi-natural authenticity and total sociation), we must therefore try to conceive of the difference between (natural) power and (social) capacity. The difficulties with which such an attempt finds itself confronted begin immediately with the fact that this

III. Joys and Horrors of Authenticity

I

The ideal of authenticity or self-realization aims to achieve a correspondence between the natural powers of the individual and the socially acquired form of the subject. This ideal, as the critique of its debased form in the ego-model of the inner core wished to show, can, however, only be rendered comprehensible if its starting point is the ontological difference between those things whose correspondence it seeks to achieve. This is the difference between nature and culture (or nature and normativity). A key insight of the ideal of authenticity is that we do not have to understand this difference as incommensurability: if the individual reflects upon himself 'genealogically', the natural powers, to use Herder's expression, may become the 'yardstick' for evaluating socially and culturally acquired subjectivity; the natural powers may take on normative power. With this insight, the ideal of authenticity or self-realization establishes the practice of a new, radical form of cultural and social criticism: the critical reflection on cultural and social forms in light of the question of whether they not only develop our natural-individual powers into social capacities, but are spaces of exploration and facilitation, which enable us to express and unfold those powers.

It is this combination of an ideal of authentic correspondence and a practice of radical criticism that I have called 'Romantic'; Rousseau and above all Herder are its first representatives. This combination also entails the formulation of a characteristic which defines the culture of modernity as a whole: the culture of modernity features the refraction of culture in nature; reflection upon and evaluation of cultural and social forms with respect to the natural powers of the individual. The Romantic ideal of authenticity, however, means more than just this; the Romantic ideal of authenticity not only demands that we judge the social form of the subject by his natural powers, but asserts that it is possible to make the social

difference is evidently not a symmetrical difference, a difference between things of the same kind. Natural powers cannot therefore be distinguished from social capacities in terms of content, in terms of what they aim to achieve. This accounts for their indeterminacy. But the difference between them lies in the very fact that this difference cannot be determined: this is not a difference between goals that can be defined in terms of content, but a difference between the *mode of operation* of powers on the one hand and capacities on the other. Thus, an explanation of this difference (diagnosed by the ethic of self-realization) would have to demonstrate an element of (normatively indeterminable and thus subjectively unavailable) power in every socially acquired capacity. Discussions with Andrea Kern made me aware of this problem, as fundamental as it is unresolved here.

form of the subject tally with his natural powers and explores ways of realizing this possibility. The Romantic view is that society and culture can be transformed, or in fact revolutionized, in such a way that individuals experience their socialization as synonymous with the further development of their natural powers – as Herder puts it: as a practice of the soul in line with what it itself wants. The young Marx may have found the pithiest formula for this claim made by the Romantic ideal of authenticity when he wrote: 'fully developed naturalism [...] equals humanism [... ;] fully developed humanism equals naturalism'. Marx calls that which this formula is meant to represent 'communism'; it is:

> the *genuine* resolution of the conflict between man and nature and between man and man – the true resolution of the strife between existence and essence, between objectification and self-confirmation, between freedom and necessity, between the individual and the species. Communism is the riddle of history solved and it knows itself to be this solution.[38]

For communism is nothing other than the structure of authenticity or self-realization once it has become the general state of affairs.

The thread which Marx is picking up here is the Romantic idea of a seamless correspondence between natural powers and subjective-social capacities. Marx's communism projects this seamless correspondence into the future, while it is a historical beginning for Herder (and Rousseau). This is the systematic meaning which the concept of 'mother tongue' has in Herder. Like all language, the mother tongue is also *learned* language. But as against everything else that is socially learned, such as any languages learned later (Latin, for example, in our case), it is not just the language learned first: 'It left its impression on us first, and at the tenderest of ages, as it was *by means of words* that we gathered into our souls the world of concepts and images that becomes the writer's treasure trove.'[39] Rather, for Herder, it is (or becomes) a language with which we are in a state of perfect harmony – to such an extent that Herder no longer uses the concept of social learning and practice, but images of natural unity: 'our way of thinking is, as it were, implanted in it [the mother tongue], and our soul and ear and organs of speach are formed along with it' (p. 408). It is 'my language' (p. 408), in which I am 'master' (p. 412).[40] Herder

---

[38]   K. Marx, *Economic and Philosophic Manuscripts of 1844* (London: Lawrence & Wishart, 1970), p. 135.

[39]   J. G. Herder, *Über die neuere deutsche Literatur. Dritte Sammlung*, in *Werke*, vol. 1 (Frankfurt am Main: Suhrkamp, 1985), p. 407.

[40]   On this metaphor, used repeatedly by Herder, see G. Plumpe, 'Eigentum – Eigentümlichkeit. Über den Zusammenhang ästhetischer und juristischer Begriffe im 18. Jahrhundert', *Archiv für Begriffsgeschichte* 23 (1979), pp. 175–96.

certainly makes use of the two-stage model outlined earlier again here: the 'dark ground' of the soul is articulated and its character defined through social learning and practice, initially that of the mother tongue. But in the unique case of the mother tongue, the social learning and practice should no longer (as Herder wrote) be the 'meaning of another', 'which imprints itself upon us'. Here, in the case of the mother tongue, there should be a perfect correspondence between that dark ground and the social form of the subject attained through learning.

The same structure which defines Herder's concept of the mother tongue also determines his concept of the individual, which he understands as a 'little world' or 'sensory universe'. For here again, according to Herder's genealogical model of human development, we must distinguish between two different levels, two different ways in which we make one out of many:[41] through our natural powers and through our socially acquired capacities. And as in the model of the mother tongue, Herder's concept of individuality conflates these two levels. As a result, though, Herder must either divest the powers already at work in the dark ground of the soul of their natural and individual character and endow them with a socially pre-established form; or, conversely, he must divest the capacities acquired through learning and practice of their social character and have them emerge from the nature of the individual (for one's inner nature is always individual). Whichever way one looks at it, Herder's explanation of the success of authentic correspondence in the models of the mother tongue and of individual totality risks losing sight of the difference which his 'genealogical' reflection on subjectification was so centrally concerned to demonstrate.

The fundamental insight of Herder's genealogical perspective was that the subject entails a dark ground of natural-individual powers *prior to* its socially acquired form. This is the insight which Herder deploys to criticize the seamless equation of subjectification and socialization.[42] It is also the insight which made the concept of authenticity possible in the first place: the idea

---

[41]   Herder, *Vom Erkennen und Empfinden der menschlichen Seele*, pp. 353–4, see also pp. 350ff.

[42]   The following remarks are also directed against John Dewey's critique of the concept of self-realization in 'Self-Realization as the Moral Ideal' (1893), in Dewey, *Early Works*, vol. 4 (London and Amsterdam: Feffer & Simons, 1975), pp. 42–53. Dewey rightly rejects the idea of the self as 'a presupposed fixed schema or outline' (p. 43), which supposedly exists in the form of the possibility or ideal and must then be realized. This he contrasts with a perspective which assumes that the self is a 'concrete specific activity', a perspective which attributes potential or capacities on this basis (pp. 45–6). At the same time, however, he identifies these with that which is already entailed in the present action in its fullest and most appropriate form (see pp. 50–1), in order to preclude a fundamental ('infinite'; p. 45) surplus of capacity beyond its realization through action.

of authenticity opposes the practice of standardization and disciplining, by evaluating the form of the subject according to *another criterion* than the ability to succeed as socially defined. This other criterion is the further development of natural-individual powers. The fact that these powers are 'natural' (or are experienced as such by the individual) means that they are categorically different from the socially acquired subjective capacities. These powers do not exist *in order to* fulfil normative standards; natural-individual powers feature no inherent normatively defined telos. In this sense they are 'undefined': they are the potential of a normatively unspecific striving and impacting. If, as Herder's genealogical perspective tries to show, such powers exist, that is, if we look at ourselves in such a way that we assume a 'dark ground' of our soul, as a means of understanding the history of our social acquisition of subjective capacities, then we ascribe to ourselves a 'nature', which may indeed be cultivated into the social form of the subject, but which remains forever a prerequisite for and thus separate from this form. The ground of natural powers thus introduces into the subject an irredeemable unfathomability. The ground of natural powers is both ground and abyss for the social form of the subject: the natural powers of the individual are never entirely absorbed into its socially acquired form and thus always go beyond its socially acquired form. There is a tension between the natural ground and the social form of the individual, which may be eased but which, for conceptual reasons, because of their categorical difference, can never be entirely resolved.[43] Herder's models of

---

[43]   The account in this paragraph follows Dieter Thomä's explanation of an authentic relationship to oneself as 'self-love'. 'Self-love' is what Thomä calls a relationship to oneself 'which makes it possible to identify an action, a decision, but also a feeling as one's "own"' (Thomä, *Erzähle dich selbst*, p. 246). One of the dimensions of self-love, according to Thomä, following Rousseau, is a sense of one's own 'existence', which he describes, borrowing from the phrasing used by Nietzsche and Plessner, as the unfathomable ground of possibility (p. 203; see also pp. 184, 206). Within the relationship of self-love, according to Thomä, the relationship of this unfathomable ground of possibility to the 'definitions' of the subject (acquired through socialization in my interpretation) is one of 'supplement' (p. 203). But this contradicts the way Thomä has previously described the 'feeling of existence' with Rousseau: as an 'ecstatic' experience possible only by turning away radically from the (social) world (see p. 198). This account, it seems to me, renders inevitable the consequence that Thomä is determined to avoid: rather than speaking of the 'complementary' relationship between the unfathomable ground of possibility and social determination, we must refer, with Derrida, to the aporetic character of the self. On the critique of Derrida, see p. 199 and D. Thomä, 'Das "Gefühl der eigenen Existenz" und die Situation des Subjekts. Mit Rousseau gegen Derrida und de Man denken', in A. Kern and Ch. Menke (eds), *Philosophie der Dekonstruktion. Zum Verhältnis von Normativität und Praxis* (Frankfurt am Main: Suhrkamp, 2002), pp. 311–30.

an authentic language, supposedly unique to the individual, and of an individual totality claimed to be whole and cohesive mislead us about this tension. It is, however, with the insight into this tension that the post-Romantic history of authenticity begins.

2

Two aspects are crucial to the post-Romantic history of authenticity: that it is *post*-Romantic, but a history of the idea of *authenticity*. 'Post-Romantic' – here, this means that it is concepts of subjectivity which cast doubt on the possibility of a total correspondence between the natural-individual ground and the socially acquired form of the subject; concepts of subjectivity, in other words, which are aware of the (ontological) rift between nature and culture running through the centre of the subject. Nonetheless, they are concepts of authenticity. For even if they cast doubt on the final step taken by Romantic concepts of authenticity, namely the belief in the possibility of a complete correspondence between the natural-individual ground and socially acquired forms of the subject, they follow them with regard to their first and fundamental step. This is the step that entails attributing a normative claim to the natural powers themselves and judging the forms of socially acquired subjectivity in accordance with this. The post-Romantic objection to Herder's concept of mother tongue and individuality is that it short-circuits the natural and the social in a way that conceals their fundamental difference: the natural powers of an individual are not constituted in such a way (for they have no 'constitution') that their unfolding could be equated with the participation in a social practice. But at the same time it is also true that the natural powers of an individual cannot possibly unfold unless a subject acquires the capacity to participate in a social practice; if it lacks the ability to participate in a social practice, the subject can do, and thus *is*, nothing at all. This is the problem with which the authentic subject is confronted; it is the recognition and above all the *having* of this problem that makes the subject an authentic one. It can satisfy the normative demand of its natural powers – according to Herder, the demand that one make use of these powers as *they* want to be made use of – only in such a way, namely through the social attainment of subjective capacities, that it fails to satisfy this demand, curtailing or even betraying the development of its natural powers. We might call this the 'aporia of authenticity'. From a post-Romantic point of view, 'authentic' means an outlook which judges the social form of the subject by its natural powers *and* is aware of the impossibility of their total correspondence.

To conclude I would like to recall two tropes, which I shall roughly outline, through which our post-Romantic culture has thought about and practised this resolution of the tension relating to 'authenticity'. The first trope conceives of the tension in perfectionist fashion – as stimulus and space for the ceaseless improvement of culture; the second trope conceives of the tension in tragic fashion – as the limit, or even the abyss of all culture.

A predicament is aporetic if there is no way out of it. But this does not mean that one can do nothing *in* this predicament. One can try to change social practice in such a way that involvement in it at least moves closer to the normative demand to develop one's own natural powers. This change may, for example, lead to the invention of new, individual and original forms of speaking. The priority here is not to speak differently from others, but to speak in a characteristic, that is, in one's own way, in a way that tallies with one's own inner nature. The attempt to find a language of one's own is the attempt to find a language other than the conventional. But this is not the attempt to find a language different from that of others. For if I can fulfil the normative demand to develop my natural powers only by participating in a social practice, such as that of speaking, then every attempt to change this language in such a way that it becomes my own is also a proposal to improve socially practised public language. Thus, if I understand my creative change of language *only* in terms of it becoming my own as a result, I am misunderstanding it. I fail to grasp that every time I invent a way of speaking peculiar to me I have in fact undertaken or suggested a change in public language, which must prove itself from this point of view: the creation of a generally better language, and that means better for everyone. By the very fact that I am trying to find a language of my own, I thus take part – whether I know it or not, whether I want to or not – in the shared project of improvement, and ultimately perfection, of public language.

This makes it clear that even a post-Romantic culture of authenticity – a culture made up of individuals concerned about their authenticity – is not an exclusively private culture. Rather, a culture of authenticity develops its own form of public sphere. But this is a public sphere of a particular kind, not a homogenous medium in which individuals appear as equal persons. Rather, it is a space of competition – a medium of contestation.[44] This is a competition in which individuals take part in order to determine whose route to making language 'characteristic' is acceptable and right for everyone else. Because the competing proposals arise from the perspectives of individuals, this competition can never be won. But more important than winning the competition is entering it and holding it, that is, not to misunderstand the attempt to improve public language in such a way that it may be considered one's own, as a case of privatism, but to understand it as a debate with others over the best, the perfect form of our common, public language.

The perfectionist understanding of the ideal of authenticity sees the constitutive

---

[44]   See Stanley Cavell, *Conditions Handsome and Unhandsome* (Chicago, IL, and London: University of Chicago Press, 1990), ch. 3.

unfathomability of the individual, which is anchored in the indefinable character of his natural powers, as a source of innovation and transformation of social practices, through participation in which the individual becomes the subject of capacities. The natural powers are thus experienced here as conducive to changing the subject, and through it the society or culture.[45] But this is only one side of the tension between natural powers and subjective capacities; the experience of this tension is at the centre of the post-Romantic ideal of authenticity. The other side is the experience that the natural powers are not only capable of being socially or culturally productive, but are also asocial and thus destructive. Indeed, that they have the potential to be socially or culturally productive only *because* they are asocial and thus destructive. This is the abyss which the ideal of authenticity has opened up within the subject through its normative reference to inner nature – and which no Romantic primitivism, or post-Romantic perfectionism, can close up again. Few commentators have described this more acutely than Lionel Trilling who, in his study of sincerity and authenticity, declares Joseph Conrad's *Heart of Darkness* the 'paradigmatic literary expression of the modern concern with authenticity'.[46] Conrad's novel deals with Kurtz, who carries on his cruel regime in the jungle of the Belgian Congo as representative of the royal trading company and who dies uttering the dark words: 'The horror! The horror!' Trilling reminds us that these words have often been interpreted by 'critics of liberal or radical [i.e. left-wing] view' as a reproach to the Belgian imperialist regime, which was in fact horrific. But according to Trilling, there is 'no ground' for this (p. 133). Kurtz's horror is not at colonial society and its cruelty, but at himself; according to Trilling's account, it is the horror which seizes the one who, with reckless truthfulness, has looked within himself.

The chorus in Sophocles' *Antigone*, which stated that Antigone lives solely according to her own law or lives her own life, has also said prior to this that much is 'monstrous', 'but nothing more monstrous than man'.[47] The chorus relates this to the fact that, despite all the knowledge and abilities that he has acquired, indeed *through* all his knowledge and abilities, the human being is a transgressor of laws: 'More than he hopes of wisdom and the skills of art, he comes to grief one time and to good another. He offends the laws and the sworn conscience of earth and the rulers of nature' (p. 81). Thus, it is the ethical ambiguity of the socially acquired capacities that the *Antigone* chorus calls monstrous. Kurtz's horror, meanwhile, resembles that which modern thinking

---

[45]   A prime example is G. H. Mead, *Mind, Self, and Society: From a Standpoint of a Social Behaviorist* (Chicago, IL, and London: University of Chicago Press, 1967), pp. 214ff.
[46]   Lionel Trilling, *Sincerity and Authenticity* (London: Oxford University Press, 1974), p. 103.
[47]   Sophocles, *Antigone*, p. 81; after Hölderlin.

about the subject sees in the figure of Oedipus: the horror at the monstrous, the terrible thing which the human being is as a result of his natural powers and wants – and the horror at the monstrous, the terrible thing which the human being must therefore do to *himself*, to his natural powers and wants, when he becomes a social subject and makes socially defined normativity his own.

10

The Status of the Enlightenment in German History[1]

Reinhart Koselleck

Si Dieu n'existait pas, il faudrait l'inventer.
If God did not exist, it would be necessary to invent Him.

This statement from Voltaire is readily cited to underline the sovereignty of the human being said to have been unleashed in the eighteenth century, when people broke free of religion and metaphysics. The human being, it is suggested, also determines the position of God and, if needed, for reasons of social control for example, may occupy His position argumentatively. Belief in God is no longer a theologically grounded, self-evident commandment; it is universally useful or, to use more modern language, ideologically fungible.

Allow me to add a second dictum now quoted just as readily to characterize the self-determination of the human being attained, at least theoretically, in the eighteenth century. 'How is it possible to have a history a priori?' asked Kant. His answer: 'If the fortune teller himself creates and contrives the events which he has prophesied.'[2] The human being is or is becoming capable, many readily conclude in light of this passage from Kant, of organizing his history according to a plan, of making his own history.

Both interpretations, presented in abbreviated form here, clearly belong

---

[1]   The first part of this lecture was first held at the University of Hamburg in January 1980 at the invitation of the Art History department; the second part (which included an interpretation of social history omitted here) was replaced by the present version, delivered in honour of the 300th anniversary of the University of Halle.

[2]   Immanuel Kant, *Der Streit der Fakultäten. Erneuerte Frage: ob das menschliche Geschlecht im beständigen Fortschreiten zum Besseren sei?* (The contest of faculties. A renewed attempt to answer the question: is the human race continually improving?), ed. H. D. Brandt and P. Giordanetti (Hamburg: Meiner, 2005 [1798]); translation by Alex Skinner.

together. If God is no longer the master of this world, who intervenes in everyday life in unpredictable ways, but at most a figure of thought, then His place is taken by the human being. The latter becomes an 'earthly god', able to steer his history in rational fashion. Those who formerly cited God and His Providence could, from the late eighteenth century, cite history, the world history of human beings who, progressing from plan to reality, are realizing their freedom to an ever greater extent. And anyone taking this interpretation of intellectual history as her starting point will also be able to conclude that the eighteenth century was in some sense an era of enlightenment. An era, whether in the sense of a turning point or a threshold or in the sense of a period with a clear endpoint after which modernity, our history, began, a time when human beings must adapt to this world, their world, without recourse to non-human or superhuman authorities. As a history of the Enlightenment's ideological impact, this interpretation – put forward by Voltaire and Kant, two of the intellectual exponents of the eighteenth century – can even lay claim to a certain plausibility. The unfortunate thing about this interpretation is that it is wrong.

At the time, both these quotations, which have now taken hold as clichés, meant something different than we find in them today. Voltaire's remark that God could be invented, if necessary, was suggestive. As a deist, God's existence was for Voltaire indisputable, the entire natural world pointed to the existence of the supreme being on whom all our lives depend. He must exist; this was Voltaire's deist postulate. This was a kind of subjective proof of God. Declared atheists such as Diderot, Holbach, and Laplace came a generation later.

Herbert Dieckmann has shown how deeply implicated the entire philosophy of the Enlightenment remained in the questions considered by Christian theology, which it tried to answer in new ways.[3] Questions were asked about the existence of the soul, life in the beyond, original sin and evil, the relationship between freedom and necessity, and similar old problems already posed by theology. And this goes for Kant as well, even for the dictum cited above. For him, this does not constitute evidence that history can be made. Rather, much like Voltaire's dictum, it is meant half-ironically. The human being who brings about the events he predicts is the anxious politician who fears the people and thus provokes the revolutions he wishes to avoid. Or the prophet of doom who unintentionally helps realize his visions by evoking them. If history is being made here (Kant refers cautiously to 'events'), then it is the opposite of what was planned. This was a 'self-fulfilling prophecy' that no-one intended.

Politically, Kant's target here are those holding power in State and Church, but his aim was not to demonstrate the potential to make history. This insight

---

[3]   H. Dieckmann, 'Religiöse und metaphysische Elemente im Denken der Aufklärung', in Dieckmann, *Studien zur europäischen Aufklärung* (Munich: Fink, 1974), pp. 258–74.

into the context thus requires us to tone down two famous flourishes of
the Enlightenment. The passages are more restrained or ambivalent than the
statements quoted above might suggest.

First, let's turn once again to the interpretations of the quotations relating to
the invention of God and the potential to make history mentioned at the start.
Both interpretations come from the nineteenth century. They already assume the
death of God, such that it was possible to reinvent Him – interpreted as a human
projection. And they refer back to a history whose potential to be produced, to be
made, could be conceived only through transcendental philosophy. The conditions
of history correspond to the intellectual conditions of its knowability.

But both interpretations are elicited from texts which had at least opened
up this possibility of an interpretation, or at least the possibility that the
authors could have thought such things. The semantics of the texts thus extend
further than the writers' intentions. A simple counter-question reinforces this
supposition: it would have been impossible to make either statement in the
seventeenth century. Both are based on the anthropological assumption that
human beings are inherently destined to make their own decisions, to become
autonomous, if they are not already. Rational self-determination free of external
authorities is an implicit condition for conceiving of the potential to construct
God or produce history, for rendering it possible to think of such things. And
if we take into account the ironical weapons and techniques of camouflage by
means of which the Enlightenment thinkers had to or wished to operate under
the restrictions imposed by censorship, our two dicta from Voltaire and Kant even
take on a cryptic meaning, which may turn out to be the intended meaning or
at least a meaning that such language has made possible. This applies to Kant's
phrase 'history a priori',[4] which, in the context of an interpretation of Job, he
expects potent practical reason to master.

Voltaire's half-ironic thought experiment concerning the possibility of
inventing God at least points to a certain human autonomy, which Kant wished
to establish through moral philosophy and extend to the possibility of mastering
future history.

Despite reservations arising from the critical analysis of these texts, we
would thus have risked identifying a trend that helps to signify an important
strand of the Enlightenment as a whole. It allows us to trace the distance from
heteronomy to autonomy, which Enlightenment philosophers saw it as their task
to cover: away from the heteronomy of Church and State, away from superstition
and belief in miracles towards a religion, founded in reason and morality, that
is universally applicable. Away from the rule of monarchs, the kind of rule not
subject to the laws which it is the task of the self-determining citizen to recognize

---

4   Kant, *Streit der Fakultäten*.

and implement politically – the citizen of a republic as the normative standard for every society.

Such statements at least outline the self-understanding of that tiny minority of the intellectual elite who identified the century they were living in as one of enlightenment during their own lifetimes. This observation has brought us to the very centre of our discussion. How are we to define the Enlightenment, whose status within German history is our concern here, in the first place?

In an initial run-through, I will offer some remarks on the history of concepts which, with any luck, open up a minimal definition of the Enlightenment in a systematic sense.

In a second stage, the newly defined Enlightenment can then serve as a criterion against which some findings relating to German history will be measured.

First, the conceptual history of that which we have become accustomed to calling the 'Enlightenment'. What we are dealing with here is an absolute semantic novelty, that of the definition of an era that also extends into the future. For it is something new in history for a generation of contemporaries to apply an epochal term to itself. It took three centuries for the Renaissance to be termed as such around 1550. The Reformation was adopted as an epochal descriptor 100 years after the theological *reformatio* and its ecclesiological consequences occurred, and the 'modern age' was endowed with its emphatic name only in the nineteenth century, the so-called 'Middle Ages' having supposedly ended as early as 1500. Set against these findings, the 'Enlightenment' is an astonishing exception. To live in the age of reason, of criticism, of enlightenment was part of the definition of the eighteenth century itself: that is, while the period itself was unfolding, it was experienced and understood as a distinct era. Thus, so-called 'humanity', self-determining in autonomous fashion, also made decisions about the chronologically unique period through which it was living – it not only thought rationally, but also historically, something which we can affirm against all the sterile debates on historicism.

But let us be cautious. In German, the epochal self-definition, the definition of the eighteenth century as a century or age of 'Enlightenment', appears only in the 1780s – triggered by Zöllner's famous question: 'What is Enlightenment?' [5] Mendelssohn was right to state that the word was a newcomer to the German language. [6]

---

[5]   The question was posed in the *Berlinische Monatsschrift* (*Berlin Monthly*) in December 1783 in reply to an earlier essay by Johann Erich Biester, one of the journal's editors.

[6]   Mendelssohn did so in his essay 'Über die Frage, was heißt aufklären?' (On the question: What does 'to enlighten' mean?) – first published in September 1784 in the *Berlinische Monatsschrift*.

If we now consider the Enlightenment to have begun in retrospect with Leibniz or Descartes, and include within it Thomasius (thanks to Halle) and Wolff (again, thanks to Halle), the term was as yet unknown as regards this so-called 'Enlightenment'. In any event, from the perspective of the stimulating debate around 1780, the new term 'Enlightenment' is an owl of Minerva, which spread its wings only at the end of the defined period. And Hegel made sure – as far as he could – that the Enlightenment be applied only to the eighteenth century. Thus, even this emphatic term of historical self-definition rapidly becomes an ex-post term.

The notion of a threshold, the use of 'Enlightenment' to initiate a new period, was thus pushed into the past and historicized within a generation. And the further back the Enlightenment was dated, its beginnings placed as early as the seventeenth century, the greater the tendency to dismiss it as outdated. But we cannot content ourselves with the semantic finding – from the perspective of those who grew up with the French Revolution.

Expressed in this single term, Enlightenment meant more than the mere self-conscious identification of a historical period. Enlightenment always lays claim to an enduring systematic, anthropological status as well, the implication being that it cannot and must not become outdated. It claims an elementary innovative potential per se. Some linguistic remarks are helpful here.

In German, the term 'Enlightenment' – *Aufklärung* – was initially a natural condition, then a metaphor, before attaining the status of standard term. In terms of everyday language, it initially referred to *serenitas*, to the brightness of that change of weather that causes the sky to clear or that leads to the rays of the rising sun, driving away the clouds or the dark night. The active verb, 'to enlighten' or 'to enlighten oneself' in a sexual sense, had long been common in the eighteenth century before it was condensed into the collective singular of an 'enlightenment in general' (*Aufklärung überhaupt*) by Schaumann in 1793.[7]

It was only through this transition from verb defining action to noun that 'enlightenment' could attain theoretical status – analogous to all terms found in philosophical, social and political, or theological language at the time. This transition took place in German (later than in the French *éclaircissement*) in the 1780s, and it led to a theoretically new, innovative dynamism that other terms lacked. *Verstehen* (understanding) led to *Verstand* (intellect) – a term referring to a specific state, *Vernehmen* (perception) to *Vernunft* (reason) – a term referring to a long-term condition, *Begreifen* (grasping) to *Begriff* (that which is grasped) – an expression that pins down and fixes, which captures conceptually that which we seek to understand. 'Enlightenment' is a different matter. Enlightenment is not only a new term appearing in the 1780s – it is also an innovative term

---

7   J. C. G. Schaumann, *Versuch über Aufklärung, Freiheit, Gleichheit* (Halle, 1793).

that introduces a process which consistently aims to change things, above all, to improve them.

Kant registered this precisely in 1784, when he revised the statement that we are living in an enlightened age: no, he asserted, we are living in an age of Enlightenment.[8] Here, it is not the goal or result that is highlighted – but rather the way and the task. As Wieland said at the time: 'Enlightenment is a means rather than an end.' 'Enlightenment' thus enters the ranks of the processual terms that were gaining theoretical potency at the time, such as progress, development, history; used transitively or intransitively, these made it possible to articulate linguistically a profound experiential shift. Enlightenment as a self-evident moral commandment to liberate oneself from self-imposed immaturity (first understood as 'emancipation' in the nineteenth century) – this is a dynamic precept that turns the verbal form *aufklären* into a permanently repeatable, reflexive concept of action. From a systematic point of view, the concept of an Enlightenment which acknowledges no authorities other than those insights one has attained rationally and by oneself, other than self-monitored will-formation – this anthropologically grounded concept can only be demanded and established if it engages in a historical development caused by this very Enlightenment. Enlightenment is thus a systematic concept, inconceivable without the historical change which is to be caused by the Enlightenment in the first place. This is the hallmark of the term.

It is unique as an epochal term and at the same time repetitive – as a constant challenge. Since 1800, it has thus been possible to apply the term historically both to the breakthrough that occurred in the eighteenth century and equally well to all historical situations understood in an analogous way: to the flowering of culture in Athens, to the enlightenments in the Middle Ages, to the Renaissance, and to numerous occasions in the nineteenth and twentieth centuries up to the so-called 'third Enlightenment' identified by Marcuse at the time of the student rebellions of 1968. This double-sidedness of the Enlightenment as a completed process discovered once and pinned down uniquely as a concept – and yet systematically capable of cropping up again everywhere, that is, the fact that it is both systematically established and historically repeatable, this double-sidedness runs through all definitions from 1780 on.

Truth, justice, maturity (*Mündigkeit*), humanity – who would wish to forego them, even if the only way to attribute any meaning to them is by Enlightenment – 'enlightenment' taken in a literal sense: 'to bring to light' injustices, acts of inhumanity, lies, prejudices, or errors? Arguments over what exactly constitutes

---

[8]   Kant's statement appeared in the December 1784 publication of the *Berlinische Monatsschrift* as part of his famous essay 'Beantwortung der Frage: Was ist Aufklärung?' (Answering the question: What is Enlightenment?).

true or false Enlightenment thus run through every camp, whether Protestant or Catholic, right or left (since the French Revolution). Looked at in this way, the Enlightenment, ever since it was phrased as such, has been concerned with achieving a minimal consensus without which it seemed impossible or inconceivable to live together in society. No historicization can oust this systematic and repeatable claim asserted by the Enlightenment.

Admittedly, at this level of generality, couched in terms with which few would disagree, the Enlightenment rapidly enters the realm of the arbitrary. Each individual enlightens herself in so far as she is able – socially, religiously, or politically, or in other ways. Since its appearance, Enlightenment (like progress and history) has become a cliché, a nebulous term that no longer allows us to make distinctions; a term, therefore, that is best avoided.

We must therefore extend our semantic investigations. Few can be unaware of the negative term *Aufkläricht*, coined by Leo (which alludes to *Kehricht* or 'rubbish'), or that of *Aufklärerei* or 'enlightening around', which accuses the Enlightenment philosophers of exhibiting a brashly impertinent know-it-all attitude, their arguments divorced from reality. This critique begins with the French Revolution at the latest. Some approvingly trace the Revolution back to the Enlightenment: the latter is believed to have been realized in the Revolution. Others trace its failure, the terror and dictatorship of Robespierre and Napoleon I to the fact that the Enlightenment had not gone far enough, that it was merely half an Enlightenment. The Enlightenment is thus never wrong – whether the Revolution succeeded or failed. Right in principle, it was merely the attempt to apply it that went wrong. Or the other elastic extreme: the Enlightenment is made specifically responsible for the disasters. Ever since millions were killed by the French Revolution as a result of the civil war and the ensuing post-Revolutionary and Napoleonic Wars throughout Europe, the Enlightenment is thought to suffer from a lack of evidence in its favour. And if it is still claimed to be right, its opponents assail it as mere ideology.

The victims of the guillotine in Paris, those drowned deliberately in Avignon, the firing squad victims of Lyon, the drowned of Trafalgar, and those who froze to death in Moscow are no longer amenable to enlightenment. In Lessing's words: 'Nothing that requires the spilling of blood is worth one drop of it.'[9]

From 1789 on, this experience changed the standing of the Enlightenment within the German vocabulary. Wieland, who initially welcomed the Revolution with optimism, seeing it as a result of the Enlightenment, is an example. In 1793 he concluded that 'the periods of the greatest enlightenment have always been those in which every type of speculation, madness, and worship of the

---

[9]   G. E. Lessing, *Ernst und Falk: Gespräche für Freymäurer* (Ernst and Falk: Dialogues for Freemasons) (Wolfenbüttel, 1778–1780); translation by Alex Skinner.

practical were most in fashion.'[10] And in 1798 he added bitterly that with the spread of the Enlightenment, we 'have refined the art of deluding ourselves to an unprecedented degree'.[11] Later, such insights were to be called the 'dialectic of Enlightenment', the analysis of which produced, as it were, an Enlightenment of the Enlightenment, a kind of meta-Enlightenment.

The art of unmasking, of ideological critique, was constantly provoked and refined anew by a ceaseless flow of historical challenges. I mention only Marx, Freud, and Nietzsche for the nineteenth century, Mannheim, Horkheimer, and Adorno for the twentieth. The Enlightenment thus proved capable of adaptation, but the naive innovative emphasis of the eighteenth century, the idea that you could force progress, was lost as a result.

We shall therefore permit ourselves another look back at the semantics of the eighteenth century. Even then, the Enlightenment came up against limits which it had unintentionally set itself, but which had not gone unnoticed. The word was mostly used transitively. Those who referred to the Enlightenment had to ask themselves: who is enlightening whom? And about what? Then, though, it emerged that this Enlightenment in the name of reason was rapidly abandoning the tolerance that it itself had postulated. Whether it was Joseph II ending restrictions on the practice of Lutheranism on the condition that individuals first completed a six-week course of religious re-education intended to win them back for Catholicism; or Kant, who diagnosed the existing Churches as historical artefacts, yet urged people to attend church regularly; or the fact that atheists continued to be fundamentally ostracized; or that Jews were emancipated only after undergoing conversion or were at least required to give up their rites and customs in the name of moral equality – an overbearing moral despotism always lurked behind the Enlightenment, the imposition of a certain view with pedagogical legitimation which all too often dispensed education in accordance with corporative or national priorities. This, too, was Enlightenment, and it quickly integrated the leading academic classes, the lawyers, theologians, philosophers, and doctors into the paternalistic system established by sovereigns and the state. Moses Mendelssohn, not sworn to progress in light of his experience, saw things more clearly. He warned Enlightenment thinkers against advancing the spread of truth merely in line with calculations of utility: 'The virtue-loving *Aufklärer* [exponent of Enlightenment thinking] will thus proceed with care and caution, preferring to tolerate prejudices rather than banishing

---

[10]   Chr. M. Wieland, *Göttergespräche* (Dialogues of the Gods), No. 12 (1793); translation by Alex Skinner.

[11]   Wieland, *Gespräche unter vier Augen* (Private Dialogues), No. 11 (1798); translation by Alex Skinner.

them along with the truth with which they are so closely entwined.'[12] This was the voice of wisdom rather than prudence, though this is audible here as well. When he defined the Enlightenment in 1784, Mendelssohn also made an observation of enduring validity. He contrasted praxis-related culture and theory-related Enlightenment, subsuming both under the overarching term *Bildung* (encompassing different meanings such as 'formation', 'education', or 'cultivation'). All three terms were new to the German language, but *Bildung* ranked above the other two as the superior term. And this was evident later on. *Bildung* did not take leave of the Enlightenment, but absorbed it. Though it emerged at the same time, it became the new key concept of the nineteenth century.

Bildung is neither *Einbildung* (imagination) nor *Ausbildung* (education in a more formal sense). The self-determination that Kant had demanded of the Enlightenment was to be realized through *Bildung*. The realms of the heart and of emotion, all too readily left out by the rational Enlightenment, were to be integrated into *Selbstbildung*, the cultivation of the self; art was to be integrated into life. Leading one's life in autonomous rather than passive fashion – this meant really taking the Enlightenment into one's own hands.

This self-generated aspiration soon influenced the forms of sociability, especially sexuality. Against the enlightened doctrine that sensuality needs to be managed and controlled, it was equated with love, with love as a kind of anthropologically grounded means of human self-constitution. This is still evident in how we use language. No *Aufklärung* about sexual relationships can surpass experience, which can only be gained through love itself. In short: the process of anthropological self-justification, begun by the Enlightenment, was greatly intensified by the concept of *Bildung*.

This includes the reintegration of religion, over which rational Enlightenment critiques had placed a question mark or which, given the pietist 'illumination', was in competition with the rational Enlightenment. Autonomous *Bildung* converted religion into religiosity, incorporating it into the activity and experience of individual lives.

Let us leave it at that. However much *Bildung* or Enlightenment are taken literally or subjected to ideological critique: the semantic valences and the diachronous sequence attest to the success of the key concept of *Bildung*, which absorbed the Enlightenment into itself. Weimar Classicism, Romanticism, Idealism – all are the result of an Enlightenment thought through to its conclusion, the result of a *Bildung* that has historically never ceased to outdo itself.

This also applies to the use of political language. In the *Volksaufklärung*

---

[12] M. Mendelssohn, 'Über die Frage, was heißt aufklären?'; translation by Alex Skinner.

(people's Enlightenment), the people always remain the addressees and objects of an Enlightenment imposed from above (there are good reasons why Goebbels' ministry of *Volksaufklärung* and propaganda bore this name). But with respect to *Bildung*, the passive addressee takes on an active role. *Volksbildung* and *Nationsbildung* at least allocate to the people or nation the role of potential sovereign, in charge of their own development, their own masters.

There is thus something to be said for the hypothesis that Mendelssohn's linguistic observation that Enlightenment and culture should be subsumed under *Bildung* was intended to put into practice what Kant established theoretically: the autonomous subject, whose arguments must be able to pass muster in the public sphere in order to be rational, develops not through Enlightenment from outside, but through the *Bildung* of the self.

As Herder affirmed in his discussion on freemasons: 'All victories over prejudice [must] be won from the inside rather than the outside [...]. It is their way of thinking, and not society, that makes human beings what they are.'[13] Who could fail to hear the voice of his Königsberg teacher? *Sapere aude* – Have the courage to use your own reason.

Our semantic stock-taking has come full circle. What can lay claim to systematic status over the long term is the minimal formula: Have the courage to use your own reason. Who would wish to contradict this? But we may also ask: who manages to summon up this courage? Enlightenment as a concept of action open to the future and open to reflexion may be compatible with this. But Enlightenment as the dictate of a moral despotism, incapable of tolerating prejudices, of letting them be – this Enlightenment rapidly becomes ideology, which has to deploy terror in order to uphold its rightness. The semantic findings are thus multifaceted to the point of contradiction. In themselves they offer us no norm with which we can assess the status of the Enlightenment in German history. To close, let us therefore make do with six conclusions which are at least compatible with what we have said about language:

1. In the German-speaking world, the Enlightenment was a primarily Protestant movement, inconceivable without the postulated autonomy of the conscience.

2. The secularization of the Catholic Church, its monasteries, its estates, and its constitutional position are also a result of the Enlightenment – notwith-

---

[13]   J. G. von Herder, *Breife zur Beförderung der Humanität*, Zweite Sammlung. Breife 26: Gespräch über eine unsichtbar-sichtbare Gesellschaft (*Letters for the Advancement of Humanity*, Second Series. Letter 26: Dialogue on an invisible-visible society), in Herder, *Sämtliche Werke*, ed. B. Suphan (Berlin: Weidmann, 1881), vol. 17, p. 132, translation by Alex Skinner.

standing the accelerating effect produced by our western neighbours, the Franks as they were then known.

3. In terms of power politics, the focus thus shifted to the Protestant-dominated north – and to the booming educated middle class emerging there.

4. Part of this process, and of key importance, is the continuing influence of natural law, framed in terms of constitutional law through Kant's philosophy, ferment of the movements for a liberal and democratic constitution.

5. Harder to assess, because it has not as yet been studied sufficiently by social historians, is the impact of the Freemason lodges. This secret interior of the Enlightenment did at least stimulate communication between the different estates and was a training ground for moral exercises and democratic principles. The great reforms in Prussia and Bavaria were initiated by masons. The Steinian municipal ordinance, formulated by Frey, and the Hardenbergian agrarian reforms, under the overall control of Scharnweber, at least made use of the language of Enlightenment, a language which worked towards the independence of all estates, including the bourgeoisie and the peasants, because as human beings they ought to be equal, and if possible brothers.

6. This brings us to one last point, to a criterion that generally distinguishes the German from the French Enlightenment. The German Enlightenment remained informed by theology. From Lessing's critique whose purpose was to protect the pedagogical revelation, through Kant's moral siphoning off of a hypothetical revelation, to Hegel's interpretation of the self-revelation of the spirit, a thread runs through their various philosophies of history, a thread which ultimately plays a key role in the worldviews of the educated middle class and which holds them together.

The *Hallische Jahrbücher*, the voice of the Young Hegelians, bears eloquent witness to this. The Young Hegelians saw themselves as the radical, true, and only consistent Enlightenment. And they were in fact more radical than all the Enlightenment philosophers in France or Britain – more radical because, as career Protestants, they retained a religious motivation.

The critical destruction of the afterlife, the sublation of religion into the interpersonal, social self-constitution did not prevent radical Enlightenment thinkers from continuing to believe in salvation. What is more, they believed that they could implement salvation themselves, whether the sacred state carried out this task or whether it abolished itself because society, its own master, sovereign and free, rendered any state unnecessary. This line of argument runs from the

Illuminati via Weishaupt and Fichte to the Young Hegelians all the way to Marx and Engels.

You will permit me one final remark, once again on language, with which we began. When the metaphors of Enlightenment language are transferred to politics, they recognize just two camps: one of light and one of darkness. Behind this opposition lurk alternatives, one of which we are compelled to accept; we are left with only one way out. For who would not wish to stand in the light, advancing towards the sun, leaving behind all creatures of the dark, eliminating them if possible or necessary? We should forgo this legacy of the Enlightenment, conveyed through the language of propaganda. May we have the courage to use our own reason.

11

The Dark Continent – Europe and Totalitarianism

Mark Mazower

I have been asked to talk about the relationship between Europe and totalitarianism, two concepts which are much used and much misunderstood. Both concepts need a little investigation before they can be used. I want to start with *Europe* by asking a perhaps odd question – does modern Europe have a history? – before going on to ask what place totalitarianism might have within it.

Eric Hobsbawm has questioned whether continents can have histories *as continents*. After all, from a purely geographical point of view, Europe is merely the western prolongation of Asia with no clear dividing line: where one makes the border – whether, following the Russian geographer Tatischev, at the Urals, or, as was once implied, along the former Iron Curtain, or perhaps along the current border with Russia – is an intellectual choice which generally rests upon various politico-cultural assumptions. Bismarck once said: who speaks about Europe, is mistaken; it is a purely geographical concept. In fact, however, it is anything but that.

The modern political conception of Europe emerged out of the divisions of Christendom and has never entirely lost those associations. It was following the Napoleonic Wars that the Great Powers took upon themselves the right to speak in the name of Europe. But when the Russians described the Holy Alliance in the 1820s as 'the great Association of Europe', it was its Christian character against the godless French they had in mind. Christianity stood for civilization against barbarism, and Europe was increasingly identified with the same emancipatory struggle. The British Earl of Clarendon in 1854 saw the Crimean War – a war fought against Russia on behalf of the Ottoman Empire – as 'a battle of civilisation against barbarism, for the maintenance of the independence of Europe', and two years later, the Treaty of Paris admitted the Ottoman Sultan to the Concert of Europe – the reformed grouping of Great Powers – on the condition that he introduced the principle of religious equality into his lands: in other words, whereas in 1815 the Holy Alliance had ruled out including the Turks (since they were no Christians), four decades later, 'Europe' was coming to stand for a set of normative principles which could even be extended to an Islamic state, a set of principles, let it be noted, with a certain conception of freedom at their heart.

But there was another important aspect of the emergence of the concept of 'Europe' in nineteenth-century diplomatic consciousness: it was associated with ideas of preserving continental peace by ensuring a balance of power among the leading states – the very balance of power which Napoleon had overthrown so alarmingly. The Concert of Europe was thus linked to the emergence of an 'international system of states'. For its Habsburg and Romanov sponsors, those states were primarily hereditary monarchies and empires. 'Peoples? What does that mean? I know only subjects', declared the Emperor Francis I. But almost from its inception, the Concert of Europe found itself grappling with the power of a new political force – nationalism – which transformed the continent through the rest of the nineteenth century, and swept away many of those, such as Metternich, who had believed they could control it indefinitely. The 'challenge of Europe', then, was the same challenge which faced Kant: how to secure peace in a fragmented world.

For the historian of Europe, the rise of nationalism poses a challenge of a different but related sort. The rise of history as a profession largely coincided with the triumph of nationalism and was indeed closely linked to the rise of the nation-state: history offered this radical new form of political organization a kind of legitimacy, and historians were highly valued. People and states – to use Carl Schorke's term – 'thought with history', and the mission of the historians was to tell the story of their nation whose present standing required a glorious past. As a result, the vast majority of historians were and still are trained in the field of one or another national history, and produce works, debates, and arguments which reflect this.

To the question, therefore, whether there is a specifically European history which stands over and above the conglomeration of national histories which fill our bookshops, scholars are intrinsically uneasy. They have given three kinds of answers. One is that which you will find in any textbook. The history of the modern world – at least between 1815 and 1945 – is nothing other than the history of Europe, understood as the rise and fall of a certain system of states, and the political and social modes of organization associated with this. This professional approach originated with the First World War, the international discussions over war guilt which followed Versailles, and the opening up of state archives. These developments permitted the emergence of diplomatic history as an academic discipline and shaped a narrative of modern European history which still dominates our teaching. In the 1970s a British scholar did a statistical analysis of the structure of a dozen commonly used textbooks of modern European history. He showed that scholars were still fighting over the old question of who started the First World War, only to this they had now added the issue of the origins of the Second World War as well. Focusing almost two-thirds of their attention on just three countries – Britain, France, and Germany – they offered differences of nuance but the same fundamental narrative – the background to 1914, the war, and the disintegration of the peace settlement, Weimar and the economic crisis, the rise of the Third Reich, collapse of the Popular Front, the polarization of the Spanish Civil War, and so on. Eastern Europe scarcely got a look in; Russia not much more. Moreover most historians evidently followed Felix Gilbert's assumption that 1945 was 'the end of the European era' since, apart from a perfunctory treatment of the Cold War, they had little to say of recent events. It was as if European history, strictly understood, had ceased to exist with the rise of the Super Powers. We should be better off, wrote Geoffrey Barraclough in the *Times Literary Supplement* in 1956, 'if we could scrap our histories of Europe and free our minds from their myopic concentration on the West. [It] obscures the fact that we are living in a world totally different, in almost all its basic preconditions, from that which Bismarck bestrode.' Only recently has the end of the Cold War encouraged historians to see the years from 1945 to 1990 as *history* too.

The second kind of European history is very different to this. It seeks to rescue and trace through time a certain 'idea of Europe', reaching back much further into the past than 1815 – sometimes indeed to Rome, the Goths, or early Christianity. This approach is generally one with its eyes firmly fixed on the present, or even on the future. The French Protestant historian-statesman Guizot saw European civilization as a blend of Germanic independence, Christian spiritual individualism, and Roman civic virtue – a brew which some still find tempting – and concluded that 'European civilisation had entered into the truth, into the plan of Providence; it advances according to the ways of God. That is the rational principle of its superiority.' A little later, Jacob Burckhardt was far less optimistic: 'European culture' was – in his view – under constant and increasing threat from the 'despotism of the masses', the rise of nationalism, materialism, and the modern state. In his mind, the idea of Europe had belonged to a cultivated elite and was essentially a cultural force. Its cosmopolitan culture was perhaps the last bastion against nationalism, which he saw all-conquering, intolerant of difference. Others again, especially in the first half of the twentieth century, defined Europe by the enemy beyond its borders. Their 'European Europe' – some parts of 'Europe' are more 'European' than others – turns out to occupy the space from the Pyrenees to the Danube, a historically Catholic space bounded by implicitly non-European Muslims and Slavs. Thus during the Cold War, for instance, Austrian historians praised the Holy Roman Empire – and its Habsburg heirs – for carrying out their 'historic mission' to defend Europe against the

Orient, while others depicted even Charlemagne as a kind of Cold War warrior. Such a perspective has done much to shape the latest reincarnation of this version – what we might call the 'Eurohistory' supported by the European Commission. Look at Duroselle's 1990 *Europe: A History of Its People* or the large history of modern Europe published two years later by Milza and Berstein, and you will find a similar – we might call it a Christian Democrat – reading of Europe's story from Charlemagne to Adenauer: need one point out its defects – its ignoring of Christian Orthodoxy (producing a most odd version of early Church history) and Byzantium; its downplaying of conflicts within European Christendom; its neglect of the role of Muslims and Jews; its discomfort with conflict in general, and Europe's mid-century drift into dictatorship in particular?

And just here is where we come to the third kind of European approach to history, the one most directly pertinent to my argument – the liberal approach. The idea that Europe's history is the history of liberty goes back at least to Hegel who saw the evolution of world events from the Orient through the Classical world to the Germanic world as a history of gradually expanding freedom. It is difficult to underplay the influence this approach has had on our understanding of Europe's past, especially as adapted over the last fifty or sixty years. The confidence of late nineteenth-century liberals was rather battered, to be sure, even in Britain, by the rise of Mussolini and Hitler. Nevertheless, it persisted: one interwar British best-selling history (by H. A. L. Fisher) insisted against all the odds in 1935 on the liberal inheritance common to Europe as a whole, while the Italian philosopher Benedetto Croce argued in 1941 that liberty 'is the eternal creator of history'. Liberty, he wrote, was still 'the moral ideal of humanity', despite what he described as 'contemporary events and conditions in many countries, owing to which a liberal order, which seemed to be the great and lasting achievement of the nineteenth century, has crumbled'.

Such views did not lack for critics. Followers of Max Weber questioned whether modern capitalism would permit freedom and democracy to flourish. Marxists criticized the liberals' assumption that their values would prevail, or were indeed the only ones that mattered. And perhaps most tellingly, Michael Oakeshott, the conservative British political philosopher, accused liberals in 1940 of underestimating their opponents and the forces ranged against them: obsessed with individual agency, and confident that their views represented the essence of humanity, they saw their enemies as individual tyrants and dictators, closing their eyes to the deep foundations upon which modern despotisms often rested.

As if to bear out Oakeshott's words, we find the eminent American historian Carleton Hayes warning in 1938 of the 'challenge of totalitarianism'. Totalitarianism was a term he applied to Russia, Germany, Italy, and Turkey, among others – the Cold War had not yet turned the last into a valued American ally. Hayes stressed the role of the dictator – irrespective of ideology – and the way a single party and modern communication allowed him absolute control. I shall come shortly to the concept of totalitarianism itself and how it developed over time. The point to note here is that Hayes' article was motivated primarily by concern at public opinion in the USA at that time. He noted with some apprehension the sense:

> particularly among the younger generation that the choice of the future is not between democracy and dictatorship, but between Fascism and Communism. To a considerable number of impressionable and volatile souls, the United States must be made over, and the only question is whether to make it Fascist or Communist.

Totalitarianism – a concept meeting the dangers from Left and Right – thus emerges here as the cry of the frustrated and deeply liberal, keen to reaffirm the values of liberty and to redefine the nature of the fundamental political struggle ahead. 'I do not prefer Fascism to Communism', writes Hayes. 'I do not want any totalitarianism. I want to stick to democracy.' As a personal political position that is clear and understandable enough. But the question here is what the impact of such an outlook has been on the writing of history. It is all very well to see liberty's enemies as the aliens, imposing their views through sheer coercion on a basically liberal populace. The trouble is that the twentieth century has posed a substantial challenge to such views. It is to the nature of this challenge that I now turn.

The First World War was supposed to end with the triumph of liberalism. US president Woodrow Wilson talked about making the world 'safe for democracy' and by late 1918 it seemed this had happened. Three empires had collapsed; there were now thirteen republics in Europe compared to only three four years earlier. A belt of democracies – stretching from the Baltic Sea down through Germany and Poland to the Balkans – was equipped with new constitutions drawn up according to the most up-to-date liberal principles. British scholar James Bryce, in his 1921 *Modern Democracies*, talked about 'the universal acceptance of democracy as the normal and natural form of government'. Yet within only a few years the challenges to this Anglo-American optimism had begun to appear. Even before Mussolini's rise to power, events in Russia, Hungary, and then Turkey showed the difficulties that would be involved in making good on Woodrow Wilson's boast.

In Russia, the first revolution of 1917 – which had been greeted by international liberal opinion as paving the way for genuine parliamentary democracy – was overtaken by the Bolshevik coup later that year. A 'bourgeois democratic' revolution was thus mastered by one fought in the name of 'proletarian socialism'. The Constituent Assembly was dissolved by Lenin and the Fifth Congress o

Soviets later approved its own constitution. But real power was wielded by the Party, and what Lenin thought of his own constitution was made clear when he wrote that 'the scientific term "dictatorship" means nothing more or less than authority untrammelled by any laws, absolutely unrestricted by any rules whatever, and based on force'. This is perhaps the first appearance of a new conception of state power that was to become much clearer in Italy and Germany later on. In Bolshevik Russia, however, there was no single dictator – not in practice at least until Stalin's rise to pre-eminence – and the Party organization was in fact never adjusted to make space for one. Hence Stalin's death – unlike Hitler's, Mussolini's, or Franco's – did not spell the end of the political system he ruled over.

The Bolsheviks came to power in what was simultaneously a world war and a civil war. A similar backdrop not only swept away the old autocratic empires, but pushed several other of the new states to which they gave birth in undemocratic directions as well. In Hungary, the end of the First World War triggered off a civil war between communists and anti-communists which the Right won. Here, the rather ambiguous nexus between war, mass democracy, and rightwing authoritarianism was made clear for the first time. Following elections in January 1920 – the first ever held in Hungary with universal suffrage – Admiral Miklos Horthy presented himself as candidate for the position of head of state. The Allied Powers had prevented a Habsburg from being nominated so Horthy offered himself as Regent. Only a little while earlier he had proposed a military dictatorship as the means to the country's renaissance, but had run up against British and French disapproval. Now parliament duly elected him and allowed him the power to name the head of government: his choice, Bethlen, was not even a deputy. Hungary embarked on twenty-four years of authoritarian rule, during which time elections were held and a powerless parliament continued to meet. Was this a dictatorship? Certainly Horthy was no democrat. Yet he never bothered with a party of his own, and enjoyed only a very modest cult of personality. After the White Terror which brought him to power, his regime was not very repressive and killed far fewer people than the communist regime which ruled the country in the late 1940s.

Let us compare two other cases more or less contemporaneous – from outside Europe. Turkey, like Hungary, was what was left of a great empire after its collapse. Like Hungary it was invaded by its enemies, and the need to defend its territorial integrity accentuated the army's role in politics. At the end of the First World War, Mustafa Kemal Ataturk emerged as the leader of a new Turkish nationalist army. Unlike Horthy he was not a legitimist. In 1921 he combined the positions of President of the Grand National Assembly and Commander-in-Chief and enjoyed powers according to which 'the orders I give are law'. Under his leadership, the Armenians and Greeks were driven out, the caliphate was abolished, and the Ottoman sultans sent into exile. From 1924 until his death in 1928, Ataturk ruled as dictator of a one-party state through his Republican People's Party. He was appointed its head in 1927 – well after he controlled the state apparatus – and after his death he was proclaimed 'Eternal Leader' and 'National Unchangeable Leader'.

In Iran, as in Turkey, the old dynasty was overthrown in the aftermath of the First World War, and an army man, Riza Khan, rose to power with a mission of national reassertion and modernization. Khan himself considered creating a republic along Turkish lines – with himself as an Iranian Ataturk – when news that the Turks had abolished the caliphate alarmed the Iranian ulema. Once they had decreed that a republic was not Islamic, Riza Shah crowned himself head of state – with the support of a Constitutional Assembly. Like Ataturk, he saw dictatorial powers as necessary for modernization and secularization; unlike him, he wrapped this in a monarchist mantle.

Let me summarize what these three cases – European and non-European – collectively indicate about the interwar drift to personal dictatorship. First, they were each the product of a war or national crisis which had bankrupted the old regime and led to a vacuum of legitimacy. Weakness bred the demand for new strength and this gave military men the route to power. Yet national assemblies continued to function in every case – an important point to which I will return. Already a great variety of constitutional forms of dictatorship is evident: in the Hungarian case, parliament voted in a new head of state and handed over powers to him as regent; in the Turkish case, it handed them over to its own parliamentary president who became head of the new republic; in Iran, Riza Khan was already Prime Minister before he was crowned head of state and founded a new dynasty. With the proliferation of dictatorships between the wars – at least twelve or thirteen in Europe alone by 1940 – the difficulties of categorization become more acute still.

The two paradigmatic rightwing dictators in interwar Europe are, of course, Mussolini and Hitler. Both were civilians – in contrast to the three figures mentioned above – with ambiguous links to the armed forces. In both cases, their power came not from a military putsch or from war, but from the political movements they founded. Hitler abjured the revolutionary road after the failure of the 1923 Beer Hall Putsch. But Mussolini had already realized this, entering power in a ruling coalition – in October 1922 only four out of fourteen members of the government were fascists – and moving gradually to the imposition of one-party rule so that it was only in 1926 that all other political parties were banned and the era of 'parliamentary fascism' came to an end.

But the vestiges of the old political system remained in Fascist Italy: there was no clean break. So far as the Italian state was concerned, the Duce was only the head of government, and although the Fascist Grand Council could in theory nominate a new Prime Minister to the King, in practice they showed no sign of doing so before the scale of Italy's military defeat became evident in 1943. What is striking is the degree of constitutional confusion that underpinned this 'personal party dictatorship'. 'Fascism does not need long statutes or complicated rules', boasted party ideologues. In fact it had precious little formal organization at all, and it was remarkable that the Duce, though head of the government, held no formal position within the Party hierarchy and organization. The manner of his election and appointment was never defined. In the Party statute of 1929 he is described as the first among the hierarch; the 1932 statute deliberately removed him from, and placed him above, the hierarchy.

In the Third Reich, Hitler – party member no. 55 – had become uncontested *Führer* of the NSDAP in July 1921. But it was only with the refounding of the Party in 1925 that the *Führerprinzip* was formally proclaimed as the basic rule of the Party, the previous system of internally electing the leader was abolished and Hitler became unquestioned leader. In contrast to Mussolini, Hitler thus established his grip over the Party well before the seizure of power and the basis of his authority was spelled out clearly through the leadership principle.

The Nazi conquest of the German state brought new constitutional complexities, mixing revolutionary breaks with the past with some surprising concessions to legal continuity. The Weimar Constitution was never formally abrogated and the 1934 Succession Act, which followed the death of President Hindenburg, combined the offices of Reich President and Chancellor in the person of Hitler. The Cabinet and the Reichstag continued to exist, and the Enabling Act, which was the true legal basis for the regime, was renewed no fewer than three times – in 1937, 1939, and 1943 – an extraordinary procedure in a state commonly regarded as being sublimely indifferent to the rule of law. On the other hand, Hitler enjoyed far greater power than even Hindenburg had done; judges were told that when applying the law they should take into account *Mein Kampf* and ignore any rulings of the Supreme Court prior to 1933 which conflicted with national socialist ideology. The state, like the Party, was being run on the basis of the Fuehrer Principle, but what this meant for the German state was far less clear than what it meant for the Party. Nazi theorists claimed the *Führerstaat* was 'rooted in the people', and saw its legitimacy emanating from Hitler's special relationship with the 'real will of the people'. This *völkisch*-mindedness explains the regime's liking for plebiscites – over withdrawal from the League of Nations, for example, or the abolition of the Reich Presidency in 1934.

In other words, what I am trying to say is that, when we look at it closely, the relationship between democracy and rightwing dictatorship in interwar Europe was by no means straightforward. On the one hand, there was a strong tradition of anti-parliamentarism and an idealization of hierarchy. On the other hand, the cult of the dictator coexisted with the mechanisms of post-war mass politics and the dictator was hailed for his ability to 'acquire the confidence of the masses' better than the old bourgeois elite of the nineteenth century had done. By the late 1930s we find the following categories of non-democratic regimes on the continent: Soviet communism; fascist dictatorships based on single-party rule by civilians (Italy and Germany); authoritarian quasi-dictatorships in Hungary, Yugoslavia, Romania, and Greece; corporative regimes in Austria and Portugal; military-backed government in Poland; and military dictatorship in Spain. In many countries there were fascist movements with their own versions of the cult of personality, but in many of them – Belgium, Britain, Romania – they failed to take power. Following the parliamentary route did not always guarantee success and could be blocked by the existing political elite.

Who says democracy must always win out? In the 1930s it appeared to be on the defensive in Europe, and commentators offered a variety of explanations. Some focused on the unworkability of the new constitutions, others on cleavages of class or ethnicity within society; others again on the difficulties of adapting nineteenth-century parliamentarism to the economic and technological demands of the modern world.

To some, however, the reason for the absence of effective opposition and for the extraordinary longevity of many dictators – often only terminated by external intervention, military defeat, or death – was far simpler. They ruled by terror and the deprivation of liberty was their crucial characteristic. In the hands of liberal observers, the notion of totalitarianism, originally coined by Italian fascists to describe the ambitions of their own political project, was turned into a new kind of political theory.

Initially, the concept of totalitarianism was used by theoreticians of fascism in a positive sense. Alfredo Rocco saw it as 'an absolute monopoly of authority by the state', while the philosopher Gentile used it to convey fascism's ambition not merely to reshape the political sphere, but to mould 'the whole will and thought and feeling of a nation'. But by the 1940s, as I have already mentioned, the term was being negatively and critically used by those who opposed both fascism and communism to mark out a liberal ground to defend. It was from such a position that George Orwell wrote *1984* and Hannah Arendt her lengthy (1950) study *The Origins of Totalitarianism*. With the onset of the Cold War, Nazi Germany and Soviet Russia merged in the American political imagination. 'There isn't any difference in totalitarian states', stated President Truman in 1947, 'I don't care what you call them, Nazi, Communist or Fascist.' This anti-communist position was attractive in Europe too, in France as a way of targeting the often uncritical Marxism of the intellectual Left, in West Germany for those uneasy with growing post-war assertions of the 'singularity' of the crimes of the Third Reich.

Most scholars recognized that there was something distinct about some of the mid-twentieth-century dictatorships that marked them out from the past. In the Third Reich, or the Soviet Union, for example, the regimes clearly aimed to shape individuals as well as the state, to invade the sphere of private life, atomize society, and abolish its autonomy at the same time as they centralized power. They were phenomena of modern mass politics which had no direct connection with the despotisms of earlier epochs. Some traced the intellectual origins of totalitarianism back to the Enlightenment, in particular to Rousseau's doctrine of a General Will and to a certain mutation of democratic practice. Thus Robert Nisbet in 1943, and Jacob Talmon a little later, talked about what they called 'totalitarian democracy' – an inherently pessimistic reading of modern society which presented the conservative, monarchical polities of the past and their traditional societies as having been better able to defend liberty than their post-Versailles successors. Others, by contrast, notably Carl Friedrich and Zbigniew Brzezinski, stressed the role of terror and coercion and saw society as a passive object of aggression from a small despotic clique.

I do not want to enter this now rather antiquated debate, but rather to draw attention to some things the concept of totalitarianism overlooked. In the first place, it fairly obviously downplayed the significance of ideology, which was reduced in many accounts to mere propaganda. (After all, Stalin's Russia was equated with Hitler's Germany!) Propaganda was clearly an important part of the way in which these regimes reproduced themselves. But, equally obviously, there were some important ideological differences between, say, Nazi Germany and the USSR, which helped shape their policies, as well as their levels of coercion. These regimes used force, not for the sake of it, but to promote and realize their goals: hence this force was directed in the Nazi case against racial threats to the German *Volksgemeinschaft*, and in the Soviet to the enemies of the revolution. To ignore ideology was to deny their whole cultural context – something no anthropologist would ever do.

Taking ideology seriously means entertaining the possibility that the relationship between state and society, between rulers and ruled, was more than a simple one-way street. Is it possible, for example, to write a *social* history of the Soviet Union? Some have clearly thought so and tried to do this, even showing how the Terror in the 1930s was not merely coercion, but also a matter of upward mobility for a new generation of Party apparatchiks. More recently, scholars have stressed, not the autonomy of society, but its complicity and participation in political life; coercive instruments such as the Gestapo and the NKVD relied on ordinary citizens, on denunciations and freely proffered information. Urban growth and industrialization were also collective projects in which enthusiasms could be mobilized. What lies at the bottom of this is the problem of belief in an unfree society – to what extent ordinary people shared goals of their leaders and what beliefs underpinned support. The idea of totalitarianism was not very good at exploring this scene, or, rather, it assumed it did not exist.

After all, despite the theorists' understandable focus on state terror, in fact levels of coercion varied hugely across regimes and within regimes across time. The killing power of the Third Reich after 1939 bears no relation to that before, while 22 June 1941 constitutes another turning point. The Nazi case was one of continuous escalation – of those killed and imprisoned (100,000 to over 1 million) – but other, more long-lived cases showed that coercion could also be scaled back – as in the Soviet Union after Stalin's death, or in China after the Cultural Revolution ended. Moreover, non-totalitarian regimes were also capable of imprisoning or killing large numbers of their own citizens – from Indonesia in 1965 to Guatemala and Argentina.

And I would add a final consideration: did not the totalitarian model ignore the role of ideological confusion, uncertainty, and what one might call structural tension within both the Third Reich and the USSR? Dictators might have power, but they did not always know what to do with it. Two quick examples – the zigzags of German population policy in Poland from 1939 to 1941 (as recently outlined by Christopher Browning), or the real dilemmas which faced the Kremlin in shaping a policy for controlling eastern Europe after 1945 – point to the importance of reminding ourselves of the difficulties those in control of these powerful state machines sometimes had in working out what to do with their power, which, like all power, was not unlimited. They were not very good at recognizing the limits to their power, and neither were many of those who studied them, struck as they were instead (and understandably) by the huge increase in the forces at their disposal compared with the past.

Finally, it may be helpful to return to the original question and conclude by summarizing Europe's relationship with totalitarianism. Insofar as Europe was at the forefront of developments in mass politics after the First World War, it also found itself witnessing the first experiments in a new kind of dictatorship. These used the mechanisms of modern mass democratic politics, and sometimes even preserved their laws and institutions – Soviet constitutions, plebiscites in the Third Reich, and so on. In the 1930s most of the new democracies which had been formed after the First World War had given way to dictatorships of the Right, which are just as much part of Europe's political traditions as democracies had been. The Bolsheviks had tried and failed to inspire imitators, despite vicious civil wars in Finland, Bulgaria, and Hungary. It was this collapse of older democratic expectations – expectations that I have tried to show were umbilically linked to a certain conception of Europe itself – that led so many liberal commentators to the new concept of totalitarianism.

After 1945, the concept acquired new uses in the anti-communist free world. But ironically, as it was spreading in popularity, so its usefulness was slipping away. Democracy revived in western Europe under American auspices, while in eastern Europe the High Stalinism of 1948 to 1953 gave way after the dictator's death to a different, more managerial kind of communist rule. Prison camps remained, but were scaled back. The political police still kept the population under surveillance – but as Beria's death indicated, they were losing influence to the managers and technocrats. Were one to map the size of prison-camp populations in Europe through the twentieth century, one would see a line rising sharply in the late 1930s and 1940s, but falling fairly quickly from the mid-1950s. It was not until 1989 that eastern Europe was also able to escape communist repression, but with the exception perhaps of Romania, the idea that these were totalitarian states had been abandoned some time earlier.

However, as I tried to indicate at the start of my article, the twentieth-century drift to a new kind of dictatorship had not been confined to Europe, and right from the start it had been visible elsewhere – in Turkey, for instance, or Iran. Decolonization, as we now know, brought liberation from colonial oppression, but in many cases soon led to new despotisms – whether monarchical, as in Morocco, Thailand, and Saudi Arabia, or Baathist (Syria, Iraq); theocratic (Iran), or communist (China, Cambodia). In the second half of the twentieth century, the concept of totalitarianism became more applicable outside the continent than inside it.

12

Value Change in Europe from the Perspective of Empirical Social Research

Helmut Thome

Introductory Remarks

When studying values empirically, social researchers apply a methodological perspective which differs substantially from that characteristic of philosophers, social anthropologists, or historians of ideas. In empirical research, values are treated as something 'measurable', measurable, above all, with the instrument of systematic surveys. This is a persistent source of irritation, and not just among non-sociologists; I shall therefore deal briefly with this methodology by way of introduction. The first thing to bear in mind is that we constantly produce rough-and-ready 'measurements' of values in everyday conversation. Referring to a colleague, for example, we say that he values his work *more* than his family; we state appreciatively of a friend that truthfulness is *more important* to him than economic profit; in a political debate, one speaker is up in arms about the Social Democrats (SPD) because they are still more concerned with 'equality' than 'freedom', while the reverse is fortunately true of the Liberal Democrats (FDP). The last example features quantification on two levels at the same time. First, the speaker compares the 'weight' of two values – freedom and equality – within a group and, second, compares two groups or parties with respect to their (dominant) value preferences. We do this kind of thing all the time. Wouldn't it make sense to render such implicit measurements explicit in order to scrutinize them in an open and amicable way, enabling us to assess more effectively whether our comparative statements are correct, whether they appropriately characterize not just individuals, but also larger groups of people? This at least is what empirical social research tries to do when it makes statements about the value orientations present in particular sections of the population, the extent to which these groups differ in their orientations, and how these change over time.

We are immediately confronted by a significant difficulty involved in this endeavour. Values such as freedom or equality, truthfulness or justice, are not directly observable; they are, as the empiricists say, 'latent constructs' measurable, if at all, only indirectly with the aid of certain 'indicators'. But this is also how we go about things in everyday life. We observe a particular behaviour in other people or we register certain utterances and come to conclusions about their values on this basis. In principle, sociological survey research proceeds in much the same way, though it is more systematic and deploys methodological (statistical) controls which make it possible, to some extent, to eliminate certain sources of error or to assess remaining errors of measurement and take them into account in analyzing the findings. Research on value-change involves both comparative statements about various groups or populations (cross-sectional analyses) and changes over time (longitudinal analyses). The main instrument here is the 'representative' opinion survey. A certain number of individuals (sample), randomly selected from the populations of various countries, are asked about their values in writing or orally; the survey is repeated at certain intervals, usually with new samples also representative (or supposed to be) of the particular population groups. The various value categories, which must be defined in advance, are typically obtained through a set of 'standardized' questions which each individual must answer. This throws up two particularly serious problems.[1] First, the questions posed must be understood in more or less the same way in each group of respondents about which we wish to produce information. Second, the terms used to express values such as 'freedom' or 'achievement' may change their meaning over time. It is not only difficult to grasp these variations in meaning in the first place. It is even more difficult to take adequate account of the shifts in the terms' semantic content when making quantifying statements about the relative importance of the values involved. I am unable to examine in more depth the methods and techniques deployed in empirical research on values in this contribution. I will, however, point now and then to certain specific features in the following sections.

For more than three decades, the international social scientific debate on value change has been dominated by the American political scientist Ronald Inglehart. He has collated the greatest quantity of empirical material for longitudinal and cross-sectional analyses and has become known primarily for his theories on materialism and postmaterialism. But he has also attached a good deal of importance to the shift in religious orientation. The cross-country comparison of value change in section 2 is largely based on Inglehart's findings.[2]

---

[1]   Gabriel (1998) provides a more detailed overview of the problem.

[2]   Despite the many criticisms which Inglehart's work has attracted, there is no

In section 3 I present a research approach developed by the sociologist Helmut Klages in parallel and in part as an alternative to Inglehart. This gives us the opportunity to have a closer look at the situation in Germany – beginning with developments in the 'old' Federal Republic and concluding with a comparative analysis of value orientations in eastern and western Germany since 1990 (section 4).

But before setting about measuring values and trying to show how they have changed, one must first clarify what is meant by 'value' or 'value orientation'. The following section attempts to do so.

1. The Definition of Values

Values are defined in a confusingly diverse range of ways in the literature. In the late 1960s one sociologist tried to count them (Lautmann 1969); in 400 specialist publications dealing specifically with values, he came across 180 different definitions. Were we to do the same today, we would probably have to add a fair number of new ones. Most definitions, however, or at least those applied in contemporary sociology, have a common core, formulated in the early 1950s by the American anthropologist and values researcher Clyde Kluckhohn (1951: 395), who was inspired by earlier studies by the social philosopher John Dewey: 'A value is a conception, explicit or implicit, distinctive of an individual or characteristic of a group, of the desirable which influences the selection from available modes, means, and ends of action.'

There are three crucial aspects to this definition:

1. To understand values as concepts, ideas, or ideals is to break with those conceptions that equated values with valued, loved, or desired objects. A classic work by Thomas and Znaniecki from 1921, for example, contains a list of possible values, such as 'a food-stuff, an instrument, a coin, a piece of poetry, a university, a myth, a scientific theory' (Thomas and Znaniecki 1984 [1921]: 58). These are undoubtedly all things that people might value, but we have not yet identified

---

alternative diagnosis of value-change of the same empirical scope and based on the same wealth of evidence. More recent books by this author (published after the German version of the present article was submitted) include Inglehart and Norris (2004) and Inglehart and Welzer (2005). Two other authors often referred to in the field of cross-cultural value studies (making up 'the big three' together with Inglehart) are G. Hofstede and S. H. Schwartz (e.g., Hofstede 2001; Schwartz 1992; 2004). Readers wishing to familiarize themselves with other cultural or social psychological approaches might also be interested in the work of Rokeach (1973) or Triandis (1995), and the textbook by Berry et al. (1997).

the 'factors' or criteria which make them valuable. But the need to find such 'symbolically generalized factors' (Luhmann) is apparent when we observe how we ourselves or others constantly exchange or replace objects and goals in the name of the values to which we adhere. It is very hard to do justice to such observations unless we do away with the object fixation characteristic of certain conceptions of values. Doing so makes it possible to vary evaluative perspectives and objects independently of one another in our analyses and to make the concept of values reflexive, in other words, to ensure that 'values' may also appear as the *objects* of evaluations. Admittedly, this throws up a whole range of other questions, but these I wish to leave to one side here.

2. The second point I want to underline relates to the distinction between *desired* and *desirable*. I am not concerned here with the question of whether it is possible to define values without a certain element of circularity. What seems important to me is the distinction between actually existing and *legitimate* desires, which may be linked with the conceptual distinction between (bodily) 'needs' and 'values'. The simple observation of something which, once again, we and others do constantly underscores the value of this distinction, namely wanting something but nonetheless refusing to pursue it and instead avoiding it because we consider it a 'bad idea', or even harmful or bad. This, of course, relates to more than just the sumptuous cake that we forego for the good of our health.

3. The third point concerns the function of values, though here again I am stifling a complicated issue, namely whether it is meaningful in the first place to make functions components of definitions rather than expressing them as empirical hypotheses. Kluckhohn draws attention to two functions of values. (a) They serve as criteria for the selection of modes, means, and ends of actions; we should add that they also guide the selection of *perceptions* (see Kmieciak 1976: 150). (b) They 'characterize' an individual or group, in other words, they represent a personal or collective identity.

In addition, values serve as a 'vocabulary' (C. W. Mills), allowing us to attribute motives and facilitate or support the formation of expectations without which social control and the coordination of actions would be impossible. The sociologist Niklas Luhmann describes taken-for-granted values as the 'medium for the supposition of a common interest' (Luhmann 1998: 343). In highly differentiated societies, they have this function of establishing consensus only if they are highly general and abstract, that is, if they do not prescribe specific actions. The openness to interpretation of values, though some find it disturbing, is an advantage rather than a shortcoming.

This brings us to the specific value orientations which have (or are claimed to have) changed markedly over the last four decades. I begin with Ronald Inglehart's theories on value change and selected findings which he has deployed to back them up. I am sceptical about Inglehart's theoretical approach (see Thome 1985a; 1985b; 2003), but will restrict myself to pointing to a few criticisms here and there. My key concern is to present empirical findings which remain relevant even if viewed from a different theoretical perspective.

2. Inglehart's Theories and Findings on Value Change

Inglehart characterizes value change primarily through a memorable conceptual couplet: he describes and interprets it as a shift in preferences away from 'materialist' to 'postmaterialist' values. He also refers to a 'shift in survival strategies', which aim initially at 'economic gains', but later – with increasing prosperity – at the refinement of 'lifestyle' (Inglehart 1997: 64); he also talks about 'survival values', whose significance is declining in favour of 'well-being values' (Inglehart 1997: 82). He ultimately expands all of this into an ambitious theory of 'modernization and postmodernization', which attempts to link cultural change with economic and political change.

In section 1 we distinguished the concept of values clearly from that of needs. Inglehart attaches no importance to this distinction, presumably because he works on the assumption that, over the long term, the value orientations that hold sway within a society must be compatible with the need structures present among the population, that is, that they develop in a coherent way. (The problematic nature of this assumption is elucidated in the chapter by Wolfgang Reinhard in this volume.) Inglehart puts his two basic hypotheses as follows (I quote them here as they appear in Inglehart 1990: 56; much the same can be found in Inglehart 1997: 33):

1. 'A *Scarcity Hypothesis*. An individual's priorities reflect the socioeconomic environment: one places the greatest subjective value on those things that are in relatively short supply.'

2. 'A *Socialization Hypothesis*. The relationship between socioeconomic environment and value priorities is not one of immediate adjustment: a substantial time lag is involved because, to a large extent, one's basic values reflect the conditions that prevailed during one's preadult years.'

The first hypothesis, as Inglehart himself points out, corresponds with the law of decreasing marginal utility as found in economics. He combines this with a theory of hierarchical needs development, which he believes may be drawn from relevant studies by the American psychologist Abraham Maslow from the 1950s. This is a somewhat more sophisticated version of the dictum freely adapted from

Bertolt Brecht and sufficiently well known in everyday communication: 'First you fill your stomach, then you think about morality.' In Inglehart's adaptation of Maslow, this is expressed as follows (Inglehart 1977: 22):

> 3. *Maslow's Theorem*: 'People act to fulfil a number of different needs, which are pursued in hierarchical order, according to their relative urgency for survival.'

On this view, the physical need for sustenance and freedom from bodily harm take precedence over all else. Only to the extent that these are satisfied – this conception tells us – do we turn our attention to the social need to belong and to be respected, and to the personal need for self-actualization. With respect to political objectives, basic needs find expression, for example, in the pursuit of economic stability and continuous growth; the need for security requires public order and protection from criminality and hostile countries; the need to belong and to be given respect motivates calls for participation in the workplace and in politics; self-actualization requires legally enshrined freedoms and opportunities to make decisions and arrange our lives as we see fit. Inglehart's idea was to ask people how urgent they consider the political goals classified here in this way.

But before looking at this more closely, I must add an explanatory remark on the socialization hypothesis. As formulated above, it may not be immediately understandable, because the temporal shift addressed above already relates to population aggregates. Earlier on, Inglehart put it like this (1977: 23):

> 2a. 'People tend to retain a given set of value priorities throughout adult life, once it has been established in their formative years.'

Here, Inglehart is not asserting that no further changes occur once people have reached adulthood, but merely that they become less likely as people get older, that is, they are *relatively* stable. Inglehart links the socialization hypothesis with a *generational hypothesis* which can be summed up as follows:

> 4. Because of the irregularities (discontinuities) in the development of the socio-economic environment, ruptures occur in the continuous succession of cohorts; these lead to the development of generations. During their primary socialization, the members of a particular generation are exposed to roughly the same socio-economic influences, which differ in relevant ways from those which impacted on other generations. (We refer for example to the pre- and post-war generation.)

The next step in Inglehart's argument involves an empirical observation:

5. In the USA, Japan, and the countries of western and central Europe, the social prerequisites for the satisfaction of material needs improved significantly for all social classes after World War II.

Let's pretend for a moment that we knew nothing about how values have changed since the 1960s and had to predict this on the basis of Inglehart's assumptions and observations as outlined above (No. 1 to 5). We would produce the following prognoses:

Prognosis 1: The generations that grew up in central and western Europe *before* the end of the Second World War will moderate their relatively strong materialist orientation only negligibly in response to the post-war economic upturn.

Prognosis 2: The generation that grew up in central and western Europe *after* the Second World War will be less materialistic or more strongly postmaterialist than the pre-war generation ('cohort effects'). The extent of the difference between the generations will depend on how rapid and intensive the change in the socio-economic environment is.

Prognosis 3: As the older cohorts are being continuously replaced by the younger ones (population replacement), we would expect an overall shift in values towards greater postmaterialism among the populations in these regions – as long as the socio-economic environment does not drastically worsen.

Inglehart believes that these expectations, deducible from his theoretical assumptions and empirical observation, are confirmed by the way in which values have in fact observably changed. In order to understand this, let's look again at the methods of data collection. In a long series of surveys since the 1970s (carried out primarily within the framework of the half-yearly *Eurobarometer* studies), Inglehart has consistently deployed the following instrument of measurement in country-specific samples.

First the respondent is presented with an introductory statement (the exact wording varies in different surveys and countries):

I would now like to ask you some questions about political goals. You can't have everything at once, and this applies to politics as much as anything else. In this list you will find some goals which politicians might pursue. If you had to choose between these different goals, which would seem most important to you personally?

They are then presented with a list of political goals from which they are to select the ones they consider most important. The goals are:

A. Protecting freedom of speech.

B. Fighting rising prices.

C. Giving the people more say in important political decisions.

D. Maintaining order in the nation.

After an initial response, the respondent is asked to identify the second and third most important goal. Two of these goals, namely A and C, are intended to convey a postmaterialist orientation, the other two, B and D, a materialist one. The answers are used to create a scale which has become known in the literature as the 'Inglehart index' (or 'Inglehart scale'). If a respondent identifies *both* postmaterialist goals as the two most urgent, he receives the code number or scale score of '1'. Inglehart refers to this group as 'pure postmaterialists'. Conversely, if a respondent gives precedence to the two materialist goals, he receives the code number '4'; these are the 'pure materialists'. Should a respondent place a postmaterialist goal first and a materialist goal second, he receives a score of '2' and is termed a 'mixed postmaterialist'. But if he puts a materialist goal first and a postmaterialist one second, he receives a score of '3' and is labelled a 'mixed materialist'. Inglehart works on the assumption that this index represents a continuum of values: the higher the scores, the greater the materialist orientation, or to put it the other way round, the lower the scores, the stronger the postmaterialist orientation. (The way you turn the scale is of no importance.)

Inglehart has occasionally deployed a more comprehensive scale featuring eight more political goals. On the materialist side, this includes economic growth and an intensified fight against crime for example, on the postmaterialist side such things as a 'less impersonal society' and a 'greater say at work'. But most of the findings presented by Inglehart are based on the four-item scale presented above. (The term 'item' is applied by analysts to denote any given element in a scale, in this case a question.) Inglehart emphasizes that the short scale always produces results that deviate only negligibly from those generated by the longer version. Yet questions have consistently been raised about the validity of the scale. Some have expressed doubts, for good reason, about whether it really measures the value poles 'materialist' versus 'postmaterialist' in a 'one-dimensional' way (see Flanagan 1982; 1987; or Bacher 1988). Is it meaningful, for example, to place 'peace and quiet' and 'price stability' in the same value category (the materialist)? How much do the results change if we replace price stability with the fight against unemployment (see Bauer-Kaase and Kaase 1998; Clarke *et al.* 1999)? These objections come into play particularly with respect to certain interpretations with which Inglehart goes beyond the content of his data and his concepts' legitimate field of application, when he moves from analyses of politics to generalizations in the field of cultural sociology (though he deploys an additional array of questions here – see below). But this does not render the information collected through the Inglehart index entirely useless. From a pragmatic point of view, two key points must be borne in mind here. (a) These measurements are not primarily intended to correctly capture the value orientations of *individuals*, but to identify group differences and trends. In calculating percentages or mean values, random, unsystematic errors in individual measurements are generally cancelled out; systematic errors of the same size and direction do not affect differences between individual scores. (b) No other approach has produced similarly comprehensive comparative data on such a large number of countries and over such long periods of time. Every account of value change that goes beyond individual countries and short periods of time depends on Inglehart's data, however selectively and critically one may use them.

This brings us to some of the key findings of Inglehart's studies. The first figure shows the results of a so-called cohort analysis, summarized for six European countries: Belgium, France, the United Kingdom, Italy, the Netherlands, and West Germany. (These findings are based on more than 240,000 interviews.)

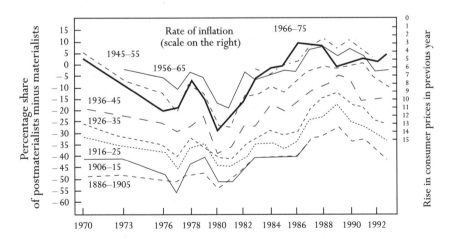

Figure 12.1   *Percentage share of postmaterialists minus materialists in eight age cohorts in six western European countries, 1973–94. Collated data from Belgium, France, Great Britain, Italy, the Netherlands, and West Germany. Source: Inglehart (1998: 196). Data from weighted random sampling for Eurobarometer surveys on behalf of the European Commission.*

The left axis of the graph shows the 'percentage of postmaterialists minus percentage of materialists'. This number is calculated for various age cohorts. The lower the dips in the lines, the larger the share of materialists; the higher the peaks, the larger the share of postmaterialists. We see straight away that the different age cohorts occupy different positions: the younger the cohort, the smaller the proportion of materialists in comparison to postmaterialists; the difference between the pre- and post-war generations is particularly marked (if we compare the lines for the 1936–1945 and 1945–1955 cohorts.) Further analyses show that members of the younger generation are particularly likely to tend towards postmaterialism if they grew up in affluent families (Inglehart 1990: 167 ff.). Both findings tally with theoretical expectations. More important than the difference between the cohorts at the beginning of the period under study is their persistence over the entire period. This shows that we are not, or not primarily, dealing here with so-called lifecycle effects. The young are not less materialist because they are young but because they grew up during a period of greater economic security. Had age been a decisive factor, the 'young' would have eventually changed over the years, becoming more 'materialist', that is, become more like the preceding cohorts. But this is not the case.[3]

The graph not only shows the cohort effects, but also a so-called period effect. According to Inglehart's theory, value orientations are dependent *primarily* on the degree of economic security. This structural influence, it is assumed, is strongest while people are growing up; this is what gives rise to the cohort effects. But the influence of the economic situation is not restricted to this period of life; its effects remain acute during other stages of people's lives as well. *All* age groups respond to current changes in their economic situation. Inglehart regards the rate of inflation as a yardstick of economic insecurity. He has included it in the graph – the thick black line – in inverted form, that is, the lower the troughs in the inflation *line*, the higher the inflation *rate* (see the right axis). The parallels between the lines are in fact startling. When the rate of inflation increases, as it did at the start of the period under observation, support for materialist political goals is stronger in every cohort; when it decreases, as in the 1980s, support declines. At the end of the period studied, however, from 1989/1990, this connection seems to disappear.

If we look at developments between 1970 and 1990 not only divided by cohorts, but also as they relate to various total populations, Inglehart's prognosis is also largely confirmed. His thesis was that the more postmaterialist younger groups are gradually replacing the more materialist older groups and that this

---

[3]   There are, however, other findings that demonstrate, at least for Germany, that the differences between the generations disappear in the late 1970s to early 1980s (see Böltken and Jagodzinski 1983; 1985; Jagodzinski 1985).

'population replacement' is bringing about an overall shift towards postmaterialism. This applies to the EU countries as they then were, with Belgium being an exception that remains unexplained (see Inglehart and Abramson 1994: 338).

Since the late 1980s and early 1990s, however, postmaterialism has begun to decline again slightly in western and central Europe. Initially, this is still compatible with the rate of inflation, which temporarily increases again slightly, though this congruence no longer applies later on. Here again, the trends in the individual countries do not run entirely in parallel. France, for example, shows no decline until 1999, unlike Germany east and west, the United Kingdom and the Netherlands (see Van Deth 2001: 27). Whether this means that Inglehart's theory contradicts the facts is subject to dispute among the experts. Perhaps the rate of inflation is no longer a useful indicator of economic security or insecurity. It may be that, once a certain level of economic prosperity is reached, we must assume that 'economic security' depends less on objective economic data than on processes of communication in which various interpretations compete within public discourse.

So far, we have been concerned only with the categories through which Inglehart describes value change and with how he explains it as a consequence of economic and political developments. But he has also tackled the question of how value change affects structures of political conflict and forms of democratic participation (see Inglehart 1990, ch. 9–11). I will highlight just a few key points here.

Within the political systems of western societies, Inglehart distinguishes between pre-industrial and industrial conflict structures. The pre-industrial are based, above all, on religious and ethnic, language community, and regional differences; the industrial conflict structure equates largely with class conflict. However, class conflict did not replace the pre-industrial conflict structures, but was merely superimposed upon them (see Lipset and Rokkan 1967). The European party systems developed out of this mesh of conflict structures, whose basic features they retained at least until into the 1970s. The increasing postmaterialist orientation inserts a new conflict into this structure which, according to Inglehart, has changed and relativized the traditional forms of class conflict and the way it is represented in the political parties more strongly than the preindustrial conflict structures. In essence, Inglehart explains this as follows:

1. As the prevailing brand of politics was for long of a materialist complexion, a higher degree of dissatisfaction with the political system spread among the postmaterialists than among the materialists – and they were more motivated to support political changes as a result.

2. As the postmaterialist group features relatively high numbers of young and

better-educated people, it has more energy and greater cognitive abilities for political participation and for the development of new, unconventional forms of political protest.

3. Traditionally, people tried to exert political influence via large corporative organizations of which they were members. It was largely left to the organizational elites to engage in politics. The new forms of participation meanwhile are not 'elite-directed' but 'elite-challenging'. The postmaterialist orientation also targets the anonymization of the individual by bureaucratic organizations. The forms of participation are thus more individualistic. This is apparent in new social movements such as the women's and environmental movement, as well as the proliferation of grassroots and self-help groups.

4. Over the course of time, increasing numbers of the younger postmaterialists in various spheres of society attain elite positions, not least in the party elites. Germany not only saw the foundation of a significant new political party in the shape of the Greens (which entered the Bundestag, the lower house of the German parliament, for the first time in 1983), but also a virtual schism in the FDP. The SPD has not formally split, but is increasingly struggling to integrate its more materialist and more postmaterialist members and supporters.

5. The long dominant opposition, based on class conflict, between 'left-wing' and 'right-wing' parties or groupings is being supplemented and overlain by a new political dividing line, which Inglehart assigns to the opposition between 'postmodern' and 'fundamentalist' values (1997; see below). This opposition manifests itself, for example, in environmental and immigration policies, as well as lifestyle issues – such as recognition of gay marriage – and policies geared towards the family and women. In Germany, the postmodern end of the spectrum is represented most prominently by the Green party, the fundamentalist end by the extreme rightwing groupings; but this dividing line runs, as mentioned already, through the longer established parties as well.

6. Postmaterialism is thus only the kernel of a greater complex, which Inglehart describes as 'postmodern' value orientations. Overall, they lead to 'declining confidence in religious, political, and even scientific authority; they also bring a growing mass desire for participation and self-expression' (Inglehart 1997: 327).

Before taking a closer look at these or similar conceptual extensions, I present some data on the development of the postmaterialist orientation among a number of occupational groups:

Table 12.1 *Value type according to occupation and age group*

	Under 35			35–49			50 and above		
	Materialist	Post-materialist	Number	Materialist	Post-materialist	Number	Materialist	Post-materialist	Number
Senior manager/administrator	19	27	1150	23	25	1415	24	15	902
Student	20	24	11,677	–	–	–	–	–	–
Freelance worker	20	21	869	20	22	608	29	15	505
Employee, non-manual labour	25	20	11,623	31	14	7166	36	11	3871
Unemployed	28	17	4958	33	11	1218	37	8	1565
Independent trader	31	12	2257	40	9	2797	41	7	2104
Manual worker	30	13	10926	36	9	6904	41	8	4817
Housewife	36	10	7787	43	8	7192	46	6	9824
Farmer	38	11	401	45	8	706	46	6	1111
Retired	–	–	–	37	11	412	46	6	19,526

Source: Inglehart (1998: 399). Data collated from Eurobarometer surveys in Belgium, West Germany, Denmark, France, Great Britain, Ireland, Italy, Luxembourg, and the Netherlands between April 1980 and November 1986.

The table summarizes survey findings from various European countries. The percentages for the three age groups confirm the general trend towards greater postmaterialism; the data for the various occupational groups show that this development is generally more rapid the higher the occupational status. Business persons are an exception here, even the younger among them being generally materialist rather than postmaterialist – and much the same can also be said of manual workers. Unfortunately, 'top management' and 'civil service' are lumped together in the table. The figures are nonetheless remarkable; they show that as early as the first half of the 1980s postmaterialist orientations are more strongly represented than materialist ones among the younger age groups in these positions of leadership. In another survey (not reproduced in detail here), Inglehart (1990: 323) cites data from a West German study of elites published in 1982 (Wildenmann et al. 1982), comparing them with the findings from his own surveys (summarized for the period 1976–1987). Among the general population, the materialists outnumber the postmaterialists by 15 per cent, among the officials of business and agricultural associations the figure is 26, among senior managers in major companies 22, and among CDU/CSU politicians 16 per cent. At the same time, however, there is a markedly higher number of postmaterialists among the senior staff of universities and research institutions, journalists, FDP and SPD politicians; even among the 85 trade-union leaders questioned, the proportion of postmaterialists is 38 per cent higher than that of materialists. (There seems to be no recent data of a comparable nature.)

As mentioned earlier, Inglehart has recently extended his system for categorizing relevant value orientations. No longer restricting himself to the dimension of materialism vs postmaterialism, he has embedded this pair of categories in the more broadly conceived dimension of 'survival vs self-expression'. He also constructs a second analytical dimension which contrasts 'traditional' and 'secular-rational' orientations (see Inglehart and Baker 2000: 24). The dimension 'traditional' versus 'secular-rational' is concerned with cultural changes occurring in the transition from preindustrial to industrial societies. Key points here are belief in God and religious commitments, respect for authorities and a high regard for one's own nation and the family. The average extent to which the respondents in a particular country approve or reject such concepts or ideals marks (in the form of so-called 'factor scores') the country's position on the axis of traditional versus secular-rational orientation. The second dimension is dealt with in the same way. This is concerned primarily with the more far-reaching differentiation of cultural modernity and postmodernity, which is occurring on the basis of increasing material prosperity. This is another application of the materialism–postmaterialism index, supplemented by additional measurements of subjective well-being, political engagement, trust in other people, and tolerance for non-conformist lifestyles (such as homosexuality).

Inglehart acknowledges in principle that these two dimensions may be combined in different ways in the different countries. While a continuous increase in economic prosperity promotes both secularization and self-expression values, this development is 'path-dependent', partly determined by cultural traditions with deep roots. Inglehart has analysed data from more than 150,000 interviews which he organized in the early and mid-1990s in sixty countries. Each country (with its average values on both axes) can now be represented as a point in a two-dimensional system of coordinates. This looks as follows (figure 17.2):

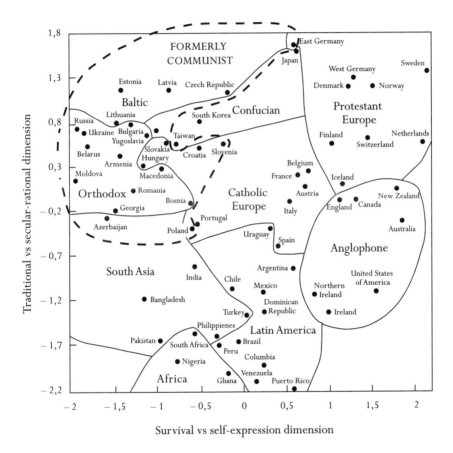

Figure 12.2   *Position of 65 countries in relation to two value-dimensions*
Source: Inglehart and Baker (2000: 29). Data from World Values Survey 1990–91 and
1995–98

Inglehart believes that his ratings are validated by the fact that the countries can be grouped in familiar cultural areas on the basis of his measurements. In the Protestant-dominated countries of northern and central Europe for example (upper right-hand corner), and the English-speaking countries (particularly the USA), self-expression values are very important, though the former are more strongly detraditionalized and secularized than the latter; in both dimensions, they have higher scale scores than the Catholic-dominated European countries. In the ex-communist countries, unless of an Orthodox Christian persuasion, traditional religious orientations have also diminished markedly, though here the survival orientation complex still clearly dominates the category of self-expression values. The position of the USA and the other English-speaking countries is also worthy of note; in their value orientations, they are all more traditionally religious in character.

If we compare the position of individual countries, however, there are a few surprises that place a question mark over Inglehart's generalizations. There are, for example, no two countries closer together if we combine both dimensions than Japan and eastern Germany; the Philippines and Peru, and Slovakia and Taiwan also make up surprisingly close pairings. This brings out how problematic it can be to use the same questions in very different cultural areas when comparing a large number of countries. It is, for example, questionable whether signing a petition in east Asian countries conveys the importance of self-expression values to the same degree as in the USA or Europe. Even more questionable is the attempt to establish the strength of religious ties in Confucian countries in the same was as, for example, in the USA through a statement about one's personal relationship to God ('God is very important in respondent's life'). From a more broadly conceived historical perspective, Inglehart's concept of secularism, the sharp opposition between religion and rationality, is also unconvincing. It suppresses the potential for modernization which religious thought has released over the course of time. (A number of the contributions in this volume offer interesting reflections on this subject.)

Nevertheless, the subsequent statistical analysis confirms the assumption that the position of the countries on *both* value dimensions depends not only on the level of economic development they have reached, but also on longer-term cultural traditions, which are in fact influenced by religion to a significant degree. These traditions are present within social institutions and shape individuals' value orientations in this way – relatively independent of their *personal* religious convictions. Inglehart concludes (Inglehart and Baker 2000: 36):

> Although historically Catholic or Protestant or Islamic societies show distinctive values, the differences between Catholics and Protestants or Muslims within given societies are relatively small. [We should probably add: in as much as there are no politicized religious conflicts.] In Germany, for example, the basic values of German Catholics resemble

those of German Protestants more than they resemble Catholics in other countries.

In what follows, we take a closer look at findings on religious orientations.

Religious orientations

As mentioned earlier, Inglehart assumes that with increasing material prosperity people's sense of security grows and 'makes the need for the reassurance provided by traditional absolute belief systems less pressing' (Inglehart 1997: 281). In light of this, Inglehart believes, we would expect a trend towards secularization in the developed industrial societies, while, on the other hand, we must also expect fundamentalist reactions. In addition, irrespective of secularization, we can assume that more people will concern themselves with spiritual matters, 'broadly defined' (Inglehart and Baker 2000: 49).

Inglehart registered religious orientation by means of two key indicators. He first asked about church attendance, noting the percentage of those who go to church at least once a month in the various countries. (Again, we should note that church attendance plays a different role within the Christian churches than, for example, in societies influenced by Confucianism.) Among other things, he ascertains that while the proportion of churchgoers declined between 1981 and 1991 or 1998 in sixteen out of twenty highly developed industrial nations, this trend was less dramatic than we might have expected: the average decrease is 5 per cent (Inglehart and Baker 2000: 46). A far above average decline is registered for Switzerland, Australia, Spain, Germany (west and east, minus 10 and 11 per cent), and Holland. The data for the individual countries must, however, be viewed with caution because of random influences affecting sampling.

The formerly communist countries have for the most part seen an increase. Alongside eastern Germany, the exceptions here are Slovenia (though only with an irrelevant minus of 2 per cent) and Poland, with a minus of 11 per cent (from a very high initial level of 85 per cent).

The findings for the developing countries are very mixed; Inglehart registers an average decline of 4 per cent.

It is interesting to contrast this indicator with the second one, based on questions about the importance of God in one's personal life. In the highly developed industrial countries, there is virtually no decrease in the percentage of those who attach great importance to God in their own lives; in the two other groups of countries, Inglehart even notes increases of 6 per cent on average (Inglehart and Baker 2000: 47). Here, there are a number of striking country-specific features. In western Germany, for example, there is no decline in the personal significance of God, in contrast to church attendance; for Spain, in even greater contrast to church attendance, there was even an increase of 8 per cent.

We should, however, note that the percentage of those for whom God is important personally is in almost all countries lower than the number of those who attend church at least once a month.

In light of his data, Inglehart concludes that even with respect to the economically highly developed countries of the west it is incorrect to refer to a general trend for religious convictions to become insignificant. Religion has many functions (Inglehart 1997: 285 ff.; Inglehart and Baker 2000: 46 ff.). One of these, Inglehart tells us, is to impart a sense of direction and of security in an uncertain world. But even if material prosperity and security are guaranteed, pressing questions remain open: 'Where do we come from? Where are we going? Why we are here?' (Inglehart and Baker 2000: 47). (This statement is, however, not entirely compatible with the conception of a bipolar model of orientation in which religious commitment is understood as an indication of cultural traditionalism, as we saw earlier.) The survey findings show that while postmaterialists adhere less than materialists to traditional forms of religious commitment, they think more intensively about the meaning of life than do the latter (Inglehart and Baker 2000: 48). For the highly developed industrial nations, again for the period between 1981 and 1991 or 1998, Inglehart observes an increase in this group of 6 per cent on average, more than in the other two country groups. Leading the field here are some of the countries for which a parallel and particularly major decline in church attendance was observed: Germany (12 and 7 per cent), Australia (10 per cent) and Holland (10 per cent); the increase in Finland and Sweden (both with 8 per cent) is also notable.

The period considered by Inglehart provides a very limited basis on which to identify trends. In an exhaustive secondary analysis of survey data from western European countries, Jagodzinski and Dobbelaere (1995a) look back two decades earlier. They point out that the decisive collapse in membership in the major Protestant churches in the United Kingdom, West Germany, Denmark, and Holland occurred in the 1960s. They define core membership not only on the basis of nominal affiliation, but also by weekly church attendance. Towards the end of the 1960s in these countries the figure was around 10 per cent, in Denmark considerably less, in West Germany more. In certain Protestant denominations, however, the core of committed members remained largely unchanged, particularly among the neo-Calvinists in Holland. In the Catholic Church, the decline was more gradual and there were significant national differences. Italy, for example, followed the general trend in the 1970s, but this then went into reverse. For Catholics in the United Kingdom (a relatively small minority), the authors record a state of near stability throughout the period examined. Nonetheless, the UK, along with France, the Netherlands, and Belgium are among those countries which exhibit the greatest overall increase in the religiously uncommitted (Jagodzinski and Dobbelaere 1995a: 105). By the late 1980s, more than half in the first three countries mentioned do not belong to a church, while in Belgium and Denmark the figure approaches the 50 per cent mark. In West Germany and, above all, Italy, the proportion is significantly smaller (see below, section 4).[4] The authors note more nuanced trends within specific countries with respect to church-based religious convictions, which differ according to gender, employment status, and education (Dobbelaere and Jagodzinski 1995). For most people, ideas about God are becoming 'more abstract'; the majority of Europeans believe 'in God' (in West Germany between 1981 and 1990 around two-thirds of respondents), but only a minority believes 'in a personal God' (in West Germany in 1981 and 1990 a good fifth; see Gabriel 1998: 41). Even among those respondents who describe themselves as 'not religious', there are many who believe in 'God'. In western Germany in 1990, for example, the figure was 25 per cent, in France 31 per cent, but in eastern Germany only 5 per cent (Köcher 1998: 61). Overall, the data attest to a tendency towards growing religious and ethical pluralism. But, Jagodzinski and Dobbelaere (1995b: 247) conclude: 'the trend is by no means as universal as often suggested'.

The following section presents studies which deal specifically with value change in Germany. We look first at developments in the 'old' Federal Republic (section 3); this is followed by a comparison of east and west for the post-1990 period (section 4). We shall be turning once again to the issue of religious attitudes in this context.

3. Value Change in West Germany

Educational goals and civic virtues

Helmut Klages has probably carried out the most in-depth research on value change in West Germany. When he began his studies in 1980, he based them, among other things, on survey data originally collected by EMNID and the Institute for Public Opinion Research in Allensbach (reproduced in figure 12.3 as presented in Meulemann 1985).

Besides other things, figure 12.3 shows that the educational goal 'independence and free will' found increasing support among respondents from 1960 on, at the expense of that of 'obedience and subordination'. Interest in politics also increases during this period, while intrinsic work motivation and frequency of church attendance both decline. With respect to educational goals, the Institute for Public Opinion Research in Allensbach also registers a marked decline in other civic virtues such as politeness and good behaviour, cleanliness and thrift since the mid-1960s. In 1978, Noelle-Neumann anxiously enquired: 'Are we all

---

[4]   On trends towards secularization in Europe, see also Y. Lambert (1998).

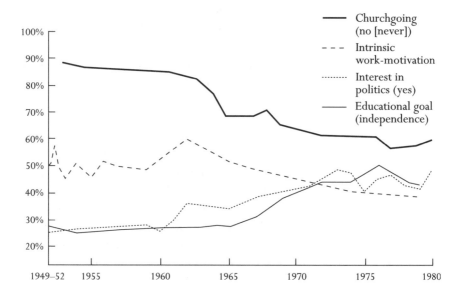

Figure 12.3   *Change of values in Federal Republic of Germany 1949–80:*
churchgoing, intrinsic work-motivation, interest in politics, independence
as educational goal. Results of population survey.
Source: Meulemann (1985: 409). Data: survey conducted by EMNID and Institute
for Opinion Polling, Allensbach.

becoming proletarians?' (Noelle-Neumann 1978). A less pessimistic tone is struck by Helmut Klages, who was inspired by the (temporary) stabilization in value indicators after 1972/1973 to refer to the 'end of the period of value change' (Klages 1985: 123–4). This turned out to be rather premature, as the following figure 12.4 showing preferences in educational goals up to 1995 lays bare (once again on the basis of EMNID surveys).

The rate of change gathers pace again in the 1980s, peaking in 1989 in this account. Karl-Heinz Reuband suspects that the temporary stabilization may have been caused by the terrorist attacks in the 1970s (Reuband 1997: 135):

> In any event, the subject of 'law and order' stands out more strongly in the public consciousness during this period [...] support for the death penalty increases abruptly [...]. However, in the early 1980s, this period of counter-trends came to an end as did the analogous trend in the evaluation of educational goals.

Unfortunately, Reuband's diagram does not include the educational goal of

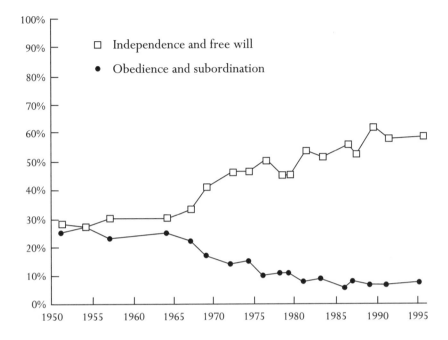

Figure 12.4 *Educational goals in the federal states over the course of time.*
Source: Reuband [1997: 134]. Data: survey conducted by EMNID.

'orderliness and diligence', which maintains a very stable level of approval of around 40 per cent, with only brief fluctuations, between 1951 and 2001. For the two other educational goals, developments after 1995 may be summarized briefly as follows (see Meulemann 2002). 'Obedience and subordination' remains at a low level, with only c. 5 per cent of respondents identifying it as a primary goal of education in 2001; in the same year, 'independence and free will' is at around 53 per cent, slightly below the level of 60 per cent in 1995. With respect to the ranking of these educational goals, there is only a slight difference between western and eastern German respondents (Meulemann 2002: 19). (As mentioned earlier, I will be looking more closely at east–west differences later on.)

The Institute for Public Opinion Research registers a particularly strong shift in sexual norms. For example, '(as late as 1967), only 24 per cent of young women found it acceptable to cohabit with a man without being married. Just a few years later 76 per cent stated that it was quite acceptable' (Noelle-Neumann and Petersen 2001: 16).

This is a good place to return again briefly to Inglehart, who also examined the complex of 'civic virtues'. Alongside the fields of religion and politics, he distinguishes those of 'respect for authority', 'sexual and marital norms', 'bonds between parents and children'. In all these fields, he discovers that the postmaterialists tend to have a more permissive attitude than the materialists. But in almost all these fields, support for libertarian positions among the total population increased between 1981 and 1991, with one significant exception: in the case of parent–child relations, the trend runs in the opposite direction in a clear majority of the nineteen countries examined. Respondents were asked for example, 'If someone says a child needs a two-parent home with both a father and a mother to grow up happily, would you tend to agree or disagree?' 'In 16 of the 19 countries for which we have data agreement with this proposition rose, instead of falling, from 1981 to 1990' (Inglehart 1997: 286). In Germany, however, the number of those who answered yes to this question was particularly small and, during the period of observation, stable. But it must be added that in Germany the number of children born out of wedlock increased only negligibly after 1960 and was only half as high as in the United Kingdom or France as late as 1985, at around 10 per cent; in Denmark the figure was four times as high (Inglehart 1997: 289).

In this regard, Inglehart points to a large number of studies which indicate that children growing up in one-parent families suffer negative effects. (There are other studies which dispute or qualify this assumption.) He suspects that the general public has become increasingly aware of the problems facing children growing up under these conditions and has therefore begun to attach greater importance to parent–child relations once again. The difference between materialists and postmaterialists remains with respect to this question as well, but in both groups, the 'conventional' orientations regarding the parent–child relationship have gained in importance again since the 1980s.[5] In a comparative analysis of German and Italian data from 1981 and 1990, for example, Meulemann (1999) identifies an increase in generational solidarity within families. Yet his conclusion that 'There can be no question of growing individualization within the family' (Meulemann 1999: 411) seems overdone, and not only because of the short period of observation. While the number of those opting for the educational goal of 'obedience' climbs slightly in both West Germany and Italy during this period, there is a greater increase in the number of those who prefer the (individualistic) goal of 'independence', especially in West Germany. Overall, the relationship between wife and husband and between parents and children has long been shifting away from a 'positional' (hierarchical) structure towards a 'personal' (partnership-based) one. Reuband (1997: 144) points to trend studies

---

[5]   In addition, those who wish to sweepingly interpret value change as 'value loss' find themselves confronted with another finding: postmaterialists tend to trust other people and to get involved in social and political life more than materialists (Inglehart 1997; Inglehart and Baker 2000: 36).

that demonstrate 'that the degree of independence enjoyed by young people has increased over the long term', while the extent and intensity of parental control has decreased. With the help of retrospective surveys of older cohorts, Reuband reconstructs a trend in certain educational *practices* since the 1920s which shows that behavioural changes preceded changes in educational goals as explicitly formulated. Around 1925, about 80 per cent of children were 'brought up strictly' (according to their later statements), by the mid-1980s, the figure fell to around 20 per cent; the decline in corporal punishment was weaker, from around 55 per cent to c. 30 per cent, with a deviating upward trend during the Nazi period (Reuband 1997: 148).[6]

Value synthesis

Let us turn again to the research approach adopted by Helmut Klages, who leans on Inglehart in his typology of values but contrasts markedly with him in one crucial respect. Initially, he also works on the basis of a bipolar dimension at one end of which lie the so-called duty and acceptance values, while self-expression values make up the opposing pole. The first category is represented by key words such as 'discipline', 'doing your duty', 'order', 'achievement', the second by 'participation', 'autonomy', 'pleasure', 'creativity' (Klages 1985: 18). But more than the dichotomy between these two poles, he is interested in the ambivalences and attempts at value synthesis. He therefore develops a different instrument of measurement than the one we know from Inglehart. Rather than asking his respondents to rank different value indicators, he has them assess a long list of about fifteen items (statements that express a particular value orientation), each independent of the others in line with its importance (the so-called 'rating' method). In other words, it becomes possible to rate duty and acceptance values as of equal importance as self-expression values. On this basis he initially constructs four and later five value types. First, the conventionalists (also referred to as 'traditionals'). These respondents rate objectives such as 'respecting law and order', 'ensuring security', 'being diligent and ambitious' as particularly important and set relatively little store by self-expression values. Those who rate self-expression values highly Klages divides into two groups: the idealists and the hedonists. The idealists define self-actualization in terms of a 'cooperative' rather than 'egotistical' individualism (Durkheim). For them, the traditional values of the conventionalists no longer play any role; neither are they keen to attain 'power and influence' or the highest possible living standard and high levels of pleasure. What matters to them is to get involved in society and politics, they wish, for example, to 'help the socially disadvantaged and marginal social groups'. The

---

[6]   For further analyses of family-related values in the context of a comparison of Germany and France, see Attias-Donfut (1998).

hedonists also reject some traditional values, but material prosperity continues to be an important goal for them, along with 'having power and influence' and being able to 'enjoy life'. 'The dominance of the pleasure principle and their efforts to get what they want as quickly as possible often cause them to test the boundaries of the socially and legally tolerable', as Klages goes on to characterize them (Klages 2001: 10). Klages' favourites are the 'active realists', who generate a synthesis of values by upholding traditional civic virtues and getting involved in society, but are also able to enjoy life. Klages concludes that they are the group 'best characterized as having a strong capacity for modernization in light of their basic mental constitution' (Klages 2001: 10). This brings us to the fifth and final group, the 'aimlessly resigned'. They are unable to rate any of these values highly; in Klages' words, they are 'the true "poor relations" of social change; withdrawal, passivity and apathy are their typical traits' (Klages 2001:10).

What proportion of the population do these five value types make up and what developmental trends can we make out? Unfortunately, comparable data exist only for the relatively short period from 1987 to 1999. Klages considers the group comprising eighteen to thirty-year-olds particularly relevant to future trends, presenting the following findings for what was West Germany (Klages 2001). The number of both the traditionalists and the resigned is relatively stable at around 10 per cent. In terms of the *total* population of fourteen years and above, the proportion of traditionalists is 18 per cent, while the resigned make up 16 per cent in 1999. Thus, markedly fewer young people are traditional or resigned in their attitudes in comparison with their older counterparts. A slight upward trend is apparent among the realists, from 32 to 36 per cent; in 1999, they made up around a third (34 per cent) of the total population.[7] In addition, realists and idealists exhibit significantly greater willingness than the other value types to get involved in the community (Gensicke 2001a: 293). The share of idealists among young people declined from 25 to 15 per cent between 1987 and 1993, while the figure for 1999 was 18 per cent. (Share of the total population in 1999: 17 per cent.) In line with this, the share of hedonists increases by 10 per cent between 1987 and 1993, from 21 to 31 per cent, decreasing again slightly by 1999 to 27 per cent. The share of hedonists, however, varies strongly with age. For the total population, Klages indicates a share of only 15 per cent for 1999. The generational difference is particularly striking with respect to this value type. If we link this with Inglehart's socialization hypothesis and 'population replacement', we would expect this type to become increasingly important within society in future. Of further relevance here are the findings of studies

---

[7]   A 1979 study, conceived rather differently as regards methodology, recorded a share of realists of a good 27 per cent among fourteen- to fifty-four-year-olds (Herbert 1991a: 39).

by the SINUS Institute, which attest to an increase in competitive attitudes (see Schnierer 1996: 70; more recent data are to be found in the business journal *Manager Magazine* 2 [2006], pp. 84–91).

The numerical decline in idealistic self-actualizers confirms the decrease in the share of postmaterialists since the late 1980s. The ongoing surveys by the Institute for Public Opinion Research in Allensbach also suggest a change of direction with respect to certain indicators. 'Politeness and good behaviour' and 'getting your work done in an orderly and conscientious way' are, for example, no less highly valued at the turn of the millennium than in the mid-1960s; 'being careful with money' and the willingness to 'fit in' have also regained support over the last decade, though without reaching the level of the 1960s; in much the same way, the value placed on work – in comparison to freedom – has also increased markedly since the mid-1990s (Noelle-Neumann and Petersen 2001: 19).[8] Certain trends, however, have intensified rather than waned. This applies, for example, to the tendency 'to place ever more emphasis on raising children to achieve, encouraging a thirst for knowledge and nurturing their technological skills' (Noelle-Neumann and Petersen 2001: 20). But, Noelle-Neumann notes, 'the trend towards prioritizing the enjoyment of life is also solid. A clear majority of West Germans under 30 years of age continue to state that they do not see life so much as a mission; the main thing is to enjoy it' (Noelle-Neumann and Petersen 2001: 21). Noelle-Neumann now has a far from negative view of this, believing that a positive attitude to work and a positive attitude to enjoying life are only seemingly contradictory. And she quotes the American ambassador to Germany of many years, John Kornblum, who when asked what had changed most during his period in office replied: 'The Germans have become more relaxed' (Noelle-Neumann and Petersen 2001: 22). Also in a positive vein, Noelle-Neumann notes that with respect to the acceptance of civic virtues such as politeness and conscientiousness at work, the generation gap has decreased markedly since the early 1990s. The number of young people who believed that their views differed from those of their parents in every sphere of life has declined (intermittently) since the mid-1980s; in eastern Germany, however, the figure has climbed slightly from 10 per cent in 1990 to c. 15 per cent in 2000, though this is still slightly below the figure for western Germany.

The trends identified by the Allensbach Institute are confirmed by the findings of the Shell studies on young people. These are summarized as follows: 'The assumption that value change is moving fairly steadily towards "postmaterialist" values of self-actualization and civic engagement and is paralleled by a decline in the values of achievement and fitting in has proved premature. The trends

---

[8]   See also Meulemann (1998a), who provides an interesting analysis of differing attitudes towards work in Germany and France.

characteristic of young people over the last 15 years have turned out differently.'[9] 'In contrast to the 1980s, young people now adopt a more pragmatic stance [...] achievement, security and power have become more important [to them] over the course of the 1990s' (Shell Jugendstudie: 3). Behaving in an environmentally aware way and political engagement are clearly less important to them. It is not only the differences between the generations which have levelled out, but also those between the genders (Shell Jugendstudie: 4):

> Girls and young women have become more ambitious, but also more conscious of security [...] 'having a career', 'gaining independence' and 'taking responsibility' are just as 'in' for them as they are for young men and they view their personal future just as positively as do the latter [...]. However, the fact that achievement and security rank highly again among young people does not mean that they have become less creative, tolerant or pleasure-loving as a result [...]. What is new is the increasing tendency of young people to combine such 'modern' values with 'old' values such as order, security and diligence.

This brings us back to Klages' idea of the (necessary, desirable) 'value synthesis', which clearly comes about when people accept traditional values such as diligence and orderliness as secondary virtues or 'instrumental values' with which one can foster 'ultimate values' such as professional success and enjoyment of life.

In the following section, I take a closer look at differing value trends in the former East and West Germany since 1990.

4. Differences within Germany East and West

Initial congruities

Let's stay with Klages' approach for the time being. In April 1990, parallel representative surveys were carried out in the then West and East Germany (by the Research Unit for Societal Development or FGE). The analyses show an astonishingly high degree of concordance between east and west immediately after unification, though both the conventionalist and materialist-hedonistic orientations were more prevalent among citizens of eastern Germany, while the willingness to help the socially disadvantaged and those on the margins of society was less developed than among their western counterparts (Herbert 1991b: 124–5).

---

[9]   Shell Jugendstudie, www.shell-jugendstudie.de/download/Hauptergebnisse_2002. pdf, p. 4; accessed 4 March 2004.

According to this study, the number of the 'resigned' was smaller in eastern Germany than in the west, the share of 'active realists' more or less the same (Gensicke 1992a: 49). Among members of the younger generation in particular, the differences between east and west were negligible at this point in time not only with respect to value orientations, but also in terms of their understanding of democracy (Herbert 1991b: 128). However, even for the brief period from May 1990 to October 1991, further surveys reveal some marked differences in the value profile of the eastern German population; while increasing importance was attached to 'money', for example, the reverse applied to 'politics' (Gensicke 1992b: 121).

Comparative data on value types is now available for 1999 as well. According to these, there are no east–west differences among conventionalists (8 per cent in each case) and the resigned (11 and 10 per cent) under thirty-one years of age. In both east and west, the realists make up the largest (35 and 41 per cent) and the hedonists the second largest group (25 and 27 per cent). Both these value types are present in somewhat greater numbers in the east than in the west, while the reverse is true of the 'idealists', who make up 21 per cent in the west and 14 per cent in the east.[10]

We have already established that the postmaterialist orientation (in Inglehart's sense) has diminished in Germany since the late 1980s. This development occurred primarily up to 1993, with the level subsequently stabilizing again. In the former GDR, the number of postmaterialists has increased slightly since 1992, from c. 10 per cent to c. 18 per cent in 2002 (ALLBUS data). By way of comparison: in 2002, the number of postmaterialists in the former West Germany stood at around 27 per cent. The figures for materialists in 2002 are almost identical: 18 per cent in the west, 19 per cent in the east.[11]

Equality, freedom, and justice: increasing divergence

It seems safe to assume that the West German social constitution offered more 'structural opportunities for individualism' (Meulemann 2002) than did the GDR, such that we can expect clear post-unification differences between east and west with respect to the assessment of inequality, achievement, political participation, and self-expression – with these orientations receiving greater approval or support in the west than in the east. This throws up the question of whether, in line with the socialization hypothesis (see section 2 above), these differences persist over the long term, whether they tend to diminish, given

---

[10]   These data are based on a personal communication between Thomas Gensicke and the present author. See also Gensicke (2002).

[11]   The data presented by Van Deth (2001: 26) from the Eurobarometer differ somewhat from the ALLBUS data cited, for example, by Meulemann (2002: 18).

that the West German social constitution was imported into the former GDR, or whether the differences tend to increase because the imported structures fit poorly with the traditional value orientations (see Meulemann 2002). The data paint a rather complex picture that resists easy summarization. This is partly because the findings of different surveys and studies occasionally contradict one another (see Scheuch 2003: 276–7). Initially, as we have seen, the differences are often smaller than the structural hypothesis assumes, and overall they tend to increase rather than decrease. Let's look first at the complex of equality and performance-based justice:

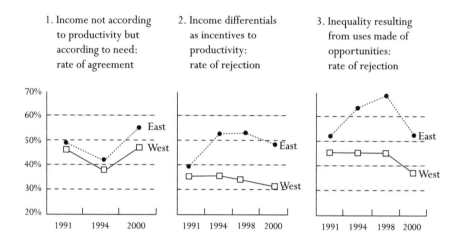

Figure 12.5 *Agreement with equality of outcomes in the new Federal Republic, 1991–2000 (per cent).*
Source: Meulemann [2002: 15] on the basis of data from ALLBUS.

The first graphic relates to expressions of agreement with the following statement in representative surveys (ALLBUS): 'Income shouldn't depend only on how much an individual works. Everyone should have what they need for a decent life.' This idea receives more support in the east than in the west, with the difference increasing slightly over time. The second graphic relates to the statement: 'Only if differences in income and social status are big enough do people have an incentive to work hard.' This time, the numbers disagreeing are noted. Here again, initially the differences are negligible. Over time, though, they increase significantly: the number of those disagreeing is declining slightly in the west, while in the east the figure increases strongly, particularly if we compare 1991 and 1994, before subsequently diminishing.

The third graphic relates to the following statement: 'Differences in social status are acceptable, because they generally reflect what people make of the opportunities they've had.' Again, the number of those disagreeing is shown. Once again, the initially small differences become larger because the number of those disagreeing increases markedly in the east by 1998; however, by 2000, this proportion has declined more in the east than in the west, though there is still a marked difference. Unfortunately, these questions were not asked in the general opinion survey (ALLBUS) of 2002.

Another question directly addresses the tension between equality of outcome and freedom (Institute for Public Opinion Research in Allensbach). The question concedes that personal freedom and a high degree of equality are values of roughly equal importance, but asks respondents to imagine that they had to choose between them. Here, barely 25 per cent of western Germans, but almost 45 per cent of eastern Germans opted for equality in 1990. Up to 2000, this difference remained more or less constant, but in both regions the numbers opting for equality increase. In western Germany they increase to slightly less than 40 per cent, in the east to slightly less than 60 per cent (Meulemann 2002: 16).

With respect to the acknowledgment of the achievement principle, however, we must distinguish between two levels. In the case of the question just quoted, the values at issue were politically relevant. The findings are different if the focus shifts to *personal* willingness to achieve, in one's job for example (Meulemann 2002: 17):

> Regardless of whether you ask people if they give work precedence over freedom or about how important work is to them [to their personal wellbeing], the results are the same. Fewer westerners than easterners find professional achievement motivating [...] and eastern Germans' greater motivation in this regard remains constant rather than diminishing [or even increases].

The younger and middle cohorts in particular increasingly accept individual differences in income on the basis of achievement; but they, too, '(support) the principle of equal distribution vehemently at the level of society as a whole' (Thumfart 2001: 12).

East and west differ more strongly in the evaluation of the *realization* of values than in their preferences for general *principles*. Here, the gap has widened significantly over the last decade. Since 1994, for example, there has been a decline in the number of those who, 'looking to the future of the united Germany, expect to see an improvement in the social safety net, the labour market and general economic security'. In mid-1997, the figure lay 'below the number of those who expect things to get worse for the first time' (Thumfart 2001: 8). Surveys carried out between 1996 and 1998 show that with respect to solidarity, social security, community life, the social recognition of achievement, and equality of opportunity, eastern Germans see the GDR as significantly better than the unified Germany in some ways. 'Only in such fields as self-determination, self-actualization and freedom is the new Germany ahead of the GDR, though only minimally in some cases' (Thumfart 2001: 7). Negative evaluations were found even with respect to freedom of choice in education and occupation, and even the administration of justice (Thumfart 2001: 8). I present a few numerical examples here. When eastern Germans were asked in 1995 and 1990 in which fields the GDR was superior to the FRG, the outcome was the pattern of answers as follows:

Table 12.2   *Claimed superiorities of the German Democratic Republic over the Federal Republic of Germany*

	1995	1990
Economy/technology	6%	2%
Standard of living	8%	25%
Provision of living accommodation	53%	27%
Well-being	57%	18%
School education	70%	33%
Protection against crime	88%	62%
Social security	92%	65%

Figures based on L. Montada/A. Dieter (1999), cited in A. Thumfart (2001: 9, n. 17).

In the general categories 'economy/technology' and 'living standards', the GDR was clearly seen as lagging behind. Five years after unification, the GDR was seen as better with respect to specific services even in cases in which West Germany was considered better in 1990, namely, provision of accommodation, the public health system, and schools.

Asked for an overall assessment in 1998, around three-quarters of western Germans stated that unification had been disadvantageous to them, but more than half of eastern Germans said the same thing; 83 per cent of western Germans believed that easterners had clearly benefited from unification, while, conversely, 75 per cent of eastern Germans thought that unification has disproportionately advantaged westerners (Thumfart 2001: 9). On the other hand, another survey from 2001 (IPOS) found that of respondents in the west only 11 per cent described unification as wrong, and a mere 9 per cent in the east (Scheuch 2003: 277). It is clearly difficult to keep sensitivities and more profound convictions apart in mass surveys.

Evaluations of profit and loss are closely bound up with assessments of justice. A study from 1997 surveyed such assessments on a fairly broad basis. In ten out of twelve pre-given spheres, eastern German respondents considered the GDR to be more just than the unified Germany. This applied to the situation of women, welfare benefits and employment opportunities, the distribution of wages and income, professional or on the job training opportunities and university education, and even, once again, the administration of justice. The new Germany is seen as more just solely with respect to opportunities for self-employment and the distribution of consumer goods (Thumfart 2001: 10).

After 1991, the number of those who prefer people of their own nationality to foreigners also increased; in 1996, the figure was slightly more than 60 per cent in both eastern and western Germany, 'with one third in both populations also exhibiting a marked intra-German ethnocentrism', as Alexander Thumfart states (Thumfart 2001: 9). Thumfart sums up his analysis of the survey findings with the thesis that (Thumfart 2001: 13–14):

it is not just that social integration in relation to norms of justice has not yet occurred; it is being hindered by *reciprocal* collective stereotypes and intensifying ascriptions [... The] acceptance of western German models with respect to individual behaviour by no means necessarily leads to the dismantling of collective dissociation and typification.

Finally, I want to take a brief comparative look at the fields of religious ties and civic engagement east and west.

Ties to the church and religiousness

In terms of religious issues, there continue to be significant differences between the eastern and western parts of Germany, and these are in fact generally increasing. Church membership and church attendance have by no means increased in the east after the collapse of the old regime. The differences between east and west have remained fairly stable in this regard. In 2000, 13 per cent (1991: 11 per cent) of western German respondents stated that they are not members of any church, while the figure for eastern Germans is 71 per cent (1991: 65 per cent) (Meulemann 2002: 21). Membership differs sharply according to generation. In 1990, 52 per cent of sixty-five- to seventy-four-year-olds but only 17 per cent of eighteen- to twenty-four-year-olds in the east belonged to a church (Köcher 1998: 56). In western Germany, these differences were significantly smaller (in contrast, for example, to France), with the biggest gap between twenty-five- to thirty-four-year-olds (83 per cent) and sixty-five- to seventy-four-year-olds (95 per cent). Particularly in eastern Germany, however, even those not affiliated to a church appear to go to church occasionally, given that only 63 per cent stated in 2000 that they 'never' do so, the figure for western Germany being 24 per cent.

The number of those in the east who state that they are 'not religious' has increased since unification. In 1990, only around 38 per cent of those asked by the Institute for Public Opinion Research gave this answer; in 2000, the figure was almost 48 per cent. The number of the non-religious is, however, still more than 20 per cent below the number of those not members of a church in eastern Germany. In western Germany meanwhile, the number of the non-religious is fairly stable at just under 30 per cent (Meulemann 2002: 20–1), which means that a significant portion of church members describe themselves as non-religious. There is no seamless match between church ties and religiousness. In western Germany in 1990, such a match applied to only around half of Protestants and two-thirds of Catholics. In eastern Germany, the link here is significantly stronger: 95 per cent of Catholics and 67 per cent of Protestants described themselves as religious in 1990. Nevertheless, 19 per cent of those not members of a church described themselves as religious in 1990 in western Germany, while in the east it was 8 per cent (Köcher 1998: 57).

Civic engagement

To conclude, here are some findings on civic engagement. The first comprehensive survey on this subject, as far as I am aware, was carried out in 1999, under the direction once again of Helmut Klages. (On the following, see Gensicke 2001b.) According to the findings, 68 per cent of western Germans and 55 per cent of eastern Germans 'participate actively' in one way or another in a *Verein* (club or association), 'citizens' group', self-help group, or similar projects.[12] In this study, those individuals who have taken on certain responsibilities or tasks 'voluntarily' within the areas of activity identified by them have been classed as 'volunteers'. With respect to all respondents, the figure was 35 per cent in the west and 28 per cent in the east. (When the survey was replicated in 2004 these figures were confirmed: 37 per cent west, 31 per cent east; Gensicke 2005: 13.) The intensity of the engagement can, of course, vary greatly. The number of those who spend more than five hours per week engaging in such activities is 11 per cent in the west, and 8 per cent in the east. If we make a distinction between different fields, it emerges that 'sport and fitness' is the most popular field for voluntary engagement, at 12 per cent (west) and 8 per cent (east). The 'social' field and that of 'politics and political causes', the key components of what we tend to understand as 'civic' engagement, amount to a mere 7 per cent (west) and 6 per cent (east). In both east and west, the prevailing organizational form is the *Verein*, which covers c. 50 per cent of such activities; in second place in the

---

[12]   By way of comparison, in the GDR, only 5 per cent of the population managed to avoid becoming a member of a mass organization and every second citizen was involved in voluntary activities (Roth 2001: 16).

west are the churches or other religious organizations at 15 per cent (7 per cent in the east), while in the east national or local institutions are in second place with 14 per cent (10 per cent in the west). Overall, the voluntary sector in the former GDR is more strongly linked with work than in the old West Germany (Gensicke 2001b: 28). Self-help activities for the unemployed are also markedly more extensive in the former GDR (Roth 2001: 17).

With respect to the motives and expectations which people associate with their own engagement, 'fun' tops the list in both east and west at 88 per cent and 87 per cent. However, the motives of 'helping others' and 'doing something for the common good' are described as important almost as often – at around 80 per cent among eastern Germans and 75 per cent among their western counterparts (Gensicke 2001b: 29). Once again, we find that mixture of duty and self-expression values characteristic of recent trends in values as a whole (the 'synthesis of values' dealt with in section 3).

There is little doubt about the positive connection between gainful employment and voluntary activities: 'The less a particular section of the population works and the lower its household income, the less likely it is to volunteer' (Blanke and Schridde 2001, quoted in Roth 2001: 20, n. 29). We can thus expect labour market trends to have an impact on the opportunities for, and willingness to carry out, voluntary activities (Roth 2001: 20). In terms of individual traits, however, ties to a church and age seem to be the key factors determining the willingness to take part in such activities (Gensicke 2000: 245).

Voluntary activities and other forms of engagement are generally viewed in a very positive light. But a warning seems in order here. 'Voluntary activities, honorary posts, membership of a *Verein*, and "social capital" must not be equated with democratic engagement or involvement in civil society', as Roland Roth states (2001: 22), pointing to German history. In terms of social scientific research, much work remains to be done to develop appropriate criteria of classification and gather relevant data.

Summary and Discussion

It is no easy task keeping abreast of research on value change; an introductory account is inevitably highly selective. In light of this, I felt it made sense to focus on studies by authors who have stirred up a high degree of interest both within the research community and among a wider public. It also seemed imperative to take at least a cursory look at certain aspects of methodology. In interpreting and evaluating the findings attained through survey research, we should keep both their potential and limits in mind. I have opted not to address issues of causal analysis as most readers will not possess the knowledge of statistical models and analytical methods that this would require.

Hypotheses about value change entail essentially two kinds of statement. The first type are claims that certain values (such as postmaterialist orientations, self-expression values) have become more important over time or have spread more within different sections of the population (or, conversely, have received a diminishing level of support) in comparison to others (such as duty and acceptance values). The second type are statements about how individual values are reconfigured, how new patterns form, in which, for example, things previously thought to be in opposition or coexisting in isolation from one another are increasingly seen as linked and compatible (see, for example, Klages' concept of value synthesis). Attempts to implement a research programme that reflects this throw up a number of problems (beyond technical and often serious organizational issues), which are not ultimately amenable to resolution, but which one simply has to deal with as best one can. These problems include, first of all, the question of which terms we ought to use to capture the various value orientations in the first place and relate them to one another. Here, empirical social research attempts to adopt the concepts of theoretical sociology or the history of ideas (such as 'rationalization', 'individualization', 'secularization', or ideals such as 'freedom', 'equality', 'justice'). But the definitions of these terms are for the most part a subject of dispute in their disciplines of origin and rather vague as deployed within a given culture. If you manage nonetheless to settle on a useable definition, you find yourself faced with a problem generally characteristic of empirical social research. How do we 'operationalize' the concepts (theoretical 'constructs') selected, that is, link them with observable reality through concrete research stages? Which questions (and answers) enable us to ascertain, for instance, whether (and with what degree of intensity) a particular individual really takes her lead from a value predetermined conceptually by the researcher (and then, on this basis, how the value orientations of individuals are distributed within smaller or larger groups)? We cannot ask someone whether she is 'secular' or 'materialist' in orientation or whether she has a 'rationalist understanding of the world'. However, the quality of the 'measurement' of values in surveys is not a matter of the degree to which the *semantic* content of the question is linguistically congruent with the content of the theoretical construct which we ultimately wish to capture. Compared with the intended conceptual content, the wording used in the questionnaire often seems silly and hopelessly inadequate to the outside observer. But the crucial thing is whether those individuals who do in fact have differing views with respect to value orientations (as interpreted by the researcher) are able to make these differences sufficiently evident in their answers to the 'silly' questions, to 'reproduce' them as it were. If this is the case (and we can test this empirically to some extent), we can work on the assumption that the questions presented in the questionnaire are a usable instrument.

Inglehart does in fact manage to show that the orientations of those respondents he identifies as 'postmaterialist' differ fairly consistently (especially with respect to political issues) from those of the 'materialists' in various spheres of life (some examples are mentioned above). In this sense, his index emerges as useable in certain fields of application. But the question remains whether his interpretation of the concept of value in terms of an economically inspired theory of needs (see 'Maslow's Theorem' at the beginning of section 2) is persuasive. It may be that materialist political objectives are backed with greater urgency in poor countries than in affluent ones. But apart from the fact that 'urgency' is not the same as 'high regard',[13] this observation by no means necessarily requires us to assume that the degree to which material needs are being met straightforwardly determines the level of postmaterialist goals. A relevant example: from 24 June 1948 to 12 May 1949, West Berlin faced a very dangerous situation as a result of the Soviet blockade (all routes in were closed off); many people starved or froze to death; giving in, in other words the withdrawal of the western protecting powers, would have alleviated the immediate suffering, but would have meant the loss of personal freedoms. We have survey data from this period collected under the aegis of the American military authorities in West Berlin (and the western German zone). Among other things, people were asked which of two types of government they preferred: (a) 'a government which offers the people economic security and the opportunity to have a good income'; (b) 'a government which guarantees the people free elections, and freedom of speech, the press and religion'. These two questions can be convincingly compared with the Inglehart index, as the respondents had to give precedence to economic needs or political freedoms. But against Inglehart's assumptions, the number of postmaterialists did not decline during the blockade, but increased, from c. 30 to more than 40 per cent; by December 1950, it had even climbed to c. 50 per cent (more precise figures in Thome 2003). When 'materialist' and 'postmaterialist' needs were simultaneously at risk, it was the special value placed on freedoms rather than the dominance of the need for physical and economic security that was most apparent.

During the periods in which Inglehart gathered his data, political and personal freedoms were at no point endangered on a comparable scale in the western democracies. It is hazardous to come to conclusions about the relative value placed on alternative political objectives on the basis of respondents' statements about their importance unless you also ascertain the degree to which they consider them to be at risk or fulfilled. The increase in material prosperity released the potential for demands for other, additional objectives, including in the political sphere:

---

[13]   Here, there is evidence of a certain analytical ambivalence, ignored by Inglehart, which arises from the equation of needs and values, an equation which he has not thought through sufficiently.

greater opportunities for participation and co-determination at work and in the political arena, opportunities for alternative lifestyles, preservation of the natural environment, etc. But the declining urgency of materialist political goals in this period is not evidence of the diminishing value placed on economic prosperity (which continued to increase). The upward trend in postmaterialist objectives ground to a halt towards the end of the 1980s in European countries or went into reverse when this prosperity was increasingly experienced as under threat in the wake of 'globalization'. Again, though, this does not necessarily mean that the value placed on postmaterialist goals (which had by then been achieved to a greater extent and still seemed not to be at risk) had actually diminished.

By introducing a second dimension of values (traditional-religious vs secular-rationalist orientations), Inglehart seems to be making an analytical distinction which attributes to various cultural traditions a greater and, above all, ongoing influence, a factor which cannot be absorbed by the developmental dynamics of economic and technological change. But this supposed distinction is problematic conceptually and operationally. While the two value dimensions are presented side by side in the empirical surveys (see above, figure 12.2) and can thus be combined in any number of ways, they are arranged sequentially in conceptual terms (see esp. Inglehart 1995); they form a sequential pattern whose postulated developmental trend – according to Inglehart – follows economic progress. The industrialization phase features a transition from value commitments anchored in tradition and religion towards values legitimized in secular-rational terms ('modernization'); with the rise of the (richer) service and knowledge society, postmaterialist orientations gain more importance compared with materialist ones as the core of a more broadly conceived dimension of *survival vs self-expression values* ('postmodernization'). The culturally specific 'path dependency', the ongoing impact of traditional interpretive models and institutions, finds expression (in Inglehart's model) in temporal delays and overlap, but not in alternative developmental trends. Within the system of coordinates seen in figure 12.2 (see above), the dominant developmental path runs from the lower left to the upper right – with variously curved trend lines. Inglehart is in fact able to ascertain that only economically poor countries are to be found in the lower left quadrant of this diagram (with a Gross National Product of less than $2000 per inhabitant), while almost all (including non-European) rich countries (with a GDP of more than $15,000 per inhabitant) are clustered in the upper right quadrant, in other words, they have largely undergone both the modern and postmodern transformation. The formerly communist countries have become culturally detraditionalized on average as much as the rich countries of the west, but have not yet reached the postmodern phase. The developing countries of South America meanwhile appear to be moving more rapidly towards 'postmodernization' (self-actualization) than towards 'modernization' (secularization, rationalization). A high degree of cultural detraditionalization is meanwhile ascribed to the small number of countries shaped by Confucianism included in the study, but (with the exception of Japan) this is combined with an ongoing major emphasis on 'survival values'. As mentioned in section 2, this categorization may be particularly problematic because the western categories of secularization and individualization may not be directly translatable, let alone amenable to operationalization with the same array of questions in this cultural area (see Vinken 2006).

But the operational definitions of the two value dimensions (their conversion into specific batteries of questions) also call into question their analytical discriminatory power in another sense. It is, for example, hard to understand why the statement 'abortion is never justifiable' is ascribed to the traditional orientation, while the statement 'homosexuality is never justifiable' is ascribed to the survival orientation. It is also astonishing that an index of personal autonomy is supposed to represent secular-rationalist thinking rather than self-expression values (Inglehart and Baker 2000: 24). Nonetheless, despite the nebulousness of the analytical categories, the United States is identified empirically as a 'deviant case', which has 'modernized' (secularized) culturally to a relatively small degree, while its level of 'postmodernization' (individualization) corresponds to that of the other rich countries. However, this correspondence itself draws attention to the fact that the category of postmaterialist orientations, expanded into the notion of postmodernism, is somewhat misconceived. The findings obtained through the original index show that US citizens, going by their level of prosperity, were only weakly postmaterialist in orientation in the 1990s (see Inglehart 1997),[14] compensated for within the conglomeration of post-modern values by a particularly strong emphasis on self-expression values.

Alongside the flawed equation of (political) urgency and (general) positive appraisal (see above), it is apparent that the equation of self-actualization and postmaterialism or the exclusion of self-actualization and a materialist orientation is also misguided. It is based on the lack of a distinction between the content and structure of values. In his reception of Maslow's theory of needs (see above, section 2; see Thome 1985a), Inglehart overlooks the distinction made by Maslow between content and motives, which grow further apart the higher the level of needs reached: self-actualization may be achieved through very different activities and pursuits, by helping the poor as much as by becoming a successful businessman.

---

[14]   Other authors even refer to a sharp increase in materialist attitudes among young Americans in the 1970s and 1980s. Rahn and Transue (1998: 545) see this as the cause of a decline in trust within society and point to Tocqueville's warning that selfish individualism rooted in materialism might become a danger to democracy.

Klages incorporates such a distinction at least partly into his typology of values. In a certain sense, his concept of values is at right angles to that of Inglehart, in that he opposes duty and acceptance values (which Inglehart ascribes to cultural traditionalism) to self-expression values rather than to the categories of secularization and rationalization. He also identifies two variants of self-expression values: hedonistic materialism and idealistic social engagement.[15] However, even Klages does not distinguish sufficiently between the *content* of values and the modes of *acquisition* of values. Duties are accepted because recognized authorities or traditions, to which the person adheres, both suggest that they should be; self-expression values are selected on the basis of convictions or beliefs to which the person has committed herself; the specific content thus varies. The purpose of this distinction is elucidated by the empirical analyses that Meulemann (1998b) has presented on the values 'achievement' and 'public spirit'. Here, 'achievement' is not an unambiguous duty or acceptance value (as in Klages' work); it tends to be so for older people, but for younger people it is a self-determination value. Self-determination values, Meulemann agrees, are not opposed to public-spiritedness, and may even foster it.[16]

The distinction between the content of values on the one hand and forms of value commitment and value genesis on the other is also relevant to the frequently asked question of whether value change ultimately leads to a loss of values or even moral decline. As we have seen, Klages understood loss of values as lack of orientation: the 'aimlessly resigned' consider nothing (or very little) important or worthwhile. But their share of the population does not seem to be increasing. Loek Halman (1995: 426) sums up his findings, gleaned from European studies on values, with the thesis that a 'moral decline' has not taken place. In a comparative

---

[15]   This recalls Durkheim's classical distinction between moral and egoistic individualism, both of which he strictly set apart from traditional collectivism, in which the 'collective' was valued more highly than the 'individual'. Recent literature, particularly in cross-cultural psychology, but also sociology at times, often works on the assumption of a bipolar dimension of 'collectivism' versus 'individualism', which is a clear step backwards with respect to the analytical potential of the Durkheimian categories because it blurs the distinction between traditional collectivism and cooperative (moral) individualism (see Durkheim 1957; 1986; 2006).

[16]   Meulemann (1998b: 261–2) distinguishes conceptually between selfish 'self-development values' and 'self-determination values', which are open in terms of content. As evidence of a general growth in public spirit in West Germany, he points, among other things, to studies which show that 'between 1953 and 1979, the number of people who readily discuss things with individuals outside of the family grew from 28 to 41 per cent, and the number of people who consult with individuals outside of the family in difficult situations rose from 5 to 12 per cent' (Meulemann 1998b: 277).

analysis of German and Italian survey data (also gathered within the framework of the European value studies of 1981 and 1990), Wolfgang Jagodzinski (1999) examined three frequently mentioned aspects of a possible loss of values: (a) the relativization of moral norms, a decline in their status as unconditionally valid; (b) the erosion of the moral consensus; (c) the increasingly fragmented nature of moral convictions, the loss of consistency and coherence. While Jagodzinski sees 'indications of greater relativization of moral norms in the post-war generations', its extent is strongly dependent on the particular sphere of norms involved. It is 'particularly marked in attitudes to life and sexuality, rather less in attitudes to selfish behaviour and youth crime and is weakest in attitudes to attacks on public goods' (Jagodzinski 1999: 481–2). Ultimately, it is an open question 'whether rigid moral supervision merely shifts ceaselessly from one sphere to another' (Jagodzinski 1999: 482). The younger age groups, according to another finding, are rather more heterogeneous in their normative orientations than the older (consensus thus seems to have diminished), and their attitudes to normative issues are less coherent (that is, attitudes to a particular moral issue leave attitudes to other moral issues relatively open). Jagodzinski, however, rightly draws attention to the fact that contemporary societies require a high degree of normative relativization, but that this implies neither greater permissiveness nor a greater willingness to engage in immoral behaviour (Jagodzinski 1999: 482–3).

To adequately convey the conceptual distinctions mentioned here (to which we could add others), empirical research on values would have to enhance its instruments of survey and measurement. It is, for example, generally possible to distinguish between universal principles and situational norms and to conceive of the sphere of values in a multi-dimensional way within an array of questions (see, for example, Schwartz 1992). We would also have to pay heed to the fact that it is easier to express individual values in highly abstract form than value hierarchies, which vary more strongly in accordance with the situation and with respect to the perceived level of fulfilment or risk – meaning that these need to be incorporated as well. The normative and social generalization of values might also be registered in a more sophisticated way (proposals on this can be found in Thome 2003). In relation to 'consensus', the task would not only be to ascertain the extent to which different people (or groups) do in fact agree, but also the extent to which they are aware of this agreement.

Representative surveys are indispensible to empirical research on values. But in this field, too, there is a need for greater cooperation with qualitative social research, which questions or observes relatively small samples of people more intensively than is possible with the tools of standard survey research. This seems to me particularly essential to the reconstruction of the various forms of the genesis of values and personal commitment to values (see the chapter by Joas in this volume and Joas 2000).

Bibliography

Attias-Donfut, Claudine, 1998. 'Generationenverhältnis und sozialer Wandel', in R. Köcher and J. Schild (eds), *Wertewandel in Deutschland und Frankreich* (Opladen: Leske & Budrich), pp. 173–205.

Bacher, Johannes, 1988. 'Eindimensionalität der Postmaterialismus-Materialismusskala von Inglehart – Ein Methodenartefakt?', in H. Kreutz (ed.), *Pragmatische Soziologie. Beiträge zur wissenschaftlichen Diagnose und praktischen Lösung gesellschaftlicher Gegenwartsprobleme* (Opladen: Leske & Budrich), pp. 215–19.

Bauer-Kaase, Petra, and Max Kaase, 1998. 'Werte und Wertewandel – ein altes Thema und eine neue Facette', in H. P. Galler and G. Wagner (eds), *Empirische Forschung und wirtschafts-politische Beratung. Festschrift für Hans-Jürgen Krupp zum 65. Geburtstag* (Frankfurt and New York: Campus), pp. 256–74.

Berry, John W., Marshall H. Segall, and Cigdem Kagitcibasi (eds), 1997. *Handbook of Cross-Cultural Psychology*, vol. 3, 2nd edition (Needham Heights, MA: Allyn & Bacon).

Blanke, Bernhard, and Henning Schridde, 2001. 'Bürgerengagement und aktivierender Staat', in R. G. Heinze and T. Olk (eds), *Bürgerengagement in Deutschland. Bestandsaufnahmen und Perspektiven* (Opladen: Leske & Budrich), pp. 93–140.

Böltken, Ferdinand, and Wolfgang Jagodzinski, 1983. 'Postmaterialismus in der Krise', *ZA-Information* 12 (1983), pp. 11–20.

—, 1985. 'In an Environment of Insecurity: Postmaterialism in the European Community', *Comparative Political Studies* 17 (1985), pp. 453–84.

Clarke, Harold D., Allan Kornberg, Chris McIntyre, Petra Bauer-Kaase, and Max Kaase, 1999. 'The Effect of Economic Priorities on the Measurement of Value Change: New Experimental Evidence', *American Political Science Review* 93 (1999), pp. 637–47.

Dobbelaere, Karel, and Wolfgang Jagodzinski, 1995. 'Religious Cognitions and Beliefs', in J. W. van Deth and E. Scarbrough (eds), *The Impact of Values. Beliefs in Government*, vol. 4 (Oxford: Oxford University Press), pp. 197–217.

Durkheim, Emile, 1957. *Professional Ethics and Civic Morals* (London: Routledge [first French edition 1950]).

—, 1986. 'Individualism and the Intellectuals', in R. Bellah (ed.), *On Morality and Society: Selected Writings* (Chicago, IL, and London: University of Chicago Press), pp. 43–57.

—, 2006. *On Suicide* (London: Penguin, 2006 [1897]).

Flanagan, Scott C., 1982. 'Measuring Value Change in Advanced Industrial Societies. A Rejoinder to Inglehart', *Comparative Political Studies* 15 (1982), pp. 99–128.

—, 1987. 'Changing Values in Advanced Industrial Societies Revisited: Towards a Resolution of the Values Debate', *American Political Science Review* 81 (1987), pp. 1303–19.

Gabriel, Oscar W., 1998. 'Fragen an einen europäischen Vergleich', in R. Köcher and J. Schild (eds), *Wertewandel in Deutschland und Frankreich* (Opladen: Leske & Budrich), pp. 29–51.

Gensicke, Thomas, 1992a. 'Wertstrukturen im Osten und Westen Deutschland', *BISS public* 2 (1992), pp. 45–53.

—, 1992b. 'Lebenskonzepte im Osten Deutschlands', *BISS public* 2 (1992), pp. 101–22.

—, 2000. 'Deutschland im Übergang. Lebensgefühl, Wertorientierungen, Bürgerengagement', *Speyerer Forschungsberichte* 204 (2000).

—, 2001a. 'Das bürgerschaftliche Engagement der Deutschen – Image, Intensität und Bereiche', in R. G. Heinze and T. Olk (eds), *Bürgerengagement in Deutschland. Bestandsaufnahmen und Perspektiven* (Opladen: Leske & Budrich), pp. 283–304.

—, 2001b. 'Freiwilliges Engagement in den neuen und alten Bundesländern. Ergebnisse des Freiwilligensurveys 1999', *Aus Politik und Zeitgeschichte. Beilage zur Wochenzeitung Das Parlament* 25–6 (2001), pp. 24–32.

—, 2002. 'Individualität und Sicherheit in neuer Synthese? Wertorientierungen und gesellschaftliche Aktivität', in Deutsche Shell (ed.), *Jugend 2002. Zwischen pragmatischem Idealismus und robustem Materialismus* (Frankfurt am Main: Fischer).

—, 2005. 'Wachsende Gemeinschaftsaktivität und steigendes freiwilliges Engagement', *Informationsdienst Soziale Indikatoren* 34 (2005), pp. 11–15.

Halman, Loek, 1995. 'Is There a Moral Decline? A Cross-Nation Inquiry into Morality in Contemporary Society', *International Social Science Journal* 145 (1995), pp. 419–39.

Herbert, Willi, 1991a. 'Wandel und Konstanz von Wertstrukturen', *Speyerer Forschungsberichte* 101 (1991).

—, 1991b. 'Die Wertorientierung der Deutschen vor der Vereinigung. Eine empirische Momentaufnahme in Ost und West', *BISS-Public* 2 (1991), pp. 119–32.

Hofstede, Gerd, 2001. *Culture's Consequences: Comparing Values, Behaviours, Institutions, and Organizations across Nations* (Beverly Hills, CA: Sage).

Inglehart, Ronald, 1977. *The Silent Revolution: Changing Values and Political Styles in Advanced Industrial Society* (Princeton, NJ: Princeton University Press).

—, 1990. *Culture Shift in Advanced Industrial Society* (Princeton, NJ: Princeton University Press).

—, 1995. 'Changing Values, Economic Development and Political Change', *International Social Science Journal* 145 (1995), pp. 379–403.

—, 1997. *Modernization and Postmodernization: Cultural, Economic and Political Change in 43 Societies* (Princeton, NJ: Princeton University Press).

Inglehart, Ronald, and Paul R. Abramson, 1994. 'Economic Security and Value Change', *American Political Science Review* 88 (1994), pp. 336–54.

Inglehart, Ronald, and Wayne E. Baker, 2000. 'Modernization, Cultural Change, and the Persistence of Traditional Values', *American Sociological Review* 65 (2000), pp. 19–51.

Inglehart, Ronald, and Pippa Norris, 2004. *Sacred and Secular: Reexamining the Secularization Thesis* (New York and Cambridge: Cambridge University Press).

Inglehart, Ronald, and Christian Welzer, 2005. *Modernization, Cultural Change and Democracy* (New York and Cambridge: Cambridge University Press).

Jagodzinski, Wolfgang, 1985. 'Die zu stille Revolution. Zum Aggregatwandel materialistischer und postmaterialistischer Wertorientierungen in sechs westeuropäischen Ländern zwischen 1970 und 1981', in D. Oberndörfer, H. Rattinger, and K. Schmitt (eds), *Wirtschaftlicher Wandel, religiöser Wandel und Wertwandel. Folgen für das politische Verhalten in der Bundesrepublik Deutschland* (Berlin: Duncker & Humblot), pp. 333–56.

—, 1999. 'Verfällt die Moral? Zur Pluralisierung von Wertvorstellungen in Italien und Westdeutschland', in R. Gubert and H. Meulemann (eds), *Annali di Sociologia – Soziologisches Jahrbuch 13. 1997 – I – II* (Trento: University of Trento), pp. 385–417.

Jagodzinski, Wolfgang, and Karel Dobbelaere, 1995a. 'Secularization and Church Religiosity', in J. W. van Deth and E. Scarbrough (eds), *The Impact of Values. Beliefs in Government*, vol. 4 (Oxford: Oxford University Press), pp. 76–119.

—, 1995b. 'Religious and Ethical Pluralism', in J. W. van Deth and E. Scarbrough (eds), *The Impact of Values: Beliefs in Government*, vol. 4 (Oxford: Oxford University Press), pp. 218–49.

Joas, Hans, 2000. *The Genesis of Values* (Chicago, IL: University of Chicago Press).

Klages, Helmut, 1985. *Wertorientierung im Wandel. Rückblick, Gegenwartsanalyse, Prognosen* (Frankfurt and New York: Campus).

—, 'Brauchen wir eine Rückkehr zu traditionellen Werten?', *Aus Politik und Zeitgeschichte. Beilage zur Wochenzeitung Das Parlament* 29 (2001), pp. 7–14.

Kluckhohn, Clyde, 1951. 'Values and Value-Orientations in the Theory of Action. An Exploration in Definition and Classification', in T. Parsons and E. A. Shils (eds), *Toward a General Theory of Action* (Cambridge, MA: Harvard University Press), pp. 388–464.

Kmieciak, Peter, 1976. *Wertstrukturen und Wertwandel in der Bundesrepublik Deutschland* (Göttingen: Schwartz).

Köcher, Renate, 1998. 'Zur Entwicklung der religiösen und kirchlichen Bindungen in Deutschland und Frankreich', in R. Köcher and J. Schild (eds), *Wertewandel in Deutschland und Frankreich* (Opladen: Leske & Budrich), pp. 55–65.

Lambert, Yves, 1998. 'Säkularisierungstendenzen in Deutschland und Frankreich in europäischer Perspektive', in R. Köcher and J. Schild (eds), *Wertewandel in Deutschland und Frankreich* (Opladen: Leske & Budrich), pp. 67–92.

Lautmann, Rüdiger, 1969. *Wert und Norm. Begriffsanalysen für die Soziologie* (Cologne and Opladen: Westdeutscher Verlag).

Lipset, Seymor M., and Stein Rokkan (eds), 1967. *Party Systems and Voter Alignments* (New York: Free Press).

Luhmann, Niklas, 1998. *Die Gesellschaft der Gesellschaft* (Frankfurt am Main: Suhrkamp).

Meulemann, Heiner, 1985. 'Wertwandel in der Bundesrepublik zwischen 1950 und 1980: Versuch einer zusammenfassenden Deutung vorliegender Zeitreihen', in D. Oberndörfer, H. Rattinger, and K. Schmitt (eds), *Wirtschaftlicher Wandel, religiöser Wandel und Wertwandel. Folgen für das politische Verhalten in der Bundesrepublik Deutschland* (Berlin: Duncker & Humblot), pp. 391–411.

—, 1998a. 'Arbeit und Selbstverwirklichung in Deutschland und Frankreich', in R. Köcher and J. Schild (eds), *Wertewandel in Deutschland und Frankreich* (Opladen: Leske & Budrich), pp. 133–50.

—, 1998b. 'Wertwandel als Diagnose sozialer Integration: Unscharfe Thematik, unbestimmte Methodik, problematische Folgerungen. Warum die wachsende Bedeutung der Selbstbestimmung kein Wertverfall ist', in J. Friedrichs, M. R. Lepsius, and K. U. Mayer (eds), *Die Diagnosefähigkeit der Soziologie. Sonderheft der Kölner Zeitschrift für Soziologie und Sozialpsychologie*, pp. 256–85.

—, 1999. 'Generations-Solidarität in Deutschland und Italien – Parallelen der politischen Geschichte und Divergenzen vorpolitischer Werte', in R. Gubert and H. Meulemann (eds), *Annali di Sociologia – Soziologisches Jahrbuch 13. 1997 – I–II* (Trento: University of Trento), pp. 385–417.

—, 2002. 'Werte und Wertwandel im vereinten Deutschland', *Aus Politik und Zeitgeschichte. Beilage zur Wochenzeitung Das Parlament* 37–8 (2002), pp. 13–22.

Montada, Leo, and Anne Dieter, 1999. 'Gewinn- und Verlusterfahrungen in den neuen Bundesländern: Nicht die Kaufkraft der Einkommen, sondern politische Bewertungen sind entscheidend', in M. Schmitt and L. Montada (eds), *Gerechtigkeitserleben im vereinigten Deutschland* (Opladen: Leske & Budrich).

Noelle-Neumann, Elisabeth, 1978. *Werden wir alle Proletarier? Wertewandel in unserer Gesellschaft* (Zurich: Interfrom).

Noelle-Neumann, Elisabeth, and Thomas Petersen, 2001. 'Zeitenwende. Der Wertewandel 30 Jahre später', *Aus Politik und Zeitgeschichte. Beilage zur Wochenzeitung Das Parlament* 29 (2001), pp. 15–22.

Rahn, Wendy M., and John E. Transue, 1998. 'Social Trust and Value Change: The Decline of Social Capital in American Youth, 1976–1995', *Political Psychology* 19 (1998), pp. 545–65.

Reuband, K.-H., 1997. 'Aushandeln statt Gehorsam? Erziehungsziele und Erziehungspraktiken in den alten und neuen Bundesländern im Wandel', in L. Böhnisch and K. Lenz (eds), *Familien. Eine interdisziplinäre Einführung* (Weinheim: Juventa), pp. 129–53.

Rokeach, Milton, 1973. *The Nature of Human Values* (New York: Free Press).

Roth, Roland, 2001. 'Besonderheiten des bürgerschaftlichen Engagements in den neuen Bundesländern', *Aus Politik und Zeitgeschichte. Beilage zur Wochenzeitung Das Parlament* 39–40 (2001), pp. 15–22.

Scheuch, Erwin K., 2003. *Sozialer Wandel*, vol. 2: *Gegenwartsgesellschaften im Prozess des Wandels* (Opladen: Westdeutscher Verlag).

Schnierer, Thomas, 1996. 'Von der kompetitiven Gesellschaft zur Erlebnisgesellschaft? Der "Fahrstuhl-Effekt", die subjektive Relevanz der sozialen Ungleichheit und die Ventilfunktion des Wertewandels', *Zeitschrift für Soziologie* 25 (1996), pp. 71–82.

Schwartz, Shalom H., 1992. 'Universals in the Content and Structure of Values: Theoretical Advances and Empirical Tests in 20 Countries', in M. P. Zanna (ed.), *Advances in Experimental Social Psychology*, vol. 25 (San Diego, CA: Academic Press), pp. 1–65.

—, 2004. 'Mapping and Interpreting Cultural Differences around the World', in H. Vinken, J. Soeters, and P. Ester (eds), *Comparing Cultures: Dimensions of Culture in a Comparative Perspective* (Leiden and Boston, MA: Brill), pp. 43–73.

Thomas, William I., and Florian W. Znaniecki, 1984 [1921]. *The Polish Peasant in Europe and America* (Chicago, IL: University of Chicago Press).

Thome, Helmut, 1985a. *Wertewandel in der Politik? Eine Auseinandersetzung mit Ingleharts Thesen zum Postmaterialismus* (Berlin: WAV).

—, 1985b. 'Wandel zu postmaterialistischen Werten? Theoretische und empirische Einwände gegen Ingleharts Theorie-Versuch', *Soziale Welt* 36 (1985), pp. 27–59.

—, 2003. 'Soziologische Wertforschung. Ein von Niklas Luhmann inspirierter Vorschlag für die engere Verknüpfung von Theorie und Empirie', *Zeitschrift für Soziologie* 32 (2003), pp. 4–28.

Thumfart, Alexander, 2001. 'Politische Kultur in Ostdeutschland', *Aus Politik und Zeitgeschichte. Beilage zur Wochenzeitung Das Parlament* 39–40 (2001), pp. 6–14.

Triandis, Harry C., 1995. *Individualism and Collectivism* (Boulder, CO: Westview Press).

Van Deth, Jan W., 2001. 'Wertewandel im internationalen Vergleich. Ein deutscher Sonderweg?', *Aus Politik und Zeitgeschichte. Beilage zur Wochenzeitung Das Parlament* 29 (2001), pp. 23–30.

Van Deth, Jan W., and Elinor Scarbrough, 1995. 'The Concept of Values', in J. W. van Deth and E. Scarbrough (eds), *The Impact of Values: Beliefs in Government*, vol. 4 (Oxford: Oxford University Press), pp. 21–47.

Vinken, Henk, 2006. 'East Asian Values Surveys. Making a Case for East Asian-Origin Values Survey Concepts', *ZUMA-Arbeitsbericht* 5 (2006).

Wildenmann, Rudolf, et al., 1982. *Führungsschicht in der Bundesrepublik Deutschland 1981* (Mannheim: University of Mannheim).

13

The Realities of Cultural Struggles

Dieter Senghaas

In the present article I attempt to bring clarity to the debate on so-called 'cultural conflicts'. However, these conflicts are discussed here only inasmuch as they are of political or, to put it more precisely, macropolitical relevance. I call *these* conflicts 'cultural struggles' and I approach this topic through a comparative analysis anchored in developmental history, my primary concern being to shed light on *contemporary* realities.[1]

1. Casting Our Mind Back

I

Let's begin with a quotation:

> The superiority she [Europe] has long maintained has tempted her to plume herself as the mistress of the world, and to consider the rest of

---

[1] I point the reader at the outset to some important texts of relevance to the present topic, supplementary to those cited later on, particularly Harald Müller, *Das Zusammenleben der Kulturen. Ein Gegenentwurf zu Huntington* (Frankfurt am Main: Fischer, 1998); Mark Juergensmeyer, *Terror in the Mind of God: The Global Rise of Religious Violence* (Berkeley, CA: University of California Press, 2000); Martin Riesebrodt, *Die Rückkehr der Religionen. Fundamentalismus und der Kampf der Kulturen* (Munich: Beck, 2000); Henner Fürtig (ed.), *Islamische Welt und Globalisierung. Aneignung, Abgrenzung, Gegenentwürfe* (Würzburg: Ergon, 2001); Thomas Scheffler (ed.), *Religion between Violence and Reconciliation* (Würzburg: Ergon, 2002); Harald Barrios and Andreas Boeckh (eds), *Resistance to Globalization: Political Struggle and Cultural Resilience in the Middle East, Russia and Latin America* (Münster and London: Lit, 2003); Thomas Meyer, *Identity Mania: Fundamentalism and the Politicization of Cultural Differences* (London: Zed, 2001); Wolfgang Schluchter (ed.), *Fundamentalismus, Terrorismus, Krieg* (Weilerswist: Velbrück, 2003); Michael Minkenberg and Ulrich Willems (eds), *Politik und Religion, Politische Vierteljahresschrift* special issue 33 (2003).

mankind as created for her benefit. Men admired as profound philosophers have in direct terms attributed to her inhabitants a physical superiority and have gravely asserted that all animals, and with them the human species, degenerate in America – that even dogs cease to bark after having breathed awhile in our atmosphere. Facts have too long supported these arrogant pretensions of the European. It belongs to us to vindicate the honor of the human race, and to teach that assuming brother moderation. Union will enable us to do it. Disunion will add another victim to his triumphs. Let Americans disdain to be the instruments of European greatness! Let the thirteen States, bound together in a strict and indissoluble Union, concur in erecting one great American system superior to the control of all transatlantic force or influence and able to dictate the terms of the connection between the old and the new world.

This statement is from Alexander Hamilton and appears in the famous *Federalist Papers* (final paragraph of no. 11).[2] It can easily be applied to the present. Hamilton's reference to 'Europe' need only be replaced by 'the West'; if we then replace the 'Americans' whom he is trying to stir to action with 'Muslims', and think, for example, of one of the well-known fundamentalist authors from the Islamic world, Sayyid Qutb (1906–1966), rather than Hamilton, this quotation could be from our own time.[3] It would remain only to substitute 'the countries of the Islamic world' for the 'thirteen states', and for the 'great American system' perhaps 'the Muslim world', the '*umma*', or, within a more limited area, with reference to the Arab-Islamic world, 'the Arab Nation', the project of a state uniting all Arabs. An updated statement might then go something like this:

The superiority the West has long maintained has tempted it to plume itself as the master of the world, and to consider the rest of mankind as created for its benefit [...]. Facts have too long supported these arrogant pretensions of the Westerner. It belongs to us to teach that assuming brother moderation. The community of Muslims, the *umma*, will enable us to do it. Disunion will add another victim to his triumphs. We Muslims must cease to be the instruments of Western greatness! Let the Muslim States, bound together in a strict and indissoluble Union, concur in erecting one great Islamic system superior to the control of all Western

---

[2]   Alexander Hamilton *et al.*, *The Federalist Papers* (London: New English Library, 1961), pp. 90–1.

[3]   On Sayyid Qutb, one of the most influential fundamentalist authors of Egyptian origin, see Gilles Kepel, *The Prophet and the Pharaoh: Muslim Extremism in Contemporary Egypt* (London: Al Saqi, 1985), pp. 61ff.

force or influence and able to dictate the terms of the connection between our world and the West.

If we understand culture to be the totality of the typical ways of life of a people, including the mental state and values that underpin them, the situation addressed by Hamilton is a cultural conflict, or to put it in political terms, a *Kulturkampf* or cultural struggle. What was at issue in the clash between Britain's American colonies and the mother country?

In the perception of those who became 'Americans' through this conflict (something which they by no means were to begin with), Europe was considered the epitome of an old world order in which life was not worth living, one from which they had escaped in 1620, the year the 'Pilgrim Fathers' landed in America. From the perspective of the Puritan colonists fleeing Europe, the old world order was characterized by feudal despotism, an extreme class society, the arrogance of the upper classes living in luxury and extreme exploitation of the peasant masses. In the eyes of those living on the other side of the Atlantic, Europe was also considered 'rotten', morally corrupt: European potentates sold their subjects like goods, and other European potentates bought them in turn, in order to deploy them in the struggle against the inhabitants of the British colonies on the North American continent. Of course, this view of Europe had much to do with the reality of Europe.

Their own world, understood as the epitome of a 'new world order', an 'Empire of Liberty', contrasted with the old in every respect. The freedom of the individual, guaranteed by matching rights obtainable through legal action, in combination with a wealth of voluntary associations which astonished Alexis de Tocqueville decades later, was intended to found a civil society. The motto was thus: individualism plus solidarity, underpinned and framed by political self-determination, that is, legitimized public authorities; this self-determination (or 'ownership' to use a term characteristic of the recent development policy debate) was anchored in religious freedoms, but also in domestic economic independence ('taxation only with representation'), and was flanked by sovereign control of foreign trade policy, which was seen as an indispensable means of achieving successful domestic economic development.

This was how the New World saw the Old, at first primarily in the consciousness of the key actors, who used the print media of the time (local newspapers), which enjoyed increasingly wide circulation, as a platform for the propagation of their ideas. But these ideas would not have had such wide appeal had not the citizens' assessment of the situation generally coincided with that of the political leaders. The 'New World', in fact nothing less than a 'new world order' – this was a *projet* in the Sartrean sense, a plan for a particular way of life and for the future. This project featured clearly recognizable components: a specific view of people and society; matching ideas regarding the kind of political order (constitution) congenial to this view; development programmes in the field of education and infrastructure; an economic programme, particularly with respect to the fostering of indigenous industry, and as part of this a plan for foreign trade intended to safeguard domestic development (Friedrich List and the 'federalists' would later find much common ground). And, last but not least, this plan of action presupposed political sovereignty, that is, self-determination.

The idea here was of a *development* project, understood in a comprehensive sense. The aim was to found something new: partly as a means of defending oneself against despotic Europe, but partly as an autonomous project. The new order was meant to be a better one. The shift, already apparent at the time, towards the idea of being a 'chosen people', towards a sense of mission, is linked with this foundation myth, which was more than mere myth, far more than a fiction. For, as history would show, this project was of tremendous significance because it was underpinned by a trend towards secularism, apparent only *in nuce* at the time. This was a 'project of modernity', understood not as the concern of a dissenting intellectual aristocracy as in the European *siècle de lumières*, but as a project and political process enjoying broad consent, that is, on a mass basis.

This first example exemplifies the most important factors in a cultural struggle: resistance to heteronomy and the resulting anti-hegemonic, anti-imperial, anti-colonial, and anti-imperialist stance. This oppositional attitude helps raise consciousness, precisely in the sense of 'concienciación' (Paulo Freire). Beyond this, it aims to mobilize effective opposing forces ('empowerment'). The oppositional attitude is supplemented by an independent model of a way of life and society, which links in with the idea of political innovation. The overall process is comprehensive in nature: it touches on the political, social, and economic order – and all three are endowed with a particular meaning. Thus, in this context, in contrast to its definition in *Duden*, the concept of culture cannot be reduced 'to the totality of the intellectual and artistic expression of a community or people'; it also incorporates the old rejected public order along with the new one that is aspired to. In this context, in which what is at stake is a model and alternative model of a public order, culture is not one dimension among others, but at bottom the epitome of the political order, because culturally informed ideas aim to organize the various spheres of life in an active fashion. Culture is thus emphatically political culture.

This example shows how the combination of oppositional stance and a perspective based on a plan for the future – at an elite and mass level – can turn a cultural struggle into a major historical conflict. In the case of America, history rewarded rather than punished the protagonists. This doesn't happen often, which makes it particularly instructive: *Tu felix America!*

2

Let us recall another historical context: Sub-Saharan Africa's struggle to achieve decolonization and follow its own developmental path more than 150 years later. Once again, prefigured by the context, oppositional attitudes were in evidence, above all anti-colonial and anti-imperialist propaganda, growing in intensity from the 1950s on, and corresponding political movements. But future-oriented perspectives were also articulated and flowed into the political debates. They may be paraphrased through certain slogans, which were more than mere slogans, which in fact brought together a number of profound ideas.[4] The idea that a process of renewal must take place in decolonizing Sub-Saharan Africa – building eclectically on indigenous tradition *and* external influences (Christian mission and Islam, the legacy of the modern colonial administrations and the laicist state) – was captured, for example, in the term 'consciencism' coined by Nkrumah. The intention here was to create a new, coherent consciousness, a new indigenous identity, out of the reality of entirely different fragments of experience ('structural heterogeneity of consciousness'): the 'African personality'. And this last not only at an individual, but also at a national or all-African level. The idea of the 'African personality' was thus linked directly with the concept of 'Panafricanism'. Here, too, political sovereignty as a result of successful decolonization was the key prerequisite for the project: 'Seek ye first the political Kingdom and all other things shall be added unto it.' These words could be read engraved in a central location in Accra (Ghana) some years after Ghana gained independence.

Other variants of this project for Africa were furnished with their own unique philosophy of life, and sometimes overlain with their own epistemology as well. Senghor contrasted western *raison analytique à distance* with African *raison-étreinte* or *raison-toucher*, that is, cool, analytical reason with a kind which remains symbiotically connected with people, the world, and nature. The latter was a core assumption of *négritude*, an identity claimed to apply to Sub-Saharan Africans.

The fate of these projects is well known. They went, like so much else, the way of the postcolonial state: from liberating awakening to ideology of domination, before finally falling into oblivion. The American example cited earlier may provide clues to the reasons why history turned out this way: above all, there was a lack of ideas concerning a project of independent economic development as foundation and underpinning of the cultural project.

This state of affairs itself, exemplified here through Africa (West Africa in

---

[4]   An early in-depth account appears in Dieter Senghaas: 'Politische Innovation. Versuch über den Panafrikanismus', *Zeitschrift für Politik* 12 (1965), pp. 333–55. On the general problem of cultural self-assurance, see Ludger Kühnhardt, *Stufen der Souveränität. Staatsverständnis und Selbstbestimmung in der 'Dritten Welt'* (Bonn: Bouvier, 1992), pp. 35ff. and passim.

particular), could also have been described with reference to other cases. It is always to be found whenever political groupings of one kind or another (tribes, peoples, colonies, etc.) rise up against foreign rule, enter into an anti-colonial struggle, and strive for political sovereignty as a result of decolonization. An oppositional stance is crucial here, as well as efforts to found an independent identity. Wherever decolonization movements were engineered in situations of colonial or informal dependency, whenever 'peripheries' have risen up against 'centres', articulating protest and, ultimately, often engaging in a military struggle against their colonial masters and so-called mother countries, what took place was also a cultural struggle, even if only in the sense of an intensified programme of anti-colonial mobilization.[5]

This state of affairs could be observed, with matching programmatic doctrines, as early as the nineteenth century; but its decisive impact on history was felt primarily in the twentieth century and especially after 1945. In this respect, south-eastern Europe played the role of forerunner to a certain extent in the late nineteenth century. It is there (in Romania in particular) that the birthplace of sophisticated doctrines regarding the relationship between 'centres' and 'peripheries' is to be found; corresponding developmental imperatives were formulated there;[6] and the requirements for the formation of a cultural identity were recognized there as well. Many varieties of later developmental socialism (African, Arab, Indian, Indonesian, etc.) were prepared in a comparable context. The historical foundation of harder forms of developmental socialism in the sense of a people's communism motivated by Marxism (such as the Vietnamese or Chinese variant) also lies in initial situations of this kind.[7]

3

This observation brings us to the recollection of a third event.

Strangely, since the 1990s, in the debate – still current or at least thought to be – on the 'clash of civilizations', the east–west conflict is interpreted as a conflict of ideologies that has now come to an end, while the 'clash of civilizations' that is now supposedly emerging is seen as a conflict of cultures and the 'cosmologies' that characterize them, rooted in the depths of history. But what was the east–west conflict? From the contemporary perspective of

---

[5]   Early, seminal analyses can be found in John H. Kautsky (ed.), *Political Change in Underdeveloped Countries: Nationalism and Communism* (New York: Wiley, 1962).

[6]   See Roman Szporluk, *Communism and Nationalism: Karl Marx versus Friedrich List* (New York: Oxford University Press, 1988).

[7]   See also Bassam Tibi, 'Politische Ideen in der "Dritten Welt" während der Dekolonisation', in *Pipers Handbuch der politischen Ideen*, vol. 5 (Munich: Piper, 1987), pp. 361–402.

1917 or 1950, even looking back from the present, two notions of people and society (and the corresponding realities), irreconcilable in terms of their favoured political and economic system, confronted one another in the east–west conflict. Representative of the western camp were and are individualism and pluralism as constitutive conditions of modern society, checks and balances as a principle of political order, the public sphere as intrinsically valuable (including the modern idea of the media as a 'fourth estate'); in addition, science, justice, and adminis- tration are generally regarded as neutral, non-partisan spheres; market and culture are seen as spheres of action important in their own right and featuring their own logic; and with regard to the economic sphere, market prices, private property, and comparative costs and advantages are a key guiding factor.

Eastern real existing socialism was characterized by collectivism, the forcing into line of politics, society, economy, and culture, and as a result: concentration of powers; deliberate partisanship in science, law, and administration; and with regard to the economic sphere, orientation towards administrative political prices, collective ownership, and a monopoly on foreign trade. There was also a crucial difference in the evaluation of the political, social, economic, and cultural conflicts inevitable in modern societies. As a rule, the western understanding considers conflicts to be inescapable or endemic; they cannot be abolished, but must be regulated by many and diverse provisions for dealing with conflict. In the east, these were seen as disruptive and dysfunctional; regulatory mechanisms were underdeveloped; there were only a few self-regulating nets capable of absorbing conflicts, and when conflicts came to a head the response was generally repressive.

This was a confrontation between two projects. It is perfectly possible to refer to this constellation as a cultural struggle, for this conflict over the form of public order was concerned with a whole range of matters (as can be observed in every comparable case). It had a social, economic, and cultural dimension, each with its own justification and meaning, which were condensed into a specific view of the political and economic system. The fact that the antagonistic developmental projects, briefly outlined here, were the core of the competition between the systems of east and west, was evident at the latest when one of the two projects, real existing socialism, collapsed and the accumulated armaments abruptly lost their function and meaning and stood around 'aimlessly'. This fact indicates that while the conflict was highly militarized and its dynamics were conveyed in part via the dimension of arms ('arms race'), militarization was a derivative rather than originary phenomenon.[8]

This conflict, too, arose in the periphery, born out of resistance and self-

---

[8]   See Dieter Senghaas, *Konfliktformationen im internationalen System* (Frankfurt am Main: Suhrkamp, 1988), ch. 2.

defence, directed against the predatory economic and cultural competition coming from the centres. *Anti*-imperialism became the quintessence of real existing socialism, which also embodied its own political, social, economic, and cultural perspective. The fact that this perspective ultimately failed to endure plays no role with respect to the original state of affairs. As in the American-British example cited earlier, the east–west conflict involved a confrontation between two different self-understandings and programmes of action. Ultimately, the undoing of real existing socialism was the fact that, in contrast to the assumptions of classical doctrine (which was, of course, oriented towards 'mature' capitalist societies), it began as a historically significant force opposed to impending or existing peripheralization – and it was undoubtedly innovative in this respect – only to fail miserably to deal with the socio-economic and cultural complexity which resulted from the surges of modernization which it *itself* had engineered. As a result, the counter-project to western modernity, the attempt to construct an eastern, real existing socialist modernity, came to an end; the competition of systems once built upon it has lost its meaning, as has the cultural struggle that underlay it.

2. Identifying Locations

I

The events recalled above reveal the basic pattern of politically relevant cultural conflicts. Abstracting from the individual cases, the following factors are the key prerequisites for cultural struggles:

- contexts of hierarchical interaction between centre and periphery, in which a power differential, in particular a gulf in economic and technological competence, gradually takes hold;

- enduring and unbalanced competition, the centre outcompeting the periphery, particularly with respect to economy and culture (peripheralization pressures);

- a danger of peripheralization and structural dependency, resulting from both of these, expressed in open colonization, informal dependency ('informal empire'), interference and penetration, and similar phenomena, with severe consequences in each case (socio-economic and mental distortions).

As a rule, a set of circumstances like this provokes defensive attitudes; these inspire the production of counter-projects. Both tend to occur when the society in question has entered into a process of social mobilization or is making rapid advances in this regard: when a subsistence economy, for example, turns into an economy characterized by the division of labour; when the depopulation of rural areas leads to massive urbanization; when illiteracy is stamped out. The expansion of dependent employment, life in cities, and mass education are the modern basis for politicization on an equally large scale – including a politicization directed against the colonial or quasi-colonial circumstances identified above, and ultimately against all forms of large-scale discrimination against collectivities.[9]

2

The milieu and the object of such politicization may be described as developmental nationalism. It is manifested in a number of variations.[10]

A first experiential realm in this regard is the world of primary developmental nationalism, which includes the American-British example mentioned earlier. This is the kind of nationalism evident in the development of the modern-day OECD countries, which led to the development of state-centred nations (as in the case of France) and nation-states (as in the case of Germany). As we know from the history of the western and northern European nation states, as well as that of the USA, Canada, New Zealand, and Australia, the space delimited by state and culture played an important role in the developmental path of these various countries. Japan is another notable example in this respect. At a time when the dominant Latin American elites threw themselves into the arms of European civilization in a kind of self-colonization, seeing no point in pursuing an independent developmental path, and in fact did all they could to oppose such a path locally, Japan reflected on its own culture and, regardless of all its borrowings from the west, began to engineer a project of its own.

In the world of those societies that later banded together to form the OECD grouping, there was a relatively balanced combination of oppositional stance and independent, nationally defined projects. The oppositional stance was initially directed against the first take-off society and economy: Britain. The developmental programme, with its individual variations, may be paraphrased through the title of a classic work of development theory (Friedrich List): *The*

---

[9]   See Karl W. Deutsch, *Abhängigkeit, strukturelle Gewalt und Befreiungsprozesse*, in Klaus Jürgen Gantzel (ed.), *Herrschaft und Befreiung in der Weltgesellschaft* (Frankfurt am Main: Campus, 1975), pp. 23–46.

[10]   The following distinction between primary, secondary, and tertiary developmental nationalism is developed with respect to comparative research on nationalism in ch. 2 of my book *Wohin driftet die Welt? Über die Zukunft friedlicher Koexistenz* (Frankfurt am Main: Suhrkamp, 1994).

National System of Political Economy – a text which clearly emphasized the cultural component of developmental processes.[11]

Leaving the already peripheralized world is a far trickier business: this is the experience of so-called secondary developmental nationalism in south-western Europe, southern Europe, south-eastern Europe, eastern Europe, and Ireland, as well as that part of the world which we have since the 1960s grown accustomed to calling the Third World. The African example discussed above is fairly representative of this context. We must also add many successor states to the Soviet Union, particularly the Baltic, Trans-Caucasian, and Asian republics, whose breaking-away from the former Soviet Union was tantamount to an act of decolonization. Ultimately, conflicts within modern-day Russia, such as that in Chechnya, can be understood in much the same way: as attempts at decolonization.[12]

The success *or* failure of secondary developmental nationalism, that is, of the postcolonial project of development, is directly relevant to the current *problématique* of cultural conflict.

The East Asian developmental path must be described as successful. It culminated in the fundamental modernization of the various economies in the region, accompanied by corresponding social restructuring. Within a few decades, traditional societies turned into societies with a modern social profile. The modernization of the political system, particularly its pluralization and democratization, is underway. Here, the western European experience is being repeated in certain respects, though in a different order. Yet why is it that 'Asian values' are presently being opposed to western values and sometimes propagated with great militancy in this region? Asian values (such as the great emphasis placed on the family, group, and collectivity, the sense for order and public morality, respect for personal or role-determined authority and age, etc.) are understood, in combination with a modern, efficient, and internationally competitive economy, as the expression of a specifically 'Asian modernity'. In reality, however, the propaganda for so-called Asian values represents a rearguard action *against the will* of those groupings which enabled the societies of this region to achieve relatively successful development through a mixture of economic and educational dictatorship: modernizing societies, which are as a result generally individualizing ones, now demand fair participation in public affairs. Asian values serve to fend off such demands. The addressees of the propaganda for Asian values are not in

---

[11]   Friedrich List, *The National System of Political Economy* (London: Cass, 1983 [first German edition: 1841]). See also Hermann Bausinger, 'Agrarverfassung und Volkskultur, Friedrich List als Volkskundler', in Dieter Harmening and Erich Wimmer (eds), *Volkskultur – Geschichte – Region* (Würzburg: Königshausen & Neumann, 1990), pp. 77–87.

[12]   Hélène Carrère d'Encausse, *The End of the Soviet Empire: The Triumph of the Nations* (New York: Basic, 1993).

fact the west and western values (both of which are significant as ideological projections), but rather increasingly emancipated, highly educated Asians who have found their political voice, particularly a new middle class. What we are seeing here is thus, first and foremost, a local conflict against the background – and this is the remarkable thing – of a relatively successful developmental path.[13]

The exact opposite is evident in Sub-Saharan Africa, the region to which our second bout of recollection was devoted. Just as the reasons for developmental success in the case of East Asia are comprehensible today, so also are the reasons for the dramatic failure of development policies in Sub-Saharan Africa. Large-scale collapse is a far from infrequent occurrence, while even those achievements of colonialism which have so far sustained many of these countries have suffered material decline: roads, railway lines, docks, public buildings, etc. In some cases, the breakdown ends up in a state of affairs that is hard to describe: a kind of regressive 'retribalization', which is accompanied by a 're-traditionalization' that defies easy understanding. In many locations, ethnicization then seems like ineluctable fate, frequently in combination with the return of warlordism, which tends to lead to a fatal situation of conflict with a dynamic all its own. This last occurs primarily when local resources (diamonds, high-grade wood, oil) are being sold profitably within a segment of the globalized black economy, thus becoming a temporarily inexhaustible source of funds for the provisioning of the parties to conflict and their clientele. But it makes no sense to refer to issues of cultural conflict in such contexts.

For the discussion of such issues, a third case is of greater significance, namely those Third World societies outside of East Asia and Sub-Saharan Africa in which the postcolonial state has produced a mixture of success and failure – with the overall result of a mounting developmental crisis. The success consists in the fact that the developmental process in these societies saw a temporarily strong surge of development featuring marked upward social mobility. But this upward mobility no longer translates into secure professional and social positions; in particular, it no longer provides jobs in the bloated postcolonial state administration and state-run firms, which formed an effective sponge soaking up the first and second generation of the postcolonial elite. In addition, the development that occurred was, as a rule, insufficiently broadly based, pushing ever greater numbers to the social margins, a document to its failure.[14] The political representatives of the

---

[13]   See ch. 2.9 in Dieter Senghaas, *The Clash within Civilizations: Coming to Terms with Cultural Conflicts* (London and New York: Routledge, 2002).

[14]   In this respect the early Latin American analyses have proved entirely correct. See, for instance, Aníbal Quijano, 'Marginaler Pol der Wirtschaft und marginalisierte Arbeitskraft', in Dieter Senghaas (ed.), *Peripherer Kapitalismus* (Frankfurt am Main: Suhrkamp, 1974), pp. 298–341.

postcolonial status quo are held responsible for this failure, with good reason. They find themselves facing threats on two fronts, positioned as they are between the frustrated, politicized, upwardly mobile middle class, and the quantitatively growing classes of the marginalized poor.

3

This constellation of factors gives rise to fundamental conflicts which reopen the debate on where development is going, indeed on the project of development overall. The questions at issue here are not only minor ones about this or that developmental variant, but relate to the question of power itself. And this question in turn is connected with an increasingly pressing social question which, *rebus sic stantibus*, there is currently no prospect of resolving. This intensely problematic set of circumstances has given birth to tertiary developmental nationalism in response to the failure of the secondary variant, its point of departure the militant reculturalization of politics. The reasons for this development? Reculturalization, motivated by developmental nationalism, is occurring because it expresses the crisis of development as a whole in symbolic form; it may arise as a defensive reaction against particularly powerful, indeed overwhelming international influences; but it may also simply be engineered in Machiavellian fashion as an obvious strategy and effective instrument in the struggle for influence and power.

This development is evident in numerous locations. It has gained notoriety in the Islamic world, particularly in the Arab-Islamic region, in Iran and with increasing intensity in Pakistan. It is occurring in explosive form in India, where there are clashes between militant forces motivated by Hinduism and Islamic groupings as well as Sikhs. A civil war lasting almost twenty-five years resulted from this constellation in Sri Lanka, where Singhalese and Tamils (and thus a politicized Buddhism and politicized Hinduism, whatever their part in the conflict may be) are engaged in a bloody struggle.[15]

That which is generally fought out at the level of the state as a whole is now taking place within specific segments of the state as well, sometimes with less intensity, sometimes in highly militant form, but always with clear cultural components – in those conflicts in which a minority suffering massive political, economical, social, and cultural discrimination makes a stand against the majority. What we are seeing here is political resistance to assimilation which, as a rule, occurs against a broad experiential background: the accumulation of persistent frustrations of many different kinds. The cultural conflict in the narrow sense (conflicts relating to schooling and language policies), inherent in this situation,

---

[15]   See, from a comparative perspective, Mark Juergensmeyer, *The New Cold War? Religious Nationalism Confronts the Secular State* (Berkeley, CA: University of California Press, 1993).

which can easily be couched in emotional terms, often becomes the immediate trigger for a general escalation of conflict.[16]

A cultural conflict of a unique kind exists in those ethnically plural societies found primarily among the ASEAN countries, where minorities (such as the Chinese communities) are economically successful but tend to be politically marginalized, while the majority populations hold the political power yet consist of second- or third-class citizens economically speaking. This situation is familiar from other parts of the world. It once played a major role in East Africa (where a dynamic Indian minority made a huge contribution to the active sectors of the economy). This finds expression in social envy, with racism adding dynamism to the situation. This state of affairs may even be found in highly industrialized countries: it was apparent in Los Angeles in the bloody clashes between newly arrived, upwardly mobile, dynamic Asians and the long-established black underclass.

In this regard, we may also mention the kind of conflict produced by an Apartheid regime, a situation, that is, in which a minority is superimposed on the majority, the former attempting to marginalize the latter (as occurred in Kosovo). This situation is rarely found today, but it, too, involves clear elements of cultural conflict: all Apartheid regimes are especially active with respect to culture, banning, for example, the language of the majority in schools and universities and the state administration, particularly the judicial system and police force. This type of conflict is characterized by culturally motivated resistance to heteronomy.

In all the cases mentioned here, it is not difficult to understand why political actors turn to culture, that is, language and religion, history and myths, to real *and* fictional, so-called 'imaginary' points of reference. But it is vital to keep in mind that this is a *modern* phenomenon resulting from *modern* developmental crises.[17]

Thus, culture, broadly understood, comes into play politically because, in light of mounting frustrations, people begin to question the postcolonial project of development as a whole, and there are objective grounds (rather than merely instrumental ones relating to the potential for agitation) for the political

---

[16]   The term 'resistance to assimilation' contrasts with that of 'resistance to heteronomy' mentioned below. Each relates to quite different contexts, as I have explained with reference to Europe in *Friedensprojekt Europa* (Frankfurt am Main: Suhrkamp, 1992), ch. 4.

[17]   See the following titles, which are still of great relevance: Peter Waldmann and Georg Elwert (eds), *Ethnizität im Wandel* (Saarbrücken: Breitenbach, 1989); Eckhard J. Dittrich and Frank-Olaf Radtke (eds), *Ethnizität* (Opladen: Westdeutscher Verlag, 1990).

formulation of a new project of development. In those places where, as in the Arab-Islamic region, cultural homogeneity rather than heterogeneity applies (all existing minorities notwithstanding) and many are turning to one source, the Koran, it would be hard to avoid a fundamental debate on the social and political order. Is not the crisis of development the logical consequence of disregarding one's own roots, one's own Islamic identity presented in the Koran? When this question is posed in specific locations, it is rarely for merely rhetorical purposes.[18]

Cultural conflicts come into play whenever a grouping embraces ethnic politics for obvious reasons, as is often found in ethnically plural societies: when disputes centre on language, religion, historical consciousness, as well as ethnic affiliation − individually or in variable combination.[19] Cultural conflicts also arise when, for want of other power resources, language, religion, and history are deliberately mobilized and instrumentalized. In such cases, actors draw on the sources of culture not for the sake of the sources but for the sake of power, and their interpretation of these sources is not motivated by their commitment to textual exegesis but by their desire for power. The 'correct' interpretation of those sources considered to be authentic then becomes an object of the cultural struggle. This was, by the way, no different in early Europe.

3. The West and Cultural Struggles

How does the West fit into these disputes?

Because 'the West', represented by specific countries, was the source of modern colonialism, imperialism, and neo-colonialism, it will always remain present in the cultural struggles being carried on the world over as long as postcolonial

---

[18] Alongside Kepel, *The Prophet and the Pharaoh*, see the highly informative selection of original voices from the Islamic world in the book edited by Andreas Meier, *Der politische Auftrag des Islam. Programme und Kritik zwischen Fundamentalismus und Reformen. Originalstimmen aus der islamischen Welt* (Wuppertal: Hammer, 1994). Also useful in this regard is Hanna Lücke, *Islamischer Fundamentalismus − Rückfall ins Mittelalter oder Wegbereiter der Moderne? Die Stellungnahme der Forschung* (Berlin: Schwartz, 1993). Of absolutely fundamental importance to the debates on the socio-political order in the context of a politicized cultural conflict within the Islamic world is the monograph by Gudrun Krämer, *Gottes Staat als Republik. Reflexionen zeitgenössischer Muslime zu Islam, Menschenrechten und Demokratie* (Baden-Baden: Nomos, 1999).

[19] An informative monographic study of general theoretical significance is Theodor Hanf, *Coexistence in Wartime Lebanon: Decline of a State and Rise of a Nation* (London: Centre for Lebanese Studies in association with Tauris, 1993).

counter-projects arise, are only partially successful, or even unsuccessful. This was and remains the first key point.

The second relates to the local postcolonial elites, which function as bridgeheads of the west in these countries and, even in those places where they did not and do not play this role, are nonetheless perceived as such. The battle with the corrupt, self-enriching postcolonial elite which frustrates subsequent generations thus almost inevitably becomes a battle with the west as well.[20] This tendency applies particularly in cases where – as in India for example – the secular state was taken over by the postcolonial elite as a legacy of colonialism, still survives in terms of its external form, but is increasingly perceived as one of the causes of the crisis of development, and thus not as an agent of its resolution. When the secular state is considered not a helpful arena for dealing with the problems of coexistence in societies that are becoming pluralist, or which are already, but as a western transplant, the west as a whole becomes a target of polemic along with it. This process may have no immediate consequences for the west, but it is of much significance to the local conflict.

The west also comes into play because now the crisis of development is interpreted – almost everywhere, even in the west, though in fact wrongly – as caused by a Eurocentric approach. But the developmental policies pursued in the postcolonial societies did *not* adhere to those priorities which underlay the paths to development typical of Europe.[21] Yet somehow this misunderstanding is insurmountable; it is testimony to an astonishing ignorance of economic history.

These three factors inspire many diverse projections onto the west, which often find expression in dramatic propaganda. When, as has happened so often, actors declare 'the' west (or sometimes a specific country, particularly the USA) to be, or want it to be, the 'devil', as a rule we are seeing an autistic allusion which, like every case of autistic enmity, is characterized by great potential for escalation and a momentum of its own. This autistic enmity is deepened and strengthened if it is then endowed with an additional emotional charge as a result of actual conflicts, in response, for example, to hostage dramas, terrorism, the condemning of individuals to death (*fatwa*), and similar cases that stir up emotions.

---

[20]   Kepel, *The Prophet and the Pharaoh*, is also particularly revealing with respect to this problem, especially his discussion of the concept of *jahiliyya*, which expresses the moral and ethical decline of societies in the real existing Islamic world.

[21]   I explain the reasons for this in Dieter Senghaas, *The European Experience: A Historical Critique of Development Theory* (Leamington Spa: Berg, 1985); see also Ulrich Menzel and Dieter Senghaas, *Europas Entwicklung und die Dritte Welt. Eine Bestandsaufnahme* (Frankfurt am Main: Suhrkamp, 1986), esp. ch. 1.

Yet, notwithstanding all the allusions mentioned above, whether real and/or projected ('imagined'), it is clear that the actual fronts in present-day cultural struggles develop locally, that there is therefore no evidence of geocultural conflicts, although the number of manifest conflicts featuring genuine or imposed cultural components has increased in recent times. In particular, Islam and the west do not face each other like a pair of opposing armies. This would be impossible, if for no other reason than because Islam as a monolithic entity exists only in the fiction of the *umma*, but not as a political reality. 'Islam' does not exist in the singular; rather, as the title of one book signals correctly, there are 'worlds of Islam'. At present, variants of the theocratic state based on 'virtue' exist in Iran and Sudan; an opportunistic relationship to Islam as a means of securing power was evident in Iraq in the 1990s; Syria is openly repressive; enlightened absolutism holds sway in Jordan; Egypt is a secular, typically postcolonial state now threatened from within; and Libya features a particularly interesting variant of an Islamic regime, heretical from an orthodox point of view. If we add to these variants the particular forms which have developed in the Maghreb, in parts of Sub-Saharan Africa, and especially in Asia, the heterogeneous character of political Islam is quite clear.[22]

Despite often similar developmental crises, this heterogeneity in turn translates into very different cultural struggles. The situations in Libya and Iran, for example, can hardly be reduced to a common denominator, and yet both countries are often perceived as if they had identical Islamic (Islamist-fundamentalist) regimes.

Much the same applies to the west. It is no doubt thoroughly 'western' in many respects, but operationally speaking it rarely presents a united front in its political behaviour. And there is no sign that western politics will proceed very differently in the future.

No geocultural conflicts are emerging in the other regions of the world that are shaping the *macro*structure of international politics in a fundamental and thoroughgoing way either. The construction of a 'collusion' between Confucianism and Islam is particularly mistaken; so far, the only observer to 'spot' this collusion is Samuel Huntington, helping him achieve unparalleled international prominence.[23] Extravagant ideas on things 'geocultural', whether true or false, always attract great attention in the media.

---

[22]   Gernot Rotter (ed.), *Die Welten des Islam* (Frankfurt am Main: Fischer, 1993).
[23]   See Samuel Huntington, *The Clash of Civilizations and the Remaking of World Order* (New York: Simon & Schuster, 1996).

4. Concluding Remarks

Politicized cultural conflicts, described here as cultural struggles, existed long before the recent debate about them. Our initial recollection of historical events was intended to bring this out. We might have cited other cases, such as the cultural struggles sparked off by the French Revolution, which once inspired some commentators to refer in retrospect to a 'global civil war', though this is surely going too far.[24] If we look far back in history, it is possible to discern a cultural struggle – perhaps the first in history, and one, moreover, that was explicitly perceived as such – in the Maccabees' struggle against the violent Hellenization of Judea being pursued by the Seleucid Empire. The Old Testament (2 Maccabees 6) provides a dramatic account of how the Temple in Jerusalem was transformed into a shrine to Zeus and of how the Seleucid rulers banned Jewish law, and of the culturally motivated Jewish resistance movement that developed out of this situation, which eventually culminated in the successful rebellion of the Maccabees (167 BC).

We as yet lack a synthesizing history of the modern era from the perspective of cultural struggle.[25] It could by no means be restricted to that period of history which has quite rightly been described as world civil war: the globalizing conflict between liberalism and communism between 1917 and 1989.[26] The reality of cultural struggles has been varied and multifaceted; it still is. Nothing suggests that this will change in the foreseeable future. For it would be a strange thing if, in the contemporary era, at the very time when large-scale structures are being dismantled throughout society, economy, and culture (wrongly called 'postmodernism', in fact the latest variant of modernity), the great civilizational aggregates such as Confucianism, Hinduism, Islam, Orthodox Christianity, Western Christianity, were to determine the course of events. That which is easily imaginable in the economic sphere, the development of even larger and more extensive regions as a result of increasing material and informational interlinkage, is quite implausible in the cultural sphere. *Within* the great cultural areas, rivalries, competition for political power, and struggles for hegemony will

---

[24]   For a summary of relevant contributions by Hanno Kesting, Roman Schnur, and others, see Thomas Michael Menk, *Gewalt für den Frieden* (Berlin: Duncker & Humblot, 1992), pp. 363ff.

[25]   Though there are illuminating individual studies, for example on the cultural struggle that arose at exactly the same time as the Enlightenment movement; see Christoph Weiss (ed.), *Von 'Obskuranten' und 'Eudämonisten'. Gegenaufklärerische, konservative und antirevolutionäre Publizisten im späten 18. Jahrhundert* (St Ingbert: Röhrig, 1997).

[26]   See Ernst Nolte, 'Das Zeitalter des Kommunismus', *Frankfurter Allgemeine Zeitung*, supplement 'Bilder und Zeiten', 12 October 1991.

be far more significant than the supposed common interests of grand fictional collectivities.[27] One need only look at the Islamic-Arab world since the 1950s for this to become immediately clear.

This empirically verifiable fact implies one advantage: namely that the concrete conflicts remain manageable as a rule, and it is thus possible to influence them in principle, though in the case of 'protracted conflicts' it often seems that cultural struggles are virtually intractable. Sadly, Ireland until recently, the Basque Country, Sudan, Sri Lanka, Kashmir, Tibet, and many other examples, all too easily give rise to such an impression. But civilizations or cultural areas per se will not collide – how could they? There will, however, be cultural struggles in many locations. The realities of such cultural struggles should not be hyperstylized into a geocultural fiction, and the thesis of the clash of civilizations should not be confused with reality. The empirical facts suggest such a conclusion, which is, moreover, advisable from a political point of view, including the politics of peace.[28]

---

[27]   Johan Galtung also assumes that such grand collectivities are capable of coherent action. See his contribution 'Konfliktformation in der Welt von morgen', in *Friedensbericht 1992* (Vienna: VWGÖ, 1992), pp. 229–61.

[28]   See Dieter Senghaas, *On Perpetual Peace. A Timely Assessment* (Oxford and New York: Berghahn, 2007).

14

The Contest of Values: Notes on Contemporary Islamic Discourse

Gudrun Krämer

People are thinking seriously about values again. They are doing so in Europe, which has been reappraising its Christian heritage since the fall of the Berlin Wall and the collapse of the Soviet empire; in the United States, which has decided to launch a worldwide crusade for freedom; and in Asia, which insists on its cultural specificity. The Muslim world, too, is debating values, internally as well as with the outside world. The debate is taking place in a highly charged atmosphere, and it is marked by a pronounced asymmetry of power. The west calls on 'Islam', that is to say, on Muslims, to engage in a process of 'enlightenment' which is not just to put them on the road to Europe, but to secure their access to modernity – not, of course, the modernity that has shaped the twentieth century so profoundly, the modernity of fascism, totalitarianism, racialism, and genocide, but the light side of modernity with its high moral ideals and values. The west calls for the rule of law and good governance, freedom, and the respect for human rights. It even promotes such principles in various ways – just as it hinders them in others.

Faced with western demands and expectations, Muslims find themselves on the defensive; this is true even for those who actually embrace these principles. They cannot do so without defining their relationship to the west (as the overpowering Other) and to Islam (as the supposedly one and only expression of Self). The debate on values thus cannot be separated from identity politics. While Europeans and Americans can speak without (positive) reference to other cultural traditions, Muslims discussing Islamic alternatives cannot do so without referring to the western experience, if only implicitly. Even those expressing themselves in strictly Islamic terms, rejecting the adoption of all 'non-Islamic' concepts, from natural law through democracy to the idea of autonomous reason, do so against the backdrop of a challenge posed by the west, and a desire to distance themselves from the west. The 1948 Universal Declaration of Human Rights can be read without knowledge of non-western documents, but the Islamic declarations of human rights produced in subsequent decades can be understood only in relation to this and other 'universal' declarations.

In this regard, as in so many others, Muslims hold many different opinions, not only Islamic or Islamist ones. We are talking, after all, about more than 1.2 billion people, the majority of whom do not live in the Middle East, and hence in the immediate neighbourhood of Europe, but in south and south-east Asia. Still, it is Muslims in the Middle East – the region between Iran, Turkey, and Morocco – who continue to be most widely heard and read internationally. Among them there are many who do not see their identity jeopardized if they allow themselves to be inspired by modern socio-political ideas and values – precisely because they do not consider them exclusively western, but universally valid, and for this reason adaptable to non-western traditions and ways of life. Yet with the exception of declared atheists (of whom there are few), even these Muslims usually make an effort to justify their position in 'Islamic' terms, testifying to the resounding success of Islamic discourse. Today it is almost impossible for anyone in the Muslim world to eschew it if she or he expresses a view on social, legal, or political issues.

It should be said that there are several variants of Islamic discourse, which resonate in different socio-cultural milieus. Here I examine a line of thought whose basic argument may not at first appear conspicuous, but which, in my opinion, is quite innovative: the argument that Islam not only features specific rules of conduct, including a set of ritual obligations, but also a stock of basic values, or principles, that guide social and political life at the individual and collective levels. This stock of basic Islamic values or principles (both terms are often used interchangeably) normally includes justice, freedom, equality, responsibility, and participation in decision making. Though rooted in the authoritative legal and theological tradition, this catalogue is manifestly modern. Notions of justice and equality can serve to illustrate the logic of the argument, and the stakes involved in the debate.

Islam as Text

Islam, as even many of its critics have come to see, is certainly distinctive, or 'different', and perhaps even 'other'. Yet it is neither uniform nor unchanging. To this extent, the critique of 'Orientalism' (which asserts such uniformity and immutability) has been absorbed into public discourse, or at least important parts of it. If we take this insight seriously and consider Islam to be intrinsically plural and changeable, it becomes impossible to make definitive statements about the canon of Islamic values. We can merely refer to concepts defined by Muslims with reference to Islam (as they understand it). In the present context, what is meant by Islam is not the totality of Muslims today or at some point in the past together with their social practices, which are or were perceived as Islamic, but rather the tradition which Muslims at all times and in all places have considered normative. This tradition consists of texts of very different character, first and foremost the Koran and the Prophetic Traditions, or Sunna.[1] According to Islamic doctrine, the Koran (the Arabic *qur'ān* literally means 'recitation' or 'reading') comprises the revelation 'sent down' by God in its final (Arabic) version to Muhammad, whom this revelation marked out as his prophet and messenger. Regardless of the different narrative perspectives identifiable in the text itself, the Koran is considered to be divine speech and thus in the most literal sense the word of God. A standard text was produced only some time after the death of Muhammad in A D 632 (precisely when and by whom and on what basis is contested among scholars). Since then, the Koran has existed in book form, comparable to the sacred books of the Jews and Christians, though a standardized text, authorized by al-Azhar University in Cairo, only became generally accessible in the 1920s, well after the introduction of printing in the Middle East. The Koran may be recited only in the Arabic original; translations are considered no more than approximations of the meaning of the authoritative Arabic text. This underscores the crucial importance of Arabic as the sacred language of Muslims and at the same time highlights the difficulty faced by those unable to read it – but who nonetheless feel qualified to speak on Islamic doctrine, law, and ethics.

More easily accessible, but also more unwieldy, is the Sunna ('cleared path', or 'normative example'), or Prophetic Traditions, a huge corpus of individual reports (Hadiths) on the statements and practices of Muhammad that are thought to be inspired by divine revelation.[2] Unlike the Koran, the Sunna does not exist in the form of a single book, but in a number of collections dating from the ninth century A D. Sunni Muslims recognize six such collections as canonical and the Shia four, the latter differing from their Sunni counterparts primarily in accepting as transmitters of Hadith only Ali and the imams descended from him rather than the wives and companions of Muhammad, including the first three caliphs Abu Bakr, Umar, and Uthman (whom the Sunnis regard as rightly guided, whereas the Shia deny their legitimacy). The Sunna is extensively cited (not least in the debate about values) but it is not recited. Nonetheless, it is considered by most Muslims to be part of revelation and thus essentially sacrosanct.

---

[1]   See Jane Dammen McAuliffe (ed.), *The Cambridge Companion to the Qur'an* (Cambridge: Cambridge University Press, 2006); Neal Robinson, *Discovering the Qur'an: A Contemporary Approach to a Veiled Text*, second edition (London: SCM Press, 2003); Hans Zirker, *Der Koran. Zugänge und Lesarten* (Darmstadt: Primus, 1999); Stefan Wild (ed.), *The Qur'an as Text* (Leiden: Brill, 1996).

[2]   See Daniel W. Brown, *Rethinking Tradition in Modern Islamic Thought* (Cambridge: Cambridge University Press, 1996).

The problem with this conception of sacred scripture is readily apparent. The Koran and Sunna document (or purport to document) social norms and practices characteristic of Arab tribal society in early seventh-century north-western Arabia, practices which may have been affected by the Koranic message, or even been transformed by it, but which cannot be simply transferred across time and space to be 'implemented' in entirely different socio-cultural settings. Many Muslims are aware of this. Few, however, conclude that the exemplary practice of the Prophet is not only situated in a particular space, but also tied to it and thus not timelessly valid and binding, at least not in its entirety. As a rule, Muslims, particularly those advocating innovative ideas, avoid discussing the prophetic era and begin their critical inquiry only some decades later, when, it is generally believed, the glory of the early years had already faded.

The stakes are high with regard to the Sunna and the prophetic era more generally. They are even higher with respect to the Koran. In much of the Muslim world today, it is virtually impossible to publicly discuss the status of the Koran as the word of God.[3] Only a small number of scholars and intellectuals have adopted (elements of) modern textual criticism, and they have done so cautiously and without casting doubt on the fact of divine revelation as such.[4] They mainly argue that the word of God is accessible to human beings only in their (human) language, and that human language is inevitably tied to a particular time and place. Few go so far as to say that the Koran itself is mute. It is easier to suggest that Koranic images, metaphors, and narratives come alive only within individual listeners and readers, who place them within their own particular experiences and intellectual horizons. This still allows for a variety of positions. These range from a radical stance that views the Koran as divine revelation expressed in human language, which can and must be read with the tools of historical criticism, to less radical positions that emphasize the complexity of the Koranic text as well as the ever-changing interpretive horizons of its recipients: the conclusion in both cases is that, in order to become alive, the Koranic message requires human agency.

This is not all new. Classical exegetes did recognize the fact that the Koranic text is opaque in parts, occasionally ambiguous and full of meanings that are

---

[3]   Along with the titles mentioned above in n. 1, see Claude Gilliot and Rotraud Wielandt, 'Exegesis of the Qur'ān', in Jane Dammen McAuliffe (ed.), *Encyclopaedia of the Qur'ān*, vol. 2 (Leiden and Boston, MA: Brill, 2002), pp. 99–142; Stefan Wild, *Mensch, Prophet und Gott im Koran. Muslimische Exegeten des 20. Jahrhunderts und das Menschenbild der Moderne* (Münster: Rhema, 2001).

[4]   See Suha Taji-Farouki (ed.), *Modern Muslim Intellectuals and the Qur'an* (Oxford: Oxford University Press, 2004); Katajun Amirpur and Ludwig Ammann (eds), *Der Islam am Wendepunkt. Liberale und konservative Reformer einer Weltreligion* (Feiburg: Herder, 2006).

impossible to define in exhaustive fashion, no matter how excellent one's command of Arabic. As a matter of fact, the Koran itself says so in more than one place. Rather, individual passages must be carefully considered, placed within the overall context of the Koran and assessed in light of other references that seem to point in a different direction. The Koran itself refers to the possibility of replacing some provisions by 'better' ones (Sura 2:106), with the later parts of revelation, logically, correcting or even abrogating earlier ones. Yet the Koran does not offer a linear narration and therefore does not provide a basis to establish the chronological sequence of provisions. At best, this may be done with the aid of extra-Koranic materials, including the Sunna and the biography of the Prophet (sīra). However, their use as historical sources is debatable, and strongly contested among non-Muslim researchers. Very few Muslim Koranic scholars have ventured to critically examine or 'deconstruct' the Muslim (and thus admittedly human and fallible) tradition concerning the age of the Prophet and the early Islamic period more generally. Even innovative Koranic scholars, who acknowledge the historical embeddedness of revelation, rely more or less blindly upon a Muslim tradition whose oldest surviving texts date back to the early eighth century, at least three generations after the death of the Prophet. The challenges of Koranic interpretation may seem all too familiar, if not downright trite, to trained textual scholars (particularly Bible scholars). Trite they are not: Islamists deny them, firmly declaring the Koranic message to be unambiguous, and critics of Islam who eagerly quote Koranic verses to demonstrate the irreconcilability of Islam and modernity do the same. Neither is concerned with the ground rules of textual criticism.

Islamic Discourse

Contemporary Islamic discourse serves to underline this point. Though by no means uniform, it is premised on one assumption: Islam is what is written in the Koran and Sunna. No idea, act, or institution can be considered Islamic (and thus legitimate and authentic) if it cannot be traced back to the Koran or Sunna. Unlike the discussions about political strategies and the status of jihad, the debate on values shows how difficult it often is to clearly distinguish between Islamists (Arabic: islamiyyūn) on the one hand and 'ordinary' believers (muslimūn, mu'minūn) on the other. All take it for granted that Islam entails more than the belief in the one and only God and his messenger Muhammad. All assume that faith demands deeds that attest to its truth before the world,[5] and that Islam

---

[5]   This position still leaves a number of questions to be addressed, such as whether the profession of faith (shahāda) is sufficient for an individual to be considered a Muslim or whether it must be continuously confirmed through action, whether grave sins render

establishes a particular way of life that translates religious values into daily actions. As indicated by the Latin term, religion *binds* its adherents. For this reason, it will have an impact on society, and cannot remain restricted to the private sphere. In this sense, Islam, as the classic formula has it, is 'religion and world' (*al-islām dīn wa-dunyā*).

Islamists go beyond this widely shared view in more than one respect, firstly in regarding the Koran and Sunna as the sole foundation of all norms and values to the exclusion of all other sources of morality and normativity. This is aimed at those Muslims who believe in the ability of exceptional individuals, notably Sufi saints and masters, to gain direct access to divine truth, with illumination rather than book learning showing the path to this truth. At the same time, it is aimed at those Muslims who accept the validity of other sources of inspiration for Muslims alongside the Koran and Sunna, provided they do not run counter to the fundamental teachings or, as it is often put, the basic values of Islam (and whether they do so is, of course, subject to debate). Why not benefit from the experience of others, especially as this was common practice throughout history?

Islamists in their majority acknowledge no such stock of shared human values. This sheds light on the radical and at the same time utopian nature of their approach. In the age of globalization and mass migration, they wish to affirm a boundary between different religions (cultures, civilizations) that was originally defined in territorial terms: the boundary between the 'territory of Islam' (*dār al-islām*), in which the sharia is enforced by the prince or state, and the 'territory of war' (*dār al-harb*), in which this is not the case, either because the rulers are not Muslims or, although nominally Muslims, fail to apply the sharia exclusively and comprehensively. According to hard-line Islamists, the *dār al-islām* must be cleansed of all non-Islamic ideas and practices and the *dār al-harb* fought by means of jihad; Muslims living there must render themselves immune against all non-Islamic ways of thought and conduct. Even those Islamists who, in recognition of present realities, acknowledge a third category, the 'territory of truce' (*dār al-sulh*) or 'of treaty' (*dār al-'ahd*), in which the state of war between Islamic and non-Islamic territories has been temporarily or permanently suspended, fail to transcend the territorial logic. And yet, the presence of millions of Muslims in the diaspora – traditionally defined as *dār al-harb* or at best *dār al-sulh* – poses the issue of boundaries in novel ways. Muslims do, of course, continue to encounter

---

an individual an unbeliever (*kāfir*), whether this leads to his or her exclusion from the community of Muslims (Arabic *takfīr*, translated rather inadequately as excommunication), and whether a jihad must be launched against such people, though it may not be launched against Muslims. These issues were major topics of early Islamic theology and politics, and feature prominently in contemporary attempts to come to terms with militant Islamism.

territorial borders, including those they did not draw themselves (such as those enclosing 'fortress Europe'). Yet they cannot mentally opt out of the present, and impregnate themselves against non-Koranic concepts and models that dominate the global market in ideas and values. Beyond small islands of retreat, the Islamist law of purity cannot be upheld.

Much the same applies to another distinguishing feature of Islamist doctrine: the notion that the divinely ordained way of life cannot be realized on an individual level, but only within the framework of an 'Islamic order' (*nizām islāmī*), in which God's law is universally enforced. Islam, it is claimed, requires the 'application of the sharia' as the body of ethical and legal rules decreed by God for all times and places. The application of the sharia in turn presupposes an Islamic state. Accordingly, Islam encompasses not just 'religion and world', but 'religion and state' (*al-islām dīn wa-dawla*). The establishment of (genuinely) Islamic states or of one unified Islamic state (in the shape of a universal caliphate for example) also addresses the problem of boundaries, as all Muslims would have either to move to the *dār al-islām* or turn their current place of residence into part of it. This leaves the question of how they are supposed to seal themselves off from global trends unanswered. How the sharia is to be 'applied' and how the 'Islamic order' is to be organized remains contested. Even committed Islamists are put off by political realities in Iran, Saudi Arabia, Pakistan, or Sudan, at least those living beyond the borders of these states, which all call themselves Islamic. There is thus no single model of an 'Islamic order'.

To sum up, the term 'Islamists' here refers to a discursive community rather than the advocates of a particular political organization or strategy. Islamists are to be found in many different places, among the opposition as well as the establishment, among intellectuals and businesspeople, judges and high-school teachers, shopkeepers and unemployed youth. They share the conviction that Islam represents a unique, self-contained, and all-encompassing system of norms and values which must regulate individual life as well as the public order, and that this system is divinely ordained and accessible solely through the Koran and Sunna, to the exclusion of all other sources of morality and normativity. According to them the canon of norms and values enshrined in the Koran and Sunna makes Islam unique and essentially unchanging, and, at least at the moral level, superior to all other systems.

Basic Islamic Values

Islamic discourse refers to the Koran and Sunna in order to render its own claims unassailable. At the same time, when addressing social and political issues, it makes use of the language of Islamic jurisprudence (*fiqh*), without necessarily retaining its logic and procedures, let alone its substance. The strategy of presenting one's own discourse as firmly anchored in the grand tradition is, of course, deliberate. It is also very common and deceptive. Anyone talking about values in the Muslim world today must speak about the sharia, and this goes, to repeat, even for those who do not wish to see it 'applied'. Very few Muslims dare to say openly that, at least in its present form, the sharia is outdated and unsuited to modern circumstances. Rather, they focus on what is meant by sharia. The relevant discussions are complex and sophisticated, and in many instances do not allow for a sharp distinction between Islamist and non-Islamist speakers. Thus a majority of Muslims will argue that the sharia is divine law in the sense that it was laid down by God (or his messenger Muhammad, which is generally less clearly stated), with respect to its fundamentals and certain specifics, in the Koran and Sunna. Accordingly, they perceive Islamic law not as a human construct, but essentially as divine statute, which is merely 'discovered', 'understood', and 'implemented' more or less correctly by human intellects.[6] The crucial distinction between God's *laying down* of all norms and laws (*shar'*, *sharī'a*) and human *understanding*, as expressed among other things in jurists' law (*fiqh*, from the Arabic verb 'to understand'), is fully acknowledged. The resulting consequences are, however, a matter of controversy.

Islamists emphasize the comprehensiveness of divine sharia, which according to them covers all spheres of life, leaving at most very limited room for human interpretation, to be exercised in accordance with the powers of judgement granted by God and, of course, in light of revelation. Meanwhile, in sharp contrast, their critics, some of whom adopt an openly modernist stance, highlight the small number of legally binding rulings in the Koran (reference to the Sunna would be detrimental to their line of argument), and extend the field of human interpretation as much as they can. Even independent legal reasoning (*ijtihād*), which has played a key role in Muslim reformist thought since the eighteenth century, featuring repeated calls for the 'opening' of the 'gate of Ijtihad' supposedly closed in the tenth century, remains grounded in the normative texts. It is free only from exclusive ties to a particular school of law (*madhhab*) with its specific doctrines and methods, ties which moulded the theory and practice of Islamic law until well into the twentieth century. Sunni Muslims tend not

---

[6]   For a useful overview, see Peter Scholz, 'Scharia in Tradition und Moderne – Eine Einführung in das islamische Recht', *Jura. Juristische Ausbildung* 23.8 (2001), pp. 525–34; for different perspectives, see Wael B. Hallaq, *The Origins and Evolution of Islamic Law* (Cambridge: Cambridge University Press, 2005); Bernhard G. Weiss, *The Spirit of Islamic Law* (Athens, GA, and London: University of Georgia Press, 1998); Mohammad Hashim Kamali, *Principles of Islamic Jurisprudence* (Cambridge: Islamic Texts Society, 1991); also Abbas Amanat and Frank Griffel (eds), *Shari'a. Islamic Law in the Contemporary Context* (Stanford, CA: Stanford University Press, 2007).

to dwell at length on what the 'opening of the gate of Ijtihad' entails for the status of human reason and freedom. Shia Muslims, in whose legal tradition reason plays a greater role, and is more generally acknowledged as valid, seem less reluctant. Yet both Sunni and Shia Muslims find it difficult to recognize the moral autonomy of the individual. At the same time, even Islamists do not entirely deny human judgement or reason, but see them based on divine will rather than natural law.

The distinction between (unchangeable divine) sharia on the one hand and (changeable human) jurists' law on the other is easier to make in theory than in practice. In the present context of angry contestation, the formula 'fiqh is not the same as sharia', helps avoid a critical examination of the sharia, which may easily be seen, and dismissed, as an attack on the very foundation and bulwark of Muslim identity. However, the strategy of avoidance does little to clarify specific issues. Ultimately, even seemingly unambiguous passages in the Koran and Sunna have to be read by humans (and this is precisely what fiqh is: the attempt to understand) and translated into practice in order to have a social impact. Those who study the substance and scope of the sharia itself go further. Two approaches stand out here, one based on contextualization and the other on abstraction.[7] Both seek to establish a hierarchy of norms and rules, one by placing them on a chronological scale, the other by assessing their relative weight and authority.

Contextualization builds on established modes of Koranic exegesis by seeking to ascertain the precise historical context in which a specific injunction is embedded (technically known as the 'occasions of revelation'). The aim here is not to contest the validity of a particular Koranic injunction, but to restrict it to its original context and thus to limit its overall binding force. Sura 4:3 and 129 serves as the classic example of this approach. In the context of providing for female orphans, it allows Muslim men to marry up to four 'believing' women on condition that they treat them equitably. The vast majority of Muslim exegetes past and present have classified this provision as generally binding, while modernist interpreters see it as providing for an exceptional case only, with no universal binding force. In terms of textual exegesis narrowly defined, this reading is perfectly legitimate, for the relevant passages are notoriously difficult to interpret. One problem, however, remains unresolved. In order to justify their conclusion, which is based on contextualization, modernists have to rely on mainstream Muslim historiography to determine the context of any given ruling, or its 'occasions of revelation'. As a rule, they do so without first engaging in rigorous source criticism. The uncritical use of history in what aims to be a historical, critical approach to the Koran does not seem to bother them.

---

[7]   For a more technical discussion, see my 'Justice in Modern Islamic Thought', in Amanat and Griffel (eds), Shari'a, pp. 20–37.

Abstraction offers still greater possibilities of rethinking the Koranic message, especially when combined with contextualization. The guiding idea is to identify core principles and values in the Koran and Sunna, in order to do justice to the 'spirit' of the sharia (or Islam, both terms often being used interchangeably in the present context) rather than remaining restricted to its letter.[8] Technically, these principles have been described as representing the 'objectives' of the sharia (maqāsid al-sharī'a), or its 'finality'.[9] Abstraction rests on the assumption that the sharia contains a canon of universal norms and values – among them justice, freedom, equality, responsibility, and participation (shūrā) – which must be adapted to the ever-changing circumstances of time and place to take effect. This assumption, innocuous though it may appear at first glance, has important consequences: according to a number of interpreters, universal principles carry greater weight than specific provisions of the Koran and Sunna and, in case of conflict, can even supersede or suspend explicit textual injunctions. This is a daring claim to make and fraught with risk. Yet its proponents can again build on the legacy of classical Islamic jurisprudence which, though it proceeded in casuistic fashion, was unable to forego a certain degree of rationally guided abstraction in elaborating positive norms on the basis of a limited number of authoritative textual references. This included developing a concept of the common good or public interest (in modern legal terminology, maslaha 'āmma) and of certain underlying goods or benefits (masālih) to be protected by the sharia. Five such goods or benefits were identified

---

[8]   For more depth, see my Gottes Staat als Republik. Reflexionen zeitgenössischer Muslime zu Islam, Menschenrechten und Demokratie (Baden-Baden: Nomos, 1999), esp. ch. 3 and 4, which discuss Sunni Arab Islamist authors. The lawyer Mohammad Hashim Kamali, originally from Afghanistan and now teaching in Malaysia, is an excellent representative of non-Islamist Islamic discourse; see, for example, his Freedom, Equality and Justice in Islam (Cambridge: Islamic Texts Society, 2002). On Muslim ethics in general and the question of whether human beings can attain certain knowledge irrespective of revelation, see A. Kevin Reinhart, 'Ethics and the Qur'ān', in Jane Dammen McAuliffe (ed.), Encyclopaedia of the Qur'ān, vol. 2 (Leiden and Boston: Brill, 2002), pp. 55–79, and Before Revelation: The Boundaries of Muslim Moral Thought (Albany, NY: State University of New York Press, 1995); also Toshihiko Izutsu, Ethico-Religious Concepts in the Qur'ān (Montreal and London: McGill University Press, 1966); Richard G. Hovannisian (ed.), Ethics in Islam: Ninth Giorgio della Vida Biennial Conference (Malibu, CA: Undena, 1985); Majid Fakhry, Ethical Theories in Islam, second enlarged edition (Leiden: Brill, 1994); Daniel Brown, 'Islamic Ethics in Comparative Perspective', The Muslim World 89.2 (1999), pp. 181–92.

[9]   See now David L. Johnston, 'A Turn in the Epistemology and Hermeneutics of Twentieth Century Usul al-Fiqh', Islamic Law and Society 11 (2004), pp. 233–82, and Felicitas Opwis, 'Islamic Law and Legal Change: The Concept of Maslaha in Classical and Contemporary Islamic Legal Theory', in Amanat and Griffel (eds), Shari'a, pp. 62–82.

by classical scholars: the protection of religion (that is, Islam), life, offspring, property, and either intellect or honour.

Reference to eminent scholars such as Abu Hamid al-Ghazali (d. 1111) and Abu Ishaq al-Shatibi (d. 1388) cannot, however, obscure the fact that modern interpreters have moved well beyond the limits established by Ghazali or Shatibi. Not only do they tacitly assimilate the five basic goods and benefits (masālih) to the objectives (maqāsid) of the sharia. They also have fewer scruples about defining the common good with regard to present needs and aspirations, and though they take great care to refer to the Koran and Sunna, they cannot do so without using their own judgment. The trust in human reason they declare and the rationalist if not openly utilitarian logic they employ renders them suspect to Islamic scholars and Islamist theorists alike, who fear for the authority of 'divine law' if men (and women) are allowed to adapt it to their own expectations.

But there are also those who find fault with the textual obsession that characterizes 'Islamic discourse' – the eager citation of shorter or longer passages of scripture, the constant reference to the masters, even if they plainly meant to say something very different from what is ascribed to them. Few have expressed their impatience with the retrogressive and ahistorical character of Islamic discourse as openly as the Islamic economist Syed Nawab Haider Naqvi:

> True, these maqāsid, i.e., (a) faith; (b) life; (c) progeny; (d) intellect; and (e) wealth, must have made an interesting list of objectives, in the time these were formulated, to address legal and metaphysical issues; yet they need to be refocused, expanded and amended to become useful guides for public policy in modern times. Leaping between totally different eras and time zones to cull nuggets of traditional wisdom is, at best, an exercise in futility.[10]

What Naqvi is attacking here is the imagined continuity across time and the unbroken authority of ideas and practices developed in the early Islamic period, combined with the sharp boundaries drawn around a Muslim community and identity that are exclusively defined in religious terms. Even Muslim intellectuals who see themselves rooted in the Islamic tradition are irritated by the claim that the only way to conceptualize Islamic authenticity should be with reference to what Muhammad and his contemporaries thought and did in the seventh century A D within the narrowly confined milieu of Mecca and Medina, rather than to present concerns and aspirations.

---

[10]   *Perspectives on Morality and Human Well-Being. A Contribution to Islamic Economics* (Leicester: The Islamic Foundation, 2003), p. 129.

Justice and Equality

The search for justice is a classic concern in both European and Islamic thought, which did not have to be 'invented' in the modern era in order to serve as a weapon in the alleged clash of civilizations. Justice regularly tops the list of basic values presented as specifically Islamic, and not only among Muslims. Justice, writes an American legal anthropologist, 'is the most essential, if indeterminate, of virtues for Muslims, because it keeps open the quest for equivalence, a quest seen as central to both human nature and revealed orderliness in the world of reason and passion'.[11] Contemporary Muslims see justice as the supreme Islamic value, overarching and integrating all others. For one Islamist author, justice is the 'spiritual pole of legitimate politics in harmony with the sharia':

> God the Highest made justice (al-'adl) – and equity (qist), which here also means justice – the essence of what is right, because it is the foundation of all the comprehensive principles and general rules the lawmaker [God] has defined in his divine law. It truly represents God's order and law (nizām allāh wa-shar'uh), preparing a straight path for humankind in this world and the hereafter.[12]

The proponent of a more modernist Islamic position says much the same: 'Justice is one of the highest values and, in its various forms, also one of the defining concerns of Islam. On the list of priorities, it comes immediately after

---

[11]   Lawrence Rosen, 'Justice', in John L. Esposito (ed.), *The Oxford Encyclopedia of the Modern Islamic World*, vol. 2 (New York and Oxford: Oxford University Press, 1995), pp. 388–91, here p. 391; see also his studies *The Anthropology of Justice: Law as Culture in Islamic Society* (Cambridge: Cambridge University Press, 1989) and *The Justice of Islam* (Oxford: Oxford University Press, 2000). Majid Khadduri, *The Islamic Conception of Justice* (Baltimore, MD, and London: Johns Hopkins University Press, 1984) is broad-ranging but ahistorical. The historical embeddedness of Muslim ideals of justice is illustrated by Franz Rosenthal, 'Political Justice and the Just Ruler', *Israel Oriental Studies* 10 (1982), pp. 92–101; Ann K. S. Lambton, 'Changing Concepts of Justice and Injustice from the 5th/11th Century to the 8th/14th Century in Persia: The Saljuq Empire and the Ilkhanate', *Studia Islamica* 68 (1988), pp. 27–60, and Boğaç A. Ergene, 'On Ottoman Justice: Interpretations in Conflict (1600–1800)', *Islamic Law and Society* 8.1 (2001), pp. 52–87. For a more technical presentation of my own argument, see my 'Justice in Modern Islamic Thought'.

[12]   Farīd 'Abd al-Khāliq, *fī l-fiqh al-siyāsī al-islāmī. mabādi' dustūriyya. al-shūrā, al-'adl, al-musāwāt (On Islamic political doctrine. Constitutional principles: consultation, justice, equality)* (Cairo and Beirut: Dār al-Shurūq, 1998), pp. 195, 196–7.

belief in the one God (*tawhīd*) and the status of Muhammad as the true prophet (*risāla*).'[13]

Again, moderns can draw on Islamic tradition, which itself assimilated antique and ancient Persian ideas, though they give them an unmistakably modern touch. In Islam as elsewhere, justice covers a broad semantic field, comprising ethical-religious, legal, social, and political issues, each couched in its own particular terms. My concern here is not with divine justice, which has greatly occupied Muslim thinkers in the past, but with justice in the context of social and gender relations. The Koran itself offers no theory of justice, but rather refers to just and righteous behaviour in specific contexts, for which it uses a variety of terms, notably *qist*, designating equity or fairness, or giving the full measure (derived from the verb 'to distribute', 'to allocate'; see for example Suras 3:18 and 55:9), *ihsān*, fair and righteous behaviour towards others, and *'adl*, which is commonly translated as justice (derived from the verb 'to be or make straight, even, or equal'). In post-Koranic usage, *insāf* was added to the list, which again describes the fair and equitable treatment of others. According to Sura 16:90, God desires humankind 'to act with justice and equity and to give to one's kind (what is their due)'; Suras 2:83; 4:58; 4:135; 6:152; 49:9; 60:8 have similar things to say. God enjoins believers to do right (*ihsān*) by their parents and relatives, the poor, the weak, and orphans (see, for example, Sura 2:83). The duty to give alms (*zakāt*), which is considered one of the five pillars of Islam, testifies to this social obligation (see, for example, Sura 9:60). Charity is also one of the objectives of the post-Koranic institution of religious endowments (*waqf, habous*), which, though legally disputed, was of major importance to Muslim societies for many centuries.

Building on Koranic references, which were gradually supplemented by Aristotelian concepts that became accessible to Muslims from the late eighth century on, Muslim lawyers and theologians developed more abstract conceptions. Accordingly, justice (*'adl*) in the broadest sense entails behaviour that conforms to God's law and for this reason is 'just' and 'right(eous)'. By the same token, it is in harmony with the ideal of good measure and moderation (*i'tidāl*), or the golden mean. Justice requires fairness, impartiality, balance, and harmony. According to Sura 2:143, God placed the Muslim community in the middle, or quite simply the right place (*ummatan wasatan*). The insistence on equity and moderation is linked with the emphatic rejection of all 'exaggeration in religion' (*al-ghuluww fī l-dīn*), which forms part of the standard repertory of early and classical Islamic scholars and also serves as an argument against religious extremism and the illegitimate use of violence in modern times. Opposites of justice, depending on the context,

---

[13]   Kamali, *Freedom, Equality and Justice in Islam*, p. 107. Kamali also highlights the features common to Islamic and non-Islamic ideals of justice.

include sacrilege, sinfulness, injustice, oppression, and disorder, which indicate that the bounds set by God (the sharia) are being transgressed. If the worst comes to the worst, they lead to unrest, anarchy, and civil strife, all included in the term *fitna*, which threatens to tear the Muslim community apart and, by the same token, to put Islam in jeopardy.

A 'just order' keeps society in a state of harmonious balance, very much in the spirit of the classic maxim 'to each as he or she is due' (*suum cuique*), which need not be an equal share of rights and duties, but a 'right' or appropriate one.[14] Justice, therefore, cannot be blindfolded. It must take account of the status and social ties of individuals and groups if it wishes to be fair and to restore order.[15] The prime responsibility for ensuring that justice is dispensed and order upheld rests with the ruler. He must see to it that 'everything is put in its proper place'.[16] What exactly this proper place might be is altogether a different matter. Muslim concepts of a just order were as variable according to place, time, and socio-cultural milieu as non-Muslim ones. The Koran and Sunna offer no detailed prescription. And yet, the sharia had the potential to act as a corrective to despotic rule, for though the ruler was above his subjects, he was not above divine law. If he violated the sharia (and that happened often enough in real life), he was infringing on God's law and would be punished, if only in the hereafter.[17]

In the modern period, the symbolic significance of the sharia as a guarantor of law, order, and justice has assumed crucial importance. At the same time, notions of justice have been subtly redefined, notably with regard to the issue of equality. Pre-modern concepts of justice were often at variance with the ideal of social equality, which the Koran endorses in certain passages and contradicts in

---

[14]   The classic formula was attributed to the Roman jurist Domitius Ulpianus (c. AD 170–228) and incorporated into Justinian's *Corpus Iuris Civilis*: *Juris praecepta sunt haec: honeste vivere, alterum non laedere, suum cuique tribuere* (to live honestly, to do no harm to others, and to give to each as he or she is due); see Otfried Höffe, *Gerechtigkeit. Eine philosophische Einführung* (Munich: Beck, 2001), pp. 49–53.

[15]   For visualizations of justice, see Michael Stolleis, *Das Auge des Gesetzes. Geschichte einer Metapher* (Munich: Beck, 2004).

[16]   On royal justice and the so-called circle of justice, see Roy P. Mottahedeh, *Loyalty and Leadership in an Early Islamic Society* (Princeton, NJ: Princeton University Press, 1980), esp. ch. 4; Jocelyne Dakhlia, *Le Divan des rois. Le politique et le religieux dans l'Islam* (Paris: Aubier, 1998); Aziz Al-Azmeh, *Muslim Kingship. Power and the Sacred in Muslim, Christian, and Pagan Polities* (London and New York: I. B. Tauris, 1997).

[17]   For a concise statement using the example of an early eighteenth-century rebellion, see Ergene, 'On Ottoman Justice', pp. 86–7.

others. Contemporary Muslims are grappling with these contradictions.[18] Many summarily declare Islam a religion of equality and justice. As quickly becomes apparent, though, they usually differentiate between the spiritual, legal, and socio-economic dimensions of (Islamic) justice. As the debate on human rights and human dignity 'in Islam' clearly shows, this boils down to a distinction between the dignity and ontological equality granted by God to all men and women on the one hand and differentiated rights and duties attributed to specific groups and individuals on the other.[19]

There is no longer any need to discuss slavery, which was still practised in parts of the Islamic world in the twentieth century, but which is now legally prohibited everywhere – though the Koran and Sunna, like the Bible and the early Christian tradition, deal with it as a social reality of the time.[20] The Koran neither prescribes nor abolishes it, but hedges it in with ethical rules. In much the same way, the Sunna prescribes the release of slaves as penance for a number of sins and offences. Slavery is one of the very few subjects about which contemporary Muslims will openly say that the relevant provisions in the Koran and Sunna are no longer in keeping with the times and which therefore, while not formally abrogated or abolished (that would be a sign of human hubris), have become irrelevant. As a rule, though, this awkward subject is passed over. The implications of what it means for certain textual references to be considered either obsolete (because they no longer accord with social reality) or offensive (because they clash with the principle of equality) are left unexplored. It would appear though that in regard to slavery, the (general) principle of equality has been given precedence over (specific) textual injunctions in the Koran and Sunna. It remains to be seen to what extent this precedent will be followed in other social domains.

A look at the two big issues in contemporary debates on values, human rights, and equality 'in Islam' – gender relations and the status of non-Muslims – reveals a different picture.[21] The debate on gender – incidentally the only one in which female voices are to be heard in significant numbers – is especially revealing. The

---

[18] See Louise Marlow, *Hierarchy and Egalitarianism in Islamic Thought* (Cambridge: Cambridge University Press, 1997); Kamali, *Freedom, Equality and Justice in Islam*, ch. 2 and 3.

[19] Mohammad Hashim Kamali, *The Dignity of Man: An Islamic Perspective* (Cambridge: Islamic Texts Society, 2002); see also Krämer, *Gottes Staat als Republik*, pp. 74–6.

[20] See William Gervase Clarence-Smith, *Islam and the Abolition of Slavery* (Oxford: Oxford University Press, 2006), and Ehud R. Toledano, *As If Silent and Absent. Bonds of Enslavement in the Islamic Middle East* (New Haven, CT, and London: Yale University Press, 2007).

[21] On the status and role of non-Muslims in an (ideal) Islamic order, I refer the reader to my study *Gottes Staat als Republik*, pp. 162–79.

gender debate is premised on a distinction between equivalence or ontological equality of men and women before God, and their equal treatment before the law. With rare intensity, participants seek to ascertain the true meaning of the relevant Koranic references, which, it emerges, are more ambiguous than is often assumed. The Koran makes it as difficult for the champions of equality as does the Bible, for it says different things in different places. According to Sura 75:37–9, God created man and woman (as partners, Arabic: *zawjayn*) from the same material, namely a drop of sperm, which developed into an embryo. According to Sura 4:1, meanwhile, both were created out of one person or soul (*nafs wāhida*). The notion that Adam was the first being and Eve his partner, formed, as stated earlier in the Bible, out of one of Adam's ribs, is not in the Koran but is part of (male) Koranic exegesis.[22] Still, according to the Koran, both men and women are responsible for their lives before God. Yet according to Sura 4:34, men are the 'maintainers of women' (of which more in a moment). This reflects a social role model that differs very little from its European counterparts (not all of them premodern). It envisages a division of roles which corresponds to the specific physical and mental qualities of men and women, which, being different, also entail different rights and duties in certain circumscribed fields. Equality is thus held to be compatible with differing levels of responsibility, with men ranking above or at least before women.

The Egyptian lawyer and Muslim Brother Sa'id Ramadan, son-in-law of the founder of the Muslim Brotherhood, Hasan al-Banna, and father of the well-known scholar-activist Tariq Ramadan, draws a lively picture in a text significantly entitled *Milestones* (*ma'ālim al-tarīq*, as opposed to *ma'ālim fi l-tarīq*, the famous text by the equally famous Egyptian Islamist Sayyid Qutb, executed in 1966):

> Just as Islam declared the basic relationship between man and woman to be one of partnership, it defined their relationship within the family by basing it on the equality of rights and obligations (Sura 2:228). The gradation between them [Arabic *daraja*, to which Sura 2:228 refers] is like an administrative hierarchy, which no commercial business can do without. In this way, the business of life has been established which produces the new generations for the community of believers.[23]

The debate on marriage, household, and the family features similar patterns of

---

[22]   See Cornelia Schöck, 'Adam and Eve', in Jane Dammen McAuliffe (ed.), *Encyclopaedia of the Qur'ān*, vol. 1 (Leiden and Boston, MA: Brill, 2001), pp. 22–6.

[23]   Ramadān, *ma'ālim al-tarīq* (Cairo: Dar al-Nashr wa-l-Tawzi' al-Islamiyya, 1987), p. 44.

thought and argument.[24] Much of it reproduces thoroughly conventional views. Yet there are also serious attempts to conceptualize gender relations in a way that responds to modern realities and realizes gender equality without abandoning core Islamic teachings and without negating what they see as the specific physical and psychological qualities of men and women. The American scholar Amina Wadud figures among the best-known proponents of this attempt to reconstruct Islamic gender roles. For her, equality, as a basic value of Islam, is compatible with a certain degree of social differentiation.[25] Riffat Hassan, originally from Pakistan and now living in the USA, who considers herself an 'Islamic feminist', proposes a simpler argument. For her, the equality of the sexes derives from divine justice. Patriarchal practices violate the teachings of the Koran and hence are un-Islamic (here she takes up the frequently made distinction between [pure] Islamic teaching and [marred] Muslim practice, contingent upon time and setting and distorted by male prejudice and misconceptions).[26] The debate on polygamy, or to be more precise polygyny – the option granted to men in Sura 4:3 to marry up to four 'believing' women provided they treat them equitably – continues unabated, even though polygyny is not widely practised and is legally restricted in many Muslim countries.

At least as instructive and relevant is the discussion on gender roles within the family, more specifically the principle of *qiwāma* mentioned in Sura 4:34. *Qiwāma* can be understood to signify precedence, dominance, maintenance, or protection, serving as a prime example of how difficult it is to translate seemingly short and

---

[24]   Barbara F. Stowasser, *Women in the Qur'an, Traditions, and Interpretations* (New York and Oxford: Oxford University Press, 1994), and Gisela Webb (ed.), *Windows of Faith: Muslim Women Scholar-Activists in North America* (Syracuse, NY: Syracuse University Press, 2000), provide good overviews. For innovative contributions, see Oumaima Abū Bakr and Shīrīn Shukrī, *al-mar'a wa-l-gender. ilghā' al-tamyīz al-thaqāfī wa-l-ijtimā'ī bayna l-jinsayn* (*Woman and gender: eliminating the cultural and social discrimination between the sexes*) (Damascus and Beirut: Dār al-Fikr, 1423/2002), esp. pp. 11–77, or Kamali, *Freedom, Equality and Justice in Islam*, pp. 61–78.

[25]   Amina Wadud, *Qur'an and Woman: Rereading the Sacred Text from a Woman's Perspective* (New York and Oxford: Oxford University Press, 1999), esp. pp. 66–78, 82–5. See also Asma Barlas, *'Believing Women' in Islam: Unreading Patriarchal Interpretations of the Qur'an* (Austin, TX: University of Texas Press, 2002), esp. pp. 184–202; or Azizah Yahia Al-Hibri, 'Muslim Women's Rights in the Global Village: Challenges and Opportunities', *Journal of Law and Religion* 15 (2000–2001), pp. 37–66, esp. pp. 50–1.

[26]   Riffat Hassan, 'Challenging the Stereotypes of Fundamentalism: An Islamic Feminist Perspective', *The Muslim World* 91.1 (2001), pp. 55–69, and 'Rights of Women within Islamic Communities', in John Witte, Jr, and Johan D. van der Vyver (eds), *Religious Human Rights in Global Perspective* (The Hague and London: M. Nijhoff, 1996), pp. 361–86.

simple Koranic passages. In the relevant literature, the spectrum ranges from male dominance, matched by female subordination ('men are above women'), to a protective relationship, in which the husband bears special responsibility for his wife and children ('men stand before women'). What remains is the husband's role as breadwinner and head of the household. At the same time, modern conceptions of marriage and family as based on partnership – though not on legal equality – between husband and wife have moved well beyond traditional role models, which assign separate spheres to them, rendering true partnership virtually impossible. Unlike in the formula 'separate but equal', these conceptions emphasize both partnership and differentiation. The basic notion, then, is that 'in Islam' difference is natural and, rather than being denied, must be accommodated in adequate fashion.

Compared to the debate on gender and family with its strident overtones and broad repercussions, debates on social justice and Islamic economics are remarkably low key.[27] Interestingly, they do not seem to include any women. It has been rightly pointed out that they revolve around concepts of a moral economy, in which ethics are at least as important as specifically Islamic institutions, such as the prohibition of interest and insurance, which have been compensated by a variety of well-established practices, some of them newly defined. Since the 1970s, advocates of an Islamic market economy that is premised on the social obligation imposed on property have come to dominate the field; they ultimately give priority to distributive justice over equality of opportunity. The prevalent moral discourse is embodied in exemplary fashion by one of the leading proponents of Islamic economics, Khurshid Ahmad, who once again extols the ideal of the golden mean:

> The middle path then is the right option. Faith, fortitude and loyalty to Divine Principles should go hand in hand with creativity, flexibility and the ability to face the ever-changing intellectual, economic, technological and civilizational challenges. Perhaps what is needed is faith with fortitude, confidence with humility, loyalty with openness, and innovations rooted in tradition. This should be the defining character of the contemporary Islamic debate.[28]

---

[27]   For useful introductions, see Khurshid Ahmad (ed.), *Studies in Islamic Economics* (Leicester: The Islamic Foundation, 1400/1980), and Timur Kuran, 'On the Notion of Economic Justice in Contemporary Islamic Thought', *International Journal of Middle East Studies* 21 (1989), pp. 171–91. Unfortunately, the important study by Olaf Farschid, 'Islamische Ökonomie und Zakāt', dissertation, Freie Universität Berlin, 1999, has not yet been published.

[28]   Khurshid Ahmad, Foreword to Naqvi, *Perspectives on Morality*, p. xiii.

It is no coincidence that this sounds like a sermon to be given on either Friday, Saturday, or Sunday: reason, yes, but without presumption; rationality, too, but within the bounds set by God; creativity, certainly, but in the knowledge of human frailty; movement, absolutely, but neither too slow nor too fast. What it reveals is a fear of the uncontrolled dynamism of critical thought, which refuses to stop at the gates of 'Islam', or at least at those erected by its guardians past and present. And yet the rational spirit that permeates Islamic discourse as soon as it refers to universal values and higher norms that are to take precedence over the specific injunctions of sharia and *fiqh* will not be easily restrained or suppressed. Only experience will show how far its advocates are willing and able to go within their self-imposed framework, and whether what they present as sharia, designed to preserve Muslim identity, is recognized as sharia by other Muslims. This experience will very likely not be uniform.

15

Does Europe Have a Cultural Identity?

Peter Wagner

In 1870, once the process of Italian unification had been completed with the creation of a nation-state after several years of conflict (including armed conflict), in much the same way as in Germany, one of the protagonists stated: 'Now that we've created Italy, we have to create the Italians' (this remark is attributed, perhaps wrongly, to Massimo d'Azeglio). Despite his efforts to fuse the territories of the peninsula together into a single political order, d'Azeglio did *not* believe that Italy already had a cultural identity. But he did think that the future Italians ought to become more aware of what they had in common, and he also thought that politics should help them to do so. This idea is also to be found in contemporary Europe. More than twenty-five years ago, to mention a small but not insignificant example, the European University Institute in Florence was founded. In a sense, one of its tasks is to *create Europeans*, who are such, not on the basis of their shared origins, but as a result of the experience of working together.

1. Does Europe Have a Cultural Identity?

This is the question I have been asked to answer. Its form recalls the questions posed in the Enlightenment contests of ideas common in the eighteenth century. Some of the most famous texts in the history of European thought were written in response to such questions, such as Immanuel Kant's 'What is Enlightenment?' or Jean-Jacques Rousseau's 'Discourse on the Origin and Basis of Inequality among Men'. In a very real way, Europe exists in these ideas. Now, I cannot compare myself with these authors and have no wish to do so. But I wish to adhere to their methodology by first elaborating the question posed more precisely.

Does Europe have a cultural *identity?*

Let us begin with the concept of identity. What does it mean to have an identity? The literal meaning of the term is 'sameness'. Ludwig Wittgenstein, perhaps the most important European philosopher of the twentieth century, once warned: 'Roughly speaking: to say of *two* things that they are identical is nonsense, and to say of *one* thing that it is identical with itself is to say nothing' (*Tractatus logico-philosophicus* 5.503). If identity means sameness, or at least similarity, then the assumption of a European identity is both dubious and problematic.

This assumption would mean, first of all, that Europeans are the same or similar. But very few people would want to claim this. Over the course of Europe's history, and I shall be returning to this subject later on, it is diversity that has generally been emphasized. Even now, debates on European unification are dominated by the motto 'united in diversity'. In contrast to the processes of national unification that characterized the nineteenth and much of the twentieth century, no-one now thinks of levelling out the diversity of Europe – and the European Commission's often over-the-top efforts to achieve standardization are probably the most common subject of criticism about the manner in which integration is being pursued. There is no lack of unity about that.

Second, identity would also mean that Europe remains the same *over the course of time*. But again, this is an idea generally associated with the nations rather than Europe itself. It was for long assumed that the various European nations would each contribute something specific to European history or to the history of humankind – and that this contribution marked out the German, French, or Italian identity. But Europe itself was not associated with such constancy. Quite the opposite: change and dynamism were often seen as part of Europe's unique path. The scientific revolution in the sixteenth and seventeenth centuries, the economic and industrial revolution in the eighteenth and nineteenth centuries, the democratic revolutions from the late eighteenth century on, made Europe one of the world's epicentres of change. Nothing stayed the same or remained stable.

What then can we mean by identity, if not sameness within Europe and constancy over time? Why do we ask about European identity in the first place?

In think this question is primarily a *political* one. It is a question about those things we share that might guide our action, and, above all, a question about that which *we* have in common and what makes us different from *others*. We see the way that identity works to guide action, for instance, in the commitment to human rights and democracy which informed the debate on the eastwards expansion of the EU. And we see the differentiating effect of identity in the commitment to social solidarity which sets Europe apart, for example, from the USA. After more than two decades of criticism of the welfare state and emphasis on the need for reform, there is still no rejection of the principle of mutual support – a principle affirmed in the Charter of Fundamental Rights adopted in Nice in 2000.

Does Europe have a *cultural* identity?

It might be objected that the question at issue here relates to Europe's cultural rather than political identity. To tackle the question of the relation between those two terms, we must first agree on a concept of culture. The term 'culture' is used discursively in at least three very different ways.

First, there is a *normative* concept, which understands culture in contrast to a lack of culture. It is linked with cultural criticism and cultural pessimism, found on both the right and left of the spectrum of political ideas within European history. We might think, for example, of Oswald Spengler's *The Decline of the West* or Theodor Adorno's condemnation of the culture industry. It is extremely difficult to emphasize normative matters without simply placing one's own culture above that of others (or the old above the new) – simply because it is one's own culture. Leading philosophers of our time have succumbed to this temptation. It is therefore unusual these days for anyone to openly use a normative concept of culture. But the question arises of whether we can do entirely without one.

Second, there is a neutral concept of culture that underlines *shared* values and norms. In my remarks on identity, I already raised doubts about whether it is possible nowadays to straightforwardly divide the world up into groups – whether we refer to them as cultures, civilizations, nations, religious communities – in such a way as to establish borders within which values are shared and beyond which they are in conflict. But as Samuel Huntington's successful book on civilizational conflict shows, such thinking is highly popular, and we will have to come back to it later on.

But what really advances our understanding is a third concept of culture which assumes that we human beings, rather than living like atoms in a world of animate and inanimate objects, ascribe values to our action and experience our world and fellow human beings in interpretive fashion. The human being is a self-interpreting being, and the resources which he deploys for purposes of interpretation define his culture. This understanding of culture generates three conclusions:

- First, our thinking must not be based on closed cultural communities. Cultural interaction occurs first and foremost between individuals rather than between groups.

- Second (of which more in a moment), we must not understand cultural commonalities and differences as resulting from a characteristic, which either is or is not part of an individual. No-one is simply or unchangeably Christian or Muslim, French or American, straight-forwardly applying his or her pre-given set of values.

- Third, this throws up the question of whether it is possible to *have* a cultural identity – as implied by the question I have been asked to address.

Does Europe *have* a cultural identity?

This is certainly the official assumption within the EU, which refers to the *acquis communautaire*, that which has been acquired by the whole community, something which we now possess. But, though the following quotation may have been flogged half to death, our classical authors already knew better: 'All that you have, bequeathed you by your father, earn it in order to possess it', as Goethe put it in *Faust I.*

In what sense does Europe *have* or not have a cultural identity? Since 1973, this is a subject which has exercised the European Commission as well. This date is worthy of note: it is the moment when the post-war momentum of European integration began to flag. The common market had been established, but attempts to go beyond it met with reluctance and resistance. The impetus of the world economy, which had lasted for the three 'glorious decades' of the post-war period, also slackened. The international monetary system shattered, the first oil crisis made Keynesian growth policies problematic, and Europe was about to experience the first real recession since the end of the war.

If the term 'identity' crops up in European documents from this point forward, the suspicion arises that Europe does not have an identity, but *would like to have* one. It is looking for sources of guidance to lead it out of the crisis, the impasse of integration, but as yet has none to hand.

In light of this, we must ask: what does this wanting-to-have mean? If the history of this entity in search of identity is marked by changes and diversity, what might be the source of identity, in the sense of value orientations capable of guiding a common course of action? The general answer to this can only be: *experiences* and their *interpretation.*

Europe can achieve an identity to the extent that it has undergone shared experiences and shows itself capable of producing a collective interpretation of these experiences – which are not simply 'there' but must be kept alive in people's minds.

This would not be a stable identity as suggested, for example, by references to 'western values' over the last year or 'Asian values' in previous years, not something which we can identify as a timeless aspect of history or which is capable of ceaseless perpetuation. Quite the reverse, such an identity would be the result of manifold experiences which may stretch across long periods of history and which may be recorded in interpretations. These experiences and their interpretations may overlap like archaeological layers – layers of time, to use the expression coined so felicitously by Reinhart Koselleck – and they change in the light of new experiences and new interpretations.

As I continue, allow me to outline, in line with this understanding, the elements of Europe's cultural identity at present. I therefore ask: Does *Europe* have a cultural identity? What is this Europe into which we are enquiring?

2. Europe

Well-springs of unity

As a geographical term, the name of 'Europe' gained currency, following the division of the Roman Empire, to refer to the western half of the empire. This also meant that Europe was associated with Western Christianity. The borders with Orthodox Christianity and (shortly afterwards) Islam were thus constitutive for Europe. The way in which these boundaries were originally set is still reflected in the debates on the eastwards expansion of the EU (with the exception of Greece, which was granted a special status as the cradle of Europe – and, we should not forget, as a member of NATO) and now on the possibility of Turkish accession.

Thus, during the Middle Ages, Europe was a religious-political-territorial unity, also known as the 'West' or the Occident.

But this unity did not necessarily mean 'identity' in a strict sense. The region was held together only very loosely. Studies of everyday life in the Middle Ages show that religious and feudal values were not widely disseminated among the general population. Meanwhile, the specific history of Europe's foundation hardly gave rise to an identity that might be traced back to unambiguous roots or a central idea. Some years ago, the French philosopher Rémi Brague brought out how Europe's self-image has always pointed to something else that existed before it. From a religious point of view, Christianity grew out of Judaism, and politically the Roman-republican tradition was inspired by the Greek democracy of the city states. Brague therefore calls European identity 'excentric' in a literal sense: lacking a core or a unique origin. And he believes we can understand the dynamism and restlessness characteristic of Europe as a result not least of this lack of sturdy roots of its own.

A history of schisms

Be that as it may, the fact is that European history was to be characterized by tensions. As a first step in our review of European historical experiences, I would like to show that there is little question of there having been a European identity and that, on the contrary, European history was for many centuries a history of political and cultural challenges dealt with through new borders, divisions, and schisms. I shall briefly mention four major stages in this history.

Reformation and wars of religion. This era of schisms began at the latest with the Reformation and the wars of religion, by which Europe was ravaged for decades. The way out of this predicament, we can state with hindsight, was the idea of state sovereignty, implemented with the Peace of Westphalia in 1648. Violent, religiously motivated conflicts subsequently became a rare occurrence in western Europe; they found their last echo in Northern Ireland. (This observation should not, however, cause us to forget anti-Semitism. One of its preconditions was the fact that the Jewry, lacking any territorial embodiment, was not included in the peace treaty.)

However, the price of this solution was the division of Europe into a system of sovereign states, which were largely pacified internally while their external relations, in contrast, remained unregulated and anarchic. Contemporary demands for an international legal system keep pointing to a problem created in the seventeenth century.

Revolution and nation. The second phase of splits within Europe was ushered in by the democratic revolutions – the French Revolution being the decisive event. Today – quite rightly – we celebrate the shift from state sovereignty to popular sovereignty that marked the political beginning of the modern world. But we often forget that this move also incontrovertibly posed the question 'Who is the people?' and that the answers to this question were often far from unproblematic. Over the course of the nineteenth century, the people, which was supposed to exercise self-determination in democratic fashion, increasingly became the *nation*, which not only developed its cultural values in a unique way but which also saw itself as struggling against the values of other nations.

In this sense, the First World War marks one of the low points, if not *the* low point of European history. It was staged as a cultural conflict in which the nations involved made the fate of humankind dependent on their victory. It was also the first war featuring mass mobilization in the sense that entire populations engaged in cultural conflict. Although democracy emerged in many countries only at the end of the war, it was also the first war of the democratic era.

The public and private sphere. Meanwhile, third, in the shadow of religious reformation and political revolution, a further separation had occurred, which made itself felt in a less dramatic way but was no less significant for that. A 'culture of individual autonomy' (Charles Taylor) slowly developed which allowed individual persons, faced with the pressures of the community and society as a whole, to think their lives in terms of self-realization. Over the course of the eighteenth century, in the run-up to the democratic revolutions as we now know, a distinction took hold between the public and private sphere that was to remain central to our political thought.

Immanuel Kant himself saw the work carried out by dependent workers (as we would say today) as private and thus subject to restrictions on freedom of expression. We now tend to see the private sphere as that in which the self develops, and the public sphere as the foundation of an informed politics which this self can then enter into. But the separation of the two spheres remains contentious – as apparent most recently, perhaps, in France and in Germany, in the so-called headscarf disputes.

Capitalism and classes. Finally, fourth, we must not forget the economic-industrial revolution and the emergence of market societies (or: capitalism). These developments produced a division into classes in Europe, classes which were often irreconcilably opposed. Referring to nineteenth-century England, Benjamin Disraeli talked of 'two nations' between which there was neither social interaction nor sympathy. This diagnosis not only touched on the growing social inequality so widely in evidence. Also at issue here was the putative irreconcilability of ways of life, that is, a cultural difference.

If the idea of linguistic-cultural identity was associated with the formation of nations, the development of classes led to a socio-cultural identity which developed, more or less clearly, everywhere in industrialized Europe. And as we know, with the split between social democracy and communism and subsequently with Soviet socialism, this opposition would lead to a political division between the states of Europe.

Processes of problem creation

We have now completed our first sprint through European history. My intention in recalling these divisions is *not* to say that Europe has no cultural identity. Quite the reverse, in light of my introductory remarks on identity and culture, my assertion is that if Europe has a cultural identity, then it must be a result of its experiences with these divisions and boundaries, and their interpretations.

But equally, I do not mean by this that Europe has something like a *negative* identity, that it is based on the mistakes and misunderstandings of the past. If we look again at the four great historical processes revolving around religion, nation, class, and the relationship between public and private, what we are seeing here are permanent problems which people have to cope with as they interact with others. We may state that, over the course of its history, Europe gradually asked itself, in an explicit and radical way, all the questions which it then gradually tried to answer – with a great deal of difficulty.

The American political philosopher Michael Walzer once described liberalism as the 'art of separation'. Liberal thought creates spheres of freedom by separating facts, and perhaps individuals as well, which would curtail such spheres if kept together. This is an important idea. But in historical reality, these separations often occur in a violent way and they are by no means always inspired by liberal thought. In a second step, I shall now briefly outline the questions thrown up by these separations in order to discuss, in a third step, the extent to which Europe's cultural identity has been moulded by these experiences.

Plurality and diversity. On the one hand, the Reformation and the wars of religion destroyed the unity of (western) Europe. On the other, though, they threw up the issue of the plurality or diversity of human life in a way that could not be ignored. From now on, it was no longer possible to condense the diversity of human endeavour into a single model of the good life. The political thought of the seventeenth and eighteenth centuries was certainly anxious to construct new models of order after the turmoil of the wars. But the great step forward that this entailed was to think in terms of the varied endeavours of individual human beings – rather than other, imposed sources of order as in the past.

The possibility of a better life or progress. With the eighteenth century – that era of Enlightenment that I touched on briefly at the start – hopes spread that such a new, self-determined, and peaceful order would in fact be possible. This is one of the elements expressed by the democratic revolutions, which were an attempt to lay the foundations for a better world through collective action. With the terms revolution and progress, which entered our political language during this period, these expectations found expression in an open horizon of the future (to borrow once again from Reinhart Koselleck).

Freedom and (collective) self-determination. If the democratic revolution stood for collective self-determination and the creation of a better order, the separation of the public and private spheres was the prerequisite for establishing and maintaining a connection between the personal freedom enjoyed by the individual and the political freedom of collective self-determination. This connection subsequently remained problematic. Some authors draw a line from the French to the Russian Revolution and even to Nazism, and thus from the promise of collective self-determination to totalitarianism. This line does not run as straight as this, but the history of democracy shows the dangers to which this phenomenon exposes itself.

Equality, prosperity, and solidarity. The development of markets and classes ultimately throws up the issues of prosperity and solidarity. Let's not forget that the promises to increase the 'wealth of nations' (Adam Smith) and – at an earlier stage – to pacify society were linked with the industrial division of labour and the self-regulation of free exchange. Those who create ties with others through trade, through doux commerce, will not want to fight them, having entered into a state of mutual dependency to the advantage of both sides. Both prosperity for the masses and peace within society were a long time coming. But in the fight against poverty and growing inequality, the concept of solidarity arose, starting out as an expression of class struggle and eventually becoming a means of organizing society within a welfare state geared towards equalization.

A trend reversal

Our second historical survey shows that with a bit of effort it is possible to read the often violent divisions of Europe in a *positive* way. European history has succinctly posed key questions about human coexistence. Without the divisions, it may have been impossible to pose them in this way.

In dealing with these questions, the expectation has consistently arisen that it might be possible to answer them once and for all and in a positive way. This was, above all, the case in the Enlightenment era, which expressed hopes that reason would be fully realized. When Max Weber translated reason into rationality more than 100 years later, such hopes had already given way to a growing scepticism. If Weber may perhaps be read as viewing the history of Europe as the history of social rationalization, he was far from entirely happy about the prospect.

In the early twentieth century, scepticism sometimes held sway in such a way that Europe's developmental path as a whole was considered disastrous. I have already briefly mentioned left- and rightwing cultural pessimism. But this negative reaction is merely the flipside of the exaggerated expectations of the Enlightenment era. We would be better off accepting that it is impossible to give answers to the questions posed that are valid for all time, but that we can adapt the answers we have to new circumstances, developing them further in fruitful ways.

In line with this, my third step in reviewing European history will consist in asking how Europe has interpreted its historical experiences and which conclusions it has come to on the basis of this interpretation.

Europe's experience as a specific entity in the world. At least since the time of Max Weber, people have wondered about the 'special European path' (Christian Meier), about Europe as a specific entity in the world. A European self-consciousness certainly existed during the Enlightenment of the eighteenth century and also subsequently in the history of nineteenth century progress. But here, Europe was seen as the spearhead of progress, the avant-garde of history, which other regions of the world would simply follow or have to follow – rather than a region with its own inimitable peculiarities. This form of self-consciousness arose first in the early twentieth century, grew stronger in the interwar period, and took on a new form in the second post-war period. Three mutually imbricated elements are characteristic of this self-consciousness.

First, the insight arose that Europe, far from being the avant-garde of history, has reached the *end of a developmental path*. The development of national societies, which increasingly expanded in imperialist fashion and opposed one another with hostility, has proved a dead end. Friedrich Nietzsche had an inkling about this situation, but it really took shape only with the experience of the First World War. Observers such as Walter Benjamin and, somewhat later, Hannah Arendt, were to speak of a temporal rupture, of the destruction of tradition and thus the disappearance of the resources that can provide people with guidance as they go about their lives.

In parallel to this realization, Europeans followed with astonishment and increasing dismay the rise of another modernity, namely that of the United States of America. The problem was not only that Europe no longer had the right to exclusively represent modernity in the world. In addition, American modernity proved superior to that of Europe in several respects. This superiority was experienced, above all, in the realms of technology and economics on the one hand and politics and society on the other. American products increasingly competed with European ones while the car factories of Detroit and the slaughterhouses of Chicago came to epitomize a kind of rationalization still alien to Europeans. Politically, the Europeans, as foreseen by Alexis de Tocqueville, had to acknowledge that American democracy was further developed than its European counterpart, thus seemingly marking out the developmental path that would have to be followed. European observers were also impressed by the commitment to social equality; the public self-confidence of American women was particularly alien to them.

Europeans conceivably could have responded to their diagnosis of American superiority in line with the motto 'catch up and overtake'. Yet this they could not do because they also regarded American society as inferior morally and culturally and did not wish to follow it in this regard. They observed the standardization of products and behaviours along with an individualization which led to isolation and loss of meaning. In this complex diagnosis, which I can only outline schematically here, lie the origins of the insight that modernity can find expression in a variety of forms – an insight which is, fortunately, more widespread today and which is also discussed in a more sophisticated way than in much of the twentieth century.

Third and finally, after the disaster of war had struck again, Europeans felt bound to change radically the course of their historical development. Gradually, after the Second World War, they developed an increasingly self-critical attitude towards their own collective memory (a memory moulded by national factors in most cases), to borrow from the French political scientist Jean-Marc Ferry. Certainly, and for obvious reasons, this was initially a German phenomenon, a way of dealing with guilt about the war and annihilation. But over the last two decades, the history of Europe has in a sense been Europeanized, with emphasis being placed on the often collective embroilment in disastrously wrong answers to the great historical and political questions.

The post-war compromise. In the first decades after the war, interpretations of the past were still national in character, and the conclusions ambiguous. The traditions of the nation-state were revived, but they were interpreted in a markedly more liberal way and in a manner that made it far easier to cooperate with others.

The political orders of post-war western Europe retained elements of their orientation towards linguistic and cultural identity, and they stabilized the beginnings of a socio-cultural identity around the commitment to social solidarity in the welfare state. They also added more developed understandings of personal freedom and political freedom as these had existed in the interwar period – though many battles, over equality for women for example, had yet to be fought out. With this commitment to multiple goals, the liberal-democratic and welfarist nation-state in the Europe of the late twentieth century was a political compromise which long proved viable, but which has now come up against its limits – to use the jargon of the day – in the face of economic and cultural globalization.

European integration. European integration is the answer to this situation, an answer that was in principle already available from the end of the war (indeed, elements of this answer were already present in the interwar period) but which had not yet been fully formulated. Born out of the post-war situation, the European project was initially developed as an economic and regulatory project which was as yet very alien to the citizens of European societies.

Things have, however, accelerated in recent decades. The reappearance of signs of crisis in the 1970s revived the debate on European identity, as mentioned in the introduction. But it was, above all, the fall of the Berlin Wall and the end of the political division of Europe which provoked the intensification of the political project of European unification. In this context, more efforts are being made to come up with a collective interpretation of historical experiences, as I have tried to outline them here.

A notable product of these efforts, whose significance is generally underestimated, is the European Union's Charter of Fundamental Rights, agreed in 2000, though remaining without legal force as the project of a treaty on a European constitution, and abandoned in 2007.

Far from being the dry product of legal and political negotiation, this charter is a constitutional document of a new kind. It goes beyond the Anglo-American inspired form of the Bill of Rights, which lists the individual's rights vis-à-vis a state. For this is a case of a polity endowing itself with its own self-understanding, in the form of principles which guide its actions. Among them we find not only the principles of freedom and equality, generally firmly rooted in the western tradition, but also those of human dignity and solidarity, which reflect specific conclusions drawn on the basis of European experiences. As one telling example among many which I might mention, the charter shows how a specific self-understanding is being developed and turned into options for action in Europe in a positive way.

3. Ways of Creating the World

Does Europe now have a cultural identity? Despite all my sceptical remarks at the outset, the answer is a cautious yes.

Europe is not rooted in its history in such a way that it might deduce its destiny from its roots. Such an idea is based in part on an inadequate concept of identity and culture, in part on a biased reading of European history. But Europe has had profound historical experiences, and has always kept on trying – during the present era as well as in the past – to interpret these experiences collectively. This gives rise to an identity which can act as a guide to action and which lays bare the differences from other action orientations.

Here, we should not imagine Europe on the model of the nation-state, as a territorial, political, and cultural unity in the world, which distances itself from others and opposes them. This would be to repeat the disastrous intra-European trends of the nineteenth and twentieth centuries on a global scale – and to dramatically aid the realization of the much-evoked clash of civilizations. If, on the other hand, so-called globalization, in a cultural sense, is an argument about how the world of tomorrow may look, then we should see Europe as a place capable of producing proposals on how to create a new world, proposals that engage critically with, and build on, Europe's own experiences.

Glossary

Assimilation
Minorities' adaptation to values, standards of behaviour, norms, traditions, and interpretations of the world considered 'normal' by society as a whole. The goal of assimilation is the total integration of minorities.

Axial Age
According to a thesis put forward by Karl Jaspers (1949), the period between 800 and 200 BC, in which the basic structure *of all* world religions and philosophies developed. In processes that occurred largely independent of one another, there was a break with the mythical worldview and transcendence was discovered. That is, a sharp quasi-spatial division was made between the worldly and the divine. The divine, as the realm of the true, was opposed to the necessarily deficient earthly domain. The tension to which this gave rise could produce impulses to change the earthly.

Centre and periphery
Used in a variety of ways in the social sciences to refer, for example, to the power differential between industrial societies and developing countries or the differences between qualified and easily replaceable workers or to express the proximity to or distance from a society's authoritative value system.

Civilization
Often used as a counter-concept to culture, particularly in Germany in the early twentieth century; was associated, on the one hand, with 'reason, Enlightenment, moderation, manners, scepticism, disintegration' (Thomas Mann) and, on the other, with (merely) material values and technological progress. This opposition is largely meaningless today.

Communitarianism
Emphasis on recalling the community-based foundations of the modern, liberal, western societies anchored in the critique of this social order.

Cultural conflicts
Conflicts between the members of different cultures.

Culture
Shared, more or less integrated ways of thinking, understanding, evaluating, and communicating.

Empirical social research
The gathering of data about real facts, events, processes, and connections; scientific working method in sociology, social psychology, political science, and social anthropology used to systematically investigate social facts.

Ethics
Theory of right action leading to real happiness.

Ethnic group
People; characteristic features of a people.

Identity
The subjective sense of (social) belonging, internal coherence, and biographical continuity.

Individualization
The dissolution of pre-existing ways of living within society and role models as the labour market, education system, and welfare state grow in importance. For individuals, this means actively and self-reflexively producing their life course.

Internationalization
The increasing importance of international involvements to social processes within nation-states.

Laicism
Ideology that demands the radical separation of Church and State.

Norm
Rule which states how people should behave in specific situations; obligatory behavioural expectation. While they may not exist in written form, norms are often viewed as customs or traditions to which people self-evidently adhere.

Periphery
(See *Centre and periphery.*)

Pluralism
The coexistence of a number of distinct groups, including ethnic groups, each of which retains its identity and social network while also being involved in a political and economic system common to all.

Postmodernity (in sociology)
According to R. Inglehart (1997), in prosperous societies materialist values (ensuring survival, career orientation) are increasingly being superseded by postmaterialist and postmodern values (liberal and democratic preferences). Differentiation and pluralization have become the cultural hallmarks of the age.

Rationality
Action carried out in line with reason. Often used in a narrower sense to mean economic rationality, that is, the economical utilization of resources.

Sattelzeit or bridge period
Term coined by Reinhart Koselleck for the fundamental shift in the use of socio-political concepts in Germany between 1750 and 1850, especially the new dynamism of terms ('revolution'), the rise of new collective singulars ('progress', 'history') and neologisms ('communism', 'liberalism'). Increasingly applied to the history of concepts in other languages and cultures as well as to other epochal processes of change.

Socialization
Process through which the fundamental elements of their culture are imparted to the new members of a society. (Occupational socialization: process in which a new employee adapt his norms, values, and convictions to those of the organization or profession in which he works. Anticipatory socialization: process through which we adapt our convictions, norms, and values in advance to a new socialization process about to be undergone.)

Social mobility
Movement up and down within a social hierarchy.

Social structure
Relatively stable, enduring patterns of social relations, social positions, and groups of individuals; patterns which individuals have little influence upon.

Sociology
Academic discipline which studies human societies, including the numerous aspects of social action and the organization of social relations.

Transcendence
The world beyond the boundaries of everyday experience (*see* Axial Age).

Value
Basic feature of every culture; a general notion shared by the majority of a group (such as a profession, class, nation) about what is good or bad, desirable or undesirable. Values are crucial to lifestyles: we link values with cultural objectifications (for example, law, morality, knowledge) and activities (such as books, paintings, museums, concerts).

Afterword

Klaus Wiegandt

Just as the first two conferences 'Evolution' and 'Humanity and the Cosmos' bore the unmistakable signature of the scientist Ernst Peter Fischer, scientific adviser at my foundation, the sociologist Hans Joas directed proceedings both in the run-up to and during the third seminar 'The Cultural Values of Europe' with much skill and aplomb. In the name of all 160 participants, I would once again like to express my heartfelt thanks to him.

For the participants, drawn from every area of society, each day opened up valuable perspectives, some of them entirely new. Towards the end of the seminar it became apparent how important cultural values have been both for developments at the level of society as well as to the way each individual finds meaning, an importance they are regaining in our time.

Regrettably, the informative interdisciplinary contributions made both during the panel discussion moderated by Gero von Boehm on the final day and throughout the conference could not be included in this book for reasons of space – this would have required another 150 pages.

Before the decision was taken to select 'The Cultural Values of Europe' as the third topic in our conference series, some of those who had taken part in the preceding events suggested that, within the framework of the foundation's activities, we ought first to tackle more important subjects which might highlight our options for dealing with pressing social issues.

On closer inspection, I believe, it has become clear to all the participants that before coming up with possible solutions to the great problems of our time, our society requires a fundamental discussion on values. How, for example, are we meaningfully to answer questions on the future of our economic order, the importance of our environment, what limits we might impose on research on genetic engineering and its application to all of animate nature, failing inter-generational contracts, the long-term level of our contribution to the Third World, or issues of increasing waves of migration, unless objectives are developed on the basis of our value system?

I would like to present here the summary I provided at the end of the conference of what seemed to me some particularly important suggestions and insights:

Over the last few days we have immersed ourselves in the topic of the cultural values of Europe. In line with a proposal from Hans Joas, we have understood 'values' as 'ideas about the desirable with a strong emotional charge'. This distinguishes values both from that which we merely desire and from emotionally neutral ideas, mere opinions in other words, as well as from norms, in which the emphasis is on their restrictive effect. By contrast, we are deeply moved by values and we feel committed to them. Rather than emerging from mere rational justification, such values are anchored in intensive experiences.

Anyone studying the cultural values of Europe will examine the significance of the Greco-Roman and Judeo-Christian traditions. We have also looked at the so-called axial age – a period when transcendence was discovered or invented. Shmuel N. Eisenstadt's lecture laid particular emphasis on the huge potential for the ethical permeation of the world to which this development gave rise. Rulers were obliged to account for their actions, because it became possible for prophets or even officials to point to divine laws and supernatural criteria. It became possible to distinguish between ethnic group and religion, making it conceivable to think in terms of universal religious communities.

Among the Greeks, the development of culture on the basis of freedom stood centre stage, freedom here meaning that enjoyed by the free in contrast to the slaves. Every freeman strove to develop himself by attaining a broad range of abilities. Christian Meier sees the origins of Greek 'rationality' in the exploration of natural laws, whether those governing relations between autonomous natural phenomena such as stars, or between free polities or free citizens.

Bishop Huber elucidated the core of the Christian message. For him, this is by no means a matter of a catalogue of moral demands, but consists of the good news of divine creation and love and the inexhaustible expectation of God's presence in the world.

In the other lectures and ensuing debates we investigated the values of inwardness (Kurt Flasch), freedom (Orlando Patterson), rationality (Wolfgang Schluchter), self-realization (Christoph Menke), and the affirmation of everyday life (Wolfgang Reinhard). We also examined the religious and cultural diversity of the Middle Ages (Michael Borgolte), how the Enlightenment and *Sattelzeit* or 'bridge period' lent dynamism to our understanding of history (Reinhart Koselleck), the contemporary value shift in Europe (Helmut Thome), as well as the dark sides of history in the shape, for example, of European totalitarianism (Mark Mazower).

It seems essential to highlight once again Peter Wagner's cautious 'yes' to the question of whether there is such a thing as a European cultural identity:

> Europe is not rooted in its history in such a way that it might deduce its destiny from its roots. Such an idea is based in part on an inadequate concept of identity and culture. But Europe has had profound historical experiences, and has always kept on trying – during the present era as well as in the past – to interpret these experiences collectively. This gives rise to an identity which can act as a guide to action and which lays bare the differences from other action orientations.

The fact that we need to go further in debating values at the present time is bound up with the most fundamental processes of change, affecting all societies, which have ever occurred in human history.

Yet we are only superficially aware of these things; we fail to grasp how our attitudes and values are affected by them in the depths of our emotional lives.

In this regard, I would like to turn again to two key intellectual challenges of the future mentioned in the discussion by Dieter Senghaas and set out in detail in his book *The Clash within Civilizations: Coming to Terms with Cultural Conflicts*. The process of upheaval affecting traditional societies and their transition to modernity, and the ongoing and accelerated changes characteristic of modern societies which have already experienced this transition, must be dealt with through a political culture of constructive conflict resolution. Here, history shows that cultural conflicts are played out primarily within a cultural area rather than between different cultures. Among the economically successful societies – particularly in East and Southeast Asia – cultural conflicts will be mitigated and balanced out within the foreseeable future. The economically unsuccessful societies – in the Arab-Islamic world for example – have reached a dead end and face a chronic crisis of development. We are seeing fundamentalist developments here, up to and including virtual civil war as in Algeria.

With respect to the protracted and controversial debate, within the context of globalization, on a new world order, I would emphasize a key insight gleaned from this week of discussion. It makes sense, first and foremost, to try to realize just a small number of universal values such as human dignity, freedom, equality, and democracy, and to retain a maximum of cultural diversity on our planet.